AMERICA'S BANK

AMERICA'S BANK

THE EPIC STRUGGLE

TO CREATE THE

FEDERAL RESERVE

ROGER LOWENSTEIN

PENGUIN PRESS | *New York* | 2015

PENGUIN PRESS
An imprint of Penguin Random House LLC
375 Hudson Street
New York, New York 10014
penguin.com

Photograph credits:
Courtesy of the Rhode Island Historical Society: Insert page 1 (top left); Library of
Congress, Prints and Photographs Division: page 1 (top right), 4 (top, bottom), 6 (top
left), 7 (bottom); Library of Congress, Harris & Ewing Collection: page 1 (bottom);
courtesy of the Jekyll Island Museum Archives: page 2 (top left), 3 (bottom), 5 (top,
bottom); Citi Center for Culture/Heritage Collection: page 2 (top right); courtesy of
the Woodrow Wilson Presidential Library, Staunton, Virginia: page 2 (bottom), 6 (top
right), 8 (top, bottom); Museum of American Finance: page 3 (top left, top right);
Library of Congress, National Photo Company Collection: page 6 (bottom); Library
of Congress, Bain Collection: page 7 (top)

ISBN 978-1-59420-549-1

Printed in the United States of America
1 3 5 7 9 10 8 6 4 2

Designed by Marysarah Quinn

TO JUDY, ALWAYS

We do not think it fair that men . . . should raise the cry of a central bank or summon the ghost of Andrew Jackson.

—Nelson Aldrich

CONTENTS

PART TWO

THE LEGISLATIVE ARENA

INTRODUCTION

So PERVASIVE IS ITS INFLUENCE that Americans today can scarcely imagine a world without the Federal Reserve. To begin with, the Fed—America's central bank—issues the Federal Reserve notes that we call "money." It sets the short-term interest rate that affects the market for mortgages, car loans, corporate debt, and even the level of the stock market. It manages, sometimes adroitly and sometimes wantingly, the supply of credit whose ebb and flow alternately buoys and batters business. It supervises—or it is supposed to supervise—the nation's banks. And as Americans were vividly reminded during the meltdown of 2008, the Federal Reserve acts as the lender of last resort, providing loans to banks when credit shuts down.

Barely a century ago, the Fed did not exist. Every other industrialized nation had such a central bank to oversee its banking system and to assure stability, yet America's financial system—if system one can call it—was antiquated, disorganized, and deficient. The United States boasted the world's largest economy, its vast territory was ribboned with railroad tracks and telephone wires, its cities were bursting with factories churning out iron and steel. Yet, almost as if history had missed a turn, its banks were disconnected and isolated, left to prosper or flounder (or fail) according to the reserves of each individual institution. As Paul Warburg, one of the heroes of this story, was to observe with his trademark acuity, America's banks resembled less an army commanded by a central staff than they did an inchoate legion of disjointed and disunited infantry. It was hardly surprising that throughout the latter half of the nineteenth century and into the early twentieth, the United States—alone among the industrial powers—suffered a continual spate of financial panics, bank runs, money shortages, and, indeed, full-blown depressions.

This book tells the story of how, culminating in the days before Christmas 1913, the Federal Reserve came to be. It was not a gentle or an easy birth, nor was it swift. To Americans of the early twentieth century, especially farmers, the prospect of a central bank threatened the comfortable Jeffersonian principle of small government. To a people for whom local autonomy was sacrosanct, the notion of a powerful bank, joined to the even more powerful federal government, was deeply unnerving. Opposition to central authority had animated the minutemen at Lexington and Concord, and the battle to establish the Fed resembled a second American revolution—a financial revolution.

America had, of course, experimented with central banking early in its history. After the War of Independence, a military success but a financial disaster, the government was saddled with debt. When in due course the Constitution was ratified, providing a greater degree of political unity, Alexander Hamilton proposed a financial equivalent, a Bank of the United States, modeled after the Bank of England. Thomas Jefferson was mightily opposed, as were his many followers. Nonetheless, President Washington was persuaded, as was a majority of Congress, and in 1791, the Bank, headquartered in Philadelphia, opened for business.

To modern eyes, the Bank was a strange beast, 20 percent owned by the government and 80 percent by private investors. It was authorized to hold the government's deposits but not, specifically, to be the nation's monetary steward or to perform other functions of a central bank. Nonetheless, the Bank began to play this role. In particular, it strengthened the previously shoddy credit of the federal government. The twenty years of its initial charter were generally prosperous, and the number of private banks, which received charters from the states, swelled from five to more than one hundred.

But the Bank was doomed by the rise of the anti-federalists, both in the White House, in the person of James Madison, and in Congress. Rechartering failed by one vote in each chamber. Thus, in 1811, America was returned to a condition of monetary innocence, or laissez-faire, money again being the business of individual banks in the states, each of which issued notes according to its respective powers. Inflation followed, and when the government's credit became overtaxed by the War of 1812, banks suspended operations, causing Madison to rethink matters. In 1816, Congress, now with Madison's endorsement, chartered the Second Bank of the United States.

The Second Bank, though endowed with more capital, was in most respects a replica of the first. It succeeded at restraining the state banks from issuing too many notes, thus keeping a lid on inflation. It worked to mute excesses in the business cycle. And the Bank's notes were widely accepted as a common currency, no small thing for a nation pushing across an unsettled continent. But the Second Bank met a fate no better than the first. Although Congress approved its recharter, the margin was not sufficient to override the determined veto of Andrew Jackson. In 1836, the national bank was, for the second time, allowed to expire. Once again, the country experienced an inflation, this time followed by a severe depression. In 1841, Congress chartered a third bank. President John Tyler, a southerner preoccupied with states' rights, vetoed it. And there, for some seven decades, matters rested.

Given the two Banks' overall effective records (and allowing for some stumbles by each), the question must be asked: Why such a haste to abolish them? Despite their success, many Americans regarded the Banks with profound suspicion. Alexis de Tocqueville, the French political thinker who toured Jacksonian America, noticed in his travels through what was still a frontier society a pair of seemingly inconsistent facts. The notes of the Second Bank were valued equally

"on the edge of the wilderness" as they were in Philadelphia, testifying to the people's general regard for its credit; nonetheless, the Bank
had become the "object of intense hatred." De Tocqueville's diagnosis
was that "Americans are obviously preoccupied by one great fear,"
which he identified as fear of a tyrannical government or, as he put it,
of "centralization." De Tocqueville was plainly bewildered. To him—
to most any Frenchman—the Bank of France seemed a natural out-
growth of the national government, no less French than the Court of
Versailles. But in America, such a bank did not seem natural. It reawakened Americans' primal anxieties, the colonials' fear that their
hard-won liberties would be crushed by a far-off king.

Even after independence, the pattern of settlement—the way that
the frontier continually pushed westward—ensured that a perpetual
class of outsiders would resent and resist the power structure in the
East and especially the Northeast. For the opposition to central banking was always a matter of geography as much as anything else. In the
vote to establish the first Bank in the House of Representatives, only
three congressmen from southern states voted in favor; only one from
the North was opposed. It was no accident that Jackson, the slayer
of the Second Bank, was a rough-hewn soldier and Indian fighter, the
first president not from the Eastern Seaboard.

Many early Americans were not merely suspicious of a federal
bank; they were suspicious of *any* big bank, a prejudice that loomed
especially large in rural areas. To merchants and city dwellers, banks
were a boon, but farmers and debtors (often the same people) resented
being hostage to banks, especially large metropolitan banks. And
most of America, for a very long time, *was* rural: when Jackson was
elected president, only one of fifteen Americans lived in cities.

Although Europe also had agrarian traditions, farmers in Europe
lived in villages. They were surrounded by neighbors, accustomed to
interdependence. In America, farmers were dispersed and isolated.
They relied less on labor (which was scarcer) and more on capital—
which is to say, they relied on banks. It has been wittily suggested,

not without cause, that American farmers hated banks because they needed loans. Jefferson in particular was suspicious of finance, a profession he considered ethically tainted. It is worth noting that Jefferson never visited a town until he was almost eighteen. Jackson similarly frowned on financiers. He squashed the Second Bank largely because, he felt, it was a tool of eastern elites.*

Jackson's heritage was remarkably enduring. Even generations later, the reformers who sought to establish the Fed could not admit to favoring a "central bank"—the very phrase was forbidden. Rhode Island senator Nelson W. Aldrich, the first legislator in the twentieth century to draft a bill for a national bank, felt as though he were doing battle not just with the populists and anti-bank agitators of his own time but also, as he phrased it, with "the ghost of Andrew Jackson."

Before Congress could consider legislation, the public had to be persuaded of or at least exposed to the idea of establishing a unifying financial institution. In the first part of our story, bankers and others launch a campaign to win over influential citizens in business, universities, and the press. The reformers were a mixed bag—economists, bankers, idealists bent on modernizing the system, and, as well, Wall Street financiers with the more self-serving ambition of enhancing profits.

New York bankers wanted a central bank in part because they wanted to assume a greater role on the world stage. The America of the late nineteenth century was an industrial powerhouse but a financial also-ran. The U.S. dollar was a second-rate currency; incredibly, the dollar was quoted in fewer currency markets than the relatively puny Italian lira or Austrian schilling. In monetary terms, America remained a stepchild of the Bank of England, whose interest-rate

---

* As a young man, Jackson had sold land in return for promissory notes from a Philadelphia merchant and endorsed the notes to pay for supplies for a store. When the merchant failed, Jackson was liable—leaving him with crushing debts. The experience forever soured the future president on high finance.

maneuvers could, and often did, plunge Wall Street into recession. Financial independence required a more resilient currency, and one whose supply was regulated not in London or in Paris but in America itself.

But what sort of bank would issue this currency and what rules would it live by? These questions had preoccupied Americans since the Civil War. They fought—unceasingly—over whether the money supply should be pegged to the country's gold reserve, or to silver, or to some other standard. Bankers of the Gilded Age were worried about inflation, as bankers always are; however, for strapped American farmers, money was in chronic undersupply. Farmers, industrialists, bankers, consumers, workers, all had conflicting interests. What became clear to all—after a disastrous panic in 1907, when the banks literally ran out of money—was that the prevailing system in which each bank stood on its own did not work.

The system's inadequacy was seen most clearly by a newcomer, Paul Warburg, a German expatriate. He was stunned by the primitive condition of American banking and relentlessly lobbied his fellow financiers to embrace reforms modeled on the central banks of Europe. As Warburg acclimated to his adopted country, he recognized the need to cultivate the political establishment, then thoroughly Republican, and recruited the powerful Senator Aldrich to his cause.

Aldrich, however, was unprepared for the progressive tide that was reshaping American politics. Social activism was on the rise and Americans—not unlike in our own time—resented the widening gap between rich and poor, evident in the palatial mansions of railroad tycoons and industrial barons. The progressive movement was an effort to balance the scales. Since progressives were all for modernization, they should have looked favorably on proposals for a central bank, but progressives were innately wary of bankers—even of reform-minded bankers. And they deeply mistrusted Senator Aldrich, who had acquired his great wealth in shady, backroom dealings with monopolists. Aldrich was so out of favor that he opted to abscond from public view, along with a band of Wall Street advisers, and rewrite the nation's banking laws in secret. Aldrich's clandestine effort, a stranger-than-fiction mission to a remote Georgia island, would forever link the Fed's founding to the wildest claims of conspiracy theorists and cranks.

In the second part of the story, as Warburg's proposals are painstakingly translated into legislation, bankers pass the baton to politicians. No sooner did this process start than, in 1912, the electorate installed the Democrats in Congress. The Democrats were hostile to a central bank. After all, they were the party of Andrew Jackson. Moreover, they were concentrated in the West and South and naturally feared that a central bank would enhance the power of the big banks in New York. But the Democrats could scarcely overlook the pressure for reform that was sweeping the country. Moreover, the Democratic president-elect, Woodrow Wilson, was a good way evolved from his small-government predecessors. Though hardly a New Deal–style activist, Wilson was more willing to balance concern for individual freedom with a desire to promote national unity and the overall health of society. On the specific issue of central banking, Wilson—a student of American government—was favorably disposed.

The task of reconciling banking reform with the party's states'-rights traditions fell, improbably, to a southern congressman—the Virginian Carter Glass. A child of the Civil War, a rebel in his bones, Glass was ambitious enough to see that modernizing banking could be his ticket to a place in the national spotlight. But he had to devise a program that did not run afoul of his party's prejudices.

Prodded by Wilson, pressured by Warburg and by Main Street bankers, Glass advanced a bill that, in its way, mimicked the constitutional experiment in federalism. The Federal Reserve would be unlike the central banks of Europe—for it would not be one bank but twelve. Power would be shared between the center and the periphery, between the federal government and the private banks that it was designed to serve. If the establishment of the Fed constituted a land-mark moment, when the direction of society veered from laissez-faire toward government control, it was nonetheless intended to be a compromise.

Glass's aim was to reconcile a set of overlapping tensions—between local and federal authority, between private and public interest, between farmers and merchants, as well as between small-town bankers, big-city banks, and Wall Street. His aim was to pool the nation's banking reserves, in accord with the principle of collective security, without creating a powerful monster that violated American traditions and the prevailing sentiment against large banks. What he and the other founders could not have envisioned was the degree to which these tensions would persist. Indeed, in the political climate of today, it is doubtful whether the Federal Reserve Act could be passed. A century later, opposition to the federal government, such as in the Tea Party wing of the Republican Party, is as impassioned as ever. In 1913, Glass had to overcome the fear that a central bank would become a tool of Wall Street; in the aftermath of the 2008 crisis, when the Fed and the Treasury provided bailouts or credit to the biggest banks, such fears run rampant. And just as opponents of the Fed's establishment protested that it would lead to inflation, the modern Fed's sustained policy of near-zero percent interest rates has prompted critics to warn that a dangerous inflation looms ever nearer. More generally, in an America still nursing its wounds from the financial crisis, both its central bank and its prominent private banks have become objects of vitriol and mistrust. Truly, the battle for the Fed in 1913 foretells our differences today.

PART ONE

THE ROAD

TO

JEKYL ISLAND

CHAPTER ONE

THE FORBIDDEN WORDS

I am in favor of a national bank.
—ABRAHAM LINCOLN, 1832

WHEN CARTER GLASS was born in 1858, the United States was an industrializing nation with a banking system stuck in frontier times. As the country put up factories and laid down rails, the tension between its antiquated finances and its smokestack-dotted towns grew ever more acute. Heated battles over "the money question" came to dominate the country's politics, but no matter how unsatisfied the people, any solution that tended toward centralization was, due to the prevailing prejudice, off the table.

America was a monetary Babel with thousands of currencies; each state regulated its own banks and they collectively provided the country's money. Officially, America was on a hard-money basis, but the amount of gold in circulation was insignificant. In any event, as a contemporary would write, it was impractical for a traveler "to carry with him the coin necessary to meet his expenses for a protracted journey." If he traveled with notes of any but a few of the biggest banks in New York, Boston, and Philadelphia, his money was likely to be refused, or greatly discounted. If he did carry gold, then, "at the hotel, in the railroad car, on the river or lake," he would be offered slips of engraved paper that, in the words of a western banker, might include "the frequently worthless issues of the State of Maine and of other New England States, the shinplasters of Michigan, the wild cats of Georgia, of Canada, and Pennsylvania, the red dogs of Indiana and Nebraska, the miserably engraved notes of North Carolina, Kentucky, Missouri and Virginia, and the not-to-be-forgotten stumptails of Illinois and Wisconsin."

In theory, these notes were redeemable in gold or in state bonds, but notes from western banks were notoriously unreliable. Bankers, not surprisingly, sought to circulate their paper as *far* as possible from the point of issue. That way, the notes might never—or not for a very long while—return, and the bank avoided the annoying detail of having to redeem its debts. There was no institution to regulate either the quality or the quantity of money, and after states adopted so-called free banking, a promoter needed little more than a printing press to set up shop. In 1853, Indiana's governor lamented, "The speculator comes to Indianapolis with a bundle of banknotes in one hand and the stock in the other; in twenty-four hours he is on his way to some distant point of the union to circulate what he denominates a legal currency, authorized by the legislature of Indiana." The system was certainly democratic—almost anyone could issue "money"—but it was just as certain to lead to credit booms and inevitable busts.

According to Jay Cooke, a Philadelphia financier, some banks issued notes equal to twenty-five times their capital "with no other security than the good faith of their institution." Since such faith was often short-lived, Cooke hardly needed to add, "confusion . . . was the order of the day." During the Civil War, the *Chicago Tribune* counted 1,395 banks in the Union states, each with bills of various denominations—some 8,370 varieties of notes in all. Even for the careful bank teller, scrutinizing this profusion of paper became an almost hopeless task. In addition to bank failures, the country was plagued by con men whose note forgeries could be worthy of a Rembrandt. So widespread were phony notes that "Counterfeit Detectors" were published, and these guides were widely circulated.

This monetary chaos formed the tableau for late-nineteenth-century reformers, and it is key to understanding how people of Glass's generation thought about money. Money—generally, gold or silver—was something of intrinsic value. Circulating paper, even though it served as a medium of exchange, was but a token, a *promise* of the real thing, discounted according to the degree to which people feared that the promise might not be kept.

Legislation during the Civil War provided a remedy—somewhat. With the government desperate for credit, Lincoln's Treasury secretary, Salmon P. Chase, was left no choice but to propose, and Congress to approve, a new system of nationally chartered banks, which were permitted to issue circulating paper money in the form of National Bank Notes. These notes were to be a new, and mercifully uniform, currency, with a standard engraving on one side and the bank's name on the other.

However, note circulation was tightly controlled. National banks had to hold a reserve and submit to federal banking examinations. Also, to issue notes, they had to invest in a proportionate amount of government bonds and deposit them with the Treasury as collateral. This requirement heightened the demand for government securities— which was, of course, Chase's purpose. By giving banks an incentive to invest in government debt, the United States contrived a means of financing the war. National banks were formed at a rapid clip, and many state banks converted to federal charters so they could qualify to circulate notes.*

---

* A legacy of the National Banking Acts, adopted in 1863 and 1864, was that banks in the United States were, even until recent times, typically denoted as the "First National," "Second National," and so on, in their respective cities.

The new notes were surely an improvement, but they had the drawback of arbitrariness. The quantity in circulation was determined by the level of investment in government bonds, and this bore no relation to the needs of trade. Perversely, circulation often fell as business activity expanded and banks found better outlets for their capital. Just as worrisome, the note supply was inelastic—banks held the quantity of bonds that they held, and no new notes could be issued in a crisis. The modern notion of a central bank to supply extra liquidity when needed simply did not exist.

It is hard to overly blame Chase because, as he said, his goal was "first to provide for the vast demands of the war." Chase was lauded for standardizing the currency and blunting the prior ability of banks to create inflation by circulating worthless paper. William G. Sumner, an influential economist at Yale, fairly rejoiced: "This system of currency has put an end at once and forever to the old bankers' trick of expansion and contraction." That economies do expand—and that currency needs to expand with them—was largely overlooked.

Also overlooked, for the moment, was the precarious manner in which the National Banking Act marshaled the country's reserves. In Great Britain or in France, reserves were stored in the central bank. In America, the Banking Act introduced an intricate and fragile system, with the reserves of one bank piled upon another.

The law recognized three distinct tiers of banks. The smallest, so-called country banks, had to either keep reserves in their vaults or deposit a portion with middle-tier banks in the city. The latter, in turn, could hold cash in the vault or deposit a portion of their reserves with banks in the highest tier, those in the "central reserve cities" of New York, Chicago, and St. Louis. In practice, since banks did not want to hold idle cash, reserves flowed to New York. And since the New York banks did not want idle money either, they lent their spare cash to the stock market. Thus, America's banking system was perched on a speculative pyramid. Whenever credit was in short supply, the entire chain backed into reverse, with country banks calling their loans, by means of urgent telegrams, to banks in reserve cities and thence to New York. This could precipitate panicky selling in the stock market. As Glass was to write, the system was a "breeder of panics," with the idle funds of the nation "congested at the money centres for purely speculative purposes."

This defect quickly became apparent. In 1873, when the new era was not quite a decade old, Jay Cooke's firm, having improvidently speculated on railroad bonds, collapsed. The failure touched off a depression, which lasted six years. In a telltale sign of the system's defects, note circulation sharply declined. Even when business recovered, the country was visited by periodic shortages of cash, or "stringencies," when interest rates would soar to as much as 100 percent. The problem was most acute in the fall, when farmers needed cash to move the crops. Farmhands had to be hired, horses fed, machinery operated, shipping procured. The agrarian economy, as it were, sprung to life and required bundles of cash. This imbalanced the relative currency demands of city and farm, resulting in regular shortages. No central reservoir existed to smooth out the seasonal lumpiness. In short, the system suffered a serious deficit: it consistently failed to generate enough money.

One obvious solution was to supply more money, but that begged the question "Who should supply it, and what *kind* of money?" Though the new National Bank Notes served as walking-around money, the United States actually had *seven* different mediums of exchange circulating in varying amounts.* During Glass's early life (the first few decades after the Civil War), Americans of every station fiercely debated how to bring order to this fiscal cacophony. In particular, they argued bitterly over whether gold should be supplemented by additional currency of some other type, including "greenbacks," the colloquial name for the paper notes issued by the federal govern-

---

* The seven national currencies were National Bank Notes, gold coins and gold certificates, silver dollars and silver certificates, greenbacks, and Treasury securities.

ment during the Civil War. Because greenbacks were not supported by any metal or tangible asset, the banking class considered them abhorrent. They were mere paper, "fiat" money (exactly what circulates today) and, to nineteenth-century bankers, an unpardonable blasphemy. In time, Congress decided to make greenbacks exchangeable for gold, and people who wanted to add to the currency shifted gears and proposed that the money supply be enhanced with notes that were backed by silver, which was more plentiful than gold. To supporters of the gold standard, silver, too, would merely cheapen the currency; it was both morally and economically repugnant.

Gold's champions tended to be creditors—people with capital. They didn't want the currency debased because they didn't want to be repaid in cheaper coin. Gold being scarcer than silver, it was more valuable. In the 1870s, much of the world had joined Britain and gone on a gold standard (agreeing to back their currencies with gold). In 1879, the United States did so as well. But Congress, trying to appease the farm lobby, directed the Treasury to also mint limited amounts of silver dollars, and at the historic ratio to gold of 16 to 1. Since the bullion value of a silver "dollar" was, by then, appreciably less, owing to a divergence in the metals' prices, bankers and Republicans regarded silver as a profane dilution. Grover Cleveland, a "gold Democrat" elected president in 1884 and again in 1892, spoke for Wall Street and for respectable opinion generally when he observed that if America went to a silver standard, "we could no longer claim a place among nations of the first class."

As a practical matter, bankers were correct that the bimetallic system of gold and silver was inherently unstable, since people would seek to cash in the poorer coin (in this case, the silver) for the richer one. But the gold standard imposed severe hardships on a great many Americans. In plain terms, the production of gold was not sufficient to support an adequate supply of money.

The issue was extremely divisive, because money shortages affected Americans unevenly. American farmers, de Tocqueville noted, were less peasants than little businessmen. They took out loans for seed and equipment. When prices fell, their debts became crushing. Credit in farm communities was exceedingly scarce. The rigid rules of the Banking Act proscribed lending on real estate, which undercut the usefulness of national banks in rural areas. Cash was even scarcer. There were fewer bank notes issued in Iowa, Minnesota, Kansas, Missouri, Kentucky, and Tennessee combined than in the tiny Eastern Seaboard state of Connecticut.

The hardship, and its palpable inequity, spawned a political awakening—a cry for redress. People blamed the money scarcity on Wall Street or on its British equivalent, Lombard Street. Carter Glass was one of those. His sense of grievance was nourished by his difficult beginnings. Glass had been born in Lynchburg, Virginia, three years before the Civil War. His mother died when he was two, and his father, a publisher and a major in the Confederate ranks, suffered painful setbacks during the war, when he forfeited a vast quantity of cotton and had to sell his newspaper. After the war, he was offered the job of postmaster but refused to work for the federal government. Major Glass also had political ambitions, but these were frustrated by Reconstruction. For his son, it was a bitter inheritance, compounded by the sight of federal troops occupying Virginia. Carter, though, was a determined lad. Frail, with sallow skin and thin lips, often sickly with digestive problems and only five foot four, he was known as "Pluck" owing to his stubbornness and fiery temper. At age fourteen, he was forced to quit school but continued his studies at night, reading his father's copies of Plato, Burke, and Shakespeare by kerosene lamp. Although Glass found work at a newspaper, his prospects were dimmed by the depression that ensued in 1873. Glass's view of this calamity was informed by his hostility to northern banks. For six straight years, as he tried to make his way in the world, the money stock shrank. Where did the money go? Gold had sucked it up—so he believed. New York and London were in on it together. He reckoned that a malign conspiracy of financiers was to blame. Because he mistrusted power, he did not want more power. He did not want a central bank.

In 1880, Glass finally got the job he wanted—newspaper reporter. Rising to publisher within a decade, Glass ceaselessly editorialized for silver. "Why should gold be minted free [in unlimited amounts], any more than silver?" he thundered in the *Lynchburg News*. Glass's crusade was as much emotional as deductive. "I confess that with all I have read on both sides of the currency questions, I understand very little about it," he confided to a comrade. "But when I see the merciless forces of corporate and individual wealth arrayed on one side, and the working, toiling masses on the other, I can but feel that you and I are right in the stand we have taken."

Silver-money advocates are often portrayed this way—as emotional and ignorant. But their distress was real. Over the course of three decades—beginning when Carter Glass was a boy—prices in America steadily declined. No American born after the Great Depression has ever experienced even *two* consecutive years of deflation but, astonishingly, from 1867 to 1897 prices skidded relentlessly lower, and over the whole of that period they tumbled well more than 50 percent. In 1867, when the future congressman was nine years old, a bushel of winter wheat fetched $2.84; thirty years later it was selling for a mere 90 cents.

Although the price of goods was falling, it is equally true, and more illuminating, to say that the price of money was rising. This was occurring for the expected reason—money was scarce. Representative Joseph Sibley of Pennsylvania noted that gold was the only commodity whose price was appreciating. "You do not want an honest dollar," he said in rebuke to President Cleveland. "You want a scarce dollar."

As America industrialized, sectional divisions in the country widened. Corporations listed on the stock exchange were able to tap capital; manufacturing firms were protected by the tariff. The system of high tariffs and a strong dollar served the Northeast reasonably well but it left farmers and debtors impoverished.

Yet the people who might have benefited most from monetary reform were also the most resistant to it. The notion of establishing a bank to regulate the money supply, although common in other countries, aroused deeply held fears of monopoly, especially in the South and West. Farmers agitated for a cruder solution: printing more greenbacks. When that crusade faded, agitators shifted their energies to silver. The point was to mint more money—any kind of money.

Bowing to the pressure, in 1890 Congress committed the Treasury to purchasing the sizable sum of 4.5 million ounces of silver a month (double its prior rate). Since the government also backed its paper in gold, a problem developed. As predicted by Gresham's Law,* miners and others exchanged their inflated silver for gold at par, the latter disappearing from circulation. As gold drained out of the Treasury, foreign investors feared that the United States would be forced to abandon gold and rushed to sell American securities.

The gold stampede bequeathed a banking panic. Depositors withdrew savings, and country banks desperately demanded their reserves from the city banks where they were parked. The system was too brittle to handle the freight. "Actual money," a commentator noted, "cannot be shipped from New York to Denver in a day, and forty-eight hours' delay may easily settle the fate of the Western institution."

The Panic of 1893 exposed, beyond a doubt, the system's flaws as well as its geographic asymmetry. Of 360 banks that failed, all but 17 were west or south of Pennsylvania. Robert Latham Owen, president of the First National Bank of Muskogee, in Oklahoma Territory, saw half his deposits run out the door in a matter of days. A future legislative partner of Glass, Owen became convinced, then and there, of the need for reform.

Cleveland persuaded Congress to repeal the silver-purchase act, but the silver lobby kept up a steady pressure for resumption, and investors remained in an agitated state. The government repeatedly

---

* Informally stated as "Bad money drives out good."

borrowed gold only to see it drain away. A. Barton Hepburn, the comptroller of the currency, was to write, "Fear of a silver basis prevailed, especially abroad, and every express steamer brought in American securities and took away gold." With gold supplies dwindling, in 1895, the President was forced to go hat in hand to J. P. Morgan, who accepted thirty-year government bonds (which he syndicated to investors) in exchange for gold to bail out the Treasury. This was a highly embarrassing demonstration of Washington's subservience to Wall Street. The private nature of the negotiations and the fact that, as it turned out, Morgan turned a profit on the syndication gave rise to charges of a conspiracy. Glass believed, on no evidence, that bankers such as Morgan had fomented the gold shortage to profit from subsequent bond sales. The Morgan deal was probably the best that Cleveland could have managed, but it left his party deeply divided.

Astonishingly, no one—least of all Glass—suggested that the government might want to supplant Morgan: that is, become its own banker. Although a central bank presumably would have provided more circulation, the mere suggestion of it stirred cries against the discredited Second Bank in the time of Jackson. That was enough to damn it. After Cleveland vetoed a measure for coining silver, Glass raged at Wall Street for urging the veto. "It is just the money power that the old United States [Second] bank used to exercise over the finances of the government," he editorialized in the *Lynchburg News*, "and would exercise at this day had not General Jackson in his might crushed out its charter."

Trying to look forward and not, for once, to General Jackson, bankers and businesspeople met in Baltimore in 1894 and proposed reforms. The phrase "central bank" was studiously avoided. However, to the conference-goers, it was plain that the Civil War banking structure had outlived its useful life. The Panic had devolved into a full-blown depression. Railroads had failed by the dozen. Thousands of factories had shuttered and unemployment had soared. In rural areas, farmers could not pay their mortgages. Virginia's farmers were ruined by debt; four in ten were forced into tenancy.

Although the depression was America's worst to date, it did not occur to Cleveland to offer federal relief. The son of a Presbyterian minister, as honest as he was corpulent, Cleveland held that people should support the government, not vice versa. This was the Democrats' laissez-faire credo. But Glass was struggling to reconcile this philosophy with the plight of his state's farmers.

The moment was highly polarizing. Populists agitated for an income tax, tariff reform, regulation of railroads, and direct election of U.S. senators (who were chosen by the legislatures). Workers erupted in sometimes violent strikes—notably, the Pullman strike of 1894, which halted much of the nation's rail traffic and led to rioting and acts of sabotage, and was ultimately suppressed by federal troops.

Discontent with the currency was the glue that united these disparate rebellions. In the same year as the Pullman strike, Jacob Coxey, an Ohio businessman, led an army of the unemployed to Washington. Remarkably, they demanded increased circulation—the first popular protest to focus on the monetary system. Meanwhile, over country hill and dale, Americans bent over oil lamps to peruse their copies of William H. Harvey's fetching parable, *Coin's Financial School*, published in 1894. Harvey was a failed silver miner turned proselytizer for silver coinage. He sold hundreds of thousands of copies.

In the next presidential election, silver was the overwhelming issue. With America mired in a depression, increasing the money supply was the perceived tonic. William McKinley, the Republican nominee, was wary of alienating the silver forces, but party bosses insisted that he stand for gold.

The Democratic convention was held in Chicago. Carter Glass, a member of the platform committee, boarded the overnight train for the Midwest in an emotional state, having buried his father only six weeks earlier. He must have ruminated on the last convention attended by Major Glass—in 1860, when the Democrats had debated slavery. This convention seemed similarly momentous, and Glass felt ready to play a part in great events. Despite the hard times, Glass enjoyed a rising prominence, having acquired the three newspapers in Lynchburg and obtained the fastest printing press in the state. His editorials, a daily barrage for free silver, were read in the highest circles in Virginia. Other social and economic issues were coming to the fore, such as labor reform and monopolies, but neither Glass nor the majority of Democrats were ready to embrace them. Glass was a *conservative* reformer, wary of measures that might divide the party and weaken the solid South. Southern democracy was founded on racial segregation, and he earnestly editorialized in support of this system. To Glass, any sort of federal interference (such as a central bank) also threatened an end to white supremacy, and was out of the question.

The Democrats, therefore, coalesced around silver as an encompassing solution for America's ills and also as a safe, unifying mantra for the delegates' lengthy list of grievances. An air of nativism, a Jacksonian Anglophobia, hung over the delegates, for whom gold represented a policy of enslavement by Britain. The platform inveighed against "financial servitude to London" and "trafficking with banking syndicates." It was a farmers' convention, steeped in the issues that mattered to farmers, and it turned to the son of an avid Jacksonian, who himself had been raised on a farm, for inspiration.

William Jennings Bryan, only thirty-six years old, had practiced law, worked as an editor, and served two terms in Congress, representing Nebraska. He was a teetotaler and a fundamentalist Christian. Many of his positions were prescient (he favored an income tax and public disclosure of campaign contributions), but his chief qualification for public life was a talent for oratory. Bryan did not analyze issues so much as feel them. While easterners judged him a dangerous radical, Bryan was driven by a yearning for the past as much as by a vision for the future. He was animated by a conservative nostalgia for small towns, religion, and laissez-faire. His early campaigns had been backed by the liquor interests, who were grateful to have found a non-drinker opposed to Prohibition. Now, he was financed by the silver interests.

Addressing the convention on the warm afternoon of July 9, 1896, Bryan recognized that leadership of the silver crusade was up for grabs, and while some of the phrases he employed had been tested in earlier speeches, never before had his rhetoric been so poetic, or so rousing. He spoke to the delegates, and to the country, as fellow farmers and rural inhabitants—as, indeed, more than six of ten Americans were. He serenaded farmers—"those hardy pioneers," he called them—"who braved all the dangers of the wilderness, who have made the desert to blossom as the rose." Indeed, Bryan spoke as a representative of "our" farms, not of "your" cities, a dichotomy he associated with silver versus gold, poor against rich, even good against evil. He paid the obligatory homage to Jefferson and Jackson, and he claimed to speak for the "producing masses," the "commercial interests," the "laboring interests," and "all the toiling masses"—only Wall Street was excluded. To bankers and to all defenders of the money system he exuded biblical wrath. "You shall not press down upon the brow of labor this crown of thorns," he bellowed in climax. "You shall not crucify mankind upon a cross of gold."

Eyewitnesses reported a momentary silence followed by a tremendous roar. The delegates erupted in cheers; they stood on chairs, gestured wildly, paraded about the hall—a few with Bryan on their shoulders. Glass felt his passions stir and joined the throng. When the frenzy broke, he dashed off a wire to his paper reporting that Bryan had secured the nomination.

The campaign that fall was bitter. McKinley had no trouble raising a war chest on Wall Street. Even some Democrats were appalled by Bryan's populism and supported a splinter candidate. Among those who voted for the gold Democrat rather than Bryan was a noted Princeton professor, Woodrow Wilson.

Nearly eight of ten eligible adults voted, one of the highest turn-outs ever. Bryan lost the popular vote by a margin of only 4 percent—not a bad showing, considering that his financial support came almost exclusively from silver mines. Having polled 6.5 million votes, Bryan was now the uncrowned king of a political movement. Not coincidentally, within a fortnight of the election, businesspeople made arrangements for a conference in Indianapolis to consider re-forming the monetary system. The organizers saw that the system was outmoded—just as plainly, they were afraid that the silverites would hijack the public debate. They wanted to reform the system before Bryan beat them to it.

The six-hundred-page report that the Indianapolis Monetary Convention was to issue bore a single, offhand reference to a "central bank." The delegates were headed in the other direction—they wanted the government *out* of banking, not mixed up with high finance. Morgan's bullion deal with the Treasury had left a sour aftertaste.

Rather than a currency based on government bonds, the India-napolis report proposed that each bank issue its own notes, backed by the loans that it made to farmers, merchants, and factories. In this way, the quantity of currency would expand and contract with ordi-nary business. Let a bank issue credit on a shipment of cotton and the bank's note would incrementally add to the money supply. Let the cotton shipper repay the debt and the currency would contract.

Loans to cotton merchants and such were dubbed "real bills," to distinguish them from speculative credit supplied to stock market traders. According to the real bills theory, such loans were inherently sound because they were backed by a tangible asset—the cotton.

A chief attraction of the real bills theory was that it took decisions regarding the money supply out of human hands. John Carlisle, Trea-sury secretary under Cleveland, maintained that issuing notes "is not a proper function of the Treasury Department, or of any other department of the Government." The task was just too difficult. Rather, Carlisle said, currency should be "regulated entirely by the business interests of the people and by the laws of trade." By the "laws of trade," Carlisle was invoking a nineteenth-century notion of natural law—of an Edenic order in which the volume of money would self-adjust.

The Indianapolis convention was guided toward this doctrine by James L. Laughlin, head of the economics department at the new University of Chicago, and the author of the Indianapolis report. According to Laughlin, an asset currency (based on each individual bank's loans) would "adjust itself automatically and promptly" as the level of trade, and therefore of bank loans, expanded and contracted to meet demand from business.

Laughlin and other theorists were supremely naïve; monetary management is far too complicated to submit to an "automatic" guide.* And they appeared not to notice that America's growing financial strength was tugging the U.S. Treasury away from the laissez-faire principles they held so dear. Indeed, various Treasury secretaries had begun to experiment with lending government reserves to banks. This is what central bankers do. Lyman Gage, secretary of the Treasury under McKinley, was a perfect illustration: even though he preached the gospel of noninterference, in practice he began to act like a forerunner of Ben Bernanke.

Born and educated in upstate New York, Gage was a former president of the First National Bank of Chicago and an enthusiastic supporter of the Indianapolis idea of getting the government out of banking. However, McKinley's high-tariff policies tended to augment Gage's power. Higher tariffs meant more government revenue to throw around in money markets. Secretary Gage, fashionably

---

* Milton Friedman would later propose an arbiter with similarly magical properties to regulate the money supply—"a computer."

coiffed in a full beard and mustache, may not have wanted a government bank but, with tariff collections streaming into the Treasury, he had one.

What further amplified the Treasury's influence was an economic boomlet, spurred by a combination of bumper wheat crops at home and a string of gold discoveries, including in the Klondike region of the Canadian Yukon. With wheat sales surging and gold more plentiful, money growth soared; deflation was finally over. In a sense, Bryan was vindicated: more money had indeed fostered prosperity. It was Bryan's ill luck that the additional metal, as it happened, wasn't silver, but gold.

Gage now faced a question unknown to his predecessors: What to do with the Treasury's surplus? As Gage was aware, the bullion stowed in the Treasury's vaults was idle; it wasn't out stimulating trade. His solution was to increase deposits in the national banks. In other words, he began to try his luck as a central banker.

War with Spain, launched by McKinley in 1898, raised the profile of the Treasury even more (wars inevitably involve governments in banking). To finance the battle of San Juan Hill, Gage offered $200 million in bonds, to which the public eagerly subscribed. The war spending ignited a genuine boom. Arthur Housman, a stockbroker who traveled the country by rail in 1899, testified to good times in a report to J. P. Morgan. "Money is plentiful throughout the country," Housman wrote in June. "In the smallest towns, money is freely offered at 5%." Chugging across the prairie, Housman approvingly observed that farmers were building new fences and barns and that ranchers were improving their breeds of cattle.

Yet the McKinley prosperity did not disguise the underlying weakness in the banking system. In the fall, country banks, needing cash for the harvest, pulled their deposits. Liquidity in New York suddenly evaporated. The city's banks had whittled their reserves to the legal minimum; now, they had little—or nothing—to lend. "The cry everywhere," said the lawyer and investor Henry Morgenthau, "was for money—more money—and yet more money."

Gage did not have to ponder long before deciding on a use for the Treasury's reserves. He loaned them to banks. Gage's idea, again, was to get the Treasury's money into circulation. Although he still affirmed the desirability of reducing the government's profile, he observed with alarm in his report for 1899 that "havoc was wrought in the regular ongoing of our commercial life." This he would not abide. The "periodical regularity" of autumnal shortages grated on him. The lack of "stability" in the currency, the want of flexibility for "needful expansion," suggested a profound inadequacy in the system.

By 1900, Gage had deposited more than $100 million of the American people's money in four hundred different banks. Outraged, Congress investigated. Legislators were irate that Gage had distributed a disproportionate sum, in particular, to National City Bank of New York. Such coziness between Wall Street and Washington inflamed old fears of bankers' conspiracies. *The Coming Battle*, a populist tract by M. W. Walbert, warned that money dealers had formed "a gigantic combination" to thwart the interests of the people.

Impervious to the criticism, the restless Treasury secretary plowed ahead. In the same year that saw Walbert's attack on banks, Gage averred, "It is a popular delusion that [a] bank deals in money." For the most part, Gage elaborated, banks deal in *credit*. Expounding on this theme, he pointed out that no more than 10 percent of a bank's daily receipts are in the form of cash. The rest consists of checks or, as Gage precisely put it, "orders for the transfer of existing bank credits from one person to another."

This 90 percent—the credit network—was where the breakdowns occurred. That credit could dry up at a time of prosperity and rising gold reserves was especially troubling. No sooner do the symptoms of trouble appear, Gage observed, than banks, guided by the "ruling principle of self-preservation," suspend or greatly inhibit their loans.

At that point, people carrying goods and securities are obliged to sell with little regard to cost. "Contemplated enterprises are abandoned; orders for future delivery of goods are rescinded." Finally, what should be an orderly contraction becomes "a disorderly flight, an unreasoning panic."

Fearing such a panic, Gage intervened in the spring of 1901, when a raid on Northern Pacific Railway shares roiled the stock market, and again in September, after President McKinley was assassinated. At the start of 1902, uncomfortable with the meddlesome style of his new boss, Theodore Roosevelt, Gage resigned. His final report was a parting shot at the venerable National Banking system. After five years in office, he had concluded that the system, admirable in many respects, had been "devised for fair weather, not for storms." He lamented that individual banks stood "isolated and apart, separated units, with no tie of mutuality between them." He lamented, too, that no association existed "for common protection or defense in periods of adversity and depression." Not since Alexander Hamilton had a Treasury secretary come so close to demanding a central bank.

Gage even spoke the forbidden words. Perhaps, he mused, the time was ripe not for a "large central bank with multiplied branches"—in view of the sure opposition it would arouse—but for a more modest institution, one restrained by constitutional-style checks. He had in mind a bank, privately owned, with authority to loan reserves from areas of the country where credit was plentiful to regions where it was scarce. Such an entity could become the object of a "perfect public confidence," he said hopefully—if its powers were properly circumscribed. "We justly boast of our political system, which gives liberty and independence to the township and a limited sovereignty to the State. . . . Can not the principle of federation be applied," Gage wondered, "under which the banks as individual units, preserving their independence of action in local relationship, may yet be united in a great central institution?"

CHAPTER TWO

PRIVILEGED BANKER, SELF-MADE SENATOR

> Under our clumsy laws, the currency supply [is] often
> largest when demand . . . is least.
> —ALEXANDER D. NOYES

> The study of monetary questions is one of the great
> causes of insanity.
> —HENRY DUNNING MACLEOD

PAUL MORITZ WARBURG, an immigrant German banker, had barely arrived in New York in 1902 when a tempest erupted on Wall Street. The drama may have seemed routine to jaded New Yorkers, but to the newcomer, it signaled that something in America's financial system was seriously amiss. Market busts were increasingly common. Beginning in 1887, there had been serious financial turmoil roughly every three years. The latest trouble had begun earlier in

1902, when the stock market suddenly cracked. Due to the fragile chain that linked the market and banks, the anxiety migrated into credit markets. Interest rates soared and reserves in the New York banks plunged below the lawfully prescribed minimum. Warburg watched in astonishment as credit quickly evaporated.

The crisis was defused by Roosevelt's secretary of the Treasury, an Iowa banker named Leslie Shaw, who sprinkled government moneys among national banks, and who assisted the banks in more creative ways as well. Critics roundly debated whether Shaw had been right to intervene. From Warburg's émigré perspective, this quarrel missed the essential point. That Shaw had been compelled to resort to such makeshift tactics was evidence of the crudeness of American banking. It proved that the system itself was the problem. "I was not here for three weeks," he would say later, "before I was trying to explain to myself the roots of the evil."

Schooled in Germany's refined financial system, young Warburg injected a sorely needed gust of fresh thinking into the stale arguments over National Banking. There was probably no one in America who better appreciated the workings of the European central banks, and how they contrasted with the system in his adopted home.

Warburg was the third of five sons, heirs to the Hamburg banking firm M. M. Warburg, which traced its origins to the time of Napoleon. He was introspective and shy, and he harbored a melancholy whose physical manifestation was a thick mustache inevitably characterized as "drooping." If his younger brothers, Felix and Fritz, were bons vivants, and Max, the second, was a headstrong banker, Paul had the soul of a poet, and the intellectual fire of the eldest brother, Aby, who became a prominent art historian. As the family biographer, Ron Chernow, noted, Paul seemed to make money without really caring for it. However, his training uniquely prepared him to be an authority in international finance.

After graduating from a European *gymnasium* at eighteen, Paul entered the family bank, spent two years in London, in a variety of jobs, and moved to Paris and to a bank specializing in foreign trade. After a year in Hamburg, the young banker was dispatched on a world study tour, commencing by train to Genoa, where he embarked on a sail-bearing steamer to Suez, followed by a luxurious British liner to India. After stops in Singapore, Saigon, Hong Kong, and Japan, he returned home via Vancouver and the United States. The trip burnished his appreciation of the role of central banking in ensuring market stability. Overall, his field study had lasted seven years.

By 1895, though still only twenty-seven, Warburg was basically running the family bank. In that same year, he married Nina Loeb, the daughter of an American financier. Like Paul, Nina hailed from a tribe of German-Jewish bankers who lavished attention on their children's education, musical training, and cultural upbringing in preparation for lives of wealth and civic involvement. Like him, as well, she carried a sadness, the result of an accident when she fell from a cart, injuring a leg and ending her dream of a career in ballet. The couple settled in Hamburg, crossing to America for summers, but Nina's ailing parents yearned for their daughter to be nearer, and in 1902, the thirty-four-year-old Paul bowed to the inevitable and moved his family to New York, where he joined his in-laws' firm, Kuhn, Loeb & Company.

Warburg was shocked by the primitiveness of American finance. Whereas banks in Germany functioned with near-military cohesiveness, banking in America, he concluded, suffered from an ethos of extreme individualism. As credit tightened, each bank pulled its loans, thereby accentuating the scarcity for all the rest. In 1903, soon after the plunge on Wall Street, Warburg let on to Jacob Schiff, his brother-in-law and the senior partner at Kuhn, Loeb, that he had penned some thoughts on the defects of American banking and how to cure them. The key problem that Warburg outlined was the lack of a central reserve. In effect, each of the country's approximately fifteen thousand banks stood watch over its own cache of gold, which neutralized what could have been a potent collective reserve. Another problem was the lack of a liquid market in so-called bills of trade—pieces of paper representing loans that were endorsed by banks. In Europe, banks could sell, or "discount," such loans to the central bank, freeing up reserves so they could issue more loans; by contrast, such loans were illiquid and inert in America. The final defect was the lack of an elastic currency. Warburg believed that each of these problems could be met by a single remedy—a central bank such as existed in his homeland.

Although his English was flawed, Warburg wielded an unusually lucid and forceful pen. The act of writing seemed to liberate him, transforming the self-effacing, studiously correct gentleman into a passionate and persuasive advocate. Schiff read Warburg's paper and agreed with the substance of it. However, Schiff said, Warburg had misread the psychology of the American people, who would "never" accept any institution resembling a central bank. He warned his junior partner not to share his paper with others. A generation older than Warburg, Schiff had immigrated to the United States after the Civil War and become one of the country's leading railroad financiers. No doubt he feared that Warburg would alienate local bankers by lecturing them on the shortcomings of their own system. But, as a teaching exercise for his protégé, he offered to show the paper, on a confidential basis, to two well-placed friends. One was Edward H. Harriman, a railroad tycoon and Schiff's sometime ally in business. The other was James A. Stillman, president of the National City Bank and one of the preeminent bankers in New York. Harriman read Warburg's memorandum and dismissively told Schiff that Old World institutions couldn't be replicated in America.

A day or two later, Warburg looked up from his desk and found Stillman looming over him. Stillman was a man of legendary laconicism, highly eccentric. He was silent now, looking at Warburg through half-closed, heavy eyes.

Finally, adopting a tone of gentle sarcasm, Stillman spoke: "How is the great international financier?" He added, somewhat defensively, "Warburg, don't you think the City Bank has done pretty well?"

Warburg agreed that it had—very well indeed.

"Why then not leave things alone?"

Warburg hesitated before daring to reply. "Your bank is so big and so powerful, Mr. Stillman, that when the next panic comes, you will wish your responsibilities were smaller."

Stillman—no longer quite so friendly—huffed that Warburg had it all wrong. America's banking system, far from being inferior to those in Europe, actually represented an improvement. Indeed, had not America tried a central bank during the Jackson era and discarded it?

Warburg put his paper on a shelf. For the moment, he had plenty else to do, learning the ins and outs of railroad finance and corporate mergers.

VARIOUS OTHER BANKERS—heirs to the Indianapolis convention—carried on the fight for reform. However, unlike Warburg, they favored establishing an asset currency, a decentralized scheme based on each individual bank's loans. Charles Fowler, chairman of the House Committee on Banking and Currency, introduced a bill to the bankers' liking, but the legislation was stillborn. For one thing, the issue was rather too technical for President Roosevelt, who preferred to expend his energies on social problems on which he could act as the nation's moral leader. Moreover, the existing National Banking system had a fierce defender in the Senate, who stubbornly and consistently blocked reform.

Nelson W. Aldrich, chairman of the Senate Finance Committee, was arguably the most influential figure in Congress at the turn of the century. In this time of Republican hegemony, his word went practically unchallenged; so great was his authority that newspapers

called him the "general manager of the United States." Strongly identified with business interests, Aldrich resisted popular efforts to regulate industry and railroads, or to protect labor. The decades since the
Civil War had seen America transformed by the Industrial Revolution, and Aldrich viewed the task of government as essentially ensuring that American business would continue its upward course. In
banking as in other fields, he reflexively defended the status quo.
However, late in life, Aldrich would experience a stunning conversion to Warburg's cause. He then became the first ardent champion
of a central bank in a position of power.

Unlike Warburg, Aldrich was of humble background. Born in
1841 in a farmhouse in the tiny town of Foster, Rhode Island, Aldrich
had high aspirations tempered by a steely pragmatism. During the
Civil War, he showed no appetite for glory, much less for risking
his hide. Assigned to guard Washington, D.C., he was enthralled
by the sight of the Capitol—"its splendid white marble staircase," in
particular—but contracted a fever and was promptly discharged. It
was not that Aldrich lacked ambition; rather, his ambition was centered on his material advancement. His father, a skilled machinist
who was learned in Rhode Island history, had been checked in his
career by periodic drinking binges. Not unlike Carter Glass, Aldrich
felt acutely his father's failure to advance in the world and harbored a
deep yearning to succeed. As a young man, he fell in love with an
independent woman of some means, Abigail P. T. Chapman, who
rebuffed him. Rejection furnished Aldrich with an urgent motive to
raise his station, a worldly zeal that persisted even after he had won
her hand, for Aldrich was to write his young wife, "I grow sick with
the thought that I am to remain one of that herd of 'dumb, driven
cattle' which makes up the mass of men."

By dint of tireless work, Aldrich elevated himself from the position of clerk at a wholesale grocer in Providence to junior partner. He
also engaged in the lively debates in the local lyceum—such public
lecture halls were a fixture in American towns of that era—on issues

ranging from the tariff to the currency. Although he was hardly rich, he identified with the propertied class, and coveted Old World *objets* as though aristocracy were his natural entitlement. While still a young man, he began acquiring land on Narragansett Bay, where the state's blue-blood families traditionally vacationed and where he himself one day would build a ninety-nine-room Renaissance château, with three sides majestically facing the sea.

Abby tried to moderate his ambition; early in their marriage, as if fighting a premonition, she expressed her "most earnest and cherished hope" that her husband might leave "an unstained record, without one single blemish." His own inner torment nearly derailed his career. In 1872, racked by insomnia, stomach pains, and mental exhaustion, Aldrich set off on a rambling tour of Europe, and though the couple had recently lost a child, his depression seemed driven by a deeper, more personal malady of the soul. He ventured from the South of France to Naples and Rome, where he gazed upon the Colosseum. Somewhere amid the paintings and palazzi, according to Jerome L. Sternstein, author of an unpublished narrative of Aldrich's early life, he rediscovered purpose, "a basis for his commitment to worldly success." As he wrote to Abby, "If I am deeply impressed with the insignificance and unimportance of man's life, I also feel what a grand thing it is to live and how much a man may accomplish even in this short and transitory existence." He returned, after a journey of five months, determined to placate the bruised sensibilities of his abandoned-feeling wife and—more than ever—to claim an august place in the affairs of men.

In the 1870s, Aldrich was elected to the city council in Providence; thanks to his close relations with local businesspeople, he also became a director of a small bank. Meanwhile, he advanced to the statehouse and then to the House of Representatives. Aldrich had no ken for dramatic speechifying. He did not give interviews, much less engage in Lincolnesque yarn spinning, and when a joke was told he smiled rather than laughed out loud. Unabashedly elitist, he had an aversion to crowds; the common touch was never his. But what Aldrich lacked in charisma or warmth was offset by his capacity to coolly analyze the facts. Over six feet tall, with a flowing handlebar mustache, he dressed in well-tailored suits and black bow ties and was a man of presence and intelligence. Rarely did he debate in public; the cloakroom, the back corridor, was where his work was done. A reporter with the *New York Tribune* noted the "side whiskers close cut" and the "brilliant dark eyes which he fastens closely upon the person with whom he is conversing." Another journalist described him, more succinctly, as "a blindness to inessentials masquerading as a human being!" Aldrich simply comprehended the issues, down to their intricate details, better than did his adversaries.

In 1881, the Rhode Island legislative bosses elevated Aldrich to the U.S. Senate. Now forty, he held a seat that was less subject to democratic challenges than it might have seemed. Rhode Island restricted the franchise to property owners and native-born citizens willing to pay a poll tax. Even when the franchise was broadened, the legislature was gerrymandered in favor of small Republican towns, shielding Aldrich from the swelling ranks of immigrants, who voted Democratic.

When he arrived in the Senate, the hot issue was the tariff. Contemporary Americans can scarcely grasp how controversial the tariff was throughout the nineteenth century. After the Civil War, business had persuaded Congress to erect a complex schedule of duties to protect textiles, manufactured products, machine tools, commodities such as sugar, and a host of other goods from imports. America was still an emergent economy, its businesses less efficient than those of Great Britain and other European states. Even as America's competitive disadvantage dissipated—that is, as the economic basis for the tariff vanished—northern manufacturers, through some combination of fearfulness and greed, supported the maintenance of high tariffs with near-religious fervor. At the same time, residents of farm states, who were consumers of industrial goods, resented having to pay more for such items. Geographically, therefore, the tariff debate mimicked that of silver, with agricultural regions fiercely resenting the tariff as an eastern, and Republican, policy prejudicial to their interests.

Aldrich immersed himself in reading on this dense topic, and had 170 volumes shipped to his home in Washington (he had a fondness for his books, mostly dry tomes). He read on both sides of the tariff issue, including Adam Smith, who in the late eighteenth century expounded the classical view that "the general liberty of trade" increased the average prosperity of all. This fine theory did not sway Aldrich, who at ground level observed that the tariff was a blessing for Rhode Island, which had the highest concentration of industry of any state in the union. Always practical in his thinking, the new senator judged that the tariff was vital not only to the manufacturers in his state but also to the "comfortable homes" and "material prosperity" of its ordinary citizens. In other words, he saw in the tariff a nineteenth-century version of trickle-down, in which factory owners insulated from overseas competition reaped higher profits and paid more lucrative wages. Aldrich did not have to be arm-wrestled into hearing out his business constituents; he avidly sought their opinion and genuinely trusted their expertise. He bonded, in particular, with the Sugar Trust, the colossus that in the late nineteenth century monopolized the sugar-refining industry. Aldrich was friends with Theodore Havemeyer, a member of the stupendously wealthy family that ran the Sugar Trust, and the owner of a mansion in Newport, Rhode Island. And the senator faithfully legislated in the Trust's interests, at times securing to the penny the tariff rate that Havemeyer requested.

On currency questions, Aldrich lined up against silver and was instrumental in 1896 in persuading William McKinley to run on a gold platform. Nonetheless, during his first two decades in the Senate, Aldrich was only intermittently involved in banking. It was the money shortages of the early twentieth century that shifted his focus. After the market break that also attracted Warburg's attention, bankers desperate to halt the never-ending succession of stringencies called on Aldrich to fashion some sort of new currency to enlarge the total in circulation and relieve the stress. Aldrich, grounded in the conservatism of the era, had no wish to dabble with the currency. He feared that supplying a new currency, by enhancing the total money supply, would likely cause inflation. Barton Hepburn, the former comptroller and now president of the Chase National Bank, urged him to support reform, to which Aldrich replied, "Our currency is as good as gold. Why not let it alone?" (Hepburn rejoined that the currency was both as good and as bad as gold, namely "quite inelastic.")

To appreciate the extent to which Aldrich was a roadblock to reform, one has to realize how influential he was not only within the Senate but with Theodore Roosevelt. Although the two did not see eye to eye on popular issues such as trust-busting, labor reform, and railroads, Roosevelt valued Aldrich's intelligence and superior financial sense. What's more, he had to deal with Aldrich's hold on the Finance Committee. As Roosevelt confessed to the crusading journalist Lincoln Steffens, "Aldrich is a great man to me; not personally but as the leader of the Senate. He is a king pin in my game. Sure I bow to Aldrich. . . . I'm just a president, and he has seen lots of presidents."

The President *did* bow to Aldrich. Behind closed doors, Roosevelt had promised Hepburn that if the American Bankers Association were to propose legislation for an asset currency, Roosevelt "would adopt it as his own." When a bill was submitted, he failed to do anything of the kind. When Hepburn sought an explanation, the Rough Rider admitted that he had cut a deal with Aldrich, as well as with Joe Cannon, the Speaker of the House, under which the legislators "let" the President have his way with "certain reforms," probably including railroad rate regulation, and kept currency and the tariff for themselves. And when Roosevelt ran for another term in 1904, currency reform was on hold.

Meanwhile, Paul Warburg continued to study the banking regime that Aldrich stoutly defended, and his critique of it deepened. Warburg found fault, in particular, with the system's rigid rules for bank reserves. The National Banking Act required banks in New York to keep a reserve equal to 25 percent of their deposits locked in their vaults, with similar restrictions applying to other banks.* This "stupid condition," Warburg concluded, immobilized the country's assets, just as if an army were required to garrison its troops in thousands of scattered barracks rather than be allowed to shift them to the front and concentrate them where they were needed most. "To a person trained under the central banking system of European countries," he would write, "such conditions seemed bewildering and strange."

In various other ways, Warburg judged that the American system, adequate perhaps for an agrarian society, was unsuited to the fast-growing industrial and commercial economy of the early 1900s. In Europe, a bank holding short-term loans could sell this paper in a liquid secondary market. (This was true both for the bills of trade mentioned earlier, which were issued by banks, and for commercial paper, which consisted of promissory notes issued by merchants and other businesses.) As a result, Europe's credit markets were fungible and highly liquid, similar to the stock market. In the United States, a bank that held such paper was stuck with a fixed, immobile asset. The lack of trading could not but be a drag on business. America needed a banking system, Warburg wrote, that was up to handling "a lively and intimate daily exchange." As business grew, the system's shortcomings were bound to surface.

Check clearing was a good example. Each bank maintained a bat-

---

* Country banks—those at the lowest level of the food chain—had to keep a 15 percent reserve, of which three-fifths could be held in interest-bearing deposits with banks in "reserve cities" (those in the middle tier) and the rest in the form of cash or gold in the vault. Similarly, banks in the nearly fifty reserve cities had to maintain a 25 percent reserve, of which half could be deposited with banks in the highest tier—that is, those in any of the three "central reserve cities" (New York, Chicago, and St. Louis)—and the remainder in their vaults.

talion of clerks to process checks and handle communications with other banks, a process that was unwieldy and at times comically inefficient. Its salient feature was a lack of coordination, in particular between banks across city and state boundaries—manifest in the seemingly simple task of routing checks to their bank of origin. A contemporary writer demonstrated the waste in the system by tracing the path of a single check for $43.56, drawn by Woodward Brothers, a general store in Sag Harbor, New York, on eastern Long Island, on its account at the local Peconic Bank and paid to Berry, Lohman & Rasch, a wholesale grocer in Hoboken, New Jersey. The check was deposited in the Second National Bank of Hoboken, which sent it along to a New York bank, which—not having a regular correspondent in Sag Harbor—bundled it with other checks to their Boston correspondent. The latter, inexplicably, transferred the nomadic debit to the First National Bank of Tonawanda, New York, near Niagara Falls. The Tonawanda bank, realizing the check had wandered off course, shipped it to a bank in Albany, which endeavored to get it nearer to home and relayed it to the First National Bank of Port Jefferson, only sixty miles from its point of issue. Alas, the check took another detour, to the Far Rockaway Bank, thence to the Chase National, the weary check's second visit to New York City. After two more stops, it was returned to the Peconic and duly laid to rest. As the writer concluded, "Once started, the poor check gets pushed along from station to station." In an economy humming with iron ore furnaces and factories, such methods were laughably archaic. In nearly every other field, combination and economy of scale were the watchwords. Industries were rapidly congealing into trusts (more than two hundred trusts were created from 1898 to 1904) and, largely in response to these giant combines, labor was recruiting workers into nationally affiliated unions. The country was knit by rail tracks and telegraph wires; electrification was advancing apace.

Only banking, or so it seemed, remained so fractured and so atomized. Even adjusting for the size of its population, America had far more banks than other countries. Most of its banks were small, rural affairs, and two-thirds were chartered by individual states rather than by Washington. Such state banks, although uninhibited by the considerable burdens of the National Banking Act, were, of course, prohibited from issuing National Bank Notes. This meant that the "national" currency was accessible to only a minority of the country's banks. As Warburg summarized this confusing picture, "there existed as many disconnected banking systems as there were States." Larger cities, it is true, had clearinghouses (local associations to provide banking functions such as check clearing and emergency liquidity), but clearinghouses were not universal, and their capacity was limited, and beyond the municipal level no collective machinery for banking existed.

Warburg frequently unburdened himself to Schiff as they walked downtown to the new Kuhn, Loeb skyscraper, a twenty-two-story token to modernity in the financial district. Schiff repeatedly insisted that, for cultural and historical reasons, America was not yet ready for a central bank. As Warburg acclimated to his new country, he came to better appreciate the political obstacles. Increasingly, his frustrations centered on the person who had the power (had he chosen to use it) to legislate reform: Senator Aldrich.

Aldrich, partly to mollify bankers, did offer his own currency bill, but it was less a reform measure than a reaffirmation of the status quo. In truth, the present arrangement suited him. High tariffs (which Aldrich largely dictated) enriched the Treasury and were used to buoy the banks in time of need. To Aldrich, the tariff, the gold standard, and National Banking constituted a sacred trinity best preserved intact. His one innovation was to suggest that *railroad* bonds be deemed acceptable collateral for government deposits in the national banks. This enraged progressives, who saw it as a plot to drive up the value of railroad securities, and thus make federal banking policy subservient to the interests of corporations.

In the marriage of business and government, Aldrich felt no discomfort. Like many politicians of the Gilded Age, he genuinely believed that society benefited when its elected leaders were guided by men of wealth. A card-playing companion of J. P. Morgan, he treated his own lack of a fortune as a providential error, one to be duly rectified. In fact, in the early 1890s, he had flirted with leaving the Senate; however, a Rhode Island business tycoon, Marsden J. Perry, offered him a way to stay in Congress and still maintain the lavish lifestyle that he, Abby, and their eight children had come to enjoy. Perry made Aldrich a partner in a plan to consolidate and electrify the state's trolleys; critically, the millions in capital needed to fund the modernization were provided by the Sugar Trust. Buoyed by this investment, Aldrich soon had a personal fortune that ran into the millions, and he could attend to his legislative work without the distraction of material concerns.*

---

* In Aldrich's private papers, there is a note from Nathaniel Stephenson, his official and rather hagiographic biographer, to the effect that John E. Searles, secretary and treasurer of the Sugar Trust, was the "gentleman" who entered into the trolley arrangements with Senator Aldrich, Perry, and another local partner, in 1893–1894, and that "the affiliation is very significant and should be studied up." But Stephenson made only passing mention in his book (pp. 98–99) of the fact that wealthy friends of Aldrich, who wanted him to remain in politics, helped him to invest in street railways. The investment was first exposed, soon after it was hatched, in a pair of explosive articles in *The New York Times,* on June 20 and June 21, 1894. The *Times* charged that the Sugar Trust forwarded $1.5 million to Aldrich to purchase stock in the Union Railway Company, a Providence trolley line. The articles were accusatory in tone and lacked corroborative proof. Due to the gravity of the accusations, Aldrich broke with his customary refusal to comment and denied the charges, save that he admitted investing in a traction (trolley) line in which Searles was also an investor— and in which each man, Aldrich maintained, had paid for his own shares. Jerome L. Sternstein's groundbreaking paper "Corruption in the Gilded Age Senate," *Capitol Studies: A Journal of the Capitol and Congress* 6, no. 1 (Spring 1978), concluded that the *Times*'s charges were in essence, even if not in every particular, accurate. Sternstein found a pair of contracts documenting that Aldrich received $100,000 in cash from Searles for the purchase of stock in Union Railway, and that Searles and his associates pledged to invest between $5.5 million and $7 million to electrify, and in other ways modernize, "four profitable but inefficient horse-drawn traction lines" servicing the Providence area. Subsequent to the acquisitions, the various lines were consolidated in a holding company, United Traction and Electric Company, in which Searles was a

Aldrich saw nothing wrong in such a convenient partnership with sugar—the industry over which he held so much power. He would have said that his votes for sugar tariffs were votes of conscience. His links to the business elite were further sealed by the marriage of his daughter Abby, in 1901, to John D. Rockefeller Jr. In a perceptive senior thesis submitted at Harvard six decades later, Michael Rockefeller, the senator's great-grandson, would write that "it became easy for Aldrich to conceive of legislation as being primarily a problem of consultation with the economic aristocracy followed by the application of personal authority."*

Aldrich generally ignored public criticism, believing that the Rhode Island machine shielded him from the vicissitudes of politics. But he was foolish to be so cavalier about his reputation. The American public was developing an appetite for scandal; journalists such as Ida Tarbell were writing hard-hitting articles exposing corruption in politics and unscrupulous behavior in business. American magazines had previously catered to a literary audience, but scandal sold better, and with technological innovations such as glazed paper made from wood pulp, publishers were able to cut prices and reach a mass audience. Many articles focused on the gross inequities in American society—the squalor of tenement living as opposed to the gilded lives of the ultrarich.

Predictably, Aldrich became a target. In 1905, William Randolph Hearst's *Cosmopolitan* commissioned David Graham Phillips, a well-known novelist, to write a series of exposés, published the next year under the overwrought title "The Treason of the Senate." The second

---

director and Aldrich president. Aldrich's trolley investment made him a very wealthy man by the time he became involved in banking legislation in the early 1900s. There is no evidence, however, that Aldrich was bribed. Aldrich did not need persuading to vote in sugar's interests. More likely, the Sugar Trust wanted to keep a friendly and powerful senator in office and provided the capital that permitted him to remain there. See the Aldrich Papers, Reel 59.

* A year after his thesis, while collecting primitive art in New Guinea, the twenty-three-year-old Rockefeller tragically disappeared.

installment—"Aldrich, the Head of It All"— vilified Aldrich as "the chief exploiter of the American people." Phillips's prose was so soaked in innuendo and overstatement that President Roosevelt objected. He likened Phillips to the mythical collector of filth in *The Pilgrim's Progress*, who could "look no way but downward, with a muck-rake in his hand." Thus "muckraking" was officially christened. Critics also thought the attacks on Aldrich were unfair. Whether the reading public was so discriminating is impossible to say. But Phillips's larger point—that Aldrich typified a Congress too cozy with corporate interests and too distant from the people—was correct.

The "Treason" series weakened Aldrich's political moorings by stirring cries for the popular election of senators. More important was the context of such articles. If the populists of the 1890s spoke to farmers, the muckrakers engaged a more urban constituency who had been put off by Bryan but who were, nonetheless, disturbed at the seeming unfairness in American society. Progressives, as these reformers came to be called, tended to be liberal-leaning city dwellers, such as lawyers and educators. While the populist and progressive movements had areas of overlap, progressivism was more focused on labor than on agriculture, more drawn to government and less fixated on laissez-faire. Progressives tapped into the unease that Americans felt over the rapid transformations wrought by industry, immigration, and technological change. The automobile was one change; education was another. From the Civil War to 1900, the number of high schools nationwide rose from several hundred to six thousand. In comparison with the America of the recent past, more people lived in cities; more worked at factories; more knew people who had been born overseas. The extreme concentration of wealth was also new. Millionaires had once been unheard of; now America had 3,800 of them. Newest of all were the giant industrial combinations supplanting local businesses. If the arbiter of society once had been a small-town lawyer or banker, now it was—or seemed to be—a huge corporation, a trust.

Theodore Roosevelt, although wealthy himself, championed progressive causes, whereas he would never have identified with a mob of farmers. Woodrow Wilson, now the president of Princeton University, who was attracting attention in Democratic political circles, shared many of the same ideals.

The question of which way progressives would lean on banking reform was complicated. Progressives applauded using the tools of social science to prescribe solutions to the problems of the day. Warburg's meticulous dissection of the banking system was consistent with that approach. On the other hand, progressives were skeptical of Big Business and of Wall Street. People in the movement did not trust banks—big banks especially—and they did not trust Senator Aldrich.

CHAPTER THREE

JITTERS ON WALL STREET

There is just as true patriotism to be found in Wall
Street as there is anywhere else in this country.
—FRANK A. VANDERLIP

WITH CONGRESS STALLED and bankers in the heartland far
from committed to reform, Wall Street began to agitate for a central
bank. The spark was a prophecy delivered by Jacob Schiff, Warburg's
older partner and a respected Wall Street sage.

Early in 1906, Schiff issued a warning to the New York Chamber
of Commerce. "I do not like to play the role of Cassandra," the
bearded financier solemnly began, but if the financial system was
not reformed soon, he averred, "we will get a panic in this country
compared with which those which have preceded it will look like
child's play."

Schiff feared that America's prosperity was endangered by its rick-
ety banking system and its shallow money market. Treasury Secretary
Leslie Shaw had tried to paper over these deficits by nimbly moving

funds around, but Schiff did not need to remind his audience what had occurred the previous autumn, when Shaw had removed $100 million from commercial banks, redeploying these funds into the government's Panama Canal project. On Wall Street, short-term interest rates briefly soared from 10 percent to an intolerable 125 percent, as if New York City were some remote financial backwater. In a more mature system, such volatility would be unthinkable. It grated on Schiff that New York, which had a new subway line admired around the world and opulent hotels on a par with those in Paris, had to suffer a financial system that was a holdover from the Civil War. "I say that is a disgrace to a civilized community," Schiff proclaimed.

The chamber was so alarmed it formed a committee to study America's much maligned currency. Significantly, the primary chore of writing the committee report was assigned to Frank A. Vanderlip, one of a coterie of younger bankers who, propitiously, did not share his elders' attachment to the hidebound National Banking system. Vanderlip had a diverse background, having worked in Washington and the Midwest as well as Wall Street. He was inquiring and ambitious, the sort of businessman whom Paul Warburg had been hoping to interest in reform.

Vanderlip had grown up on an Illinois farm and begun his career as a reporter, specializing in financial news. He was an enterprising journalist, cultivating high-level sources, and in 1897 he moved to the Treasury as assistant to Secretary Lyman Gage. In Washington, he rubbed shoulders with Theodore Roosevelt, then the assistant secretary of the Navy, whom he judged to be an egotistical warmonger. When the Spanish-American War broke out, Vanderlip arranged for the sale of war bonds and became familiar with scores of bankers, including James Stillman, the highly successful though reclusive president of National City Bank (and the gentleman who had curtly dismissed Warburg's memorandum on a central bank).

Impressed with Vanderlip's quickness, in 1901 Stillman offered Vanderlip a position as vice president. Immediately, he began to groom him as a successor. Notwithstanding that Stillman lorded over his staff—each morning at his house on East Seventy-second Street, servants ferried four eggs on a tray upstairs and anxiously awaited the master's judgment—he took to Vanderlip as if he were a son. The two went motoring on Sundays, and the ordinarily delphic banker shared with Vanderlip the secrets of the business, which Stillman had built by developing a roster of prized clients, including William Rockefeller of Standard Oil and a host of other magnates. Fusing a traditional loan business with underwriting, Stillman had made City the largest bank in the United States. Meticulous in manner and impeccably dressed, he did all he could to mold Vanderlip into a worthy heir, which included providing his protégé with a mansion on the Hudson, fully furnished (in the English style), and sponsoring him for membership in the right Republican clubs.

Despite their closeness, Vanderlip did not share his mentor's hostility toward monetary reform. Stillman regarded financial panics as natural and worthy rituals that cleansed the market of excesses that he himself studiously avoided (National City was fondly known as "Stillman's money trap," an homage to his prudence). Vanderlip, nearly twenty years his junior, took a more pragmatic view, judging that America's lack of a lender of last resort was needlessly holding back its progress. Even though the U.S. economy had grown to be the world's largest, with 40 percent of total banking capital, it remained a stepsister in international finance. National banks were not even authorized to operate foreign branches, much to Vanderlip's frustration.* And owing to the lack of confidence in American markets, short-term interest rates were higher and more volatile than they were in the United Kingdom (this amounted to a penalty paid by American businesses and other borrowers). Nor was the dollar used in set-

---

* Some private banks, which fell outside the National Banking Act, did do business overseas. These included J.P. Morgan & Co., which was an unincorporated partnership, active in both commercial and investment banking.

tling international balances. To the mortification of financiers such as Vanderlip and Schiff, merchants in Philadelphia buying goods in China or South America had to settle their transactions in Paris, London, or Berlin. Wall Street was tired of paying tribute. And as long as the United States was visited by periodic panics and money stringencies, there was little chance that the dollar would overtake the pound as an international currency.

Vanderlip, who was forty-one when he set to writing the chamber of commerce report, quietly handsome with narrow eyes behind thin spectacles, had no doubt that this state of affairs could be rectified if the government were to assume a more active role. His report bristles with the frustration of a metropolitan banker whose lofty ambitions in high finance were checked by the prosaic demands of the countryside. The harvests and the marketing of the crops, he complained, had strained the banks, which were "unable to make use of their credit, but are obliged to take lawful money from their reserves and send it into the harvest fields."

Vanderlip blamed the same culprit as did Warburg—the stifling requirements of the National Banking Act, which, in particular, put a crimp on circulation. The law imposed particular burdens on rural areas. In the cities, people had bank accounts and were accustomed to writing personal checks, which were simply an unregulated form of money. On the farm, people relied on bank notes—but the note supply was, of course, highly constrained. Vanderlip's aim was to fashion a more flexible supply—not more money on average, but a greater elasticity in either direction. For this, he proposed a central bank "of issue" (that is, with note-issuing powers) that would deal only with banks; it would be controlled by a board of governors appointed, at least in part, by the president of the United States. This is a fair description of the eventual Federal Reserve Act.

But Vanderlip's prescience in one respect failed him. Although he included, as a fail-safe, an alternate, less draconian reform, he naïvely assumed that what New York bankers advised, the rest of the country would gladly endorse. Having talked to bankers in the interior, Vanderlip was convinced, as he put it with stunning lack of sensitivity, that "a majority of the bankers of the United States appreciate the necessity for a variable and elastic element in the currency and will heartily co-operate with the bankers of New York City." Sounding even more elitist, he lauded the day, not long in coming he must have imagined, when "the lawful money reserves of banks in financial centers would no longer be depleted in the autumn in order that harvest hands in Kansas, Nebraska and Dakota might receive their wages."

If the onetime farm boy had difficulty empathizing with Dakota harvest hands, it reflected Wall Street's widening distance from the rest of the country—even from other bankers. As American industry assumed corporate form, many companies established headquarters in New York and turned to banks to finance growth. Leading financial institutions in the city were gradually morphing into investment banks, peddling securities, trading bonds, and dabbling in foreign exchange. This was a momentous evolution, presaging a culture of finance that was wholly foreign to ordinary Americans. Thomas F. Woodlock, editor of *The Wall Street Journal*, observed that "New York bankers are, with few exceptions, steeped in the atmosphere of the stock-market business, and the ticker takes a good deal of their attention."

Sensitive to attitudes west of the Hudson River, Schiff tried to soften Vanderlip's recommendations when he again addressed the chamber, in November 1906. "If you go away from New York City and discuss this subject of a central bank," Schiff began, replicating the admonishments he had delivered to Warburg, "if you . . . discuss it with the people of this country all the way across its three thousand miles, you will find grave distrust in the proposition." The American people, he explained,

> at the time of Andrew Jackson, and more so today, do not want
> to centralize power. They do not want to increase the power of

government. . . . They do not want to have this mass of deposits, which the government would have to keep in this bank, controlled by a few people. They are afraid of the political power it would give and of the consequences.

The chamber of commerce approved the Vanderlip report (without the softening suggested by Schiff) the same day. The group's boldness perhaps was spurred by the urgency of events. Money markets had experienced unusual turmoil that year, exacerbated by a devastating earthquake in San Francisco that caused three thousand deaths and destroyed most of the city. The quake set off a transatlantic movement of gold that destabilized world markets. In that era, financial calamities were shadowed by the physical movement of bullion. Foreign insurers had to pay claims on San Francisco policies, and banking capital, unavailable at home, had to be imported. Gold shipments were the most practical means of supplying it. Nine days after the quake, on April 27, Vanderlip reported to Stillman, who was spending considerable time in Paris, where he resided in a gray-green mansion on rue Rembrandt, "The immediate effect has been the transfer of a very large amount of gold to San Francisco."

Just as Paul Warburg had predicted, in the absence of a government bank, National City's preeminent position thrust on it much of the responsibility of dealing with the disaster. For the moment, Stillman's money trap was up to the task. One week later, Vanderlip reassured his mentor,

The drain which California has put upon us gives indication of being at an end. Shipments there ceased two or three days ago. The total withdrawals of funds by California banks from New York and other centers will considerably exceed $30,000,000. . . . We have arranged to import $2,500,000 more gold which brings the total of the City Bank's importation, as I am cabling you, up to $31,000,000.

But money markets remained turbulent. In April and three times later that year, reserves in the New York banks fell into deficiency. Legally, this prevented them from extending new loans. What the banks needed was someone to supply them with additional reserves.

Leslie Shaw did his utmost to facilitate gold imports—including providing a short-term loan of $10 million to National City. The Treasury secretary boasted that thanks to his efforts more than six carloads of gold, "largely in bars," were imported from Europe, Australia, and South Africa. Moreover, he widened the practice of depositing and withdrawing government funds at strategic moments. It is worth listening to Shaw's recounting of the languid summer of 1906, when

> granaries and warehouses were empty, freight cars stood on sidetracks, business men fished in mountain streams or rested at vacation resorts. Meanwhile the banks were comfortably well supplied with money, and interest rates were low. Everything seemed serene . . . except to those who recognized that in this latitude crops mature in the fall.

Taking precautions, Shaw withdrew $60 million from national banks, lest it be used as tinder for stock speculation, and temporarily "locked it up." Then, as cooler nights brought the approach of autumn,

> business men returned to their desks fresh for more intense activities. Crops began to mature, granaries and warehouses began to fill, freight cars were put in commission, checks and drafts were drawn in multiplied number and in multiplied amounts, while the people naturally carried in their pockets more ready cash than at other seasons. The strain inevitable [*sic*] began to develop. Interior banks [those in the country] called their loans. . . .

With credit now in short supply, Shaw restored a portion of the funds previously withdrawn, "with great benefit," he judged, "to the business interests of the country."

Shaw was not trying to increase the money stock, only to smooth the seasonal fluctuations—a modest goal by the standards of today. The total funds at his disposal were also modest. But his actions were seen as radical by his peers. It did not help matters that fully 11 percent of the government's bank balances were parked with a single bank—National City. A Chicago banker, incensed over Shaw's close relations with City (which was also the bank to Standard Oil), fumed that the public "had begun to smell kerosene on his wardrobe." *The Nation* charged Shaw with aiding "a ring of powerful Wall Street speculators." A similar charge had been leveled in the 1790s at Treasury Secretary Alexander Hamilton and, indeed, would be brought against the Federal Reserve during the financial crisis of 2008. It is a truism of capitalism that if money is injected into the system, no matter the intent, some of it will end up benefiting well-connected financiers. Shaw had at least tried to sprinkle his deposits around the country according to demand—in Boston, Louisville, Kansas City, New Orleans, Minneapolis, Buffalo, Omaha, and other cities—but the money ended up where interest rates were highest: in New York. "Money," he dolefully observed, "is almost as liquid as water and finds its level about as quickly."

The charge of favoritism was, in any case, only a sideshow. The more elementary criticism was philosophical: that Shaw was encroaching in the money market, and this was still not thought to be the government's concern. If the Treasury secretary could intervene in credit markets, the liberal *Nation* fretted, as if bewitched by a premonition of a modern central banking maestro, what would prevent some future "autocrat" from intervening in the stock market? In a more comprehensive critique, A. Piatt Andrew, a young assistant economics professor at Harvard, charged Shaw with skirting the law in various ways (which he had), and flatly declared, "Gold imports are not a matter of government concern." No European central banker would have agreed.

Andrew saved his most sizzling critique for the end. Why was it, he wondered, that the New York banks had fallen into deficiency with much greater frequency under *this* particular Treasury secretary? "Never before," he noted, "had a Secretary declared that it was the place of the Treasury to intervene in banking operations outside of times of panic." Evidently, he surmised, banks felt less need to keep their own reserve knowing that the Treasury was ready and eager to assist. This anticipated the "moral hazard" arguments against bailouts in the 2000s. "Outside relief in business, like outdoor charity," Andrew concluded, "is apt to diminish the incentives to providence." Andrew did not belittle the defects of the American system, or the need for reform, but he rejected "arbitrary and lawless interpretations" by an official "over whom Congress has little or no control."

Nearly everyone wanted to reform the banking system, but no two groups agreed on the remedy. Wall Streeters did not much worry that a central bank might favor powerful bankers (that was part of the attraction). Bankers in Gotham believed that American leadership in finance would redound to the country's benefit, and also to their own. They had unselfish reasons as well as opportunistic ones, although it is unlikely that they examined their motives so finely. They simply felt that a stronger credit system would be good all around.

Rebuffing Wall Street, Shaw immodestly suggested that the Treasury secretary himself be endowed with czarlike powers, which, he said, would enable him to avert any and all panics in the future. Senator Aldrich applauded this idea, which he believed would strengthen the existing currency, and dashed off a bill to enhance the secretary's authority.

Aldrich and Shaw were opposed by yet another constituency, Chicago's bankers, who were concentrated on La Salle Street. Chicago bankers disliked Shaw's proposal because they feared, justifiably, that an activist Treasury would work closely with banks in New York. For similarly parochial reasons, La Salle Street was opposed to a central bank.

The Chicago bankers were important because they were a potent industry voice outside of New York; they also dominated the councils of the American Bankers Association. Under the leadership of James Forgan, president of the First National Bank of Chicago, the ABA championed a bill to expand the currency by letting big-city banks operate branch offices, through which they could distribute their own notes.

But the prospect of branch banking horrified yet another group—small-town bankers, who reckoned that if banks in the city could open branches in rural areas, country banks would be overrun. And country bankers wielded considerable clout in Congress (more than a few congressmen *were* local bankers). With the banking industry so fractured, and with Roosevelt not daring to break the impasse, reform efforts were stalemated. As one western observer put it, "The bankers are still divided; who shall decide when doctors disagree?"

Nicholas Murray Butler, president of Columbia University, acknowledged the lack of leadership on a visit to Germany, where he was received by Wilhelm II. The Kaiser inquired who managed the confusing business of American finance. With a fatalistic air, Butler replied that the system was run by "God."

Warburg diagnosed the Americans' malady as a fear that any reform would result in either the government's or Wall Street's gaining control, each an outcome dreaded by the public. Warburg would write that an "abhorrence of both extremes"—he might have said an abhorrence of power—"had led to an almost fanatic conviction" in favor of complete decentralization.

Thus far, Warburg had followed Schiff's advice and kept his views from the public. However, at the end of 1906, he found himself at a dinner with a group of bankers and economists at the home of Columbia professor Edwin Seligman. The discussion turned to the financial outlook, which many considered ominous. Warburg distilled, with his trademark clarity, just why the American financial system remained so vulnerable. His host was spellbound.

"You ought to write. You ought to publish," Seligman said.

"Impossible. I can't write English yet—not well enough for publication."

Seligman insisted. Appealing to Warburg's growing attachment to America, he added, "It's your duty to put your ideas before the country."

The gestation period was remarkably brief. On January 6, 1907, readers of *The New York Times* awoke to Warburg's first published American article, "Defects and Needs of Our Banking System."

"The question of the reform of the currency system is uppermost in the minds of all," Warburg began. Mincing no words, he likened America's system to that of Europe "at the time of the Medicis," that is to say, in the fifteenth century.

Warburg stressed that a central bank was a requisite for developing deeper, more liquid credit markets. Even in a second tongue, Warburg waxed poetic over the centralized systems of Europe, where "the credit of the whole nation—that is, the farmer, merchant, and manufacturer . . . becomes available as a means of exchange." Warburg wanted Americans to see that their system was weakened by its lack of unity. He vividly compared its banks to the infantry in a disorganized platoon. "Instead of sending an army," he admonished, "we send each soldier to fight alone."

By the time his article appeared, New York bankers had grown exceedingly edgy. The longer the boom went on, the more it relied on credit, and many felt that credit was overextended, as in a party too merry with drink. While no domestic authority existed to take away the punch bowl, America was highly sensitive to the decisions of European central banks, in particular the Bank of England.

The view in Britain was that America's feverish economy could use some cooling down. With loan growth so rapid, the pyramid of credit was perched on a precarious base. Was this a bubble? The Bank of England only knew that it would no longer be responsible for financing America's expansion—particularly because the boom in the United States had been draining England's gold. As Vanderlip was to report to Stillman, "The Bank of England is extremely nervous on the subject of gold exports."

In the fall of 1906, the Bank of England took away the punch. London raised its interest rate from 3.5 percent to 6 percent. The Reichsbank in Berlin raised rates as well. Since international capital ever flows to where the yield is highest, these moves inevitably induced investors to ship their gold back across the Atlantic. The Bank of England further insulated the mother country from the overheated American economy by directing British banks to liquidate the finance bills—short-term loans—that they provided to American firms, thereby tightening credit. In the aftermath of the ensuing panic, Oliver Sprague, an assistant professor at Harvard and a reputable financial writer, judged that this was the turning point. Eighty years later, Richard T. McCulley reached a similar conclusion. When the Bank of England reversed the gold flow, McCulley wrote, "the Wall Street boom punctured as easily as a soap bubble."

Wall Street tried to replace British loans with domestic credit, but American banks, having grown so quickly, had reached a point of exhaustion. Toward the end of the year, the stock market broke. Preparing for the worst, National City tightened its lending. Vanderlip protested, but Stillman smelled a recession, possibly a nasty one. "I have felt for some time," he wrote early in 1907, "that the next panic and low interest rates following would straighten out a good many things that have of late years crept into banking." Stillman's bank had emerged from the Panic of 1893 in a stronger position relative to competitors; he expected that prudence would pay off again. "What impresses me as most important," he informed his chastened subordinate, "is to go into next Autumn ridiculously strong and liquid."

The economy remained resilient into April, the mood in the

heartland one of "buoyancy and hopefulness"—so reported George W. Perkins of the House of Morgan to J. P. Morgan, America's most eminent financier. But the view on Wall Street, Perkins noted, was darker.

What bankers found depressing was that banks were refusing to lend. Firms with illiquid assets were becoming nervous. As Perkins wrote to Morgan in May, there were "a great number of people and houses very very closely tied up with assets that they cannot either sell or borrow [longer-term] money on." A subsequent note was nearly despairing. "As to money," Perkins wrote, "there is still a distinct disinclination on every one's part to make loans for any length of time."

Shaw had exhausted the capacities of the Treasury—always more limited than his critics granted. What's more, the pounding from the press had taken its toll. In March, he resigned, replaced by George Cortelyou, a political adviser and intimate of Roosevelt who was rather more timid.

Senator Aldrich, sensing the limited room for maneuvering, steered his currency bill through Congress, but it was altogether a modest one. When the bill was enacted, on March 3, the *Times* gratefully exhaled, describing the Aldrich bill as "a partial fulfillment of hopes that have long been entertained by the financial community for a betterment of our monetary system." It was, in fact, no such thing.

Just as the bill was signed, stocks broke again—this time sharply. Many railroad stocks fell 50 percent before the month was out; Union Pacific, a bellwether issue, plunged 25 points in a single day. In May, business began to contract. Although the recession of 1907 began as a modest one, at the end of May, Perkins confided to the venerable Morgan, who was spending much of his time on the Continent, "No [one] seems to have confidence in anything. . . . Call money is almost unlendable." Longer-term funds were even scarcer—and the crops were still on the vine. With an eye on the unforgiving harvest calendar, Perkins concluded gloomily, "There seems to be a general feeling that we are likely to have a pretty serious time next Fall."

CHAPTER FOUR

PANIC

A panic grows by what it feeds on.
—Walter Bagehot

Who is to be Mr. Morgan's successor?
—Ida Tarbell

In the fall of 1907, America suffered the worst breakdown in the history of the National Banking system. Overnight, banks were stripped of reserves and the country was plunged into a severe depression. Cash (or its equivalent in gold) was all that people wanted, and cash vanished from circulation due to people's very attempts to secure it. No agency of government was able to stem the panic. George Cortelyou, the new Treasury secretary, had neither the capacity nor the desire. "The present head of the department," he wrote of his own relatively modest efforts to relieve the crisis, "has not assumed the obligation willingly and would be glad to be relieved of it at least in part by suitable legislation."

The word "panic" springs from Pan, the mythological god of the wilds, depicted as a man with the horns, legs, and tail of a goat, who played on panpipes and who aroused fear among solitary travelers in the forest. The Panic of 1907 generated, according to Frank Vanderlip, a "sudden, unreasonable, overpowering fright" that swept through "all the human herd." In the thick of the crisis, Vanderlip encountered a prospective client, a promising young author by the name of Julian Street. He was clutching fifty thousand-dollar bills—his wife's inheritance. Previously, Street had kept the money in a trust, a lightly regulated form of bank. He had gone to the trust to withdraw his money. There, the trust officers tried to dissuade him. They argued with him and cajoled him. "For your own good, Mr. Street," the officers wailed, beseeching him to leave his funds. "Cash!" roared the author. "I want the cash!" Came the reply—"Not so *loud*, please, Mr. Street." But Street's cries echoed throughout the city, then throughout the land.

After a decade-long boom, Americans had come to think of prosperity as a given and of the financial system as robust. Rapid electrification, new techniques for mass production, and a population that had soared to 80 million had made the nation an industrial power. Businessmen believed America would never again have a panic such as in 1893. Except for the urgings of a few financiers, mostly in New York, the impetus for banking reform had languished. Most Americans were uninterested, content with the quaint decentralized system of National Banking. The Panic of 1907 shattered their complacency overnight.

Even Wall Street was caught off guard. Such crises always arrive as a shock, even to those who had sounded alarms. That summer, the level of industrial activity was weak but far from alarming. George Perkins, the Morgan partner, wrote to his eminence of "a little let-up in general business." The New York money market tightened in the fall, but bankers had seen that before. In October, Theodore Roosevelt felt relaxed enough to disengage from his constitutional duties and spend a fortnight hunting in the wild canebrake country of Louisiana (on the thirteenth day, the President shot and killed a black bear). More telling was that J. P. Morgan, having returned from Europe in mid-August, took leave from Wall Street again. The banker, who when not working or acquiring art took his greatest solace in religion, was in Richmond, Virginia, attending a convention of Episcopalians. The missives he received from Perkins were singularly soothing. "There is nothing special to report," the latter wrote him reassuringly. On October 12, Perkins dwelled on pleasantries, noting: "We are all very well, and having fine weather, and hope you are as fortunate."

The trouble started with a case of misbegotten speculation that arose, as is often the case, in a remote province of Wall Street. A well-known and rather notorious Montana copper magnate had managed to seize control of a modest New York financial institution, the Mercantile National Bank. He then used the bank to finance an attempt to manipulate a copper-mining stock. In October, the manipulation collapsed, putting the Mercantile in jeopardy. The bank's depositors now displayed a keen interest in withdrawing their money, and the Mercantile sought help from the New York Clearing House, the institution that settled balances among member banks and could also provide emergency loans to members. Assistance was provided to the Mercantile on condition that its wayward president resign. There, the disturbance might have ended.

However, banking in New York was particularly exposed due to the emergence of the trusts, whose assets had swelled over the previous decade because of their willingness to pay higher rates of interest. Trusts had begun as quiet repositories for trust funds and estates, but over time they started to mimic the lending and deposit-taking operations of banks. They also invested in riskier assets than banks, such as real estate. Trusts could do this because they existed outside the regulated ecosystem of National Banking—not unlike the way, in a future generation, special off-balance-sheet vehicles would help commercial banks to circumvent the rules. Indeed, in the panic that began one hundred years later, it was a non-bank, Bear Stearns, where the trouble started, and for similar reasons. In 1907, more than 40 percent of all deposits in New York were parked in trusts—on the periphery of the financial system. And while a dollar in the national banks was backed, on average, by 25 cents of cash in the till, each dollar in the trusts was supported by only 6 cents. This meant that trusts had far less protection for a rainy day.

Not only were the trusts vulnerable individually, but they (like banks in general) were linked by a chain of interlocking boards or, as it were, by a chain of reputation. The collapse of the Mercantile drew attention to another of its directors, a certain Charles W. Morse, who had interests in, and sat on the boards of, no fewer than six other local banks, three of which he controlled. Morse was a shady operator; his business methods, Oliver Sprague tactfully observed, "had been of an extreme character."

Now, with unease spreading, two of the Morse banks were forced to seek assistance from the New York Clearing House. In return, Morse resigned *his* positions, a development *The New York Times* reported with relief. However, Morse seems to have ratted out one of his confreres, Charles T. Barney, a central figure in developing the New York City subways and the president of a considerably larger institution, the Knickerbocker Trust Company. Barney and the unsavory Morse were partners in various deals, and their association rattled the Knickerbocker's depositors. Thus the bad coin passed from hand to hand. By Saturday, October 19, when the seventy-year-old Morgan boarded a private railcar to return to New York, he was aware of a widening crisis.

The next day, Morgan assembled a command staff consisting of himself, James Stillman, and George F. Baker, who for thirty years had been president of the First National Bank of New York. This venerable trio appointed a small team of younger bankers to evaluate the worthiness of troubled banks and determine which might merit assistance. Henry P. Davison, vice president of Baker's First National, directed this team. Davison was immediately confronted with a crisis at the Knickerbocker, which, as a trust and a non–Clearing House member, was deemed ineligible for assistance. The New York Clearing House, in other words, took a narrow view of its role, and no institution with a broader mandate existed. Barney resigned and, with time running short, Davison dispatched Benjamin Strong, his thirty-four-year-old protégé, to inspect the failing trust's books.

The Knickerbocker was housed on Thirty-fourth Street and Fifth Avenue in an opulent, Corinthian-columned temple designed by Stanford White. The sidewalk in front was besieged by a mob of depositors, some of whom bore satchels with which they hoped to carry off sackloads of cash. Inside the bank, "stacks of green currency, bound into thousand dollar lots, were piled on the counters beside the tellers," so reported the *Washington Post*.

As Strong went over the books in the rear of the bank, he could hear depositors in the green-marbled public area clamoring for their money. He later wrote, "The consternation of the faces of the people in that line, many of them men I knew, I shall never forget."

By a little after noon on Tuesday, October 22, the Knickerbocker had paid out $8 million; it then suspended operations. Strong reported that he could not, in such little time, vouch for the Knickerbocker's solvency. Morgan, therefore, decided not to intervene. In letting the Knickerbocker fail, Morgan knew he would be unleashing frantic runs on every other trust in the city. The resulting panic, as Schiff had predicted, made previous debacles look like child's play indeed.

Secretary of the Treasury Cortelyou hurried to New York on the afternoon train. He met that evening with a coterie of bankers—"with Mr. Morgan presiding," the *Times* reported. In a later era, no private banker would think of holding court over his federal overseers. Notwithstanding that Morgan's was a private bank, far smaller than the big commercial banks, Pierpont Morgan had, by a country mile, more prestige than any other banker in America. By force of reputation, he stood the best chance of corralling other banks into a cooperative rescue effort, and he was the man to whom the others turned.

The next day, a furious stampede struck the Trust Company of America, the city's second-largest trust, and also other trusts. Strong, once more, was sent to inspect the books. When he returned to the Morgan office, at 23 Wall Street, he found Morgan with Stillman, Baker, Perkins, and Davison. He told the group that although Trust of America's surplus had vanished, it remained solvent. Calmly, Morgan said, "This, then, is the place to stop this trouble."

Morgan had not been previously acquainted with Strong. He placed confidence in him on the say-so of Davison, whose unflappable steadiness was perfectly calibrated to put the eminent banker at ease. Harry Davison had been reared in Troy, Pennsylvania, the son of a farm implement salesman. He was orphaned early and went to work for a small bank, where he laboriously copied figures in a leather-bound book. Davison was a striver, ambitious but possessed of an easy manner and gracious charm, qualities that sped his rise from small-town banking to the pinnacle of finance.

Davison was close to Strong partly because the latter had also tasted hardship. Strong had been raised in a comfortable family, but his father suffered a financial setback, forcing Strong to forgo college—a bitter pill. He entered the trust field and caught the attention of Davison, who was five years his senior, and his neighbor in the bedroom community of Englewood, New Jersey. Through Davison, Strong joined the up-and-coming Bankers Trust, and seemed on the verge of a bright future. In 1905, however, Strong's wife became depressed and, one day, while her husband was at work, availed herself of a revolver that had been purchased to ward off burglars, and shot herself. Davison, recalling his own lonely childhood, felt compassion and took in Strong's children. Thus the two had a bond.

By the time Strong reported to Morgan, Trust of America had less than \$200,000 in the till. The Morgan group approved an emergency loan, on condition that the borrower show sufficient collateral. Employees of the beleaguered trust ferried boxes of securities to 23 Wall Street, and Strong and Morgan sat around a table assessing their worth. "Mr. Morgan," Strong recalled, "had a pad in front of him making figures as we went along." When Morgan was satisfied as to the collateral's value, he would notify Stillman, who was in an adjacent room. Then, Stillman telephoned his underlings at National City Bank, which promptly supplied the requisite cash, with the loan to be divided among a syndicate of banks.

But the panic did not subside. On Thursday, October 24, frightened trusts pulled their loans to the stock market—laying bare the domino-like fragility of American credit. Desperate stockbrokers offered to pay 125 percent interest on call loans (short-term loans that were callable at any time). With dozens of brokers on the verge of failure, the president of the New York Stock Exchange threatened to shutter the market. Morgan felt that closing would be a mistake. He summoned the bank chiefs to his office and in roughly a quarter of an hour obtained a pledge for \$23.5 million to shore up the market. National City committed to the largest share, \$8 million. Stillman was discovering—true to Warburg's prophecy—that his bank's granite strength foisted on it unwanted responsibility in a crisis. The next day, the fifth straight of panicky conditions, the call rate on the stock exchange for overnight loans soared to 150 percent and the Morgan syndicate had to pledge \$10 million more.

By then, a new crisis was erupting: New York City was running desperately short of cash. Morgan summoned Baker and Stillman to his private library, a palazzolike structure adjacent to his home on Madison Avenue and, once again, the bankers arranged for an emergency loan, which kept the city government afloat.

Morgan, of course, was not the only one to provide assistance.

Over a period of four critical days, Secretary Cortelyou deposited $35 million in the city's banks. However, at that point, the Treasury's surplus was exhausted.

Now more than ever, Morgan became indispensable. He filled the vacuum of central banker like a Medici prince, holding council in the evenings in his library, which was studded with hanging tapestries, ancient Bibles, and rare medieval manuscripts. Frequently he met with Baker and Stillman, and with the unflappable Davison, into the late hours. One night, as the group debated the merits of a rescue, Frank Vanderlip was also present; Morgan puffed on his cigar, which was rolled in his particular style, forming a bulge at the outer end. After a bit, Vanderlip noticed the hand that was holding the cigar had relaxed on the table, and Morgan's head had sunk forward. Vanderlip would write: "We sat quietly, saying nothing. The only sound that could be heard was the breathing of Mr. Morgan."

Morgan's centrality was so critical that the *Times* reported, worryingly, when he caught a mild cold, which was blamed on exposure to night air. Briefly, this private man was the toast of the town. Floor traders on the stock exchange burst into an ovation in jubilant thanks for his efforts. Grateful tributes streamed in to 23 Wall Street, some from far-flung correspondents. The letters, which pinned to Morgan's chest the medal of savior, raised the question of his role in the economic system and whether it could be relied upon in the future. Jacob Schiff bluntly declared, "You stand between us and financial chaos." A handwritten note from a banker in Memphis asserted that it was the general impression that "the safety and welfare of the financial structure of this country depends almost entirely upon you."

But Morgan was edging into retirement, as were Stillman and Baker. They would not be around forever. And Morgan's efforts, however laborious, were not enough. New York's trusts lost a remarkable (and devastating) 48 percent of their deposits. Even worse, at the end of October the New York Clearing House was forced to take the drastic step of authorizing banks to settle accounts with one another via certificates—paper substitutes for money—rather than with cash. The Panic had now reached epic proportions. The Clearing House "loan certificates" were backed by loans of the member banks. They were IOUs—promises to pay cash when cash became available. They were a form of invented money.

With panic spreading, clearinghouses and bank associations in scores of other cities minted their own versions of clearinghouse money. Some were elaborately engraved to give the appearance of normal currency. The certificates were intended to be used only among banks, so that cash could be preserved for ordinary depositors. In a crude way, they added to the money supply—later a function of the Federal Reserve. However, in more than a score of cities banks were forced to hand out loan certificates not just to their fellow banks, but to ordinary depositors.

Many railroads, mining companies, and shopkeepers paid workers with bank checks instead of with cash; those that didn't had little choice but to suspend operations. In Birmingham, Alabama, banks distributed checks signed by their cashiers in denominations as small as one dollar to local employers—who used this scrip to pay their workers. Retail establishments generally accepted such paper, since that was all that many customers had.

By mid-November, approximately half of the country's larger cities were using loan certificates "or other substitutes for legal money," according to a survey conducted just after the Panic by Harvard's Professor Piatt Andrew. Loan certificates had been used in previous panics, but never so extensively. In some smaller towns where no clearinghouse existed, the local bankers improvised, setting up a temporary committee, as it were, on the front porch. Bankers tried to reassure the public, noting that certificates were backed by "approved securities." Some added piquant details. In Portland, Oregon, the clearinghouse boasted that banks had deposited notes secured by "wheat, grain, canned fish, lumber . . . and other marketable products." Monetary exchange was reverting toward barter.

Andrew estimated that $500 million of cash substitutes of one form or another were circulated nationwide. And in two-thirds of cities with populations above 25,000, banks suspended cash withdrawals "to a greater or less degree." For example, in Council Bluffs, Iowa, a limit was imposed of $10 per customer; in Atlanta, $50 per day and $100 per week. Banks in Providence, Rhode Island, adopted a convenient policy of "discretion," vetting withdrawals case by case. Although such actions had scant legal footing, officials not only looked the other way, in many states they encouraged banks, for their own protection, to curtail teller operations. Bank holidays were proclaimed in a handful of states, with California's enduring until late December. Small wonder that Andrew termed it "the most extensive and prolonged breakdown" of the credit system since the Civil War.

Even though clearinghouse certificates provided a measure of relief, they were generally recognized only in their city of issue, which was a serious drawback. A New York banker lamented that "drafts on Philadelphia, Boston and other banks sent for collection are being returned on the plea that momentarily it is impossible to remit New York exchange. Each city issuing its own Clearing House certificates . . . builds a Chinese wall against other centres." Through November and much of December, the United State monetary system devolved toward the polyglot moneys of the early nineteenth century, when itinerant peddlers did business with different moneys state to state and territory to territory.

Money, in fact, traded at a premium. Those who needed cash were forced to write checks for more than 100 percent of the desired sum. Money lost its normal, fungible characteristic—it was worth more in one place than in another. Brokers placed ads offering to buy and sell currency at premiums, the size of which was in constant flux. Out-of-town exchange was often unavailable at any price.

Even the suggestion that banks were short of cash frightened depositors—many of whom withdrew funds while they still could. In New York, there was a run on the rental of safe-deposit boxes.

Nationwide, bank deposits plunged by $350 million, much of which ended up stashed in bedroom dressers and kitchen drawers.

However, hoarding by individuals did not cause as much harm as hoarding by banks. As Secretary Cortelyou noted, "It is said that many of our people have hoarded money. This is undoubtedly true, but so have many of the banks." Country banks pulled deposits from reserve cities; middle-tier banks in such cities yanked money from New York, Chicago, and St. Louis. Country bankers were not without reason for taking precautions. Some found their deposits at reserve city banks to be temporarily frozen. James E. Ferguson, a bank president in Temple, Texas, got a telegram from his reserve city bank announcing that it would not ship currency, because the reserve bank, in turn, had been frozen by New York. As Ferguson later told a congressional committee, "We were broke with a pocket full of money." It did not take many such experiences for small-town bankers to start hoarding currency.

Banks in San Antonio, Indianapolis, Wichita, and Portland bolstered their reserves to 35 percent of deposits, well above the 25 percent required. Banks in Galveston, Texas, went to 49 percent, a veritable fortress of financial redundancy, and a bank in Indiana bragged it had a cash reserve of 67 percent—a good portion of which, Vanderlip sourly surmised, had been pulled from vaults in New York. The surplus reserves represented, in effect, the banking system's wasted resources. In contrast, New York banks at least tried to supply liquidity by assuming the loans of failing trusts—and in so doing, ran their reserves to well below the legal minimum.

Charges and countercharges flew; the question of blame became impossible to untangle. Did country bankers needlessly hoard reserves, as Vanderlip believed, or did New York's risk taking leave the country exposed? Each accusation was correct. And while many out-of-town banks thought only of stuffing their vaults, they had every right to protect their own institutions.

The problem was that the system inspired a competition for

reserves, so that much of the country's banking capital, though substantial *in the aggregate*, was never put to use. Reserves were disaggregated bank by bank and city by city. This rendered them sterile. Warburg likened the system to a town without a fire department in which each family maintained a pail of water to quench blazes in its own house.

The contrast with Europe could not have been starker. In the British system, the Bank of England performed the job of "leaning into the wind"—that is, lending funds when funds were otherwise scarce. Not coincidentally, Britain had not experienced a banking suspension since the time of the Napoleonic wars. America had been scorched by five severe banking crises, in addition to more than twenty lesser panics, in little more than a generation. As the writer Richard Timberlake put it, "All institutions had to run with the wind; none could lean into it."

Quickly on the heels of the Panic, the economic contraction deepened. As bank reserves dwindled, banks were forced to curtail loans. The stock market plunged approximately 40 percent. Iron and steel production was severely reduced. Many factories shuttered or went part-time due to the lack of currency for wages. The severity of the depression astonished businesspeople, not least because it had struck during a period of prosperity. The country's railroads had been profitable, its farmers rich.

Such chaos in the midst of plenty convincingly demonstrated, at least to bankers such as Warburg, that the system had to be redesigned. Morgan's heroics notwithstanding, America's finances were too complex to rely on a single banker or group of bankers. What Strong had witnessed on the pavement outside the Knickerbocker led him and other Wall Street bankers to strongly endorse reform.

Morgan was disinclined to join a crusade; however, Stillman, burdened by the responsibility of propping up failing banks, experienced a change of heart. Several weeks into the Panic, he ventured the short distance to the offices of Kuhn, Loeb. Unannounced, he made his way to the émigré banker he had first met four years earlier. He found him there, as he was before.

"Warburg," he barked, "where is your paper?"

"Too late now, Mr Stillman," Warburg replied sadly. "What has to be done cannot be done in a hurry. If reform is to be secured, it will take years of educational work to bring it about."

Soon after this encounter, Warburg reignited the public debate with a letter to the *Times* in which he argued that only "a modern central bank" could cure America's ills. By "modern," Warburg meant "European"—that is, managed by private bankers. Warburg was mistrustful of American democracy, which was too popular (or populist) for his ordered Germanic tastes. He feared leaving banking in the hands of politicians and proposed a central bank governed by "our best trained business men." Progressives, on the other hand, saw banking as a public trust. To farmers, westerners, and others, the Panic was proof that Wall Street and business in general were unworthy of such a trust. Critics tartly observed that even in their rescue efforts, Morgan and other bankers were seeking a profit. The farther from the Hudson River one traveled, the less benign their motives looked.

One episode in particular soured the public on Wall Street. At the beginning of November, Moore & Schley, one of the most prominent brokers on the stock exchange, was suddenly threatened with bankruptcy. Since Moore & Schley owed money to banks up and down the Eastern Seaboard, Morgan had reason to fear that its failure would spark fresh waves of panic. The solution he hit upon was to unload a major asset of Moore & Schley, its holding of stock in Tennessee Coal, Iron & Railroad Company. The difficulty was that the natural buyer for Tennessee, and the one to whom Morgan turned, was the giant U.S. Steel Corporation. Morgan had a personal attachment to U.S. Steel, a prized client, which he had organized in 1901 to consolidate (some said monopolize) the steel industry. And although the sale of Tennessee achieved his aim of averting a major brokerage failure, this solution was not as disinterested as Morgan's other rescues. Also, U.S. Steel obtained, on an expedited basis, a personal assurance from President Roosevelt that the acquisition would not be attacked on antitrust grounds. Thus, the deal reeked of political favoritism as well.

The fairest conclusion was that private industrialists should not be entrusted with the degree of power wielded by Morgan (the deal itself, given the severity of the crisis and the lack of other buyers, was probably in the public interest). However, Morgan's standing with the public suffered. Some critics asserted that Morgan had contrived the entire panic. Senator Robert M. La Follette, a Wisconsin progressive and enemy of corporate power, charged that a "group of financiers who withhold and dispense prosperity" had "deliberately brought on the late panic, to serve their own ends." The President, who respected Morgan, wrote disapprovingly to his brother-in-law that the public had "passed thru the period of unreasoning trust and optimism into unreasoning *dis*trust and pessimism." (Such cycles are not unknown today.) People were so shocked by the repeated scandals and by the "trickery and dishonesty in high places," Roosevelt wrote, "they have begun to be afraid that every bank really has something rotten in it."

Since the time of Jackson, anti-banker hysteria had been a predictable American response to financial turmoil. Wall Street was often depicted as scheming and conspiratorial and, indeed, omniscient and all-powerful. Barely had the Panic ended when Alfred Owen Crozier, a prominent Ohio attorney and critic of Wall Street, penned *The Magnet,* a novel that depicted the Wall Street "machine" as an "inscrutable and mysterious power" that serves "its invisible master, undetected, with . . . infallible accuracy." Crozier was outflanked by the better-known Upton Sinclair, whose 1908 novel *The Money Changers* featured a Morgan-like figure who deliberately orchestrates a panic. The view of Morgan as inciting a crisis was a gross misreading of the man. His signature projects, such as consolidating bankrupt railroads and organizing trusts, always served the goal of greater order in commercial life. That his deal making tended to replace cutthroat competition with more gentlemanly collusion, and to augment profits, is without a doubt. Morgan's business arrangements were based on his deep-seated preference for stability and his loathing for the chaos that capitalism often produces. In 1907, Morgan had done his level best to forestall the chaos, and it was not enough.

One more nuanced analyst was Woodrow Wilson. Formerly an economics lecturer, the university president was as unsettled as were many Americans by Wall Street's risk taking and by the concentration of Wall Street power. Bankers, he insisted, should be "statesmen"—leaders in society—rather than mere profiteers. Wilson was dismayed by corporate greed and wrongdoing, which he believed to be widespread, yet he acknowledged there was nothing in the Constitution that forbid "accumulation" by business. The only way to reconcile the conflict between human avarice and the general welfare, he suggested in an interview in the *Times* soon after the Panic, was to put society on a moral footing. Where Wilson differed from many progressives was that he was willing to recognize morality, or at least civic purpose, in men of business and finance. He saluted Morgan, albeit with the air of a high-minded professor looking down on the Wall Street scrum. "I am glad to see," Wilson said puckishly, "that in the midst of all this turmoil of undefined wickedness, Mr. Morgan's name has not been among the celebrities. He seems to have kept his hands clean and his reputation clear of any dishonor." But not even Wilson thought morals alone could do the trick. Currency reform was long overdue, he said: "The European currency system is far better than our own."

Reform was suddenly the rage. Proposals poured into Congress. Over the winter of 1907–1908, Columbia University sponsored a series of lectures by prominent bankers, including Vanderlip, Perkins, and Barton Hepburn. The symposium was organized by Edwin Seligman, the professor who had prodded Warburg to publish, and who now persuaded him to appear, for the first time, on an American stage. Warburg unapologetically advised that America's system was inferior to those in Europe. In fact, he said, it suffered in comparison with that of the ancient Babylonians. Warburg made the trenchant distinction that banks in Europe, being "fully protected" by balances with their central banks, could lend freely in times of distress, whereas, during the recent American panic, as if in some topsy-turvy universe, "the banks, instead of disbursing their cash, begin to accumulate and actually to hoard currency." The Columbia lectures, which were published in book form, introduced the arguments for centralization to a wider public.

However, the Warburg view remained a minority one. Even most bankers were fixated on an asset currency—the idea floated at the Indianapolis convention for a currency based on individual bank loans. Because this would further fracture the country's money, it was the opposite of what Warburg hoped to accomplish. He recognized that the political climate was hostile to a complete remake of the system; therefore, he craftily styled his newest plan a "modified" central bank. His "modified" bank was an attempt to split the difference— in effect, it was an umbrella organization of clearinghouses that would issue currency and provide a unified source of support for banks, even if it was less than a full central bank. The fear of arousing popular opposition tilted him toward a federal structure, a pattern that would recur down to the very day of the Fed's enactment.

Although Warburg's arguments appealed to a handful of journalists and professors, he had no audience where it counted—in Congress. As a German national, Warburg had no entrée on Capitol Hill, where the asset currency notion held sway. Frustrated at being ignored, Warburg harbored a particular resentment of Senator Aldrich, who wielded the power in the upper chamber and who, as Warburg understood it, would never permit the system to truly change.

Aldrich, now sixty-six, had spent a quarter century defending the status quo in money, tariffs, and railroad regulation. He was enamored of the system of National Bank Notes secured by government bonds, and his usual contribution to the subject of reform had been to propose more such bank notes. He had little appreciation for the system's vulnerability, and much less had he foreseen the recent trouble. He had gone on his annual sojourn to Europe in the spring of 1907 and returned to Warwick, the magnificent estate he was building on Narragansett Bay, in July, in time to supervise the installation of a greenhouse with a multitude of orchids. His enjoyment of such labors was cut short by the sudden collapse of the banking system. The magnitude of the Panic jolted him. At a minimum, Aldrich realized that, for political reasons, legislation would be necessary. The Republicans could not face the electorate in 1908 without having enacted a reform. He also experienced, if not full-fledged doubt, a stirring of curiosity about what had gone wrong.

With banking conditions returning to normal, in late December the senator made inquiries on Wall Street, and found his way to Kuhn, Loeb. His ostensible purpose was narrow: he wanted to question Jacob Schiff about the law under which Germany issued government bills. Schiff called in a colleague who, he said, was better informed: Paul Warburg. Gazing on Aldrich for the first time, Warburg was struck by the sharp nose, the piercing eyes, the high color framed by the bushy eyebrows and mustache, and, above all, the "strong and clear forehead, the head erect upon the broad shoulders." In spite of his resentment, Warburg could not resist trying to engage the senator. The conversation became broader; Warburg ventured into the forbidden territory of centralization. Perhaps to quiet this simmering volcano, Aldrich said that Warburg could send him material for further reading. As Aldrich departed, Warburg mused to himself, "There goes currency reform."

Schiff advised that it would be a grave mistake to write to Aldrich. Warburg ignored him. The next day, he sent the senator a copy of his "A Plan for a Modified Central Bank." Four days later he wrote to him again. Now that the volcano was uncapped, there was no restraining it. "Did not the last panic show that we are suffering from too much decentralization of our banking system and from the absolute impossibility of securing any concerted action as to the free use of our reserves?" the banker demanded. He continued with a diatribe pleading for order, coherence, centrality—all the traits he found lacking in banking in his adopted home.

Senator Aldrich did not reply.

CHAPTER FIVE

THE CROSSING

This central reserve, or whatever name we may give to
it, must be a sacred institution, run for the public weal.
—PAUL WARBURG

Well timed reform alone averts revolution.
—THEODORE ROOSEVELT, *citing Turgot*

IN THE YEAR FOLLOWING the Panic of 1907, Congress crafted
a legislative response that was, for the most part, disappointing. It
had not thought to study the Panic; its legislation was guided by
politics. But almost as an afterthought, Congress did move the ball
forward. Before the year was out, an American delegation led by
Nelson Aldrich would fan out across Europe for the purpose of understanding just how banking on the Continent differed from that
in America. Aldrich himself made a remarkable swing toward reform. Somewhere between the old bookshops in London and the

elegant hotels of Paris, the senator, perhaps for the first time since his youth, became inspired by the classical models of Europe. His transformation was nothing short of startling. After Aldrich's return, Paul Warburg began to think that serious monetary reform just might be possible. Realizing he had become hooked on his mission in the New World, Warburg took the decisive step of applying for American citizenship.

But 1908 did not start auspiciously for reformers. The two chambers of Congress—each of them, like the White House, in Republican hands—wrangled over distinct bills, Aldrich being the author of the Senate version and Representative Charles Fowler, the champion of asset currency, leading the way in the House. Neither bill had the ambition or scope that a meltdown such as the Panic of 1907 demanded. Warburg sent a congressman a copy of his "modified" central bank plan, hoping Fowler would introduce it. The gambit went nowhere. Central banking was too hot to handle even had the members favored it, which most did not.

The Aldrich bill proposed, controversially, to let banks issue notes backed by their investments in railroad bonds. This gift to the railroads (similar to an earlier Aldrich proposal) betrayed his peculiar knack for inflaming the popular will against him. Railroads were widely resented, as much for the sumptuous mansions in Newport where industry barons summered as for their allegedly unfair rates. Western senators would not abide a favor to the rails, and the provision was stricken. That still left Congress splintered. Since Aldrich could not get his plum for the rails, he favored the status quo: currency based on government bonds. The House bill authorized currency supported by individual bank loans—precisely what La Salle Street had long demanded. Late in May, George Perkins updated J. P. Morgan, who was in London, on "the final failure" of the bill, adding, "We are all thoroughly disgusted over the condition of things in Washington."

But Congress fashioned a compromise after all, an odd slice of legislative sausage known as the Aldrich-Vreeland Act. The law, adopted at the end of May, authorized banks to form local currency associations and, with the approval of the Treasury secretary, to issue additional National Bank Notes in an emergency.* There was little enthusiasm for the bill among bankers, and none among the public. Warburg feared that Aldrich-Vreeland, which did little for his cherished idea of centralizing reserves, would defuse support for genuine reform. In short, it might be worse than nothing. The saving grace was that the law would expire in 1914. Thus it was a stopgap, not a solution. To underline the point, the law provided for the establishment of a National Monetary Commission, consisting of eighteen members of Congress, to study the defects in America's banking system and offer an enduring remedy. In this circuitous way, the bill offered possibility.

Aldrich was named the commission chairman; many assumed he would use the post to bury reform for good. On the Senate floor, however, he let slip the suggestion of bolder purpose, as if envisioning the potential for crafting a legacy as he entered the twilight of his career. "Thoughtful students of economic history," Aldrich noted, in a clear allusion to Warburg, "who are led by the experience and practice of other commercial nations . . . favor some plan for a central bank of issue." Although Aldrich gave himself political cover by insisting that America was not yet ready, he expressed a belief that, eventually, the country would adopt such a plan. This was a major concession.

Given carte blanche to do as little or as much with the commission as he chose, Aldrich ordered a vast research effort, which led to the publication of a shelf of books covering the monetary history and

---

* The emergency currency would be backed first by bank investments in government securities, as Aldrich preferred, and, second, by their holdings of commercial paper, or short-term loans. This was—in limited form—a first experiment in the United States with asset currency.

practices of nations around the world. It was a boon to the obscure field of financial history, as the financial historian James Grant would cheekily point out, and a few volumes, such as Oliver Sprague's *History of Crises Under the National Banking System*, are studied to this day. If most of the commission's work would ultimately gather dust, Aldrich sensed that an ambitious project required a proper foundation, a bibliographic heft, to be treated with the requisite gravitas.

From the beginning, Aldrich treated his fellow commissioners as ciphers. Few had either banking experience or clout on the Hill. Aldrich controlled the meeting agendas as well as press statements, which were studiously bland and designed to keep the commission out of election-year news. Aldrich did seek help—just not from the other commissioners. At the suggestion of Charles William Eliot, the long-standing president of Harvard University, Aldrich hired Piatt Andrew, the economics professor, as his assistant and in-house expert. Aldrich also sought the advice of J. P. Morgan, who urged that Aldrich enlist the services of the banker Harry Davison.

Morgan had been so impressed by Davison's efforts during the Panic that he sought permission, over a friendly dinner with George Baker, head of the First National, to lure Davison to Morgan's. The move did not occur until the end of 1908, but Aldrich was fully aware that the Monetary Commission was taking on an adviser who answered to the most powerful man on Wall Street. Aldrich, of course, saw nothing wrong with government and business joining forces. Perkins, a less-than-discreet Morgan executive, let fly in a cable to the boss: "It is understood Davison is to represent our views and will be particularly close to Senator Aldrich."

Such a communiqué, had it become public, would have destroyed the commission before it even got started. It is worth noting that, even while one Morgan lieutenant (Davison) was teaming up with Aldrich, another (Perkins) was furiously lobbying Congress to weaken the antitrust law, imploring the administration for gentle regulatory treatment of select Morgan clients, and overseeing a collusive effort by rival railroad executives to jack up freight rates. Lending a trusted man to a public commission was wholly congruent with how moguls of the era operated. Quiet alliance with the government was always preferable to noisy confrontation.

Although the Monetary Commission was bipartisan, the likelihood of its having an impact, Aldrich knew, hinged on whether the Republicans could keep control of the White House. In June, the Republicans nominated William Howard Taft, the secretary of war and a close friend of the President (the forty-nine-year-old Roosevelt had voluntarily, and mystifyingly, opted to retire). Taft publicly supported the commission and sent Aldrich a flattering note, expressing his eagerness to meet with "the levelest headed man in the country."

Three weeks later, the Democrats nominated William Jennings Bryan. A great orator though a twice-failed candidate, Bryan had no use for a commission run by Aldrich. At any rate, the Democrats backed a very different banking reform—deposit insurance. Oklahoma, a newly admitted state, had enacted deposit insurance the previous December, with the aim of discouraging bank runs. This solution dismayed orthodox bankers, who feared that insurance would serve as an invitation to reckless banking. If depositors had no reason to seek out well-managed banks, what would motivate bankers to discipline their lending? James Laughlin, author of the 1897 Indianapolis report, reacted as did many experts—with haughty disapproval. Deposit insurance, Laughlin said, was a vain attempt to "make men good by law. It is purely populistic or socialistic." He said depositors should rely instead on the "skill, integrity" and "good management" of banks.

Coming so soon after the Panic, Laughlin's evocation of bankers' professionalism sounded much as it would a century later—laughably naïve. Deposit insurance was popular with voters and came to be adopted, over the next year, in Kansas, Nebraska, and Texas, and in

ensuing years in a handful of other states.* Taft denounced the
Oklahoma plan, but as the presidential campaign progressed, he
wisely backed away from the issue. Republicans needed their own
monetary strategy; their hopes came to rest, entirely, on Aldrich's
broad shoulders.

Aldrich told the press his aim was only the modest one of refining
the Aldrich-Vreeland Act. This is scarcely credible, since within
weeks he was plotting a lengthy fact-finding mission to Europe.
Meeting at the recently opened Plaza Hotel in New York, the commission duly seconded his plan. Eight of the members would make
the ocean crossing.

Passage was booked on the German-built *Kronprinzessin Cecillie*,
departing New York for England on August 4. Aldrich reserved a
$260 suite for his wife, Abby, and himself and a lower berth for
Mathilda Schonberg, listed on the shipping manifest as their maid,
for $82.50. (Davison had sailed ahead to arrange appointments with
European bankers, with Morgan providing introductions.) Aldrich
exhaustively prepared for the inquiry. Liberated from the mesh of
daily politics, he reveled in the opportunity to practice statecraft as a
purely intellectual challenge. The senator was so eager for the project
to be seen as creditable that he took unusual precautions to guard his
reputation, insisting that his adult children in London not reside at
his hotel, lest he be accused of palming off family expenses on the
taxpayers.

At Aldrich's suggestion, Professor Andrew brought banking textbooks for the voyage to tutor his fellow commissioners. They could
scarcely have asked for a better teacher. Andrew hailed from La Porte,
Indiana, where his father, a Civil War veteran turned local banker,
had a proud record of never having foreclosed on a mortgage. Piatt

---

* When farm prices collapsed in the 1920s, state insurance schemes collapsed or
ceased to function. But federal deposit insurance, established in 1933 despite the initial
opposition of Franklin D. Roosevelt, generally succeeded.

had fully imbibed his father's conservative banking ethos. An incisive if not an original thinker, he had sparkled in academia and was no stranger to men of influence and privilege. At Princeton he had studied under Woodrow Wilson and at Harvard he was teacher to the young Franklin D. Roosevelt, with whom he went riding in the environs of Cambridge.

Economics in the Gilded Age was a liberal discipline, not the forbidding maze of mathematics it later became. Andrew thought of banking as a Renaissance pursuit, intellectually on a par with the Ibsen and Shakespeare plays he attended in Cambridge, the operas of Paderewski, and stimulating lectures by the likes of the Arctic explorer Lieutenant Robert Peary. A devotee of the outdoor life, somewhat in the model of the Harvard graduate Theodore Roosevelt, Andrew skated on Hammond Pond and engaged in strenuous running and swimming. He loved his home in Gloucester on the sea and found Harvard difficult to leave. But the thirty-five-year-old bachelor had a romantic spirit. "These autumn days are too lovely—warm and fragrant," reads a typical diary entry. The prospect of a European adventure thrilled him. Moreover, banking theory was just that— theory. Here was a chance to translate ideas into action, at the princely government salary of $3,000. With a palpable sense of excitement, he wrote in his diary, "My new life begins."

Central banking in Europe, as Andrew no doubt informed his pupils, had begun with the Riksbank, created to make loans to the King of Sweden in 1668. The Bank of England was established a generation later, in 1694, by private capitalists, also as a banker to the throne, which had been impoverished by an ongoing war with France. Over time, the Bank of England acquired other functions, such as issuing notes, acting as the government's fiscal agent, determining interest rates, protecting the nation's gold reserve and the value of the pound, and recognizing an (implicit) duty as lender of last resort. The process of becoming a public institution was gradual and, judged by modern standards, incomplete. In 1908 the Bank of England re-

mained private, a servant to the state but not of it. The important
point to the Americans was that the Bank's directors recognized the
need, in times of crises, to resist what is every banker's natural instinct to tighten credit. The only workable option when all others
were hoarding funds was for the Bank to be an open spigot. In the
famous phrase of Walter Bagehot, the Victorian-era journalist, the
central bank "must lend to merchants, to minor bankers, to 'this man
and that man.'" The Bank would insist on good collateral but, make
no mistake, it would "lend freely."

Many central banks (by the early 1900s, there were roughly twenty
in all) had been organized in response to a war or another inflationary episode. The Bank of France was chartered in 1800 as an antidote
to the financial turmoil of the French Revolution. The early American experience was similar. The first Bank of the United States was
created to mop up debts from the Revolutionary War, and the Second
Bank after the War of 1812. They improved America's credit, but the
special privileges they enjoyed fostered resentment—from Andrew
Jackson in particular. In that light, it should be recalled that corporations were often chartered with special privileges. Parliament granted
the Bank of England the exclusive right to circulate notes, just as it
had given the East India Company a monopoly on tea. Over time,
the privileges were matched with responsibilities. The various bankers to the state morphed from primarily profit-seeking institutions
into ones that, while still shareholder owned, acknowledged a first
duty to the public. Except, of course, America's Banks didn't evolve.
Congress let them expire.

Aldrich focused on the big three of European banking—England,
Germany, and France. Each of their central banks was owned by private shareholders and held the national reserve, but in important ways
they differed. The Bank of France possessed far more gold—more, in
fact, than the other two combined. Also, the French bank was controlled by the state; England's was defiantly independent. Surprisingly, directors of the latter were wealthy merchants rather than

bankers. In Germany, management was in the hands of trained professionals—experts such as Warburg. The German chancellor held supreme power over the Reichsbank but rarely used it.

The Aldrich mission docked at Plymouth, England, on August 10, 1908, and was welcomed to dinner at Morgan's London home, with Lord Rothschild present. Morgan lost no time in requesting a favor, complaining to Aldrich that the tariff on importing art was interfering with his plan to donate European treasures to the Metropolitan Museum in New York. Interviews at the Bank of England got off to a slow start. The commission group was unwieldy; the Americans struck their hosts as naïve and unprepared. Matters improved after a few days, when two commissioners returned home and several of the others struck out on their own. From then on, Aldrich worked with a core group including Andrew and Davison. Knowing he would need the support of western bankers, Aldrich also enlisted George Reynolds, a former Iowa store clerk and head of the Continental National Bank of Chicago, who cut short a vacation in Italy to join them. (In turn-of-the-century America, Chicago was still considered "western.") Davison took the lead in interrogating foreign bankers and leavened the sessions with his playfulness and wit.

The resilience of British banking made a strong impression on Aldrich. Commercial banks kept very little cash; they didn't feel the need. Even the Bank of England had relatively little gold, but faith in the institution obviated the need for more. The Americans could not help but notice how the monetary landscape was inverted from their own: the United States had far more bullion, but confidence in the national currency was greater in England. Also, as a businessman with investments in Mexico and Africa, Aldrich appreciated the ease with which British merchants financed trade. After their interview sessions, Aldrich and Andrew went rummaging through London bookstores, Aldrich liberally buying economics books for the library he was planning for Warwick. He also hunted down a print of Sir Robert Peel, the British prime minister responsible for the 1844 law that gave the Bank of England the exclusive right to issue notes. Why did Aldrich want a picture of Peel? Andrew had the strong sense that the senator had discovered his purpose; he wanted to become America's Robert Peel.

At the end of August, the group ventured to Berlin, where Andrew and Davison took in the Turkish baths, Andrew went to a production of the Strauss opera *Salome,* and more rounds of interviews commenced. Then they took a train to Paris. In the City of Light, Aldrich gazed wistfully at a dispatch written by Napoleon, just after the battle of Austerlitz, in which the general advised that the Bank of France was as critical to the Republic as were his victories in battle. The Aldrich group dined with James Stillman, the most distinguished American banker in Paris, who suggested that Aldrich gather some trusted bankers at Warwick and draw up a plan in secret. The next day, Andrew and the Davisons motored out to the country château of the U.S. ambassador.

At each central bank, the Americans were given to feel like the representatives of a primitive system, one barely above contempt. Their astonishment at what they heard was palpable (the interviews in Germany and France were assisted by an interpreter). The Europeans portrayed their institutions as effortlessly superseding parochial or private interests; their policies seemed universally accepted. The interviews, of course, took place at the apogee of the social harmony of prewar Europe. Had Aldrich gone to Europe in the 1920s, much less in the 1930s, the picture would not have been so harmonious.

Davison and Aldrich pressed their hosts on the question of reserves: Who held them? What were the requirements? What were the rules regarding the holding of cash? The Europeans' consistent response, phrased in varying ways, was that the confidence reposed in their centralized systems obviated the need for the rigid regulations of American banking. London bankers could not relate to the American fetish with "elasticity." How then, the Americans wondered, did the Bank of England adjust the currency supply to meet demand? A Bank official, rather a delphic one, said this occurred "automatically." (He meant that as bills of trade were discounted— that is, accepted by the Bank England in return for its notes—Bank notes entered circulation.) At the Reichsbank, the mechanics of discounting were gone over in detail. Exchanging bankers' loans for notes of the Reichsbank was a critical function, an official explained: "We could not stop it." On form, once a central bank was established, the other banks adapted—became dependent. The German continued, "If we did [stop] it would bring about the greatest panic that we ever experienced."

It was in France where the visitors were truly humbled. Davison explained that, in the United States, "the question of the proper relation between cash in hand and liabilities is considered very important." What, he inquired, was the rule in France: What portion of deposits were backed by cash reserves?

M. Pallain, the governor of the Bank of France, shook his head with a weary sigh. "I think you pay more attention to the quantity [of reserves] than to the quality."

But surely France had laws, regulations, some stipulation governing the proper proportion?

"*Non.*" The reserve requirements so dear to America, Pallain replied, were insignificant in France, "on account of the facilities offered by the Bank of France for the rapid conversion, in a crisis," of portfolio assets into ready money.

The Americans persisted: What, they demanded, determined the fluctuations in the volume of notes? Pallain, despairing of his ability to explain the power of a central reserve to these stubborn Yanks, waxed philosophical. "It is the sun," he said, "or it would perhaps be more correct to say, the alternating seasons."

The problem that Aldrich had come to investigate did not, on this side of the Atlantic, appear to exist. Throughout fifty-eight meetings with central bankers as well as with diplomats, editors, and local financiers, the overriding sense was one of internal coherence—of a system that worked. At the very least, Europe employed its reserves while America largely squandered its own. George Reynolds, the Chicago banker, maintained it was in Berlin, in the luxurious lobby of the Hotel Adlon, on a sofa behind the bend of the stairway facing its giant marble columns, where Aldrich "converted" to the central bank idea. At any rate, when he docked in New York on October 20, after an absence of fully eleven weeks, Aldrich was a changed man.

The November elections bolstered his sense of possibility. In the presidential contest, Taft trounced Bryan, whose appeal was confined to the South and a sprinkling of states in the West. The outgoing Roosevelt helpfully announced that he would get out of the way and leave the limelight to his successor—specifically by going on safari in Africa. Just as important, the Republicans won commanding majorities in both the House and the Senate. Aldrich's timing could not have been better.

That fall, the Monetary Commission held a hearing at the Metropolitan Club of New York, a perfect opportunity for Aldrich to unveil his agenda. The interregnum between election and inauguration was traditionally a period for showcasing new ideas. But Aldrich revealed nothing. Paul Warburg, invited to present his thoughts, noticed that some of the other commissioners looked downright drowsy—almost comatose. After the session, though, Aldrich summoned the banker.

"Mr. Warburg," he began, "I like your ideas. I have only one fault to find with them."

Warburg, momentarily stunned, asked about the fault.

Aldrich shot back, "You are too timid about it. You say we cannot have a central bank, and I say we can."

As Warburg was to recall in poignant terms, "It is easy to imagine, but hard to describe, the mixed feelings of joy and bewilderment into which this remark threw me, for suddenly I found our roles reversed." Whereas previously the banker despaired of persuading Aldrich of the merit of a central bank, now he feared that Aldrich would jeopardize the project by being too ambitious. Warburg explained that a bank with broad powers, such as existed in Europe, was politically impossible due to Americans' deep-seated prejudices against federal power. They debated the point, without resolution. Their difference notwithstanding, Warburg left elated. "For the first time," he would write, "I felt confident that genuine banking reform was within grasp of the United States."

Warburg jumped into the fray with his trademark energy. In the short space of a couple of months, he wrote an essay on the discount system in Europe, read a paper on central banking before the American Economic Association, and joined the currency committee of the Merchants' Association of New York. Business groups were becoming interested in currency reform because the panic had wreaked such havoc on trade. Even though the Merchants' Association did not favor central banking, Warburg became a fifth column, relentlessly indoctrinating the other members. "Many an afternoon and night I sat with them," Warburg was to write, "struggling to win them over to the gospel of centralized reserves."

Aldrich, meanwhile, began telling friends he would not run for another term in 1910, and that he would focus, during the time left to him in office, on monetary reform. He had visions of a central bank as the crowning work of his career—a monument to his decades in the Senate. The truth about his decision to retire was more complicated. Vilified for opposing progressive causes, and tarnished in the public eye ever since the "Treason of the Senate" exposé in *Cosmopolitan,* the senator was growing weary of divisive battles. The ugly political cartoons (invariably showing corporate money slushing in his pockets) had taken a toll. A perceptive reporter observed that, despite Aldrich's image of implacability, "he doesn't like being pilloried continually in newspapers and cartoons as a corporation Senator, the representative of 'special interests.'"

Aldrich intended to devote a full two years to crafting a bill. He wanted to work at a safe remove from politics, studying banking as if it were a purely academic or technical subject. The commission certainly had plenty to do; it had to hire writers and gather facts and figures on banking and money in each of forty-six states and overseas. Such information was difficult to obtain; New York's banking department did not even have a spare copy of the state's banking laws.

Nonetheless, Aldrich should have set a brisker pace; politics is always a question of seizing the hour. He believed he could legislate at leisure, but he misjudged the gathering strength of progressives, who were pushing for reforms such as an income tax, direct election of senators, labor protections, corporate regulation, and (taking dead aim at Aldrich) reduction of the tariff. These forces were challenging Aldrich's dominion in the Senate and redefining the national agenda. Aldrich overlooked the need to engage the public, even on what he hoped would become his capstone achievement. In a stopover in Milwaukee, soon after he returned from Europe, his response to a reporter's question about his commission work ran to seven words: "Really, gentlemen, I have nothing to say."

Aldrich's aloofness chipped away at his eroding political strength. Murray Butler, the president of Columbia University, hosted a dinner at which Aldrich was to discuss his progress. Interest was so great that Butler asked whether Aldrich would mind if a reporter or two were present. The senator replied that he would *very much* mind— another opportunity squandered.

Within the Democratic Party, Aldrich was already toxic. Woodrow Wilson turned down an invitation to another dinner, this one hosted by Vanderlip, with Lord Revelstoke, a prominent British banker—purely because Aldrich was on the guest list. In theory, the Democrats were irrelevant for the next two and probably the next four years, but monetary reformers needed the Republicans to stick together. And Republican cohesion was under threat from the tectonic forces of progressivism.

The departing Roosevelt had been veering more stridently into the progressive camp—more so than Taft. This put Republican cohesion in some doubt. The two men had an intensely personal friendship, dating to the early 1890s, when both had been appointed to posts in the administration of Benjamin Harrison, and their friendship had deepened through scores of intimate letters and by Taft's steadfast service in Roosevelt's cabinet, including the difficult post of governor general of the Philippines. However, their temperaments were dissimilar. Taft, who hailed from a political family in Ohio, was not a crowd-pleaser like the endlessly quotable and ever charismatic Roosevelt. Taft's ambition had been to become a judge—to preside in the quiet of a courtroom. He shared none of Roosevelt's affinity for leading a crusade. "What I am anxious to do," he noted shortly before he took the oath of office, "is to *do* something, and not to make a pronunciamento." Although Taft professed an eagerness to carry on the Roosevelt agenda, he declined to retain certain members of Roosevelt's cabinet, which bruised his mentor's ego. When the Tafts stayed at the White House March 3, the night before the inauguration, the conversation at dinner was strained. Even in late January— five weeks ahead of inauguration day—Vanderlip was writing, "It is coming to be an open secret that there has been a distinct break between the President and the President-Elect." This was ominous for Republican cohesion and ominous for the Aldrich agenda.

CHAPTER SIX

PROGRESSIVISM

Neither the political prejudice of the past nor the
ghost of Andrew Jackson . . . will stand in the way.
—Nelson Aldrich

Financial questions are perplexing and elusive ones.
—William Howard Taft

As the Taft administration got under way, Nelson Aldrich's work on monetary reform was sidetracked by an explosive
issue—the tariff. Always a contentious subject, the tariff heated the
political stove and energized Aldrich's many opponents, including
within his own party. Just when he was on the cusp of proposing the
first serious banking reform in half a century, Aldrich put himself at
risk of becoming a marginal—even a hated—figure.

Republicans had always supported high tariffs, but by 1909 there
was a consensus that duties were too high. They were seen by the

party's progressive wing as a burdensome tax on trade and unfair to farmers, who depended on selling goods into export markets. Since the tariff tilted the economic playing field, benefiting favored industries while jacking up prices for consumers, it was hated by laissez-faire Democrats as well. Taft, a principled but politically maladroit leader, called on Congress to enact significant reductions. This put Aldrich in a delicate spot: he could either legislate against the interests of his business friends or antagonize his party's progressives, whose support would be vital on the issue of banking reform.

Even a glimpse at Aldrich's mail gives a hint of the tariff's critical importance, and of the enormous influence that Aldrich wielded in the Senate. He was bombarded with pleas from corporations who regarded trade protection as their sovereign right. U.S. Steel lobbied him on steel duties; National Biscuit sought help on biscuits. Aldrich heard from producers of iron, of vanillin, of plate glass, of glass bottles, of jewelry, of leather hides, of lead pencils, of newsprint, of wallpaper, of glue, of umbrella frames. He especially heard from the textile industry in New England, which had long enjoyed his particular protection. The stakes were high. An agent of the Royal Weaving Company in Pawtucket, Rhode Island, typified the pressure, bluntly stating, "I would like to feel sure that our industry is taken care of."

Against these letters Aldrich had to balance, or at least consider, a deluge of pleas from foreign embassies. Cuba wanted duty-free entry for pineapples, Brazil for coffee, Great Britain for "canned kippered herrings." France sought lower barriers for silk muslin, Norway for sardines, and Turkey for raisins, figs, dates, and, indeed, "crude opium."

The tariff battle showcased Aldrich's legislative prowess. Its complexity played to his mastery of detail. Always at ease working in the shadows, Aldrich negotiated with the House leaders in secret, sometimes absconding for lengthy motorcar sessions in Washington's Rock Creek Park. Meanwhile, Paul Warburg despaired of making progress on monetary reform while its foremost statesman was absent. "I pray every day," he scribbled to Piatt Andrew, "for a speedy end of the Tariff wrangle so that the deck may be cleared for action on the currency question." Andrew at least kept the Monetary Commission humming, overseeing its research, corresponding with economists, and hobnobbing with politicos. Andrew basked in the notion that he was helping history unfold. An economist with a sense of larger purpose, he took a day off from commission work and motored to Gettysburg; on another, he went to watch Orville Wright attempt to fly in an "aeroplane."

The tariff work thrust Aldrich together with Taft, leading to a friendship that was useful to Aldrich but politically risky for the President. The senator became a regular at the White House; in the warm evenings the two hashed out duty schedules on the White House portico. Taft pressed Aldrich to lower duties, but the affable chief executive found it difficult to confront the senator, whom he increasingly admired.

The President had more success on the related matter of an income tax amendment. The issues were connected, as progressives hoped that income taxes, once approved, would displace the tariff as a revenue source. Economists such as Columbia's Seligman believed that a progressive tax could be a tool for social equity and level the disparities that the tariff supposedly created.

Aldrich did agree, reluctantly, to Taft's call for a resolution for an income tax amendment (which now would need three-quarters of the state legislatures for ratification). But on the more central issue of lowering the tariff, he was unwilling to betray his business cronies, who, he felt, had always stuck by him. Despite the disapproval from many in his party, and despite the pleadings of his president, Aldrich produced a tariff that was highly favorable to textiles and to industry overall. While Taft did win some battles, the lack of substantive reform may be judged by the praise heaped on Aldrich by the National Association of Manufacturers, whose president gloated that the bill "meets the full approval of the manufacturers represented at this association." Broadly speaking, the Payne-Aldrich tariff (the House sponsor was the fiercely protectionist Sereno E. Payne of New York) slightly reduced the duty, but the structure of protectionism remained intact.* Aldrich had been handed a chance to champion reform and had smothered it. He would soon pay a price.

Effectively, Payne-Aldrich marked the beginning of a civil war within the Republican Party. Taft was branded as incapable of standing up to Aldrich—not exactly the enemy of progressives but no longer useful to their cause. The senator himself was the enemy. Aldrich had been hoping to use this time to quietly work out details of currency reform. He now became the subject of bitter attacks.

Senator Jonathan Dolliver of Iowa shouted at Aldrich on the Senate floor that he would have to accept the "moral consequences" of the tariff, on cotton in particular. Robert La Follette and other progressives smoothly shifted gears from attacking Aldrich on the tariff to savaging whatever he might be cooking up in banking reform. Iowa's other senator, Albert B. Cummins, told an audience in Chicago he suspected that Aldrich's prospective remedy would be "a central bank" and that his "scheme" would be intolerable, for it would subject the currency to the authority of a few selfish men and, ultimately, "enslave the financial world." Cummins knew nothing about banking, but he sensed Aldrich's vulnerability.

A perceptive journalist wrote that Aldrich, on whom his party's hopes for currency reform depended, was now "distrusted, disliked, even hated and vilified as few other men in public are hated and vilified." The portrait wasn't entirely bleak. The writer applauded his legislative skills; indeed, he saluted Aldrich as "the ablest man in the U.S. Senate." But a chasm separated Aldrich from the public. He was too chilly and remote to appeal to people's "sentiment." His hair thinning, now a wispy white, he was barely *known* to the public, for, as

---

* Aldrich also slipped in a proviso for Morgan, eliminating the duty on original artworks at least twenty years old.

this critic lamented, "nobody has really given us an intimate view of the man."

As if to escape the hostile political climate, in August 1909 Aldrich and Andrew embarked on a second European study tour. In England they met with the cream of British political life, including the young president of the Board of Trade, Winston Churchill. Aldrich may have hoped that political conditions at home would improve in his absence, as if progressivism were only a passing storm. The bankers in his circle, frustrated at Aldrich's leisurely pace, tried to push matters along. Harry Davison, now in the upper echelon at Morgan's, arranged for dinners and speaking engagements for Aldrich upon his return. George Reynolds, who had accompanied the Monetary Commission the previous summer, hatched the idea of the senator's making a barnstorming tour in the West to repair his political standing. Warburg gave him a nudge. These banker-advisers, a generation younger, took it upon themselves to lighten the older man's burden. In Davison's case, the difference in age aroused a mutual interest and friendship.

Davison also looked after Aldrich financially. When Bankers Trust, of which Davison was a founder, sold public stock, Davison allotted one hundred shares to Aldrich at a price of $40,000—well below the market value. "I am particularly pleased to have you have this stock, as I believe it will give a good account of itself," Davison wrote helpfully. "It is selling today on a basis of a little more than $500 a share [$50,000 total]. I hope, however, you will see fit to put it away, as it should improve with seasoning." Davison did not think of this gift as at all unethical. Morgan's habitually looked after its friends, which accorded with its self-image as a benevolent institution. In truth, feathering the nest of a politician who was charged with reforming the banking laws was hardly an act of altruism; it was very much in Morgan's economic interest.

Aldrich, of course, was accustomed to leveraging his position for private gain. Over the summer he wrote to the president of Mexico,

Porfirio Díaz, asking him to intervene regarding "some interests of mine"—most likely rubber—threatened by an action in the Mexican courts. Aldrich by now was a very wealthy man, devoting significant time to rebuilding his house at Warwick—windowsills were a particular concern—and to his securities transactions and buying a yacht.

The focus returned to banking in September, when *The Wall Street Journal* published a series favorable to a central bank. Even ordinary Americans began to show interest. The school superintendent in Oberlin, Ohio, made inquiries to the Monetary Commission; T. R. Brandt, cashier of the First National Bank of Tombstone, Arizona, sent Aldrich suggestions, as did an anonymous writer who signed his letter "A Business Man." Books rolled off the presses, including *Money and Currency* by one D. W. Ravenscroft, who modestly described himself as "having had no education." Currency questions had always stirred the imagination of cranks, but a genuine intellectual ferment swirled around the topic of a central bank. The most interesting proposal was that of Victor Morawetz, a railroad lawyer, who argued that the United States was too big and diverse a territory for a single central bank. Instead, Morawetz proposed a system of independent regional banks.

President Taft did not get more than superficially involved in the issue, though his occasional comments were supportive. In the fall of 1909, he spent some of his dwindling political capital on Aldrich, expressing his full confidence that whatever remedy the Monetary Commission proposed would be free of "Wall Street influences." This was becoming the litmus test of monetary reform—a Jacksonian condition that any new institution be free of the taint of either Wall Street or Washington. And it was into Jackson territory—nine midwestern cities, starting with Chicago and finishing in Detroit—that, in the first part of November, Aldrich was bound.

Given that it was unfriendly terrain, Aldrich made a reasonably good showing. His handlers had prepared a full schedule of lunches with local notables and lectures in the evenings. The senator stressed that a healthy banking system was vital irrespective of geography. "Our system," he told the Commercial Club in St. Louis, "must be one which will satisfy the manufacturers of New England, the agriculturists of the Mississippi valley, and the miners of the Rocky Mountains and the Pacific Coast, and the merchants of all sections." He encouraged farmers to support him on the grounds that they were also capitalists. Local coverage tended to be more favorable after his appearances than before. A newspaper in Milwaukee, barely concealing its surprise, declared, "Senator Aldrich does not in the slightest degree suggest the czar-like manipulator of the Senate that some have painted him." Aldrich had to be pleased in Omaha when a man in the audience exclaimed, "You must be an elk because you shed your horns so easily."

However, there was also ominous criticism of Aldrich in nearly every city. The influential *Kansas City Star* published bitingly satirical "questions" for the visitor, such as "What do you do when you are not running the Senate? Do you know any insurgent Senators by sight? Did you ever see a voter? What did he look like?" More disappointing, few critics bothered to reflect on his message or evaluate central banking on its merits.

Aldrich had read enough of the commission histories to realize that talk of a central bank set off profoundly American fears of federal (or Wall Street) domination. He felt he was fighting a phantom, he said: "the ghost of Andrew Jackson." Although Warburg and he were not in frequent touch, they arrived at similar conclusions and used strikingly similar turns of phrase.

Warburg by now was well versed in the country's political traditions; indeed, in his papers there is a tantalizing scrap from the diary of Philip Hone, a one-term mayor of New York, who wrote, on the occasion of Jackson's death in 1845, "The universal American nation is in mourning. Stripes, black . . . darken the columns of the newspapers. . . . Now, to my thinking, the country had greater cause to mourn on the day of his birth than on that of his decease." Warburg would never have voiced such disrespectful musings, though he may have felt them. But Jacksonism, he held, was not incurable. Warburg believed that if Americans were exposed to the arguments for a central bank, their fears would melt before the steamroller of (as he saw it) his irrefutable logic. Popular antagonism, he maintained, was due to "ignorance" rather than "the ghost of Andrew Jackson."

Aldrich, similarly, thought the public had to be educated before he could propose legislation. When the commission met in late November 1909—its first formal meeting in a year—the members were eager to draft a bill, but Aldrich decreed that the next stage would be to blanket the country with educational literature. After his battering out west, Aldrich had no desire to face the public, though he was amenable to airing his ideas in forums he judged to be safe. The Economic Club of New York, which held its gala dinner in the Hotel Astor at the end of the month, was just such a refuge, with Davison, J. P. Morgan, and Andrew looking on approvingly from the head table. Aldrich's address suggested just how much he had come under Warburg's spell. He touted the idea of a central reserve that banks could draw upon "as water is drawn from a great reservoir"—a distinctly Warburgian image. And Aldrich made plain his favorable impression of the European central banks, whose distinguishing features he described in some detail. He stressed that commercial banks in Europe held only a thin wedge of "till money," rarely more than 3 or 4 percent of their deposits. They felt confident keeping so little cash, he noted, because they believed "a credit at the central bank is better and safer than a corresponding amount in their own possession." To New Yorkers for whom the 1907 Panic was still a recent memory, this was an arresting thought.

Banking reform and the progressive movement each hurtled ahead, like separate freight cars approaching a fateful junction. While progressivism appealed to people in each of the major parties, progressives within the Republican camp were increasingly rebelling against the party leadership. Early in 1910, Frank Vanderlip fretted to

James Stillman, "The insurgents have been showing growing strength and the President increasing weakness." The Taft-Aldrich wing was losing ground.

Aldrich was unprepared to deal with the progressives. He did not fully appreciate that the movement was about more than just a series of laws regulating food safety and railroads fares. Progressivism embodied an attitudinal shift toward a more benevolent and representative society; it was concerned with elevating the condition of the poor and giving a greater say, and a greater role, to the swelling ranks of the middle class. Its guiding ethos was that education and empirical research could foster scientific, nonpartisan reform—although very little that progressivism achieved was actually nonpartisan. Its effects were seen over a wide range of topics: settlement houses, worker pensions, primary elections, corporate regulations, and the growth of public schools.

To judge from newspaper sales, the public was more interested in and better informed on these issues than ever before. But Aldrich was unaccustomed to courting public opinion (he was chosen by the legislature, one recalls, not by the Rhode Island electorate at large). His success at accumulating a fortune had made him less—not more—tolerant of his social inferiors. He had little faith in the ability of the mass of people to govern themselves, and he had little interest in the vast sections of America outside his ken—farmers, for instance, or what farmers thought and felt about banking. It is true that much of what passed for political discourse on banking was unsophisticated and demagogic, and often wrong. But Aldrich did not try to engage these other opinions, or even debate his rivals in the Senate. Despite his ability to get things done behind closed doors, he did not really subscribe to democratic give-and-take. As his authority in the chamber waned, his interest flagged. Also, for much of the winter of 1910 he was laid up by a troublesome cold. He had one solace and searing ambition, which was to reform the country's banking system.

Warburg alternately prodded and encouraged him. When a poll of bankers responded, conditionally, that they favored a central bank, Warburg wrote to the senator, "One cannot help feeling very confident." But he was careful not to alienate Aldrich by moving too quickly, for he knew that the senator was not yet ready to publicly commit to a central bank.

Warburg also delivered a pair of speeches that showed his keen understanding of the American character. His "United Reserve Bank" lecture at the YMCA of New York, in March 1910, offered a twist on his earlier "modified central bank." For one thing, the term "central bank" had been banished. His new appellation, "united bank," suggested a more federal structure, patterned on the federal government itself. To allay the fear that it would reincarnate the Second Bank (the long-ago dragon slain by Andrew Jackson), Warburg envisioned a network of twenty reserve banks scattered around the United States. And rather than belittle the fear of centralization, he made it sound familiar, not an unfortunate current in American thought so much as a distinctive element of Americana, one to be respectfully accommodated. Warburg's scheme, therefore, was an adaptation: "It is a scheme based upon conditions peculiar to our country and our form of government. It recognizes the vast territorial area of the United States, the diversity and dissimilarity of interests, and even the traditional, sectional, and partisan prejudices of the people."

Although Warburg was building on Morawetz's concept of sectional banks, there was a key difference. Morawetz was proposing *unconnected* banks; Warburg's would be joined. "These sectional reserve banks," he stressed, "must in the end act as a unit." To avoid repeating the catastrophic experience of 1907, when the banks of each city or region had to fend for themselves, reserves at the various branches of Warburg's "united bank" would be part of a single larger reserve. Notwithstanding his seductive nomenclature, Warburg ultimately envisioned "one big bank."

In a second lecture in 1910, before the Academy of Political Science, Warburg tried to establish a link between central banking and

America's frontier traditions. He argued that a central reserve would be a plus for country banks, freeing them from the need to depend on Wall Street. Indeed, he argued, "central banks are not oligarchic but democratic institutions." This was turning Jacksonism on its head.

The "United Reserve Bank" lecture paid a serious dividend: the Merchants' Association, the group that Warburg had been methodically lobbying, abruptly dropped its opposition and endorsed a central bank. This ratified Warburg's suspicion that businesspeople were fluid in their thinking and would succumb to his efforts at persuasion. He boldly capitalized on his alliance with the Merchants' Association by persuading it to distribute thirty thousand copies of his address. By the late spring of 1910, Warburg could claim considerable progress.

It was roughly then that Theodore Roosevelt, having emerged from his African hunting expedition to civilization in Khartoum, got news of Taft's capitulation on the tariff and of other supposed heresies of the President. An uneasy correspondence between the two men followed. In June, after a string of regal visits to European capitals, Roosevelt disembarked in New York to a hero's welcome—an exuberant throng met him at the dock. For five miles along his route, people stood to greet the former president. Out of respect for Taft, Roosevelt promised to stay silent on politics for sixty days. After four days, he broke his pledge. Soon, he traveled to see Taft at his summer home in Beverly, Massachusetts. Pleasantries were exchanged, noble sentiments professed, but the friendship was over.

While not yet ready for a public break, Roosevelt privately charged that Taft was corrupted by his alliance with Aldrich. Writing to his friend Senator Henry Cabot Lodge, Roosevelt fumed, "We have had no national leadership of any real kind since election day 1908. Taft is absolutely connected in the popular mind with Aldrich . . . and company." Roosevelt conveniently overlooked the working arrangement that he, as president, had forged with Aldrich as well as his own cowardice when it came to tariff reform. In fact, he overlooked his own letter to the same Henry Cabot Lodge of precisely a year earlier, in which he had observed, "My intercourse with Aldrich gave me a steadily higher opinion of him." But his judgment that Aldrich had become political dynamite was correct.

As progressives battled for control of the party, particularly in the Mississippi Valley, they wielded the shame of the Payne-Aldrich tariff as a cudgel against Taft and the party regulars. Aldrich now was less a leader of his party than its greatest liability. In midsummer, Senator Joseph L. Bristow, a Republican from Kansas (yet another Aldrich detractor from the Plains), accused Aldrich of having raised the tariff on rubber to boost the value of his personal holding in Intercontinental Rubber Company. The Kansas Republicans were in the midst of a vicious primary battle, and Aldrich was a useful target. The insurgents swept the primary, winning six of eight contested seats. It happened that Bristow's charge was groundless: Payne-Aldrich had raised the duty on manufactured rubber goods, but Intercontinental exclusively sold crude rubber. Because there was no domestic supply of the raw material, duties were irrelevant. Due to the seriousness of the allegation, Aldrich broke his customary policy of refusing to comment and issued a lengthy denial, which included the sentence "The Senator's statement that I had any pecuniary interest in the [tariff] change is absurdly false in every particular." Bristow never attempted to substantiate his charge.* Nonetheless, Aldrich's reputation was further tarnished.

With the Payne-Aldrich tariff weighing on voters' minds, Roosevelt boarded a private railroad car for a tour of sixteen states that provided fresh evidence of the progressive juggernaut. In town after town he was greeted like a faith healer. Vanderlip reported, "Roosevelt is certainly making a triumphal progress through the West. . . .

---

* Bristow, who served one term, is remembered, if at all, for provoking a famous wisecrack. While he was delivering a lengthy oration in the Senate on the country's "needs," Vice President Thomas Marshall grew so impatient he whispered, just loudly enough to be audible, "What this country needs is a really good five-cent cigar."

The popularity of the man is amazing." Significantly, Roosevelt proposed a far more radical agenda than he had pursued as president—steeply progressive taxes, workmen's compensation, child labor protections, the right of the "community" to restrict private property for the general good. He called for a more representative political system, for a "moral awakening" of the people, and for a considerably more active federal government.

In another time, Aldrich's scheme for a central bank might have fit neatly into this agenda. Aldrich envisioned a central bank as an antidote to individualism run amok. This was an enlightened idea—a "progressive" idea—but at that moment, nothing proposed by Aldrich would be entertained by his party's liberal wing. When it came to banking, western so-called progressives were backward-looking and prone to conspiracy theories. Roosevelt, an eastern progressive, was not an enemy of bankers, but he did not have the patience to study the issue in any depth. Although he supported the notion of financial reform, it was only in the vaguest terms.

Aldrich intended to wait out the 1910 midterm elections, continue with the Monetary Commission after he retired from the Senate in 1911, and draft a bill. But the bankers around him were worried. With the Republicans weakened by internal strife, their ability to effectively legislate was in doubt. In October, Perkins anxiously wrote to the overseas Morgan, "The political pot is boiling here."

Shifting tactics, Aldrich decided to escape from Washington and craft a plan for banking reform in virtual solitude, accompanied only by a few of his trusted allies. He was feeling battered from so much personal criticism and under pressure from the bankers to show some tangible results. The idea of a working trip in a warmer climate appealed.

Then, in late October, his plans were delayed again. Aldrich, who was in New York, exited a trolley at Sixtieth Street and Madison Avenue and began walking west, toward the apartment of his son Winthrop, when he realized that Winthrop's apartment, on Park

Avenue, was actually to the east. The senator, a fortnight shy of his sixty-ninth birthday, pivoted and started toward Park without noticing a trolley headed southbound. The collision hurled him several feet and knocked him unconscious. He awoke in a confused state, described as "a slight shock." Taft, who had remained loyal to his friend, immediately cabled, "I am greatly distressed to hear of the accident to you and sincerely hope the injury is only slight. I shall be glad to be assured on this point."

On election day, Taft and the Republicans received a shellacking. The Democrats won the House, decisively, for the first time in sixteen years. In the Senate, the Democrats gained twelve seats, enough to combine with Republican insurgents and effectively control the upper chamber. Thus, the entire Congress was suddenly tilted toward the progressives. Democrats also picked up a stack of governorships, including that of Woodrow Wilson in New Jersey. The leftward shift in the electorate seemed to reflect a more general upheaval in American society. As the historian Frederick Jackson Turner remarked the following month, "It is hardly an exaggeration that we are witnessing the birth of a new nation in America." This nation counted over 90 million people, of whom more than a third were immigrants or the offspring of immigrants, largely eastern and southern Europeans, and of whom 8 million belonged to labor unions. The days of building a political stronghold on small Rhode Island towns were over.

Aldrich, for so long a leader in a conservative era, was now in the strange position of having to appeal to a Congress he barely recognized and to a political consensus from which he was excluded. His only hope was that the commission plan—once it was written— would be judged impartially. "We shall appeal to the thoughtful men of this country," he told a posh crowd of seven hundred, largely bankers, at the Hotel Astor. And yet any hope that the new Congress, in the heat of its crusading fervor, would grant Aldrich an unbiased evaluation, strictly on the merits, he must have known was a pipe dream. He was dejected by his party's loss at the polls and saw no hope in conventional politics. Sufficiently recovered from his accident, he reinstated his plan for a working trip. His plan was so secret that when the Monetary Commission met after the election, Aldrich did not even mention it.

Two years earlier, Stillman had suggested that Aldrich convene a private bankers' group at Warwick, but November was no time to be in Rhode Island. Instead, Aldrich opted for a rendezvous on Jekyl Island, in the warm waters off the coast of Georgia. At long last energized, he hastily assembled his team of bankers.

CHAPTER SEVEN

JEKYL ISLAND

A Banker uses the money of others; as long as he uses
his own money he is only a capitalist.
—DAVID RICARDO

Public utility is more truly the object of public banks,
than private profit.
—ALEXANDER HAMILTON

THE MISSION TO JEKYL ISLAND was undertaken in rare seclusion. Today it is a lost art, but in 1910, a prominent U.S. senator and
some of the leading men of Wall Street could drop off the grid without a trace and plot a complete overhaul of the banking system.

Nelson Aldrich insisted on absolute secrecy, knowing that any
plan would be doomed if it could be traced to Wall Street. He deliberately picked bankers who were senior enough to be able to leave
work and cancel appointments on a moment's notice. Harry Davison,

with whom Aldrich felt a close connection, helped to compile the list and was included as a matter of course. Davison approached Paul Warburg on November 15 and asked if he could cut loose for a week or two on an expedition to an unspecified location three days hence. Davison must have said something about the purpose of the trip but made it clear that Warburg could not tell his partners or anyone else where he was going and on what errand.

Aldrich also recruited Frank Vanderlip, president of National City, and Professor Piatt Andrew, who had taken a job as assistant secretary of the Treasury. Andrew had to pledge not to disclose their mission to his boss, the Treasury secretary—not even a cabinet member was to know! The final member was Arthur Shelton, Aldrich's personal secretary. In all there were six co-conspirators—three bankers, a senator, his secretary, and a senior Treasury official—charged with drafting a new banking regime in the remote pine and palmetto groves of southern Georgia.

It was Davison who arranged for the group to stay at Jekyl Island, an exclusive club where J. P. Morgan was a member. The ruse was that they were going duck hunting, and so Warburg, feeling faintly ridiculous, obtained a hunting rifle and cartridges that he had not the slightest idea how to use. On a frigid night, softened by falling snow, the voyagers, traveling singly and incognito, made their way to the Pennsylvania Station across the Hudson River, where Aldrich's private railcar was attached to the rear of a southbound train. The blinds were drawn, with slivers of amber light marking the window frames. Inside, the car was all polished brass, mahogany, and velvet. Warburg found Vanderlip on board; Davison was soon to arrive. This trio represented the elite of American banking—Kuhn, Loeb; Morgan's; and National City—yet none had a typical Wall Street pedigree. Davison had weathered a Dickensian upbringing in Pennsylvania; Vanderlip, bred on a farm, had come to banking via newspapers and government; and Warburg, though heir to a family bank, was a foreigner and a Jew. Each was enough of the outsider to see the system for its faults.

As the engine purred in preparation for departure, Vanderlip convivially inquired of Warburg, "On what kind of an errand are we going, anyhow?"

Warburg replied portentously, "It may be a wild goose chase instead of a duck shooting party, and it may be the biggest thing you and I ever did. That all depends on the courage that you and the others will show."

Warburg, having plotted a central bank for so long, was edgy. He had doubts about whether this small group could pull it off—doubts about the banking establishment in particular. He wondered whether Vanderlip's National City, the largest and most powerful bank, would support a reform in which its prodigious reserves would be moved from its vaults to whatever new institution they might create. "When the test will come will you cling to these old conditions or, will you show courage enough and self-confidence?" Warburg demanded.

Aldrich set a workmanlike tone, launching the group into their task at breakfast amid the clattering of cups and saucers in the rattling train car. They remained huddled around the table as the train sped southward, making little progress at first, but settling on certain preliminaries. To preserve secrecy, they were to address one another only by first names. Vanderlip offered to write down any point on which they were agreed, thus keeping a log of their progress. Aldrich was indisputably the head of the group; Warburg was the most knowledgeable (and the most opinionated) on monetary questions, although Vanderlip was a quick study. Davison's role was to smooth out the human element—to inject a note of the lighthearted in a week of tense labors and to maintain a harmonious spirit.

After a day's journey they disembarked in Brunswick, Georgia, where they planned to board a launch to the island, with an ostentatious display of rifles and loud talk of hunting. The stationmaster cut them short. "Now gentlemen, this is all very pretty, but I must tell you that we know who you are and the reporters are waiting outside," he said. The travelers were crestfallen; was their cover blown already?

Davison took the stationmaster by the arm, with his gentle touch, and said, "Come out, old man, I will tell you a story." The two left the depot and strolled outside. What the story was Davison never revealed. He returned a moment later with a twinkle in his eye and reassured the others, "That's all right, they won't give us away." For the next eight days the travelers were sequestered, without even a telegraph or telephone link to home.

The Jekyl Island Club, founded in 1885, had been described by *Munsey's* magazine as "the richest, the most exclusive, the most inaccessible" club in the world. The members, ranging from William Vanderbilt to Joseph Pulitzer, often arrived by yacht, but the premises were comfortable rather than opulent. The idea was to enjoy the natural setting—some 240 acres along the intercoastal seaway abutting marshlands and woods stocked with duck, pheasants, wild hogs, turkey, and deer. Members hunted and golfed and resided in pleasant little cottages. In winter, the club was a bustling, self-sufficient community of several hundred guests and staff. However, as Morgan had arranged that no other guests be present, the senator's party stayed in the main house, a rambling, turreted Victorian structure with wooden floors and a captain's walk with a timbered porch.

Davison and Andrew generally arose at daybreak for a ride or swim, pausing on their return to admire the massive live oak trees laced with Spanish moss. After breakfast, which was prepared by servants, the plotters—masking their identities from the staff—gathered in a meeting room by a fireplace and worked through the day. "We were working so hard that we ate enormously," Vanderlip would recall. "Without our ever stopping to hunt, deer, turkey and quail appeared on the table; there were pans of oysters not an hour old when they were scalloped."

After dinner they would remove to a more comfortable setting for a digestif and a cigar, with Davison grabbing the plushest chair. They worked well into the evening, Aldrich set the pace and he was indefatigable. Naturally at home in an exclusive setting, he strove to craft a plan on a latticework of detail. Clearly, he favored a central bank, but his ideas on how to structure it were not at all crystallized, and many questions had to be resolved: Who would put up the capital and own this bank? Who would run it and how would they be chosen?

Warburg favored a stronger government role than Aldrich did, to assure the public that Wall Street would not be in charge. Warburg also preferred a federal structure, as in his "United Reserve Bank" plan—again, to mollify the public. However, Aldrich had his heart set on a central bank like the ones he had seen in Europe.

Over the long days of work, tension arose between the two strongest-willed figures, Warburg and Aldrich. The senator disliked the tenacity with which Warburg pressed his points. Often Aldrich cut him off in midsentence, though he might later return to Warburg's point, cloaking it as his own. Warburg felt so passionately about reform that, when silenced, he could not help but smolder.

The pair reached an impasse over the structure of reserves—the building blocks, as it were, of the system they were creating. The point may seem a technical one, but it bears a moment's thought, for the entire edifice of the new central bank would hinge on how these reserves were defined. If a bank were to deposit assets at the central bank, it would be credited with a reserve—on this much all were agreed. But if the bank, say, traded a loan for a note of this new central institution, would these notes, deposited in a bank's own vault, also count as reserves?

Warburg insisted that they should (as, indeed, the modern Federal Reserve recognizes). The note, after all, represented a promise from the central bank—it was an asset no less than a deposit was. To Warburg, the integrity of the entire system hinged on this point. Aldrich disagreed. Warburg's conception, he believed, countenanced a dangerous inflation (the more reserves a bank possessed, the greater the volume it could issue in loans).

In all of his previous plans, Warburg had devoted intense thought to the issue of inflation. Since the central bank notes would circulate as money, the danger of excessive circulation was clear. Therefore, he devised an elaborate set of rules governing which sorts of paper would be eligible to be exchanged for notes. In simplest form, he proposed that notes be exchanged only for short-term paper (such as commercial paper) of the most reliable character, generally loans endorsed by banks. He thought this system, modeled on Germany's, would foster an elastic currency but also guard against abuse. Nonetheless, he could not convince Aldrich, or any of the others, on the question of reserves. Warburg and Aldrich had a heated exchange and came to the point of falling out.

When the session adjourned that night, Davison led Warburg for a walk in the island darkness, with Warburg numbly repeating, "The notes must count as reserves." "Paul," Davison interjected, "you cannot force Mr. Nelson [Aldrich]. If you try to, you will lose him. Drop the matter for the time being, and see whether you can take it up again later on." Even though Davison had no expertise in monetary matters, his calming presence and human understanding proved just as valuable.

Thanksgiving fell toward the week's end; the group feasted on wild turkey and oyster stuffing. With the basic points of the reform plan settled, at least for the moment, the conspirators opted to take a day off for a duck shoot. The party took out a boat, with Davison drolly attired in khaki hunting clothes and moccasins. No ducks were found.

The final, crucial task was to sculpt their oral discussions into a written blueprint. Warburg declined the job of draftsman, fearing that his style and language would be recognized and that the plan would be condemned as the Wall Street concoction that it was. The task went to Vanderlip, who wrote in a newspaperman's popular style, and whose views were close to Warburg's.

Aldrich prevailed on the issue of reserves, but the general outline was faithful to Warburg's idea of a federal structure. In many ways, what came to be known as the Aldrich Plan resembled Warburg's "United Reserve Bank," although the name was changed to "Reserve Association of the United States." Essentially, it was a plan to pool reserves and create a new elastic currency, a Reserve Association note, backed by a gold reserve, that would supplant the old National Bank Notes.

Both Aldrich and the bankers recognized the danger that their creation would be seen as a central bank, and thus did everything they could to avoid that dreaded appellation. That meant building in safeguards against domination by either the government or Wall Street. To mollify fears that the plan would be seen as radical, Aldrich built on the familiar tapestry of the local clearinghouses, standardizing their form and knitting them into a cohesive nationwide organization.

Each participating bank would belong to a local association, which would act as a more stable form of clearinghouse. The local associations would, in turn, send representatives to a district branch—with fifteen branches spanning the country. At the apex of the pyramid stood the Reserve Association in Washington.

Governance in the association was to be strictly democratic, with boards at each level (local, district, and national) elected by members. While larger banks would own more shares (subscriptions were set at 20 percent of capital), the overall scheme was egalitarian. A system of one bank/one vote prevailed, so that no cabal of banks—not even of the biggest banks—could hope to assert control.* The only plum for the big New York banks was that the rules would be liberalized to let

---

* Elections were cleverly divided, with a plurality of board seats awarded on a one bank/one vote basis, and a minority of seats apportioned on a per-share basis, which is to say bigger banks getting more votes. The spirit of this compromise was retained in the eventual Federal Reserve Act. Today the smallest banks in each district, the middle-tier banks, and the largest banks each elect directors to their local Reserve Bank, thus preserving diversity according to bank size. Furthermore, of the nine directors at each Reserve Bank, only three are bankers (although six are chosen by banks). The other directors are selected, at least in theory, to represent of the public.

national banks do business overseas. For Vanderlip, hungrily eyeing international expansion, this was a major coup.

The Aldrich Plan was deliberately tailored to American traditions; it was democratic in governance and federal in structure. But it was not a central bank like those in Europe. As Warburg was to write, "It was strictly a bankers' bank."

To avert the impression of a threatening colossus, the district branches would act as the operating units. They would hold the reserves of member banks and issue the new currency, through a process known as "discounting." In contrast to the existing arbitrary regime, in which the volume of currency depended on investment in government bonds, the circulation now would have an organic relationship to ordinary banking activity. In brief, member banks would go to their respective branches and exchange short-term loans such as commercial paper, suitably endorsed, for reserve notes—the new paper money. The branches also would handle routine functions such as check clearing.

The Reserve Association in Washington would control policy and oversee the branches (including when one region needed emergency reserves from another). In conception, Aldrich envisioned a single bank visible to the community in the guise of its fifteen operating branches. Importantly, Washington would set a single interest rate for the entire country. Warburg had wanted each district to set its own rate, but Aldrich, who felt that a uniform rate would seem fairer, overrode him.

To avoid the suspicion that the association would favor political factions or their friends, bankers—not government—would be in control. The President would choose the Reserve Association governor from a list provided by its directors. However, thirty-nine of the forty-five directors were either bankers or industry representatives chosen by bankers; only six were government appointees (and even they were a grudging concession, forced on Aldrich by the politically sensitive Warburg).

Although Aldrich recognized that the public had a vital interest in banking, he was adamant that the Reserve Association avoid the possibility of political influence, which, as he saw it, was the critical weakness of the Second Bank in the time of Jackson. He rationalized the near-exclusion of the public by casting monetary policy as merely a *banking* problem. "These are business questions," he said. "They are not political questions." To further keep the ghost of Jackson at bay, the association's powers would be limited. It could buy and sell securities on the open market (much like the eventual Federal Reserve), but it could not be a banker to the community at large, such as by taking deposits. It would serve the banks, not compete with them. It could not even compel individual banks to join (membership would be voluntary, reflecting the drafters' laissez-faire bias).

Just as the association would be protected against power grabs by politicians, it would also be immune to exploitation by banks, or so the drafters believed. Association dividends paid to member banks were capped at 5 percent, with a portion of the profits directed to the Treasury.* Thus, while bankers were in control, they could not expect more than a reasonable return.

It was an inventive and thoughtful plan, honestly wrought. Aldrich, who had been so wedded to the old currency based on government bonds, showed courage in supporting a new currency based on private loans. The chief deficit of the plan was that it looked backward, to the era of private bankers. The drafters could not quite envision that, in the twentieth century, progressivism and like movements around the world would insist on public control of financial institutions.

As they were leaving the island, the collaborators resolved to seek the support of Wall Street's old guard. Aldrich would talk to J. P.

---

* This feature would be honored in the eventual Federal Reserve Act; the individual Reserve Banks would earn income and pay fixed dividends to member banks, with the surplus profits distributed to the Treasury.

Morgan and George Baker; Vanderlip would consult with James
Stillman. The real work would be persuading bankers away from the
Eastern Seaboard.

Warburg suggested they also organize a league of businessmen to
promote reform. Aldrich thought this preposterous. "If you can do
that, God bless you!" he said mockingly. The others had a hearty
laugh. Once again, Warburg seethed. But despite the tension between
them, the week had enhanced his respect for Aldrich—who for all his
tendency to dominate was willing to do the hard work of understanding the issues.

The group disbanded quietly, in agreement over the blueprint
despite many points of friction. Vanderlip considered the episode a
high point of his life. Writing Stillman the next day—a violation of
his secrecy oath—Vanderlip declared, "I am back from Jekyl Island,
and have had as keenly interesting a time as I can remember ever to
have had."

Given the total makeover of Congress, now tilted toward progressives, Vanderlip was not optimistic on the Plan's immediate prospects.
Nonetheless, he predicted that eventually "something along these
general lines will be enacted." Using Stillman and Vanderlip's private
code for Aldrich, Vanderlip added, "Zivil was greatly pleased with
the result of the conference, and desires to keep in very constant
touch."

Aside from a couple of vague allusions, the Jekyl conspirators did
not refer to the trip in subsequent correspondence. Although they
would continue working together, the trip itself disappeared from
view. Six years later, in 1916, the journalist B. C. Forbes (then laying
plans for *Forbes* magazine) mentioned the bare fact of the trip in *Leslie's Weekly*. But his article received scant notice, and the secret was
essentially preserved. Even as late as the late 1920s, when Warburg
was writing an account of the Federal Reserve's origins, he said only
that he had been "invited to join a small group of men who, at Sena-

Senator Nelson W. Aldrich. Unknown, n.d. Albumen print photograph. Graphics. Anonymous. RHI X17 141.

TOP LEFT: From the time he entered the Senate in 1881, Nelson W. Aldrich was a bastion of conservatism and a stout defender of the decentralized Civil War banking structure. His cool exterior masked a melancholy nature and a yearning to leave his mark.

TOP RIGHT: William Jennings Bryan, depicted soon after his stirring "cross of gold" speech at the 1896 Democratic convention, lost the election but won the support of farmers and working-class Americans who thought the banking system favored the wealthy. Wall Street regarded him with contempt.

LEFT: Carter Glass, the son of a Confederate soldier reared on the gospel of states' rights, was determined to reform the banking system without creating a dread "central bank."

TOP LEFT: The young financier Paul Warburg moved to America in 1902 and joined his in-laws' firm on Wall Street. He was horrified by the primitive condition of American banking and passionately crusaded for a system of centralized reserves like the one he had left behind in Germany.

TOP RIGHT: The onetime farm boy Frank Vanderlip, heir apparent at National City Bank of New York, was upset that reserves were siphoned off to the countryside at harvest season, depleting metropolitan areas of funds. He agreed with Warburg that America needed a central bank.

RIGHT: Although Democrats opposed a national bank, the young president of Princeton University, Woodrow Wilson, had written favorably of Alexander Hamilton's original experiment and was sympathetic to the cause of reform.

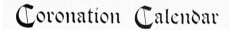

Coronation Calendar

WOODROW WILSON

"I am glad on't; 'tis a worthy governor!"

Princeton...

October 24th and 25th, 1902

WALL STREET DURING THE BANKING PANIC

TOP LEFT: During the Panic of 1907, one man—J. P. Morgan, shown beside an ornamental vase in his library—fulfilled the role of "lender of last resort," which in other nations was played by the central bank

TOP RIGHT: Even Morgan's efforts were not enough, as this scene from the Panic of 1907 demonstrates. Despite the efforts of Morgan and his colleagues to organize loans, banks around the country ran out of money and had to circulate scrip.

LEFT: In 1908, the Harvard professor Piatt Andrew (shown at his home in Gloucester, Massachusetts) guided Aldrich and other members of the National Monetary Commission on a tour of Europe, studying central banking operations in London, Berlin, and Paris.

In Europe, Aldrich did an about-face and became convinced of the need for a central bank.

The rising progressive movement trained its sights on one villain in particular: Nelson Aldrich. In this political cartoon, typical of the era, Aldrich is depicted as a spider trapping needed reform efforts in its web.

TOP: Desperate to enact a reform while the Republicans still held power, Aldrich absconded to remote Jekyll Island in Georgia with Piatt Andrew and three leading Wall Street bankers. Working in absolute secrecy in this still-standing clubhouse, the conspirators drafted the Aldrich Plan.

LEFT: During the week at Jekyll Island, tension simmered between Aldrich and Warburg. The light touch of Henry P. (Harry) Davison cooled them down.

By the time William Howard Taft succeeded his good friend Theodore Roosevelt as president, the growing strain in their relationship was visible in their mutually stiff poses. Roosevelt's ultimate break with Taft cleaved the Republican Party in two and dealt a fatal blow to the Aldrich Plan.

The political operator Edward M. House, known by the honorific "Colonel," dedicated himself to making Wilson president. His first task was winning the endorsement of William Jennings Bryan.

Inauguration day, March 4, 1913. Wilson pledged to reform the banking system, but he reassured bankers that he would "restore" rather than "destroy."

TOP: Treasury Secretary William G. McAdoo—businessman, progressive, and southerner—epitomized the new administration. He boldly proposed his own banking plan, putting Glass's Federal Reserve bill in jeopardy.

LEFT: Robert L. Owen, chairman of the Senate Banking and Currency Committee, and a disciple of Bryan, demanded that control over the Fed rest in the federal government. Glass wanted private bankers to retain some control.

With farmers, bankers, progressives, and westerners each insisting on distinct amendments, it was left to Wilson to break the logjam in Congress. He wrote to a friend, "The struggle goes on without intermission."

Signing of the Federal Reserve Act, December 23, 1913, painting by Wilbur G. Kurtz. From left to right: Lindley Garrison, secretary of war; Josephus Daniels, secretary of the Navy; Franklin K. Lane, secretary of the interior; Albert S. Burleson, postmaster general; Senator Owen; Champ Clark, Speaker of the House; Secretary McAdoo; President Wilson (seated); Representative Glass; Representative Oscar Underwood; William B. Wilson, secretary of labor.

tor Aldrich's request, were to take part in a several days' conference with him, to discuss the form that the new banking bill should take." He added in a footnote, "Though eighteen years have since gone by, I do not feel free to give a description of this most interesting conference concerning which Senator Aldrich pledged all participants to secrecy." However, in 1930, an authorized biography of Aldrich finally revealed a few details.

Thanks to its secrecy and its glittering cast, the cloak-and-dagger retreat would give rise to legions of conspiracy theories. For gold bugs, anti–Federal Reserve zealots, and flat-out cranks, the 1910 escapade would come to assume mythic significance. Over the decades, its suspicious character seemed only to grow larger. In 1952, Eustace Mullins, a Holocaust denier and conspiracy theorist nonpareil, described the "secret meetings of the international bankers" as a conclave of the Rothschild family linked backward in time to Hamilton and forward to Winston Churchill, Franklin D. Roosevelt, and Joseph Stalin. Mullins was inspired to probe into the central bank during a hospital visit to the fascist sympathizer Ezra Pound and devoted his career to a lunatic blend of anti-Fed and anti-Semitic diatribes. Some years later, G. Edward Griffin transformed paranoid theories into a lucrative cottage industry. A onetime writer for the John Birch Society and for Alabama governor George Wallace, and the author of a previous book espousing a miracle cancer cure, in 1994 Griffin penned *The Creature from Jekyll Island*. This book, which became a steady seller, argued that the bankers who came to the island in 1910 did so to establish a cartel, with the aim of suppressing competition in banking and confiscating the people's wealth.

For such writers, Jekyl became a metaphor for central banking, supposedly an international plot to bury civilization in debts. Since central bank notes are a form of obligation, each dollar issued by the Federal Reserve, each pound minted by the Bank of England, was, it was alleged, an added enslavement. A leitmotif in such arguments was that debt itself was pernicious, and in fact a strain of credit-phobia persists in America to this day. In 2010, the centenary of the Aldrich mission, Jekyll Island* was host to a conference at which a contemporary naysayer claimed that the Federal Reserve was nothing but a confidence game. These arguments against money and credit have gained wide—at times fanatical—adherence, perhaps not surprisingly, since many financial disasters are accompanied by waves of debt failures.

Credit has often been abused or overused, but it is hard to imagine a society advancing beyond the most primitive stage without some means of exchange between those possessing surplus funds and those in deficit. Otherwise, money would sit idly in the vaults of the rich. People could try to borrow from rich people directly, but most people's personal credit, and even that of most firms, is limited to a relatively small circle of acquaintances. This is the gap filled by banks. As Vanderlip put it to Carter Glass, "the main business of a bank is to exchange its credit for the credit of its customers." The point of a central bank was to be a banker to banks, to use *its* credit to supplement that of each individual institution.

The bankers who journeyed to Jekyl Island had no notion of monopoly. They wanted a more resilient banking system. They espoused greater cooperation, but it was for the purpose of collective security as opposed to, say, fixing interest rates. They certainly thought Aldrich's "Reserve Association" would redound to their institutions' benefits. Confidence in the credit system could only help their bottom lines. More specifically, Vanderlip's correspondence makes emphatically clear that he was eager for National City to expand overseas, and a central bank would further such efforts. Vanderlip, himself a former Treasury official, envisioned the U.S. government as potentially a helpful partner to international banks just as, say, planters in Central America might hope to call, now and

---

* Jekyl Island was spelled with a single "l" until 1929, when a second "l" was added.

then, on the U.S. Marines. However, the bankers accompanying Aldrich did not envision, or want, a *government* central bank. They generally held to a laissez-faire view that private credit was more dependable than government debt—and therefore, that "money" should consist of private, rather than government, notes. They were interested in a system of *self*-regulation for banks. They wanted a framework in which banking reserves could be pooled—centralized or at least regionalized—and this, they believed, would indisputably be to the greater society's good.

While sequestered on the island, the bankers spoke with bitterness at having to steal about as though they were criminals. In their own minds, and in any fair rendering, they were attempting to achieve a worthy public reform. They were conspirators, but patriotic conspirators.

Once home, they orchestrated a two-pronged attack. Aldrich reached out to leading bankers in the West. Meanwhile, Warburg surgically inserted himself into the deliberations of various commercial groups who were debating monetary reform. Coaxing these bodies toward a position consistent with the Aldrich Plan involved a nimble pirouette—because Warburg, of course, could not reveal that he knew what the Plan was going to say. Thus, he was anxious for Aldrich to go public.

Barely had he been home a week than Warburg bombarded Aldrich with seven pages of suggestions as the senator prepared a final draft. He also wrote to Andrew, whom Warburg frequently used as an alternate channel to communicate with Aldrich, relaying his impatience. Warburg had been made head of the New York Chamber of Commerce's monetary committee—an influential group—and he was especially eager for Aldrich to divulge his plan so that Warburg could openly recommend it to the committee. "Will you please find out from Mr. N [Aldrich] what he wants me to do and what he intends to do," Warburg asked Andrew, barely concealing his frustration. "I have not called together my committee up till now, but I cannot delay that very much longer." As usual, Warburg supplied a carrot as well as a stick. "Not a day passes," he exclaimed, "without some new evidence that the Central bank is wanted."

Aldrich briefed his colleagues on the Monetary Commission without breathing a word of the trip to Jekyl. But a whisper of great tidings was in the air. During December, Warburg was introduced to Taft. "Warburg," the rotund President said good-naturedly, "I hear all kinds of things that Senator Aldrich is doing. What, really, is going on?" At such moments Warburg felt his foreign roots keenly. While replying evasively to the President, he could not help but wonder about the strange workings of the American political system, in which the head of state was forced to inquire of a rank outsider about events within his own party.

Aldrich also appeared at the American Academy of Political and Social Science in Philadelphia, where he hinted about the nature of his forthcoming plan and promised the goods "in the near future." Warburg and the other conspirators awaited publication, but as the holidays approached, Aldrich greeted them with silence. Warburg suspected the delay was owing to the senator's tendency to procrastinate, but as the calendar turned to 1911 it became clear that Aldrich's health was deteriorating, physically as well as psychologically.

Although Aldrich's family tried to hush it up, press accounts grew steadily more worrisome. "Senator Aldrich Ill; Friends Worried over Reports That He Has Throat Trouble," the *Times* reported on January 6, 1911. A week later, the paper retracted the report of throat trouble, divulging now that Aldrich was "quite ill at his home." It closed menacingly, "He is abed and does not receive even his secretary."

It seems clear that Aldrich was suffering an aggravated form of the nervous melancholia that he had experienced as a younger man— in short, a breakdown. His Jekyl confreres tactfully attributed his illness to the mental strain of his work on monetary reform. Abby's diary attests to her husband's "spell of feeling very nervous" and to his recurrent sleeplessness. Presumably, more than hard work was at issue.

Aldrich had finally completed a blueprint embodying three years of intensive study—a document that he fancied incorporated the height of banking wisdom. But his term expired in March, and the incoming Congress was unlikely to show any interest. The realization that his crowning work could conceivably wind up on the scrap heap may have pushed him over the edge to depression. There was little that doctors could offer for his condition other than the advice of rest. The senator's personal physician counseled that he avoid all "excitement."

Aldrich's ill-timed absence posed a vexing issue for Warburg, who had managed to gain the joint endorsement of three commercial groups for a reform plan very much resembling the still under-wraps Aldrich Plan.* An assembly of such groups under the auspices of the National Board of Trade was to convene in Washington on January 18. Warburg felt it was vital for the Aldrich Plan to be surfaced before that date, so the Board of Trade could offer its endorsement.

But Aldrich was confined to his bedchamber, leaving Andrew to try to steer the Plan to the finish line. Andrew spent New Year's with the Davisons on Long Island, then returned home for a weekend of high-stakes meetings to win over James Forgan, the acknowledged dean of the Chicago bankers. On Friday, January 6, Andrew hosted Forgan and James Laughlin, the University of Chicago economics professor, at lunch. Saturday evening the group dined at the White House, and the following day they met with Treasury Secretary Franklin MacVeagh. Andrew was not immediately persuasive. As Forgan and Laughlin made for the train back to Chicago, Forgan cackled derisively, "Laughlin, did you ever see such a mess of a banking bill?"

Warburg, meanwhile, was fending off inquiries from Wall Street, including a pesky suggestion from Samuel Sachs, who wanted assurance that private banks such as his small firm, Goldman Sachs, would

---

* The three were the New York Chamber of Commerce, the Merchants' Association of New York, and the Produce Exchange.

be permitted to deal directly with the new central bank. (Goldman was an investment bank, whereas the Aldrich Plan envisioned a cooperative of national, or commercial, banks.) Warburg's reply was evasive, but he recognized—a century in advance of Lloyd Blankfein—that coziness with the likes of Goldman was ill advised. "My own view," Warburg replied, "is that it would be better not to open the door for the criticism that private interest might enjoy undue favoritism with the central bank."

On January 15, with still no plan before the public, the Jekyl conspirators minus Aldrich reassembled in Andrew's one-room apartment, a few blocks from the White House. Andrew had dined at the Aldriches' two nights earlier, and the senator had asked that a letter be prepared to accompany the Plan. The group worked on it through the day, with Vanderlip doing the drafting. Then, Davison shepherded the letter to Aldrich, who penciled in some changes and signed.

The Aldrich Plan was released two days later. It was presented as the work of Aldrich personally, addressed to his fellow members of the Monetary Commission. The letter took pains to characterize the Reserve Association not as a "central bank," but as an institution more suited to American needs. The goal was to bring about three seminal changes: a more unified banking system; a more logical basis for the currency; and the development of a market in bank paper, so that liquid funds would be loaned to businesses rather than to stock market traders.

In an effort to disarm the inevitable critics, the senator's letter affirmed that the provisions of the Plan had been submitted to the commission and to the American people "for their criticism and action, and not as the last word that can be said on the subject." Aldrich himself was absent. His doctors had ordered him, urgently, to go south. Even as the plan was making news, he was headed back to Jekyl Island for an enforced rest.

The New York Times obliged Aldrich by roundly proclaiming, "Aldrich Money Plan Avoids Central Bank." Immediately, Leslie Shaw, the free-swinging former Treasury secretary, retorted that the Reserve Association was a central bank "under false colors." Thus the debate over the Aldrich Plan was framed: a debate less over its merits than over terminology—over whether it was, or was not, a central bank.

The hostile political climate ruled out trying to enact the Plan for the moment. By a quirk of history, monetary reform had become linked in the public's mind not to progressivism, where it belonged, but to the archconservatism that Aldrich symbolized. His colleagues' strategy was to galvanize public opinion and hope that the opposition would soften under a deluge of favorable publicity. Warburg, with his customary brio, led the way. He had developed surprising cunning in politicking in his adopted home. He managed to be quoted in the press effusively praising the Plan while neglecting to mention that he was one of its primary drafters. He appeared in Washington not as the author of the Plan but as a fervid supporter, representing the Chamber of Commerce and two other commercial bodies. In this guise, he won the coveted endorsement of the Board of Trade. To top off this juggernaut, Warburg persuaded the board to adopt his resolution to form a "Business Men's Monetary Reform League" to spread favorable publicity. Warburg was careful to stipulate that the new league have its headquarters in Chicago so as to avoid the suggestion of Wall Street influence.

The release of the Aldrich Plan—a first draft, as it turned out, for the future Federal Reserve Act—marked an important milestone. After years of denial and then debate, a genuine, if imperfect, program was on the table. It spelled the end of the period in which bankers were the generals in the reform campaign. Now that a plan existed in the public arena, the torch passed, uncertainly, to politicians.

PART TWO

THE

LEGISLATIVE

ARENA

CHAPTER EIGHT

INTO THE CRUCIBLE

We want the views of all men to be put into the
crucible.
                                    —NELSON ALDRICH

PAUL WARBURG HAD VETTED his ideas through Nelson Aldrich
and with bankers, but his plan now faced a series of different, more
difficult challenges. What had been theory now moved into the realm
of practical politics. What had been debated by financial men would
be tested in the realm of the press and of the public. Reform would
require many iterations, especially as American politics was swiftly
radicalizing, becoming ever more hostile to bankers. Thus, the Aldrich gang would gradually recede. Warburg would remain a significant influence, if often in the background, but the direct
responsibility for reform shifted to Congress—that is, to legislators
who were not themselves financial experts. Inevitably, lawmakers re-
sorted to extensive debate and horse-trading, not to mention acrimo-
nious charges and, at times, sheer demagoguery. As elected politicians,

they faced the consummate challenge of reconciling Warburg's arguments for centralization with the public's abiding mistrust of large financial bodies.

Perhaps there might have been no Federal Reserve had Congress not launched a series of sensational hearings that, while not precisely germane to monetary reform, warmed the public to the idea of legislation. And even when a bill advanced, reform-minded bankers found it in some respects unrecognizable and also unpalatable. Bankers had been schooled in traditional doctrines of money, meaning money backed by gold or by the assets of banks. In the early twentieth century, populists such as William Jennings Bryan had begun to advocate the previously heretical idea of "fiat money"—money issued on the whim of government. The debate was part of a larger disagreement over who should control the financial system. In keeping with the laissez-faire tradition, Wall Street had mostly been able to run itself. But when Woodrow Wilson would attempt to steer reform through Congress in 1913, he would be confronted by a demand, emblematic of the times, that the banking industry be controlled by the public.

The most significant lawmaker in the process was Carter Glass, a cautious reformer if ever there was one. The Virginia Democrat was politically acute, deferential to bankers, wary of the public's fear of centralization, and fearful of antagonizing either constituency. He was also ambitious and, while admirably aware of his limitations in finance, thoroughly committed to substantive reform.

When the Aldrich Plan was drafted, the Democrats had only just won control of the House, and Glass had yet to emerge from obscurity. Republicans still held the White House but looked increasingly shaky, and the Aldrich gang, aware that they faced steep political odds, rolled out a strategy for legislation. The first task was to gain the prized endorsement of the American Bankers Association (ABA), along with support from the business community, and use these as a wedge to make inroads with the public. Then, the Aldrich Plan could be formally introduced in Congress as a reform proposal with broad backing. With Aldrich on Jekyl Island, his colleagues, emphasizing the need for industry support, secured the approval of James Forgan and George Reynolds, the two prominent Chicago bankers. Hoping to capitalize on their momentum, the senator's allies thought to invite twenty or so carefully selected bankers to a retreat in Atlantic City. Wary of disturbing Aldrich's rest, but needing his approval, Harry Davison gingerly cabled, on behalf of Frank Vanderlip, Warburg, and himself: "I am very sorry to bother you with this. Frank Paul and I believe this is a psychological time to have a meeting called of . . . prominent bankers in various sections of the country to discuss your proposed plan. Are you willing that I should instruct Arthur [Shelton] to invite the men in your name?" Aldrich responded three days later in the affirmative but stressed he could not be involved in any of the preparations.

The retreat took place over three days in February 1911, hosted by the entire Jekyl cast save Aldrich. The bankers quickly endorsed the general outline of the Aldrich Plan—presumably because it conformed to their laissez-faire tastes. But the bankers had conditions. They wanted state banks, not just national banks, to be eligible to join the Reserve Association. They wanted more lenient rules to govern the discounting of paper, so that bankers could exchange virtually any type of loan for Reserve Association notes (and thus convert such loans into money). Even more brazenly, the bankers demanded a hike in the 5 percent ceiling on dividends that the Reserve Association would pay to member banks. Most worrisome of all, they objected to even the bare element of political control agreed upon in the original draft.

Piatt Andrew protested that the price of the bankers' endorsement would be a plan so friendly to the industry it would be unacceptable to the public at large. However, there was enough common ground to move forward with a presentation to the ABA—whenever, that is, Aldrich returned from Jekyl Island.

Aldrich found it hard to be away from the action but saw no alternative. "Every attempt to do my work or to think seriously on any subject," he wrote to William Howard Taft, "brings back my sleeplessness." The President replied, affectionately, "I long for your presence. I feel as Scott said of Roderick Dhu—'A blast upon your bugle horn were worth a thousand men.'"* Groping for a silver lining, Taft added that since there was nothing the matter with Aldrich "organically," according to Aldrich's physician, the senator needed only to rest "to rid yourself of the notion that you are breaking down."

Through January and early February, Aldrich remained in a highly agitated state. His nights were racked by insomnia, which put a strain on Abby as well. "Am improving so slowly I find it imperative to avoid all excitement of new questions," he cabled Davison. His household devoted meticulous attention to his condition and care. On February 12, Abby found it worth recording in her diary that the senator "slept well two nights." As his strength returned, he took walks on the Georgia beach. He went trout fishing under the turquoise sky; in the evenings he played bridge. By the end of the month his appetite had returned and he was playing golf. In the first week in March, the desperate cloud having lifted, the Aldriches went home to Rhode Island.

Aldrich was now a retired senator. However, he faced the serious business at the end of March of negotiating with Forgan, who represented the currency committee of the ABA, over the revisions demanded by the bankers at Atlantic City. Aldrich capitulated on nearly every point. In particular, he agreed to weaken the control of the President over the leadership of the Reserve Association. In the draft composed on Jekyl Island, the President would select the association's governor and two deputy governors—and could remove them at will. Forgan demanded—and Aldrich agreed—to let the President name

---

* Roderick Dhu is a hero of *The Lady of the Lake*, a narrative poem by Sir Walter Scott (1810).

only the governor, and to vest the power of removing all three officials in the banker-dominated board. (To his credit, Aldrich refused
to yield on raising the dividend cap.)

The result was to make the Reserve Association, while unchanged
in its essentials, more fully the creature of the banking industry. Forgan also had a useful marketing suggestion—that the name be changed
to the *National* Reserve Association, a more public-sounding body.
Finally, Forgan insisted that member banks should be able to count
the association notes that they held in their vaults as reserves—thus
resolving in Warburg's favor the dispute that had flared on Jekyl
Island. Aldrich, no longer concerned with this detail, did not object.
He now had the working endorsement of the country's singular financial body and could set his sights on ratification by the full ABA,
which was to meet in the fall in New Orleans.

Warburg, while reaping a victory on the issue of reserves, was
busy laying the groundwork for the new businessmen's group—the
National Citizens' League for the Promotion of a Sound Banking
System. The aim of the Citizens' League was to attract businesspeople to the cause by enticing them with the prospect of making credit
more available and sustainable. Its purpose was to show that Main
Street was just as enthusiastic about banking reform as Wall Street.
In order to craft a heartland image, its executives were recruited exclusively from the Midwest—its president, John V. Farwell, was a
Chicago dry goods wholesaler, and its board was composed of the
cream of the Chicago business establishment, including Julius Rosen-
wald of Sears, Roebuck and Cyrus McCormick Jr. of International
Harvester.

James Laughlin, the economist (and author of the Indianapolis
report), was tapped as the executive head. Laughlin went on full-time
leave from the University of Chicago. Shrewdly, he told the press the
league was "not an organization of bankers"—it represented not lenders but borrowers. This description was considerably less than the
whole truth. As Warburg would later recount, bankers were among

the league's most liberal contributors. Moreover, Warburg was chairman of the organizing committee and responsible for setting up the branch in New York, as well as other branches, and he was intimately involved in the organization's planning.

The Citizens' League's publicity was similarly sugarcoated to appeal to Americans wary of a central bank. Its constant refrain was that it favored "cooperation, not dominant centralization." In fact, the league was backed by men, such as Warburg, who favored as much centralization as the political process would permit. Nonetheless, officials tried to portray the league as a spontaneous creation of local communities, a financial version of a 4-H Club. When addressing audiences outside of New York, they took every opportunity to distance themselves from "Wall Street." This pose of being unconnected to Gotham was deliberate; as Warburg later admitted, "it would have been fatal to launch such an enterprise from New York."

The league's strategy was also controversial. Formally, it would support principles and goals that very much resembled those of the Aldrich Plan without specifically committing to the Plan itself. Laughlin thought this necessary to make a nonpartisan appeal and to establish a reputation as an independent voice. Aldrich feared it would merely sow confusion. Since the Citizens' League's mission (in his view) was to promote the Aldrich Plan, why not just say so?

But Laughlin had a prickly, self-important streak. And he was hearing from all sides that to sell reform—in particular to Democrats in the House—it was vital that the movement not be associated with Aldrich. Two of his former students, the journalist H. Parker Willis and Theodore Roosevelt himself, forcefully argued that Aldrich was too toxic politically. Thus, Laughlin began to consider submitting a plan of his own. This would have cut the legs out from under the Aldrich Plan.

Over the summer of 1911, Aldrich became newly despondent over the thought that the Citizens' League was a fifth column that would destroy his creation from within. A rift opened between Laughlin and the New York chapter of the league. The latter was a front for Warburg—who developed a strong dislike for the professor.

Relations were further strained when Laughlin decided that Aldrich should retire from the crusade. He aired this sensitive idea with the senator, in the company of Davison and Warburg. To add to the pressure on Aldrich, the possibility of his withdrawal was leaked to the *Times,* which saw great practical sense in divorcing the unpopular Aldrich from his cause. "The credit of his achievement can never be taken from him," the paper editorialized in an unctuous tone. "Mr. Aldrich would be the last man in the world to let the pride of authorship stand in the way of . . . adoption." Not quite.

Aldrich would not consider withdrawing. And his allies in New York put intense pressure on Laughlin to rally around the Aldrich Plan. Trying to reach a modus vivendi, Laughlin held a parley on Aldrich's yacht with Andrew, Davison, and Warburg as well as Ben Strong, the banker who had helped J. P. Morgan sort out good banks from bad in 1907. Annoyingly to the New Yorkers, the league continued to assert its independence, although it stopped short of proposing a rival plan.

Surprisingly, in spite of this internal turmoil, both the Aldrich Plan and the Citizens' League steadily gained momentum. By the late fall, the league had branches in more than thirty states and it was circulating a bimonthly newsletter with a circulation of 20,000, in addition to producing a handbook on banking reform. Laughlin also made impressive strides at broadening the constituency for reform. Touring the South, he plausibly stressed the benefits to farmers if bills for cotton shipments were to be convertible into Reserve Association notes. He also tried to make reform more than a one-party crusade, arguing that it was "high time for Democrats" to get involved.

Meanwhile, endorsements rolled in. No fewer than twenty-nine state banking associations signed on; the Aldrich Plan was beginning to look like an unstoppable juggernaut. President Taft again expressed his approval, although that was the extent of his support. Treasury Secretary MacVeagh was harder to crack. MacVeagh recognized that the Aldrich Plan would reduce the department's role in monetary matters; he also was resentful of the time that Andrew, his subordinate, was spending with Aldrich, with whom his relations were chilly. Nevertheless, MacVeagh threw in the towel and endorsed the Plan.

Aldrich's return to action provided a spur. Under his leadership, the Monetary Commission snapped to life with public hearings intended to rope in farmers and representatives of labor. Aldrich made a round of speeches in the West, pleading that people study the Plan and not reject it out of hand or due to political preconceptions. A latecomer to reform, he could taste the potential for an achievement that was more enduring than his endless revisions of the tariff. He worked relentlessly on incorporating the ABA's points into a revised draft. He also was buoyed by favorable press—in the East, at any rate. The *Journal of Commerce* commented approvingly that under the Aldrich Plan, Wall Street control would be "impossible."

But in the interior of the country, fear of Wall Street domination would not go away. To midwestern progressives it was axiomatic that the Aldrich Plan was a tool of New York bankers. They saw it as a stalking horse for the "Money Trust"—a hazy expression understood by ordinary Americans to mean the Wall Street cabal that, it was said, manipulated the levers of the country's finances.

And in mid-1911 the Money Trust was catapulted onto the front pages—with disastrous consequences for the Aldrich Plan. The first inkling of trouble arose in June, when Vanderlip's National City Bank divulged a plan for a new affiliated unit, to be known as National City Co. The affiliate would have the same shareholders and officers as the bank but a separate corporate identity. In plain terms, it was an end run around the law. The affiliate was intended, as Vanderlip candidly put it in a circular to the bank's shareholders, to "make investments and transact other business, which, though often very profitable, may not be within the express corporate powers of a National bank." One of those purposes was to purchase stocks in other banks. And no sooner was the affiliate established than it scooped up shares in fifteen of its competitors, including controlling stakes of several small banks in New York.

The disclosure set off a tempest. To casual observers, National City resembled a would-be monopolist. A big bank buying shares in smaller banks seemed akin to a Rockefeller buying a string of oil refiners. New York banking was already a clubby affair, in which Morgan, Baker, and Stillman/Vanderlip tacitly agreed to restrict competition to well-defined lines of business and openly colluded in others.

What truly sounded alarm bells was the seeming linkage between the National City affiliate and the Aldrich Plan. It was easy to imagine that if the Aldrich Plan was adopted, a chain of banks, jointly owned by a holding company such as National City, might gain voting control of the National Reserve Association. The Citizens' League was alarmed, for the mere possibility of such a vehicle undermined its strategy of marketing the Aldrich Plan as a democratic reform. As the *Times* put it, "It is a waste of breath to urge upon the people of the country the acceptance of the Aldrich plan so long as one National bank, through a holding company, may control twenty, fifty, or one hundred other National banks."

In actual fact, there was not much prospect of National City's controlling the Reserve Association. America had well more than twenty thousand banks of various types—Wall Street's collusive tendencies notwithstanding, banking remained far more competitive than oil, steel, sugar, or any of the industries dominated by a classic trust. And the Reserve Association, were it to be established, would dwarf the assets even of National City. Warburg tried to placate worried officials of the Citizens' League, but his sarcasm got the better of him. Writing to the league's president, he drily remarked that taking over the Reserve Association "was as remote to the managers of the National City Bank as the Northpole [*sic*]."

Laughlin was not amused. Even if New York did not appreciate the damage done by National City, he reproachfully replied to Warburg, the news "could not have come out at a more unfortunate time."

Laughlin was right: National City Co. represented an aggressive thrust by the country's biggest bank, and the public's suspicion of its motives was perfectly understandable. In fact, Vanderlip himself had foreseen it. In a letter to Stillman on June 20, just a week before Vanderlip's circular to the shareholders, Vanderlip raised the alarming possibility that the government might seek to bring antitrust cases against the big banks. The Supreme Court had, in recent weeks, ordered the dissolution of both Standard Oil and the Tobacco Trust, so Vanderlip was paying more than his usual nervous attention to the Justice Department. "My intuition is that there is going to be a great deal of talk about banking combinations and concentrated financial power," he prophesied. "It is going to come from demagogues, but not from them alone."

Vanderlip's creation of a new affiliate did much to make his prophecy a true one. Vanderlip had been impatient to expand National City's charter and to win for national banks some of the freedoms of lesser-regulated state banks. Frustrated with the slow pace of reform, he had committed a colossal blunder.

Washington reacted quickly. Attorney General George Wickersham concluded that National City Co. violated the spirit of the banking law. However, since Treasury Secretary MacVeagh disagreed, Taft ordered the papers sent to him so that he could resolve the issue.* Since any decision would anger either progressives or bankers, the President dithered. In November, Vanderlip wisely defused the issue by disposing of the affiliate's investments and, in effect, admitting his error.

However, the political outcry would not be quieted. Even as

---

* MacVeagh was worried because quite a number of other banks had also formed affiliates, although none as large as National City's. He feared a wholesale disruption to the banking industry if the practice was invalidated.

Wickersham was launching a government probe, Charles August Lindbergh, a Republican congressman from the Sixth District of Minnesota, a hotbed of prairie populism (later the seat of Tea Party militant Michele Bachmann) called for a congressional investigation of the Money Trust. Lindbergh was the son of a bank embezzler who had fled from Sweden, and the father of the future aviator. He was a serious, scholarly lawyer who also sat on the board of the First National Bank of tiny Little Falls, Minnesota. Like so many midwestern progressives, he feared that East Coast financiers were conspiring to hijack America's economy, and the revelation of National City's investment affiliate struck him like a call to Jesus. Lindbergh saw a parallel plot at work in the Aldrich Plan, which he said was a device to take away from communities the local funds that, rightly, should stay in those communities. His call for an investigation rocketed across the progressive firmament with, in short order, dramatic consequences. The backers of the Aldrich Plan now faced the impossible burden of disproving that they were agents of the Money Trust.

Among the first to strike was William Jennings Bryan. The Great Commoner privately acknowledged that some reform would be necessary, but was repelled by the two most salient features of the Aldrich Plan—centralization and banker control. Bryan had sketched out a very different idea for dividing the banks into regional associations, with each association being able to borrow, on liberal terms, from the government. In some ways, this was closer than the Aldrich Plan to the eventual Federal Reserve Act. However, Bryan's plan was not developed, nor did he engage the Aldrich plan on the merits. Rather than admit the complexities of an issue, Bryan always preferred to simplify. Typically, he went on the attack, baldly declaring that the Aldrich Plan would lead to nothing less than "absolute commercial and industrial slavery." Despite his three failed presidential campaigns, Bryan remained the most revered of Democrats, and his opposition was a serious matter.

Even more damaging was the antagonism toward the Aldrich

Plan from within the Republican Party, which percolated along with the insurgents' growing dissatisfaction with Taft. By the middle of 1911, Senator La Follette was openly mulling a challenge to the President the following year. The Wisconsin senator, famous for his pompadour and fighting spirit, had received acclaim when, as a lawyer in Madison in the early 1890s, he claimed he had been offered (and had rejected) a bribe by a party leader. The episode convinced him that the Republicans had betrayed their liberal origins. La Follette then began to champion such popular causes as direct election of senators— which was finally moving through the Congress—voter primaries, a minimum wage, progressive taxation, and corporate regulation. As his state's governor from 1901 to 1906, he promoted a working relationship between the statehouse and the University of Wisconsin, in the belief that government policies should be founded on competent research. He was sufficiently earnest that Warburg spent an evening with the senator's adviser on banking, laying out the supposed advantages of the Aldrich Plan.

As a progressive, La Follette was in favor of "reforming" the banks, but he feared that any powerful body run by bankers would draw capital, and influence, away from the small communities of the Midwest. In particular, he feared that a national association would come under the sway of metropolitan bankers—not an unreasonable opinion. Although the Aldrich Plan had genuinely democratic safeguards, La Follette's opinion of it was tainted by his acid view of Aldrich. Finally, La Follette had a political self-interest in distancing himself from the Republican mainstream that Aldrich represented. As with Bryan, he made no attempt to debate the Aldrich Plan on its particulars; rather, La Follette proclaimed that it was simply a plot to siphon "the people's money" to monopolies and trusts. Indeed, he would declare by the end of the year that the Plan was "the greatest menace to competition at the present time."

Lurking in the shadows of the La Follette challenge to Taft was the specter of a more potent bid by Theodore Roosevelt to reclaim the

White House from his former friend. Roosevelt agreed not to publicly criticize the Aldrich Plan, as a favor to Laughlin, his old instructor at Harvard. Nonetheless, the Rough Rider represented a powerful threat to Republican solidarity, and that in itself put the Aldrich Plan in serious trouble.

Vanderlip sized up the turbulent politics of 1911 in a stream of letters to his Paris correspondent, and his reports grew steadily darker. Taft's chances seemed to have evaporated; the progressive idea was showing remarkable persistence; the fortunes of New Jersey's Governor Wilson seemed to be on the rise; Aldrich had bungled his chances for a bill. And so on and so on, letter after letter.

The political pot came to a boil late in October, when Taft's Justice Department brought an antitrust case against U.S. Steel, a Morgan-created trust that had always enjoyed Roosevelt's favor. Since the suit charged that U.S. Steel's acquisition of Tennessee Coal, Iron & Railroad—which Roosevelt had approved during the heat of the Panic of 1907—was illegal, and implied that Roosevelt had been duped, the former president regarded it as an affront to his honor. His break with Taft was now irreversible.

Morgan, who had been troubled all year by the gathering pace of investigations, spent a weekend in Vermont huddled with Aldrich, Baker, and Davison to review the ramifications of the U.S. Steel suit. Morgan and Aldrich were both pessimistic—not just about the case but about the drift toward progressive politics in general. Aldrich, Vanderlip reported, "felt that all the old moorings were cut loose politically and that the outlook was only that a bad situation might get still worse."

In November, the Aldrich group reunited in New Orleans for the ABA convention. Warburg spoke stirringly. He observed that in Europe credit was actually more useful than cash—a condition he judged that, with the passage of the Aldrich Plan, could be replicated in the United States. But the spotlight belonged to Aldrich. Appealing to southern bankers, he noted that America had exported $650 million of cotton in the previous year—most of it financed in Liverpool, London, Paris, or Berlin. He implored the crowd, was it not worth taking the United States "out of a condition of dependent helplessness"? Once more, Aldrich insisted that his plan was nonpartisan, that it dealt purely with "business questions," that it envisaged not a bank but a cooperative union of *all* banks. He pleaded to the assembly, "We have a right to expect that the plan presented will be considered fairly on its merits. We do not think it fair that men who admit they have not read the Plan should raise the cry of a central bank or summon the ghost of Andrew Jackson."

The ABA leadership stifled dissent from country bankers, and the Plan was approved without discussion. As in the original draft, the Reserve Association would be a self-regulatory body of bankers, democratically governed. Wall Street applauded the greater dose of centralization; Chicago approved because the federal government was mostly excluded. Banks were given greater license, such as the right to lend on real estate. But a flaw in the Plan was that, since participation was voluntary, scattering reserves among local banks would still be possible.

Aldrich received a five-minute ovation, but he knew even before he left New Orleans that he faced a brutal resistance. La Follette was making opposition to Aldrich a linchpin of his insurgency. In a noonday speech in Hamilton, Ohio—part of an early winter campaign swing through the Midwest—he declared, "The Progressives are prepared to fight because they understand what Aldrich is trying to do for those he represents." Newspaper coverage was withering. In general, critics focused not on the plan but on the man behind it. A devastating observation, probably accurate, in the *Rocky Mountain News* held that "the only thing the country feels sure about the Aldrich currency plan is that it is devised by the author of the present tariff."

Aldrich and his fellow plotters were partly to blame, for they had ignored a crucial tenet of progressivism—accountability to the public.

Although the Reserve Association, according to its creators, would be a body with "semi-public" powers, including acting as chief fiscal agent of the U.S. government, the public was nearly excluded from its deliberations. In this, Aldrich and his comrades badly misjudged the temper of the times.

In December, Representative Lindbergh formally introduced a resolution to investigate the Money Trust. Meanwhile, the Monetary Commission met in nearly daily session, preparing the Aldrich Plan for submission to an increasingly hostile Congress. For appearance' sake, the commission further weakened the influence of Wall Street. In the finished document, New York banks, which held 20 percent of the nation's banking capital, could elect no more than three of thirty-nine representatives to the board of the Reserve Association—a disproportionately small share.

Aldrich confessed to Taft that he would gladly retire from public life once his plan was enacted. But although the President was his ally, his chances of being reelected—and actually helping Aldrich—seemed ever more slim. The backers of the Aldrich Plan might well have to cultivate some other patron in the White House. Roosevelt, perhaps? Andrew sent the former president a complete set of the Monetary Commission publications, some thirty-five volumes. Roosevelt graciously accepted them, but it is unlikely that he gave them any thought; political economy was never his cup of tea.

The other possibility was Woodrow Wilson. By late 1911 the governor was a leading candidate among several contenders for the Democratic nomination and perhaps for the White House. Vanderlip reported that the "current is drifting very strongly toward Woodrow Wilson." Whether Wilson would be open to the Aldrich Plan was a matter of intense speculation.

Although Wilson was not a financial expert, he was well versed in the Founding Fathers' early conflicts over central banking. Wilson's upbringing favored laissez-faire, but his professional training had steered him in the direction of centralism. The son of a Presbyterian minister, born in Virginia and raised in various communities in the South, Wilson attended Princeton, where he gobbled up the study of American government. After dabbling at law, he opted for a career in academia and wrote a widely praised doctoral dissertation in which he strongly criticized congressional domination of the executive branch.* By then, Wilson was convinced of the virtue of a strong central government; indeed, he was to say of his life after Princeton, "Ever since I have had independent judgments of my own I have been a Federalist." As a mature political scientist, he heaped praise on Hamilton, the father of the first Bank of the United States, labeling him "one of the greatest figures in our history." He was distinctly cooler to Jefferson, that hater of banks, whom he dubbed "a great man, not a great American." In 1902, the same year Wilson was named president of Princeton, he published his massive *A History of the American People*, which included the distinctly anti-Jacksonian passage: "The supporters of the second bank were in a measure justified in claiming that for such a purpose the very government itself had been set up." And not only had the Second Bank shown potential, according to Wilson; it had "proved itself" to be "a great commanding bank." For a student of American government, these were strong words. It is worth noting that even then—some eight years before Wilson ran for elective office—he confided to the historian Frederick Jackson Turner, "I was born a politician and must be at the task for which by means of my historical writing, I have all these years been in training."

Most bankers had not read Wilson's scholarly writings, but they were aware of his reputation for thoughtfulness. It was known that he had declined to support the silver campaign of Bryan in 1896. Indeed, it had been a conservative magazine editor, George Harvey of *Harper's Weekly*, who had nurtured Wilson's entrée into politics, for the

---

* *Congressional Government: A Study in American Politics* was published in book form in 1885.

very purpose of establishing a potential Democratic leader who was not a populist like Bryan. Voted by students the most popular professor at Princeton six years in a row, Wilson was an inspiring figure. And from the moment he entered politics, his first serious biographer noted, Wilson had his eye on the White House. His rise was exceptionally rapid.

Bankers were also aware, however, that in the year since Wilson's election as governor, his positions had moved left and his rhetoric had turned against Wall Street. In the statehouse he was solidly progressive, extending the reach of the public utility commission to give it power over utility rates, establishing a liberal workmen's compensation program, and successfully pushing for primary elections. Significantly, he fought to break the power of political bosses (including the one who had spearheaded his nomination). And as Aldrich sought to popularize his plan, Wilson made increasingly caustic comments about bankers. In June 1911, in Harrisburg, Pennsylvania, he told a cheering throng that "the greatest monopoly in this country is the money monopoly," adding that "all of our [financial] activities are in the hands of a few men." Later that summer, he told an interviewer that a banking measure bearing Aldrich's name "must have been drawn in the offices of the few men who, in the present system of concentrated capital, control the banking and industrial activities of the country."

Wall Street was naturally stung by such comments. It was said with some exaggeration that "everyone south of Canal Street was in a frenzy against Wilson." For sure, J. P. Morgan despised him. New Yorkers felt a hint of betrayal, for Wilson had distanced himself from Harvey, the editor who had been his champion—and whose support he now considered an embarrassment. The *Times* was moved to editorialize, "We deeply regret that Gov. Woodrow Wilson should permit himself to talk, for publication . . . in a manner ill-befitting his character, standing and aspirations."

Sensing his potential, conservatives wanted to believe that Wilson had not truly forsaken them. And Wilson, at least, acknowledged that banking reform was a complicated subject. It was, he said in Harrisburg, "the greatest question before the country." He added, "I have not given sufficient study to this question," which was a way of avoiding a definitive position. Bankers still had hopes for Wilson, if for no other reason than that his intellectual capabilities were clearly of the first rank.

In the fall of 1911, Andrew sent Wilson the Monetary Commission volumes. Noting that he had studied economics under Wilson at Princeton, he entreated the governor to get in touch with him and lend his "great influence" on the determination of the fate of the Aldrich Plan. Wilson was cordial but no meeting occurred. A representative of the Citizens' League also tried to get an endorsement; clearly, the group around the Aldrich Plan was envisioning Wilson as a presidential aspirant who might be open to reform.

The emissary who got furthest was William Garrett Brown, a contributor to *Harper's* and a North Carolina Democrat who was committed to financial reform and, furthermore, felt that Wilson could do more than any other Democrat to help the cause. Brown was ailing and residing in a sanitarium but, with plenty of time for letter writing, he implored Wilson to study the Aldrich Plan and to refrain from criticizing it in the meantime. Wilson seems to have agreed.

However, at about the same time, Wilson began to receive entreaties from Edward M. House, a politically ambitious meddler with rodential features known by the honorific "Colonel" (although he was not one). Born in Houston in 1858, the son of a weathy cotton grower, House studied at schools in the East and returned home to manage the family business. He also wrote a utopian political novel and, more purposefully, became a Democratic political operative in Texas. He had since moved to New York, where he entertained national ambitions, and fixated on Wilson as a man to be president. Had House's letters been any more cloying, Wilson might have been put off, but House struck just the right note of flattery and intimacy; it was as if they were co-conspirators and friends from his very first letter.

How Wilson must have brightened to receive House's dispatch of November 18, 1911: "I have been with Mr. Bryan a good part of the morning and I am pleased to tell you that I think you will have his support." Wilson knew he had no chance of securing the nomination without Bryan. But that had seemed a tall order. Wilson had made unflattering remarks about Bryan in the past, and of course had not voted for him in 1896 (although he had in 1900 and 1908). Since becoming governor, Wilson had sought to mend their relations. The previous spring, when Wilson's wife, Ellen, learned that Bryan would be speaking in Princeton, she shrewdly telegraphed her husband, who was out of town, to hurry back. Bryan came to dinner and was a gracious guest; Wilson found him "captivating," with greater "conviction" than he had anticipated. If that was the beginning of a thaw between the two, House's letter proffered a full-scale detente. Wilson met with House for the first time several days later.

By December, House was coaching Wilson on how to deal with the Aldrich Plan. William Garrett Brown had been pressing Wilson to announce himself as either for the Plan or, at the least, favoring a nonpartisan consideration of it. House, knowing how Bryan felt about the Aldrich Plan, urged Wilson not to do this. He should simply say he would reveal his views at the "proper time."

Wilson was deeply grateful for this advice. House's friendship soon became a source of emotional as well as political support; Wilson began addressing him as "My dear friend." Wilson did not make male friends easily (he did have a close woman friend), perhaps because he did not like challenges to his authority. There was no such possibility with the deferential House. Wilson was supposed to have said, "He is like my second personality."

House pursued Bryan's support by sending him articles that testified to the enmity with which Wilson was regarded on Wall Street. The tactic succeeded in heightening Bryan's interest, but he wanted harder evidence of Wilson's conversion. On December 30, with the campaign season approaching, House conveyed to Wilson what was, in effect, the bill for Bryan's support. It came in the form of a letter from Bryan to House, with the relevant part quoted for Wilson's benefit. "If he is nominated it must be by the Progressive Democrats and the more progressive he is the better," Bryan declared. Warming to his role as a kingmaker, Bryan advised that Wilson declare himself at the party's annual Jackson dinner on January 8, which "will give him a good chance to speak out against the trusts and the Aldrich Currency scheme." There it was: Bryan's price for supporting Wilson was nothing less than a full repudiation of the Aldrich Plan.

CHAPTER NINE

THE GREAT CAMPAIGN

The Democratic members of the committee are
absolutely unfit to ever produce anything.
                              —PAUL WARBURG

No one class can comprehend the country; no one set
of interests can safely be suffered to dominate it.
                              —WOODROW WILSON

AS THE 1912 presidential campaign unfurled, the candidates sought
to curry favor with progressives, and progressives continued to regard
banking reform with profound suspicion. Thrust onto the defensive,
the reformers in the Aldrich gang would be forced to angle for position with whoever emerged as the winner. From a political stand-
point, their timing could not have been worse.

During the first week of the new year, Professor Piatt Andrew
and Senator Nelson Aldrich worked around the clock getting the

National Monetary Commission report (the Aldrich Plan) ready for submission to Congress, which had set a deadline of January 8. Since Congress was not in session, confusion arose over how the report should be "filed." Hours before the deadline, Andrew drove signed copies to the residences of the vice president (representing the Senate) and the Speaker of the House. Brimming with pride, he wrote to his folks in Indiana, "I got in the motor and tore around Washington in a storm of sleet and rain." Elated from finally finishing the long labor, the young professor hyperbolically described their report as "probably the most farreaching [sic] and most scientifically prepared legislative proposal upon any subject in the country's history, at least since the early days." With the report submitted, the Monetary Commission promptly went out of business.

Coincidentally, while Andrew was negotiating the wet streets of the capital, Woodrow Wilson was also in Washington, at the Jackson Day dinner, where he called for public oversight of banks. The governor, a careful politician, did everything to fulfill William Jennings Bryan's request that he condemn the Aldrich Plan—except refer to it by name. "This country," said Wilson, "will not brook any plan which concentrates control in the hands of the bankers. . . . The bankers of the country may have the highest and purest intentions, but no one class can comprehend the country; no one set of interests can safely be suffered to dominate it."

In the presence of newspapermen, Bryan put an arm around Wilson, signaling that the governor had made important strides. However, Wilson faced three rivals for the nomination, the most formidable of whom was Champ Clark, the progressive-leaning Speaker of the House, who had the support of the Hearst newspaper chain and of many organization Democrats. Another contender, Oscar Underwood, the Alabama representative and House majority leader, drained support from Wilson's natural base, the South. Wilson needed Bryan, who let it be known he would favor whichever of the candidates was most opposed to "predatory wealth," a phrase as charged then as a later day's "the 1 percent."

However, Wilson's condemnation of the Aldrich Plan was less than absolute. He objected to banker control but, unlike Bryan, he said nothing about centralization, which was the core idea. In fact, back-channel sources suggested that Wilson—a lifelong student of the machinery of government—was intrigued by the prospect of a reforming institution. Soon after the Jackson dinner, Paul Warburg heard from a well-connected journalist:

> In conversation with Mr. William F. McCombs, 96 Broadway, who is Governor Wilson's manager, told me this morning "not to be quoted" that the Governor was in sympathy with the Aldrich plan. The matter of control and the Board of Governors was the one question still undecided in his mind.

While Wilson's position on banking remained something of a mystery, Warburg found an opportunity to lobby Theodore Roosevelt at the end of January. He and Andrew were invited to a luncheon hosted by the *Outlook* magazine, where Roosevelt was a contributing editor. The former president, who had yet to commit to a position on the Aldrich Plan, subjected Warburg to a battery of questions. Warburg's replies were smoothly persuasive. Victor Morawetz, who advocated regional banks and was also present, protested it would be impossible in a country as expansive as the United States to manage a single central bank. Roosevelt burst out, "Why not give Mr. Warburg the job? He would be the financial boss, and I would be the political boss, and we could run the country together!" Although Roosevelt's budding radicalism frightened bankers, Warburg concluded that the Rough Rider would at least be open to considering a central bank.

In February, Roosevelt formally declared his candidacy for the White House. Even though the news was expected, Taft took it hard.

Years earlier, his wife, Nellie, had warned him not to count on Roosevelt's loyalty. But she had suffered a devastating stroke, and the President no longer had the full support of his closest companion as he headed into a wrenchingly personal battle.

The challenge from Roosevelt effectively nullified Taft's ability to advance legislation. Banking reform became a hostage to the campaign. Republicans were embarrassed by the Aldrich Plan and Democrats were beholden to oppose it. As a formality, the bill was introduced in the Senate, but no committee considered or discussed it. With the movement backed into a corner, Aldrich's allies played for time. They concentrated on lobbying the parties to at least refrain from including language in their platforms that would preclude legislation later on.

Meanwhile, the country was gripped by an anti–Wall Street and anti-banking fever. In a new book aimed specifically at the Aldrich Plan, *U.S. Money vs. Corporation Currency,* Alfred Owen Crozier posited that control of the money system would be the political campaign's "secret issue." Crozier championed a signature belief of Bryan: that only government currency could be trusted, and that bank notes (the currency endorsed by Aldrich) were strictly a means of enriching bankers.

Reasonable arguments could be made for either private or government money, but Crozier, the son of an abolitionist preacher, did not make them. He was more interested in the supposed evils that lurked behind the Aldrich Plan, which was depicted in the book as a coiled cobra, ready to sink poisons into the bloodstream of the people. Crozier's method was to assume a sinister motive and look for a guilty party. He blithely deduced that financiers had an interest in fomenting panics, and therefore must have concocted them. "Why should not Wall Street have panics once in a while?" Crozier rhetorically mused. "And if Providence won't send a panic, why not make one, when it is so easy and will be so useful and profitable." Crozier further averred that financiers had caused the Panic of 1907 in the full knowledge that it would bequeath the Aldrich Plan, which he termed "a huge private money trust to monopolize and forever control the entire public currency . . . of the United States." It had all been planned—the Panic, the European expedition, Aldrich's conversion—down to the last detail.

Crozier belonged to a long line of American conspiracists, arguably stretching from the witch-hunters in the Massachusetts Bay Colony to Oliver Stone. The shared link was that they saw in history's unpredictable twists and turns a carefully plotted script. No misfortune could ever be random; every happenstance had to have a culprit. Such arguments had a powerful grip on the American heartland, further poisoning public sentiment against the Aldrich Plan.

Thoroughly tired of such controversy, Nelson Aldrich himself quietly withdrew. He turned down all speaking invitations, although he nourished the hope that Taft would be reelected along with a Republican Congress and that they would then pass his plan. Meanwhile, he tended to his stock portfolio and to his now finished mansion, whose centerpiece was a grand marble stairway in the entrance hall. The exterior, a rather "grim granite and slate," his descendant was to write, seemed to have been designed to withstand a "siege."

With public passions so inflamed against Wall Street, Representative Charles Lindbergh's resolution for an inquest into the Money Trust obtained new urgency. Democrats in the House had opposed Lindbergh, on partisan grounds, but they needed some alternative to the Aldrich Plan—that is, they needed a banking program that was more than just oppositional. The Money Trust hearings would be their response.

The Democrats wrangled over the scope of the inquiry. Bryan favored wide-ranging hearings under the mantle of Robert L. Henry of Texas, the populist chairman of the House Rules Committee. Conservative Democrats resisted, fearing this would lead to a circus that would taint the party with "Bryanism." Bryan prevailed—mostly.

The House approved a broad mandate to investigate concentration in banking, backed by subpoena powers to compel testimony. However, the hearings were assigned to the Banking and Currency Committee, whose chairman, Arsène Pujo of Louisiana, was less provocative than Henry. Pujo was president of a small bank and had served under Aldrich on the Monetary Commission. Since Pujo was not very forceful, much would depend on whom he picked as committee counsel.

It is hard to overestimate the fear of bankers at the prospect of being put on the stand. Doubtless, some had secrets to hide. And bankers were not accustomed to being held accountable. In the modern era such hearings have become a familiar ritual; in 1912, however, neither Morgan nor Baker nor Vanderlip had ever had to face the public. J. P. (Jack) Morgan Jr., being groomed as heir to his father's business, perceptively wrote to Davison, "The questions will be put in such a way that no answers that we could make could do us any credit."

Nevertheless, Vanderlip saw a potential upside. He reckoned that nothing could emerge from the hearings that would be as bad as the "wild imaginings that seem to have taken possession of a great many people." And whatever the committee uncovered, the drama would reignite interest in reform. Indeed, he confidently, if curiously, predicted that the investigation would "plow the ground for the proper consideration of the Aldrich Plan next Fall."

In March, the Banking Committee made a decision that did seem to revive the reformers' chances. While a subcommittee under Pujo's direction would conduct the Money Trust inquiry, a separate subcommittee would be in charge of drafting remedial legislation. Splitting the committee would hopefully insulate the legislative work from the high political theater of the hearings.

The chair of the legislative panel was Carter Glass, a newcomer to the monetary debates who was suddenly thrust into a leading role. Despite his decade in the House, the fifty-four-year-old Virginian was little known. He was combative and hot-tempered, but a pragmatist underneath. He was partisan but not ideological.

Glass was a Bryan Democrat and a Jackson Democrat, but he was also a successful newspaper publisher, sensitive to the value of credit. He identified with the small businessmen and farmers in his district (the white ones, at any rate). After his stirring experience at the 1896 Democratic convention, he had entered politics more actively, serving as a delegate to rewrite the Virginia constitution, in 1901–2, for the express purpose of disenfranchising voters of color, whom Glass unashamedly referred to as "misguided Negroes." He was elected to Congress soon after, thanks to the Democrats' stranglehold on Virginia politics, which was founded on ironclad racial discrimination. For Glass, every political issue was interpreted through the narrow prism of its potential effect on white supremacy. Any position that might drive southern bankers into the arms of the Republicans threatened to uproot the system of racial exclusion—and was to be avoided at all costs.

When Glass went to Washington, D.C., he was assigned to the House Banking Committee—a topic on which he knew nothing. However, he had no false pride, and set to educating himself. By the time the Democrats claimed the majority in 1910, Glass had been in the House for eight years. Although he had little to show for it, he had read more than a hundred books on banking and chewed over the system's defects with countless businessmen and bankers.

Glass's first move as subcommittee chair was to hire a legislative aide, H. Parker Willis, the banking expert who had studied under Laughlin and who, in turn, had taught economics at Washington and Lee University to Glass's two sons. Willis's regular job—writing about banking for the New York–based *Journal of Commerce*—obviously conflicted with his legislative assignment, but neither Glass nor his newspaper cared.

The important point to Glass was that, in the thirty-seven-year-old Willis, he had snared a technician familiar with the salient ideas for reform. Since Willis was close to Laughlin, having collaborated with him recently on the handbook for the Citizens' League, he was

also quite familiar with the Aldrich Plan. Although Willis did not
support the plan (in public, at any rate), it is significant that as the
Democrats assumed an active role, the person charged with drafting
a bill was at least open to the Jekyl Island notion of a central authority. Warburg, who did not put much faith in the Democrats, seized
on this connection to protect his "baby." "The Democratic members
of the committee," he fretted to Laughlin, "are absolutely unfit to
ever produce anything; they simply have not got the knowledge." The
only option, Warburg cynically advised, was for Laughlin to control
Willis and Willis to control the subcommittee.

As a southerner, Glass was suspicious of federal power and predis-
posed to be hostile to centralization; his instinct was to organize un-
affiliated regional banks around the country. However, with Warburg
prodding Laughlin and Laughlin coaching Willis, the latter took
steps to soften the congressman's resistance. A letter Laughlin wrote
to Willis in June suggests that the pair were tacitly conspiring to
change Glass's views:

> From recent information, I am inclined to think that Mr. Glass
> is willing to go further than was indicated at the time I last saw
> you. That is, I think you accomplished your purpose of leading
> him one step at a time; and that it is quite likely he would be
> willing to take a further step in regard to an organization that
> would be more unified than that suggested by a considerable
> number of separate institutions of rediscount.

Openly imitating the Aldrich Plan was out of the question for the
Democrats. However, there was much in the Plan that clearly had
merit and could not be avoided. The subcommittee finessed this delicate issue, according to Willis's later recollection, by agreeing that if
any "desirable feature" was found in any other plan, "that should
commend it rather than militate against it." This was Willis's tor-

tured way of justifying the decision to adopt useful points from the Aldrich Plan.

That spring, Willis scratched out the beginnings of a bill. Glass encouraged him, but over the summer he was in Lynchburg (and temporarily absent from legislative work) to face a primary challenge. Willis continued to correspond with Laughlin on what the new banking bill should look like.

Meanwhile, in the other House Banking subcommittee, Pujo named Samuel Untermyer, a sharp-elbowed corporate lawyer, to head the investigation of the Money Trust. The choice of Untermyer as staff counsel made bankers quiver. Untermyer had made a fortune organizing financial syndicates and corporate combinations. Then, in midcareer, he had become an outspoken critic of trusts and of Wall Street. Bankers suspected that his conversion was politically motivated. Untermyer, a lifelong Democrat, had sought a U.S. Senate seat and was said to harbor grudges over his defeat; he also was shadowed by whispers of unethical business practices.

What frightened bankers was that Untermyer, an investor who participated in lucrative stock deals and cultivated orchids in his leisure, knew where the Street's secrets were buried. Jack Morgan cabled his father that he expected the probe to be "unpleasant." Untermyer made quiet overtures to Warburg and Vanderlip, trying to assure them his intentions were noble, but the bankers surely regarded Untermyer as a wily operator to be handled with care.

Glass was also worried about Untermyer. The congressman was warned that he should quickly occupy the legislative space or—despite the agreement to split the committee—Untermyer would encroach on his turf. Coincidentally, Untermyer had been born in Lynchburg, just two months after Glass. Untermyer was also the son of a Confederate soldier, but he had moved north after the war, attended Columbia Law School, and, at twenty-four, become a partner in a New York firm.

In fact, Untermyer did have designs on the bill drafting, a plum he hoped would follow from the hearings. He sensed an opportunity for glory in rewriting the banking laws and was to become a serious threat to Glass. Probably, he felt that Glass could be shoved aside at an opportune time. In May, Untermyer began to collect information from Wall Street banks; then he started to call witnesses. The hearings would be recessed in June for the duration of the political campaign, but Untermyer was laying the groundwork for a series of explosive cross-examinations after the election.

The campaign was one of the most exciting ever. It featured heated races in both parties, primaries in a dozen states, and women voting in California and other jurisdictions. Moreover, with Wilson, Roosevelt, and La Follette all vying for one or the other party's nomination, the possibility loomed that America would veer in a radically new direction. While candidates hit the stump, suffragettes paraded in New York City and Congress adopted the Seventeenth Amendment; once the requisite number of states approved, no future Aldrich could reach the Senate without a popular vote.

The patriotic spirit was mirrored in surging crowds to watch baseball, which newspapers were calling the national pastime. Grandstands were festooned on opening days with flags and bunting; three new concrete and steel stadiums debuted, including Fenway in Boston. "Baseball men are more optimistic than ever this season," so reported the *Times*. Taft, who had begun a tradition of throwing out the first ball, had burnished the game's status as a unifying American ritual.

The Democrats had something to learn from the sport, for they had yet to cohere as a national party. They had won only two elections since the Civil War and, to a large degree, were still a patchwork of white southerners, western farmers, and urban ethnics. Even though Wilson was every bit a segregationist (his father had owned slaves, and Woodrow was opposed to "social relations" between the races), he was the most unifying of his party's candidates and the one with the greatest appeal to progressives and independents. He was also the only Democrat whose view of central banking was more than a rehash of Jacksonism, even if his views on the subject were far from settled. While Champ Clark, seen as the front-runner, did not campaign, Wilson crisscrossed the country to give scores of speeches that testified to his faith in what a democracy could accomplish.

But the primaries did not go well for Wilson. The governor was a virtuoso orator in a time when Americans admired oratory, his biographer Arthur Link observed, but his idealistic sermons appealed "chiefly to men's minds" rather than to their "passions." He finished behind Clark in a slew of primaries, including Illinois, Nebraska (Bryan's home state), Massachusetts, and California.

Meanwhile, Bryan beseeched Wilson to declare himself plainly—and publicly—on banking reform. Wilson no doubt had Bryan in mind when he told an audience in Albany, Georgia, "I have heard a great many people object, and I must admit that I am myself opposed, to the idea of a central bank." This departed from his previous comments, and reflected desperation more than conviction. Indeed, as if to hedge his own statement, Wilson quickly added, "But we have other agencies in the United States that are much more powerful than a central bank." Once again, he turned his fire not on centralism in government but on the supposed power of Wall Street. Sincere or not, his rhetoric in Georgia helped to rescue his campaign. Colonel House was able to procure a statement from Bryan that he would consider either Wilson or Clark acceptable as a nominee. Wilson also collected endorsements from influential newspapers, including the *Kansas City Star* and the *Raleigh News and Observer.* And he reeled in contributions from well-heeled friends. As the primary season ended, Wilson finally racked up a string of victories.

The Republican contest was personal and bitter. La Follette, whose campaign was underfinanced and underorganized, resented Roosevelt for stealing his thunder, but their enmity was nothing compared with the Shakespearian drama between Roosevelt and Taft. The two old friends turned foes wounded each other as only intimates can. Taft called Roosevelt a "dangerous egotist" and a "flatterer of the people." Roosevelt labeled Taft a "fathead" and a hypocrite—a strange charge to level at such a candid public servant. Little was said about banking reform—Taft did not want to emphasize his support of the Aldrich Plan, and Roosevelt was not so interested in it—but this contest was never about issues: it was about Roosevelt's inability to let his successor govern on his own. Roosevelt's stated reason for running was that Taft had betrayed his ideals; he was not a true "progressive," for he had cultivated the support of party bosses like Aldrich (that much was true, although Roosevelt had once cultivated the same party bosses). On the issues that Roosevelt had championed as president, Taft had a generally sound record. On conservation, he had been just as vigorous at protecting public lands from development as had his predecessor. On antitrust, Taft had brought far more cases—indeed, more than Roosevelt thought were warranted. Taft also created the Department of Labor and signed legislation mandating an eight-hour day for federal contractors; he also promoted the income tax amendment. But Roosevelt, in 1912, advocated a more strident progressivism than he previously had. Far more than Taft, he wanted the government to pursue social justice and redistribution. Throwing his lot with "the people," Roosevelt advanced the ill-thought idea of letting voters overturn decisions of judges, which Taft, himself a jurist, regarded with horror. Since their differences were largely ones of temperament, or of degree, much of Wall Street regarded Roosevelt as an opportunist. "In years past he has done some excellent things," Thomas Lamont, a senior Morgan adviser, said of the former president. "But studying his campaign of the last few months I cannot help believing that his chief object at the present time is to get back into power."

Taft controlled the party organization; Roosevelt's only chance would be to light a fire in the primaries. At the beginning of April, he drubbed the President in Illinois and then in Pennsylvania. Two days later, Piatt Andrew, who was campaigning for Taft, dined with

Warburg at the Willard Hotel in Washington, where they surely discussed the sobering election news and the outlook for reform. After dinner they heard some truly awful news: after a glancing collision with an iceberg, the RMS *Titanic* had sunk into the North Atlantic. One of those who perished was the President's military aide, Archie Butt, whom Taft regarded almost as part of his family (Butt had also devotedly served Roosevelt). The President and the nation were plunged into gloom. Vanderlip, trying to explain the momentary pause in business, reported to Stillman, "The horror of the thing has affected everybody's mind." Taft cleared his schedule and skipped the baseball opener. Little was going well for the President.

On April 19, Taft was thrashed in two more primaries. Presidents in that era did not campaign, but Taft felt compelled to counter Roosevelt on the stump. He headed into Massachusetts, making whistle stops in Springfield, Worcester, and many smaller towns, where he rebutted Roosevelt's charges and what he claimed were the former president's distortions of his record. Roused from his usual torpor, Taft attacked with brio, denying that he had ever been disloyal and accusing his mentor of pursuing a divisive strategy of stirring "class hatred." However, he had no relish for this battle with "an old and dear friend." At one stop he professed, "This wrenches my soul." Concluding the day in a packed arena in Boston, Taft said his challenger was consumed with personal ambition and unfit for office. A reporter encountered the President after this bitter tirade, on the train home, slumped on a lounge. "Roosevelt was my closest friend," Taft said. Then he began to weep.

As the campaigns peaked, the Citizens' League mounted a furious publicity blitz. Regardless of who was nominated, James Laughlin was intent on securing platform statements favoring reform. With the Republicans due to gather in Chicago, followed by the Democrats in Baltimore, the league ratcheted up its spending to create a reformist groundswell at the conventions. Laughlin organized an artful campaign (even as he and Warburg continued to tussle over policy and the budget). Speakers were booked around the country; newspapers were relentlessly courted. The league bulletin was sent to every Washington correspondent, generating a stream of dispatches. According to an internal league memorandum, "Many of the fundamentals of banking reform, as advocated by the League, have become matters of common knowledge in editorial rooms." Laughlin realized that—just as Vanderlip had predicted—the Money Trust inquiry had reawakened interest in banking; the league's job now, as another internal memo put it, was merely "directing public opinion into definite channels." A shining example was an editorial that appeared in the *Lexington* (Kentucky) *Herald* on June 4—two weeks before the Republican convention—which confidently, if rather inaccurately, explained the Aldrich Plan as a bill for protecting America from the Money Trust.

Laughlin was hopeful that businessmen would rally delegates in their local communities. In Arkansas (one of forty states where the Citizens' League was active) businessmen received agitated calls to action, portraying the league as a David battling for a sounder currency against the supposed opposition of Wall Street. These efforts were carefully coordinated, in advance of the conventions, with pitches to Arkansas editorial writers.

Laughlin's earlier insistence on keeping the league nonpartisan proved shrewd, for he was able to court both parties. As Chicago neared, he dared to hope that the Republicans would endorse the Aldrich Plan outright. While expectations for the Democrats were more modest, Laughlin thought supportive language in Baltimore could have great effect, because it would bolster Glass and Willis's legislative effort. In several southern states, Laughlin lobbied influential Democrats, urging them to adopt pro-reform planks at their state conventions. Whether his hosts understood the fine points of banking was beside the point, as Laughlin underscored in a note, redolent with irony, to Warburg: "The Democratic plank in Texas first damned

Aldrich and then used practically our [exact] language" in proposing a reform, he confided.

Laughlin also wrote to Bryan—and, appealing to his sense of history, pleaded with him to soften his resistance. Knowing that Bryan would dominate the platform discussions in Baltimore, Laughlin implied that moderate language on banking would help the party snap its string of defeats:

> The country will, in the present campaign, be studying to see whether the Democratic Party can be trusted on a great new constructive measure affecting our credit organization. It ought not to be maneuvered out of position on an issue appealing to classes whose votes it wants. . . . Seldom has a greater opportunity presented itself to a public man than to you in these very days before the Conventions to win favorable regard.

In Chicago, Andrew planned to head up efforts to steer the Republican platform to the Aldrich Plan. Before he left Washington, Andrew's boss, Treasury Secretary MacVeagh, rejected Andrew's request to be absent from work. This signaled that MacVeagh's patience with Andrew's reform work was exhausted. It also signaled that the Taft administration, in the midst of its battle with Roosevelt, had no political capital to spare on banking.

Unwisely, Andrew headed for Chicago all the same. He quickly discovered that, for those who defy their political patrons, Washington has no mercy. No sooner did Andrew return to the capital than MacVeagh demanded his resignation. Andrew had the temerity to ask the President, with whom he had a passing social relationship, to intervene—and also leaked word of his unhappiness, resulting in a public row. Taft curtly informed him, "I can not think that you were well advised in deliberately disobeying the plain direction . . . from Mr. MacVeagh." Andrew was out.

He was even less effective at the convention. Chicago was the scene of a political fratricide, with Taft and Roosevelt stalwarts engaging in fistfights at the Chicago Coliseum. Although Taft had been shellacked in the primaries—even in his native Ohio—his control over the party machinery gave him a lead in delegates. He had also outmaneuvered Roosevelt in the state conventions. But Roosevelt challenged nearly a quarter of the delegates as being fraudulently chosen. The Republican National Committee had to resolve these disputes. Robert La Follette (Aldrich's nemesis) held important swing delegates, and Taft would do nothing to aggrieve the Wisconsin senator. The platform committee, not surprisingly, studiously ignored Andrew or any mention of the Aldrich Plan and approved a bland and meaningless plank—"Our banking arrangements to-day need further revision," it weakly offered, to "prevent the recurrence of money panics and financial disturbances." No mention was made that a congressional commission had already proposed such a "revision," and that it had been endorsed by the incumbent president. As a stand-alone proposal the Aldrich Plan died in the convention hall. Republican unity died as well.

Andrew had a ringside seat, recording in his diary the endless quarreling and balloting on credentials, the "fever [of] excitement." The night before the convention began, he saw Roosevelt tell delirious supporters at a packed auditorium, "We stand at Armageddon, and we battle for the Lord!" The Rough Rider was now the man on the white horse, the savior, and when he couldn't win, he declared he had been cheated and led his forces out of the Coliseum and out of the party.* Taft was renominated with a thin majority. Woodrow

---

* Roosevelt was clearly the choice of the Republican rank and file in the primaries. But the party, according to rules approved in 1908 by then President Roosevelt, had a process for choosing delegates that concentrated power in the national committee. That the committee was dominated by Taft people is unquestioned, and that some of its decisions were unfair also seems clear. Whether a completely scrupulous and

Wilson observed to a friend, "The Republicans have met—and done their worst."

The Republicans, who had long been the patron of banking reform, had nothing left to offer the cause. Taft's chances for victory in the fall had been gravely weakened—fatally so if Roosevelt went ahead with his plans for a third-party challenge. Reformers, out of necessity, took a longer look at the Democrats.

Laughlin, Willis, and Andrew converged on Baltimore, where, they knew, Bryan was crafting the Democratic platform. The convention delegates were disgorged from trains into a carnival atmosphere. Brass bands marched in the streets; every inch of the city seemed festooned with the candidates' pictures. Wilson, conveniently, was tracking the proceedings from the governor's summer cottage in Sea Girt, New Jersey, several hours up the coast. As he and his family waited for the balloting to start, he idled away time with a note to his intimate friend, Mary Allen Hulbert Peck: "The day is gray and grizzly. We have had to light a fire in the huge fire place to keep our spirits (and our temperature) up." Wilson also sent an ingratiating note to Bryan, concurring with Bryan's view that Baltimore must be "a convention of progressives." Wilson still trailed Clark in the delegate count, but he was very much a contender.

---

apolitical process (virtually unheard-of in American history) would have swung enough delegates to Roosevelt to change the outcome is unclear. Doris Kearns Goodwin (in *The Bully Pulpit*, p. 700) reckons that it might have prevented a first-ballot victory by Taft, after which "anything was possible."

CHAPTER TEN

WOODROW'S MIRACLE

> A democratic nation is richer in genius than any other nation because it releases genius.
> —WOODROW WILSON

> The Aldrich Plan is 60 to 70 percent correct.
> —WOODROW WILSON,
> *private conversation during the 1912 campaign*

WILLIAM JENNINGS BRYAN DRAFTED most of the Democratic platform himself, and it placed yet another dagger in the heart of the Aldrich Plan. Disregarding James Laughlin's plea for restraint, the Great Commoner struck a direct hit: "We oppose the so-called Aldrich bill or the establishment of a central bank." The plank approved at the Baltimore convention went on to espouse a "systematic revision of our banking laws" to free the country from panics and depressions. Carter Glass might reasonably infer that he had latitude to legislate almost any bill that did not resemble the Aldrich Plan or establish "a central bank." However, the platform also stressed states' rights and asserted that credits for farmers—always Bryan's first constituency—were "of equal importance with the question of currency reform."

This muddled prescription for banking reforms bespoke a larger truth: the Democrats were a party in transition. The platform was progressive, stressing stronger antitrust laws, a ban on corporate campaign contributions, and an income tax. However, the party was still too traditional to embrace women's suffrage or a minimum wage—either of which would have offended its southern base. Whether the Democrats would emphasize urban progressivism or agrarian mistrust of Washington would depend on their choice of a leader.

At the outset, Bryan threw the convention into an uproar by proposing that it refuse to nominate anyone beholden to J. P. Morgan, to two of his putative allies who were delegates,* or to "any other member of the privilege-hunting, and favor-seeking class." Morgan not being remotely in a position to control the Democratic convention, Bryan's suggestion was sheer demagoguery. It carried overwhelmingly, although there were scattered cries for Bryan to be lynched. Rumors spread through the Fifth Regiment Armory, home to the convention, that he was seeking to promote his own candidacy; more likely, he wished to establish his bona fides as a power broker. Bryan's vote for presidential nominee, ordained on the first ballot by the Nebraska primary result, went for Champ Clark. The Missouri representative captured a sizable plurality, 440½ votes to Wilson's 324. But Wilson had an offsetting edge; his supporters were more fervent and more committed.

At Sea Girt, the governor anxiously read the telegraph bulletins as

---

* Thomas Fortune Ryan, a tobacco magnate with investments in the New York subways, was a delegate from Virginia; fianancier August Belmont Jr., a delegate from New York.

the balloting proceeded. He had no visitors with him—only Ellen and his daughters. Always content in scholarly solitude, he spent the day engrossed in a biography of William Gladstone, the nineteenth-century British statesman also known for his oratory, religiosity, and liberal views. Hoping for news, Wilson stayed awake past midnight.

The next day, Saturday, June 29, the New York delegation shifted its votes to Clark, giving the Speaker a majority. Ellen was teary-eyed, and Wilson was on the verge of releasing his delegates. However, the party required a two-thirds majority. The stampede for Clark never materialized. On the fourteenth ballot, Bryan announced that as the New York bloc—controlled by the corrupt Tammany machine and sympathetic to Wall Street—was with Clark, he, Bryan, was switching to Wilson. From then on, the balloting resembled a war of attrition. On the thirtieth ballot, the lead finally changed hands. Not until July 2—on the forty-sixth ballot—did Wilson claim the prize. He wrote to Mary Peck, "My nomination was a sort of political miracle."

Woodrow Wilson was fifty-five, with dark brown hair turning iron gray and a square jaw that seemed to thrust him forward. He was a southerner who had spent the last three decades in the North, a conservative admirer of British parliamentary rule reborn as a progressive. Historians have never settled on why Wilson changed his spots. Opportunism was a factor, as were his battles with privileged elites when he was running Princeton. But there was more coherence to his evolving views than is often acknowledged. Wilson believed in laissez-faire—the right of people to determine their affairs—and devoutly believed in the power of competition to restrain business from harmful excess. This was pure Jeffersonian democracy. From his minister father, he had inherited a moralistic view of public life, and his own idealism persuaded him that business leaders would work for the civic good. By the time he left Princeton, however, he had concluded that business could not be trusted to regulate itself. But he never doubted the primacy of private enterprise. Where Wilson wanted the federal government to intervene—notably, in antitrust—it was to level the obstacles to fair competition.

To Wilson, the genius of American democracy lay in its perpetual power to reinvent itself from below. "Every nation is renewed out of the ranks of the unknown men," he said on the stump in Frankfort, Kentucky. He was genuinely alarmed by the appearance of giant trusts, and by the large, impersonal scale of modern industry. He feared that the individual was being "submerged." In a phrase strikingly evocative of contemporary times, Wilson fretted that the "middle class is being more and more squeezed out by the processes which we have been taught to call [those of] prosperity."

Just how conservative Wilson remained may be seen in comparison to Teddy Roosevelt, who was nominated by the hurriedly formed Progressive Party. Roosevelt deemed that big trusts were efficient economic agents and necessary to prosperity; his proposed solution was not to abolish the trusts but to regulate them. Wilson mocked this "government by experts." Roosevelt's eerie-sounding "new nationalism" proffered a partnership of (very) big business and government; Wilson wanted to use government to, when necessary, break up the trusts and restore Jeffersonian balance.

Two aspects of Wilson's philosophy guided him toward banking reform. First, he had few misgivings about federal authority, even if he sometimes parroted southerners' concerns for states' rights. His academic work was essentially a long discourse on the use of power in a democracy, and on how the central government could be made *most* effective. Early on, he had admired the British system because he judged it to be more purposeful than the American-style separation of powers. Indeed, he once mused that had he been alive in 1776, rather than see the nation split into thirteen ragtag fiefdoms, he might have been a Tory.

Also, Wilson saw the banking issue as a subset of the monopoly issue. He feared that giant financial combines were restricting the individual's, and the small business's, access to credit. In his acceptance speech, which he delivered at Sea Girt, he conflated financial and other trusts, denouncing the "vast confederacies . . . of banks, railways, express companies, insurance companies, manufacturing corporations, mining corporations . . . and all the rest. . . ." Although not illegal, he said, such confederacies "may control, if they please . . . both credit and enterprise."

Wilson's economic analysis was unsophisticated and not quite responsive to the specific banking problem. Individuals did lack credit, but not merely—not even primarily—due to monopoly. He ignored the larger issue identified by Paul Warburg—the need to pool reserves to ensure a continual flow of loans. However, Wilson quite candidly acknowledged his lack of expertise in what he called "the complicated and difficult question of the reform of our banking and currency laws."* Indeed, he admitted, "I do not know enough about this subject to be dogmatic about it."

A fair reading is that Wilson was galvanized by his distaste for monopoly to address what he surmised were similar problems in banking. Even if the issues were not strictly analogous, the one gave him license to advocate a serious revision of the other—and to adopt banking reform, at long last, as a progressive cause.

The campaign was highly captivating, even if the outcome was not in much doubt. Roosevelt was strong in the Northeast and upper Midwest, but he and Taft inevitably pulled votes from each other. Meanwhile, Wilson ran virtually unchallenged in the South and West. The four-man struggle—it included the Socialist candidate, Eugene V. Debs—forced a realignment of the major parties. The Democrat ran to the left of the Republican, setting a pattern long to endure. No single issue dominated the campaign, nor were the candidates' differences particularly sharp, but people sensed the election augured a new direction.

---

* People still spoke of the "currency" question even though, by 1912, the issues centered on banking.

Wilson began by stressing reform of the tariff, which he abhorred as an unnatural distortion in trade, but the tariff issue had lost its sting. After consulting with Louis Brandeis, a Boston lawyer making a name for himself as a strident advocate for government regulation of business, Wilson switched to a more potent theme: breaking up monopolies. Even then, he had a tendency to lose his audience in oratorical clouds and airy distinctions. When Wilson declared, "I am for big business and I am against trusts," listeners, most of them, scratched their heads.

Roosevelt's strategy was to attack Wilson as a conservative in disguise. He made the fair point that trust-busting alone could not level the playing field for workers who clamored for the right to organize, or for higher wages. Wilson also supported labor, but his enthusiasm for it was of recent vintage; by contrast, Roosevelt, a wealthy New Yorker with a common touch, had a more intimate connection with factory workers and other urban laborers.

Wall Street was as divided as the rest of America. George Perkins, formerly of Morgan's, was a leader in Roosevelt's campaign, which led to a bitter rift with his former firm. J. P. Morgan and Andrew Carnegie supported Taft, the most pro-business candidate. But many financiers—including Paul Warburg and Jacob Schiff, who typically favored Republicans—donated to Wilson. Wall Street moneymen considered Wilson a lesser evil than Roosevelt, and more electable than Taft. Untermyer, the House Banking Committee lawyer, gave $10,000 to Wilson for reasons of his own (he was plotting to hijack the committee's legislative mission, and wanted Wilson as an ally). Noticing that Jewish bankers were siding with Wilson, Frank Vanderlip sniped that the "Hebrew element" was aligning with the presumed winner—a slur that reflected an anti-Semitic bias typical among bankers of the day.

With Wilson's election looking increasingly likely, bankers angled for a clearer sign of the Democrat's agenda. In public, Wilson refused to be pinned down; he told an editorial writer he didn't want to divert the country from principles to details. His campaign utterances on banking were platitudes.

However, in private Wilson sounded ready to abandon the party's traditional opposition to a central bank. Conferring with Vanderlip in the home of a key supporter, he complimented Vanderlip's understanding of the currency question, while shrewdly deflecting Vanderlip's criticism of his own reticence in public. "You don't understand politics," the candidate chided the banker. "It does not make any difference what I think ought to be done. I've first got to be elected." Wilson went even further with Henry Morgenthau, a real estate investor prominent in the Democratic Party who visited the governor in September 1912 at his home in Princeton. Morgenthau reported to New York bankers that Wilson believed the Aldrich bill to be 60 to 70 percent correct. They would have to craft another bill (with another name), Wilson added, but before they were finished, they would get 80 percent of the Aldrich bill.

But even as he sent hopeful signs to bankers, Wilson continued his courtship of Bryan. On a stop in Nebraska, Wilson stayed with the Commoner, the two talking into the night. Bryan also campaigned vigorously for the ticket, raising the possibility that he would have influence—possibly a cabinet post—in a Wilson administration.

Roosevelt supplied the campaign's most dramatic moment. In October, he was in Milwaukee, bound for a speech, when a man at close range drew a pistol and fired. The bullet pierced the candidate's rib and bloodied his chest. Irrepressibly curious, Roosevelt demanded of his assailant, a deranged bartender, "Why did you do it?" He refused a doctor's injunction to get treatment and went directly to the auditorium. Relishing his show of courage, the onetime warrior and big-game hunter informed the crowd, "I have just been shot, but it takes more than that to kill a Bull Moose!" He spoke for fifty minutes. Only then would he go to a hospital. But his heroics came too late.

Wilson won forty states and half again as many votes as Roosevelt (6.3 million votes to 4.1 million, with Taft trailing at 3.5 million). In a sign of the electorate's leftward shift, Debs captured 6 percent of the vote—the most for a Socialist in America before or since. Although Wilson was held to under 42 percent of the popular vote, his victory was decisive. The Senate turned Democratic for the first time in twenty years, and Democrats won a commanding two-thirds of the House.*

Buoyant from his triumph but fatigued from the campaign, Wilson made plans for a holiday in Bermuda. Before he sailed, three would-be banking reformers besieged him for an audience. How Wilson chose among these suitors would go a long way toward determining the fate of reform.

James Laughlin was the only petitioner with banking expertise. He regretted that the Citizens' League—now winding down—had not authored its own reform plan, and hungered for recognition. Ill advisedly, Laughlin telegraphed the president-elect and requested a "short interview" before his trip. Wilson declined.

With more bravado, Samuel Untermyer contacted Wilson the day after his victory, professed to have urgent business, and requested "the better part of an entire day." Wilson diplomatically put him off.

Wilson also heard from Carter Glass, who wrote that he and his assistant, Parker Willis, had "formulated, tentatively, a substitute for what is known as the Aldrich bill." This considerably overstated their progress, but Glass accurately reflected their purpose. "I think the committee would not like to proceed without some suggestions from you." Wilson replied—with more warmth than he had to Untermyer—that he would be eager to "commune" with Glass as soon as practicable.

What Wilson described as a "short vacation" was in fact a four-week sojourn. Maneuvering by the various parties during Wilson's absence was intense. The jousting began with a conference between Willis and Untermyer, instigated by Untermyer. The ostensible pur-

---

* Although it was not yet constitutionally required, some states already chose senators in general elections.

pose was that Untermyer wanted Willis, who remained at his day job at the *Journal of Commerce*, to write favorably about the Money Trust hearings, which were scheduled to resume at the end of November. However, Untermyer also revealed that, despite the agreement to split the Banking Committee functions, he himself "was planning to have the Money Trust Sub-Committee introduce legislation this winter." In other words, he was intent on usurping Glass.

Willis communicated this alarming news to Glass the following day. As Willis summarized matters, "Mr. Untermyer contemplates a general campaign [aimed at] gathering to himself all the functions entrusted to the Banking and Currency Committee."

Equally disconcerting to Glass, Untermyer appeared to be in league, or at least in agreement, with some of the very financiers whose operations were to be explored in the hearings. Willis reported that the brash attorney was adamant that any banking bill include a "central reserve association," which sounded far too much like a central bank to Glass. Indeed, Untermyer was explicit that the legislation preserve "the main ideas of the Aldrich bill."

Glass's personal rivalry with Untermyer now assumed the character of a holy crusade. Furious, and realizing that his ability to lead the reform was at stake, Glass wrote to the committee chairman, Arsène Pujo, denouncing Untermyer's "impertinent activity" and seeking Pujo's reassurance. Pujo did reaffirm Glass's authority over currency legislation, but Glass hardly expected Untermyer to back down so easily. Pujo was retiring at the end of the session, and the prospect that Untermyer would influence the selection of the next chair drove Glass nearly to despair.

According to Laughlin, Glass blamed Untermyer's political machinations on Jewish financiers who were "prompting" him from the shadows. Laughlin himself could not resist sniping at the supposed deviousness of these bankers. He wrote to Willis, "Moral: Put not your trust in Hebrews." The gentile establishment regarded Jews as usurpers, welcome in finance only provisionally and on condition that they behave with particular discretion. Even though Untermyer undeniably was a slippery character, Laughlin was also being counseled by the industry (in his case, by the leading bankers in Chicago), and he, too, believed in a central reserve. Perhaps more to the point, the threat from Untermyer got the process moving, for it spurred the desultory Willis, as well as Glass, into action. During the fall campaign Willis and Glass had not even been in contact. And while Willis, as he put it, had "been working on various phases of the banking question," he had not done any writing or drafting. Now, Glass and Willis got busy.

In mid-November, Glass hosted Laughlin at the Raleigh Hotel, his Washington domicile, and asked Laughlin to sketch out a bill as an aid to Willis's drafting. According to Laughlin, Glass made not a single suggestion with regard to "particular provisions." His only concern was that the draft not "antagonize" the Democratic platform. Glass, in fact, had a copy of the platform in his pocket, underscoring his fidelity to party doctrine. Laughlin mildly suggested that they *might* be able to go a bit beyond what the platform permitted, to which Glass made no reply. The two agreed the issue could only be resolved by Wilson.

Glass, in fact, was still laboring to understand the principles of banking. He and Willis freely sought advice—although, as the scholar Robert Craig West pointed out, they were churlish when it came to sharing credit. The congressman was a deliberate pupil, but once he formed an opinion he fought for it tenaciously. Perhaps because he was unsure of his footing, he clung to his beliefs obstinately.

Glass tended to view the world conspiratorially, suspecting people with contrary views of being motivated by nefarious interests. As Glass admitted of himself, he was "too prone to be suspicious." This hurt him in his efforts to cultivate support among the banking industry. Glass knew he needed the industry's support, but he refused to take bankers into his confidence. Most bankers, therefore, heard only rumors of what Glass and Willis were up to. "Mr. Glass," recounted a frustrated Warburg, "allowed little or nothing to become public."

Stymied in his efforts to cultivate Glass, Warburg made his influence felt through the circle around the president-elect. Colonel House, Wilson's intimate friend, was eager to hear Warburg's views, and Warburg skillfully lobbied House of the virtues of central banking. Morgenthau, another Wilson adviser, asked Warburg to prepare a plan that would bridge the gap between the Democratic platform and "sound banking" principles. Wilson also read an article by Victor Morawetz, the railroad lawyer who advocated a network of regional banks. Through these channels. Wilson, upon his return, would be exposed to Wall Street's ideas, and they generally reaffirmed his own convictions. Although the president-elect had no firm agenda, broadly speaking he was more favorable to some form of centralization, and less hostile to Wall Street, than Bryan and the Democratic rank and file.

Glass got his first inkling of the gulf between House Democrats (who were mostly faithful to Bryan) and the embryonic White House when he was introduced to Colonel House at a Washington dinner. Wilson's mysterious friend pulled Glass off to the side and, speaking in private, advanced the merits of a central reserve. Glass instantly objected that the party platform "precluded" his committee from proposing such a remedy. House cuttingly replied, "I fear, Mr. Glass, you attach too much importance to party platforms." While this exchange surely unnerved Glass, the encounter boosted his standing, because House recognized that the determined Glass could be a useful partner. He wrote to Wilson, "I think the quicker you see him the better it will be. You will find him ready to cooperate with you to the fullest extent."*

---

* Trying to convince Wilson that a central bank was permissible, House misquoted the Democratic platform as forbidding "the so called Aldrich Plan *for* the establishment of a central bank" [emphasis added]. Based on this fallacious wording, House argued that, therefore, the platform would tolerate other central banking plans. The actual platform objected to "the so-called Aldrich bill *or* the establishment of a central bank."

. . .

IN DECEMBER, Untermyer turned the Money Trust spotlight on the captains of Wall Street. The Pujo hearings (though named for the chairman, they were dominated by Untermyer) did not bear directly on reform legislation. Nonetheless, by exposing an unsavory collaboration among Wall Street bankers, they helped to shape a political climate in which banking reform, of one sort or another, was seen as inevitable. In a series of highly charged cross-examinations, Untermyer sought to show that bank credit and corporate underwritings were in the grip of a small, collusive group of Wall Street bankers, at whose center was the seventy-five-year-old J. P. Morgan. Untermyer's style was prosecutorial and contentious. He elicited the answers he sought by posing barbed—often sarcastic—questions that witnesses found difficult to evade. He refused to allow witness counsels to intervene.

Morgan himself was the marquee witness. He remained America's most celebrated financier, even though he spent half his time in Europe while Harry Davison managed his bank. Morgan regarded public testimony as highly distasteful—a spectacle unbecoming to a private banker. Compelled to testify, Morgan left for Washington "by special train with half a dozen of the most distinguished counsel in New York, several of his partners, and various women relatives"—so Vanderlip reported. "The papers tell how he had twenty rooms at the Willard, and generally moved as a crowned potentate would."

On the stand, Morgan uttered a line that history would remember. Untermyer asked if the disbursal of credit wasn't primarily based on the borrower's assets. Morgan said: "No, sir; the first thing is character." This was an endearing description of nineteenth-century banking. The trouble was (as later witnesses would demonstrate), it was no longer true. More relevant to the twentieth-century question of monopoly, Untermyer got Morgan to admit that he saw nothing wrong with rival bankers collaborating with one another. Gentlemen did not compete, or not too savagely.

> UNTERMYER: You are an advocate of combination and coopera-
> tion, as against competition, are you not?
> MORGAN: Yes; cooperation I should favor.
> UNTERMYER: Combination as against competition?
> MORGAN: I do not object to competition, either. I like a little
> competition.

Untermyer deliberately zeroed in on railroads, the dominant industry of the era and one that Morgan had helped reshape through numerous mergers and securities offerings. The rails were lucrative Wall Street clients, and Untermyer tartly asked whether railroads that did business exclusively with Morgan's wouldn't be better served by a process of competitive underwriting. Implausibly, Morgan denied that they would. In the same vein, Untermyer charged that the bank maintained a too cozy relationship with its putative banking rivals, including George Baker's First National Bank. Morgan admitted that he and Baker had been close friends and associates "for a great many years . . . since 1873, at least." And if the First National wanted in on a Morgan deal? Morgan responded candidly, "I always offered them anything I had."

To the public, Morgan came off as trustworthy but a figure from a bygone world. Vanderlip ruefully observed that his performance had at times been "blundering." It seemed to confirm that Morgan could no longer be counted on for the sort of heroics he exhibited during the 1907 Panic, and that some new type of guardian was needed. The hearings, which were to continue into 1913, received extensive newspaper coverage and made a deep impression on the public.

Perhaps not coincidentally, reform proposals blossomed. In December, Laughlin delivered three successive drafts to Willis. In essence, Laughlin proposed that monetary policy be run by district associations, similar to the regional branches in the Aldrich Plan, and coordinated by a central board composed of a mix of bankers and presidential appointees. Warburg also dashed off a fourteen-page prescription, which he conveyed to Morgenthau and ultimately to Wilson. This latest Warburg model sported a central bank in Washington with twenty branches. Each of these plans featured a degree of federalization; the controversy revolved around the extent of control wielded by the center. It was this debate that unsettled Glass. Even though he probably did not see the Warburg plan right away, he was well aware of the bankerly pressure for centralization. Glass also met with Piatt Andrew, who made a renewed pitch for the Aldrich bill. In addition, Glass complained, he was "deluged with letters from people who have currency schemes."

Glass's every instinct was to try to control this process. He stymied Untermyer's attempts to poach on his turf, and by year end he had won assurance that he would succeed Pujo as committee chairman.* Glass also decided to stage hearings early in the coming year. He may have hoped to draw attention from the still ongoing Untermyer hearings, but Glass's primary purpose was to solidify the public's negative opinion of the Aldrich Plan and of central banks in general. Glass and Willis spent many hours reviewing lists of potential witnesses—screening out, when possible, adherents of a central bank. Palpably trying to stack the deck, Willis advised that they invite E. D. Hulbert, vice president of the Merchants Loan and Trust Company of Chicago, noting: "Mr. Hulbert is a very sharp critic of the Aldrich plan and has taken an extremely destructive point of view with regard to it." Glass also began to pull away from Laughlin. The professor, who had worked so closely with Willis, had clearly hoped to join the inner circle of the drafting party—he even asked whether

---

* The resourceful Untermyer did not stop trying. In December he sought to have the two banking subcommittees combined, so that he could serve as counsel to the entire panel. The Glass subcommittee rejected him.

his name could be included on the legislation! Glass put off seeing him. The sensitive Laughlin reacted with shock and self-pity ("I was considerably taken aback," he wrote to Willis).

The only audience Glass wanted was with Wilson. He wrote again on December 14, apologizing for adding to Wilson's "burdens" and humbly seeking an appointment for Willis and himself. Two days later, after an Atlantic voyage of forty hours, the president-elect, looking becomingly tanned, docked in New York. Newspapers reported that Wilson cheerfully signed autographs for fellow passengers. Back in Princeton, his most pressing chore was assembling a cabinet. He also tackled legislative priorities, including banking reform, which remained a horse with rival jockeys. Barely home a day, Wilson placed his bet. He invited the congressman from Lynchburg, and his assistant, to the statehouse.

CHAPTER ELEVEN

THE PRINCETON DEPOT

The ghost of Andrew Jackson stalked before my face
in the daytime and haunted my couch for nights.
—CARTER GLASS

I do not care what you call it, if you centralize the
control. It will be a central bank in its final analysis.
—FESTUS J. WADE, *testifying before
House Banking Subcommittee*

CARTER GLASS's date with Woodrow Wilson was set for the governor's office, in Trenton, at two-thirty on the afternoon of December 26, 1912. Glass was anxious to meet Parker Willis in advance; he fretted that this would require his leaving Lynchburg, Virginia, on Christmas Day, but then, Glass's nature was to fret. He was intensely agitated by the pressure from bankers for a centralized scheme and worried that bankers had gotten to Wilson (a suspicion, of course, that was entirely correct). His anxiety rose when, just before he was to leave home, he received an urgent telegram: "Confined by attack of cold. Would you be kind enough to come to Princeton?" The change in plans, redirecting the pair to Wilson's home, jolted Glass. He had met the president-elect only once or twice and worried whether Wilson, in his sickly state, would truly be attentive. Further upsetting Glass, his train was late—he telegrammed Willis that he would not reach Washington until after midnight.

As he traveled north, Glass wondered how he would gain the confidence of this eminent scholar—this university president. He surely took comfort that Wilson was also a southerner—born barely a year before Glass. The South, with its passion for states' rights, had overwhelmingly supported Wilson,* and the South, Wilson had said, was "the only place in the world where nothing has to be explained to me."

Yet Glass had cause for suspecting that Wilson's sectional ties were more diluted than his own. Glass's family had been in Virginia since 1648; Wilson's had been southerners for only a generation. Wilson's years in New Jersey had scrubbed his diction free of any southern accent, and his heart was unburdened by the resentments that had festered in the South since the Civil War. The president-elect loved the South, he had said, but rejoiced in its defeat. Carter Glass, a conquered soldier's son, knew no such rejoicing. A more fundamental divide marked the two men's characters. The diminutive Glass tortured himself with worry; Wilson was preternaturally self-confident, convinced by the time he grew into his full five feet eleven inches that he was destined for great things. As one biographer said, "He did not doubt."

Princeton was bitterly cold and buried in snow that day. Glass and Willis arrived on a train that chugged behind a horse-drawn plow.

---

* The only states in which Wilson won popular majorities were the eleven former members of the Confederacy.

From the Princeton depot, they traveled by carriage to the half-timbered house on Cleveland Lane. A butler led them past a blazing fire to Wilson's bedchamber, where the president-elect, looking gaunt and obviously suffering a severe cold, was propped against pillows. Glass was painfully aware of his lack of formal education in the presence of two college professors, but Wilson's bedraggled condition, the fact that he was attired in a mere robe, had a calming effect on Glass, as though putting him on a more even plane.

Glass had brought with him a few sheets of paper on which he scrawled some notes—nothing so formal as a draft. With trepidation, he began to outline his plan, calling on Willis to flesh out the details.

What Glass and Willis proposed was a series of Reserve Banks—fifteen or twenty spread about the country. Ordinary banks would subscribe to shares in the nearest Reserve Bank; thus, the Reserve Banks would be privately owned.[*]

The Reserve Banks would have several duties. They would issue notes—a new form of money, replacing the National Bank Notes based on government bonds. This new money would be issued to banks in return for assets. In other words, a bank that held a loan—say, from a local merchant—could exchange it for the new reserve paper, and turn illiquid assets into currency. Banks would have more access to ready cash to lend; the system would be less vulnerable to panic.

The Reserve Banks would also hold government deposits, including gold, providing a backstop for the currency. Glass also proposed that the Reserve Banks guarantee bank deposits, an idea that bankers—metroplitan bankers especially—detested. Since the Glass plan did not include any feature to bind the regional banks together, it was less

---

[*] True to Glass's vision, today's Federal Reserve Banks are private in the limited sense that their stock is owned by for-profit banks, to whom they pay dividends fixed by law. However, the stock cannot be transferred, all surplus profits are sent to the Treasury, and the Banks are subject to supervision by a federal agency, the Reserve Board in Washington.

centralized than the Aldrich Plan—which was, of course, his point. Indeed, it was far less centralized than the eventual Federal Reserve.

Glass and Willis laid out many of their items as talking points, testing to see how far Wilson was willing to push the banks. Would Wilson, for instance, be willing to compel the banks to join the new system against their will, or should the system be voluntary, like the ill-fated Aldrich Plan?

The most important feature—and one on which Glass and Willis were unambiguous—was that the banking system should be organized along regional lines. Thus, banks would be forced to place their reserves not with big banks in New York (as they did at present), and not in Washington, but in the vaults of the new Reserve Banks. The intent was to furnish, as Willis was to write, a "local field" for local funds. Put differently, they hoped to replace the New York–centric Money Trust with silos of credit dispersed across the length of the country.

What Glass had proposed was close to the laissez-faire ideal: each area represented by a bank that was its own duchy, autonomous, private, its size comfortingly tailored to nineteenth-century proportions.

Wilson listened intently. Something about the plan provoked him.

Bluntly, he inquired, "What have you done in regard to centralization?"

Glass stiffened. He replied that his Reserve Banks would report to the comptroller of the currency, the federal banking regulator established in 1863. This cursory check was not enough for Wilson. The president-elect suggested that though a central bank was impossible politically, it was desirable economically. Some compromise had to be worked out. Finally, Wilson issued what amounted to a command.

"You are far on the right track," he began, but the plan needed something more—"a capstone." Wilson explained that he meant a central board in Washington, sitting above the Reserve Banks. Wilson had surely been briefed in advance; his idea of a "capstone" may have been inspired by Paul Warburg (who had recently provided his plan to Colonel House).* In any case, the suggestion for a capstone reflected Wilson's deepest-held values, for he was telling Glass that he wanted the banking system to mirror the federalist design of the U.S. government itself. It was a masterly stroke.

Glass was horrified. As he left, he tried to reassure himself that Wilson wanted merely a supervisory "capstone," but he feared that Wilson had in mind an active, operating body that would resemble a central bank.†

Two days later, on Wilson's birthday, the president-elect was honored with a parade and a reception, in Staunton, Virginia, his birthplace. Glass attended the festivities, hoping for "perhaps, an hour with Mr. Wilson on currency matters." This was exceedingly myopic of Glass. The president-elect was in no mood for currency questions, and so Glass wrote to him asking for a follow-up meeting. Although Glass intended to sound reassuring, he betrayed his anxiety with a signature note of uncertainty—"We may ourselves have in readiness such a 'capstone' as I understand you to suggest," he awkwardly wrote to the president-elect. Glass was more frank when he recorded his thoughts to Willis. "It is clear to me," Glass began, adopting a conspiratorial tone, "that Mr. Wilson has been written to and talked to by those who are seeking to mask the Aldrich plan and give us dangerous centralization; but we shall have to keep quiet on this point for the present." In the next breath, Glass attempted to downplay the "tentative views expressed by the President-elect"—although Wilson had not been tentative at all—and advised Willis it would be well to prepare a capstone as an "emergency," in other words, as a feature he

---

* According to Glass's memoir, Wilson also told Glass their plan should provide for overseas banking. This feature was long sought by Wall Street, and Wilson would scarcely have thought of such a detail on his own.

† Colonel House, in a diary entry shortly after the Princeton conference, said Wilson remarked that the plan "was like building three stories of a four story house, with the expectation that a fourth story would be demanded." This suggests that Wilson did indeed hope that the capstone would evolve into a central bank.

hoped would not be implemented. "Speaking for myself," the congressman added, "I would cheerfully go with the President-elect for some body of central *supervisory* control, if such a body can be . . . divested of the practical attributes of a central bank. In my judgment," he went on, "this is the point of danger." Not the point of *disagreement*, but of "danger." A few days later, Glass worried that he had already ceded too much ground. "I am not entirely convinced that we need any 'capstone,'" he wrote to Willis, though he acknowledged they should have the "mechanism" ready.

Willis immediately began to revise the plan to include a capstone and to reflect other points discussed at Princeton, and he and Glass mounted a campaign to win the support of bankers. The pair focused not on Wall Street but on the (mostly midwestern) bankers who dominated the councils of the American Bankers Association—and, through it, the small-town bankers who were influential across the country. A prime target was Barton Hepburn, the chairman and retired president of the Chase National Bank. Although presiding over a New York institution, Hepburn, who had been born on a farm and was chairman of the ABA's currency commission, carried weight with bankers whose support Glass considered vital, such as George Reynolds and James Forgan of Chicago and the St. Louis banker Festus J. Wade.

Chicago bankers had warmed toward the central bank idea, but they remained mistrustful of any plan that smacked of New York dominance. Even though they were open to a regional approach, they had come to appreciate the Warburg argument for centralization. Willis's talks with Hepburn resembled a minuet, in which Willis probed to see how much decentralization Hepburn and his colleagues would tolerate, and Hepburn delicately pushed back. Forgan, the leader of the Chicago faction, was particularly insistent that control be centralized.

Glass used his subcommittee hearings to persuade the industry that its best—probably only—hope for reform was to rally behind him. Willis later called the hearings an exercise in "testing public opinion," which is exactly what they were not. Glass and Willis did not even disclose they had written a draft, presumably so that witnesses would not be tempted to offer criticisms. Rather, they stage-managed the proceedings to mold public opinion. As early as December 31, 1912, Willis assured Glass that both Hepburn and Warburg were "in good humor toward the hearings" and disposed "to assist by giving moderate and reasonable testimony."

Hepburn led off, and while he admitted a preference for the Aldrich Plan, he generously allowed that "no one would claim that the Aldrich bill is the last word of wisdom." This was the "reasonable" middle ground that Glass aimed to exploit. Bankers had their own reasons for rejecting a European-style central bank—namely, central banks in Europe did business with ordinary customers. American bankers were afraid of the competition from a central bank (when their self-interest was threatened, staid commercial bankers could sound downright populist).

However, the bankers also rejected the Bryan alternatives of government fiat money or federal deposit guarantees. Bryan's approach represented a contrary philosophy—rather than a strong network of private banks, a strong hand of government. The bankers feared that either of Bryan's remedies would lead to inflation. Their pushback was useful to Glass, who shied away from either extreme and who needed leverage to resist the committee members loyal to Bryan.

The one witness who did not play along was Warburg. He had come too far to muzzle his convictions now. Warburg testified that a regional system would perpetuate the flaws in the existing order. He vividly recounted to the subcommittee his horror at the money shortages when he first arrived in New York, in 1902. Now emboldened by his status as a U.S. citizen, he accused his adopted country of ignoring what worked in banking elsewhere. The country's most pressing need, he said, was to centralize reserves—without which the currency would never be truly elastic. "Elastic currency" was a buzzword among

Americans of the day; Warburg used it knowing that it resonated, but went on to define it in vivid terms. America, he noted, was hostage to the "stupid condition" whereby each of the country's seventy-five hundred national banks had to freeze a quarter of its funds "and put them into a safe-deposit box, where they are of no use."

Glass attempted to frame Warburg as an absolutist.

> THE CHAIRMAN: Would you say that we should do nothing if we can not at this time get a central reserve association?

Warburg refused to accept Glass's all-or-nothing formulation, but he pointed out that in a system with multiple reserve banks, those in New York and Chicago would surely dominate—precisely the outcome Glass wanted to avoid. And Warburg doubted that regional banks would cooperate with one another any more than individual clearinghouses had in 1907. Nonetheless, he tried to offer the subcommittee a face-saving compromise by insisting it could achieve a centralization of reserves without establishing, in formal terms, a "central bank."

> THE CHAIRMAN: That is what you are trying to arrive at, the centralization of reserves?
> WARBURG: It is not that I am trying to arrive at it, Mr. Chairman. It is to my mind—and I have studied this thing very, very carefully for a great many years—the only way, the fundamental way, in which every other country in the world has been treating this.

Victor Morawetz provided a counterweight to Warburg, offering a cogent case for regional reserves. Presumably, regional banks would respond more nimbly to local credit conditions, particularly in an era when distances loomed so large. And as Morawetz pointed out, the individual banks could always be merged later.

Glass repeatedly trotted out the Democratic Party platform restrictions, which he said "confronted" the subcommittee and "precluded" it from pursuing a central bank. He referred to the party's "traditional hostility" to central banking as though it were a perhaps-regrettable—but unbreakable—chain about his neck; this was also the tone of his memoir, in which he referred to the memory of Jackson, who had abolished the Second Bank, as a ghost that "stalked" and "haunted" him. Because these arguments did not address the substance, they raised the question of why a central bank so terrified Glass. Although he shared with Bryan a vague aversion to bigness, it is hard not to think that Glass's primary concerns were political.

They were, in any case, effective. The hearings convinced bankers, as Warburg put it, that "no scheme would be considered seriously by Mr. Glass and his colleagues unless it embraced the regional reserve bank principle." Prominent bankers such as Hepburn and Wade, and even Forgan, agreed to back a regional framework, even though they intended to keep pushing to make the individual parts cohesive.

Warburg recast his latest plan so that it comprised four regional banks (many fewer than in Glass's plan), *mutually responsible* for one another. This version was delivered to Henry Morgenthau, and also to Willis, who shared its thesis with Glass. Warburg's point was that with too many banks, the system would suffer a lack of coordination and, in the weaker regions, a lack of capital.* But a quartet of closely knit banks could preserve the principle of collective security. "The tantalizing puzzle," Warburg offered, was how to unify the system for the purposes of fluidity of reserves while nonetheless endowing the individual banks with sufficient independence—"otherwise they will be nothing but [glorified] safe-deposit vaults." Although Warburg's criticisms were constructive, Glass didn't trust him as he did other bankers, perhaps because the perfectionist Warburg was so difficult

---

* This was prescient of Warburg; lack of coordination among the Reserve Banks contributed to the Fed's ineffectiveness during the Great Depression.

to satisfy; he suspected that Warburg's true purpose was resurrecting the Aldrich Plan. Warburg returned the favor, regarding Glass as a mere politician who did not have the business mind of Aldrich.

Wilson was eager to have a bill when he took office (presidents in that era were inaugurated on March 4). Willis completed a draft on January 15. As the hearings progressed, he continued to tinker with it, still taking extraordinary precautions to keep its provisions secret. In one series of letters, Willis painstakingly queried of Glass how many people should be allowed to see the draft; agonized over whether to exclude James Laughlin, who was still advising him; and finally suggested they show the bill only to a small group in executive session after which they would "call in all copies." In their way, Glass and Willis were as conspiratorial as the bankers on Jekyl Island. Laughlin desperately sought to procure a copy, but now that Glass had the ear of Wilson, he no longer needed Laughlin. At the end of January, Glass presented Wilson with a formal draft, this time at the governor's office in Trenton. At this meeting, Wilson endorsed Glass's basic regional design. Laughlin miserably concluded he had been left "outside the breastworks."

The document Glass took to New Jersey had been softened to mollify bankers; for instance, deposit guarantees were out and the Reserve Banks were limited to taking deposits from other banks, not from ordinary citizens. Thus, the Trenton plan envisioned a "banker's bank." Nonetheless, the Reserve Banks were permitted to conduct open market operations such as buying bonds, later to become a favorite tool of Ben Bernanke. Contrary to what bankers sought, membership was to be compulsory, and Glass blithely ignored Warburg's admonition to reduce the number of Reserve Banks—Glass specified "not less than fifteen."

In other respects, the Trenton draft bore a striking resemblance to the much renounced Aldrich Plan. Both bills proposed a new currency backed by bank assets and a gold reserve. Each envisioned a new institution (or multiple institutions) to hold bank reserves, governed by local boards of bankers and a supreme board in Washington. Where Glass wanted fifteen or more banks, Aldrich envisioned fifteen branches. And notwithstanding the frequent charge that the Aldrich Plan was elitist, the bills were similar in providing for democratic governance and local representation.

The bills were also similar in scope. Each proposed a new agency to become the fiscal arm of the United State government. Each set up a system of bank examinations and check clearing. Willis even mimicked the Aldrich bill's phraseology.

Of course, the plans also differed in important respects. The biggest was that Aldrich and Warburg had conceived of "branches" around the country subservient to a central organ. Glass was proposing regional "banks" with greater local independence—although arguably, this was a matter of degree. Another distinction was that Glass-Willis compelled the banks to shift their reserves to the new Reserve Banks, ending the perilous "pyramiding" of reserves from the farm to the city to New York. Aldrich, not wanting to offend his banker colleagues, had been mum on this important point.

As the Glass legislation evolved, other significant differences would emerge. Willis would contend in his memoir that the Federal Reserve Act was the product of many bills and ideas from which its authors selected, revised, sifted, and so forth. It is true that few transformative ideas emerge from thin air; nonetheless, Willis was on shaky ground in asserting that the Act "was not derived from, or modeled after, or influenced even in the most remote way by other bills or proposals currently put forward." In fact, the Aldrich Plan was its direct and recognizable forebear. But for political reasons, as well as the desire to inflate their own roles, Glass and Willis each felt compelled to disown the connection to Aldrich.

AS INAUGURATION DAY NEARED, Wilson agonized over whether to give a cabinet role to Bryan; ultimately, he reckoned that Bryan would pose less trouble inside the tent than out. The Commoner was given State—a relief to bankers, whose worst nightmare would have been to see Bryan at the Treasury. Colonel House, who had great influence on the selections, discouraged the inclusion of another corporate critic—Louis Brandeis—probably because Wilson clearly admired Brandeis, and House saw him as a threat. With reluctance, Wilson acquiesced. (House cannily turned down a cabinet role for himself, preferring the offscreen role of adviser at large.)

The most important slot for banking legislation was Treasury. At the suggestion of House, Wilson made an inspired choice—William Gibbs McAdoo, a businessman and one of the managers of Wilson's campaign. A southerner—as were over half of Wilson's choices—McAdoo was born in Georgia, into "bitter poverty" during the Civil War. His family moved to Tennessee, where McAdoo studied law, set up a practice, and invested his meager resources in a venture to electrify streetcar lines in Knoxville (the industry that had led to Nelson Aldrich's fortune). When the venture failed, he moved to New York. With few resources, and six young children to feed, he attempted to resurrect an abandoned project to dig a rail tunnel under the Hudson River, linking New Jersey and Manhattan. The project faced high hurdles, engineering and financial; improbably, McAdoo succeeded. (The tunnels today serve the heavily trafficked PATH trains to midtown and downtown New York.) Although Morgan provided financing, McAdoo was not a Wall Street insider, and his battles with bankers left him with a jaundiced view of the financial world. He fancied himself a public-service-minded executive and adopted the motto "The public be pleased" (a clever inversion on the infamous saying of the railroad tycoon William Vanderbilt, "The public be damned"). McAdoo's slogan was certainly calculated to further his political ambitions. But he backed it by operating clean, well-lit cars, instituting a box for customer complaints, and—unusually for that era—paying equal wages to women.

As a businessman reformer and a southerner to boot, McAdoo

was perfect for Wilson. The country had been governed by Republicans for so long that business was unsettled by the prospect of a Democrat; McAdoo was a Democrat whom business could tolerate, while also clearly aligned with progressive ideals. He firmly believed that government should have a say over the economy—not leave it to the moguls with whom he had formerly crossed swords. Wiry with a dark complexion, derby hat, and black suit, he moved with quickness and vitality and, unlike the president-elect, preferred action to theorizing.

Wilson decided to begin his legislative assault with the tariff, a simpler issue than banking reform. Shortly before he took office, the Sixteenth Amendment (sanctioning an income tax) was ratified; this provided a further rationale for tariff cuts, since Wilson could now seek to replace lost tariff revenue with taxes. However, tariff cuts were a partisan cause, pleasing to the South but perceived as anti-business. Wilson did not want to be seen as a "southern" president. Putting a progressive gloss on his agenda, he made a point, in an address in January to the Southern Society of New York, of rejecting sectionalism.

Partly for this reason, the Democrats were eager to move on banking reform, which appealed to businesses irrespective of geography. Wilson saw the Glass bill as a program to benefit banking customers, not just the narrow universe of banks. His goal was to unshackle business by establishing new centers of credit. Wilson was also licking his chops over the prospect of bringing Wall Street to heel; he imagined that if the Glass bill was enacted, the new Reserve Banks would level the influence of the New York financial houses. According to Joseph Tumulty, soon to be Wilson's White House secretary, the president-elect said he wanted "to take away from certain financial interests in the country the power they had unjustly exercised of 'hazing' the Democratic Party at every Presidential election."

As if another rationale were needed, days before the inauguration Samuel Untermyer submitted the final report of the Money Trust investigation. It was a scorching indictment of the old-boy network that dominated American finance. Untermyer's relentless cross-examinations and eye-catching charts had documented the web of interlocking directorships that knit Wall Street and corporate America. (Frank Vanderlip testified, to his embarrassment, that he held directorships in thirty-five corporations.) Just as damning, Untermyer proved that competition in securities was a farce. None other than George Baker, Morgan's friend, supplied the crucial testimony.

> UNTERMYER: Have you ever competed for any securities with Morgan & Co. in the last five years?
> BAKER: I do not know that we have competed with them.
> UNTERMYER: You divide with them, do you not? You give them a part of the issues when you have it?
> BAKER: We are very apt to.
> UNTERMYER: And if they take a security, they give you a part of the issue, do they not?
> BAKER: Yes.

Untermyer affirmed that a Money Trust did exist—assuming, he wrote in the report's most quoted section, that the term was taken to mean a "well-defined identity and community of interest between a few leaders of finance which has . . . resulted in a vast and growing concentration of control of money and credit in the hands of a comparatively few men." Untermyer identified J. P. Morgan, James Stillman, and George Baker as the "inner circle." To his credit, he admitted that no conspiracy had been found—no price-fixing or plot. It was enough to say that the Money Trust existed—Wilson and the Democrats rightly regarded even the potential for abuse as serious.

Public revulsion was nearly uniform; even *The Wall Street Journal* grudgingly acknowledged that concentration on Wall Street was excessive. The hearings, as much as anything, convinced progressives that banking reform demanded immediate action. The increasingly influential Brandeis further galvanized public opinion with a widely read series, "Breaking the Money Trust,"* which was published in *Harper's Weekly* as Congress debated the Glass bill.

Surprisingly few observers noticed that Untermyer's description of a trust applied more to securities than to ordinary banking. America, after all, had twenty-five thousand individual banks—roughly half of them founded since 1900. Nor was the industry particularly profitable; net earnings of the national banks totaled only $161 million (about $3.8 billion in today's money), and a return on assets of less than 2 percent. Moreover, banks in New York City held a smaller share of the country's banking resources in 1912 than they had in 1900. It is true that within New York, assets were more concentrated than previously, and that the boards of the biggest banks were decidedly cozy. But on balance, conventional banking did not exhibit the cartel pattern of Wall Street. In this sense, the "Money Trust" was merely a convenient label to sell reform to the public.

Untermyer was on more substantive ground when he attacked the lopsided distribution of power to marshal reserves in a crisis. Regarding the market turmoil of 1907, he bore in on R. H. Thomas, the retired president of the New York Stock Exchange:

UNTERMYER: When Mr. Morgan gave the word, did that change the panic conditions?

THOMAS: It certainly had a very decided effect upon relieving the situation.

UNTERMYER: Then, it rested with one man to say whether the panic should go on or should end, did it?

Spurred by Untermyer, the journalist Ida Tarbell zeroed in on one of the system's weakest links: the New York Clearing House. Tarbell

---

* Published in book form under the title *Other People's Money and How the Bankers Use It*, in 1914, it became a progressive anthem.

claimed that this private bankers' club was "exercising power which it had been gradually gathering to itself." It was ill equipped to provide security. Its authority was citywide, not national; it was not even universally subscribed to within New York and it dispensed its powers arbitrarily. "If Congress . . . had given us any good, wholesome currency legislation, such as they have in other commercial nations of the world," Tarbell fairly screamed, recalling the desperate attempts to furnish paper IOUs in the last panic, "there would never have been any question of issuing Clearing House certificates." Such arguments did not escape the attention of Congress.

On March 4, 1913, Woodrow Wilson rode to the Capitol alongside William Howard Taft, a gracious loser. Soldiers had pushed the crowd away from the speaker's platform, where they were nearly out of earshot. Wilson sent an aide with the instruction that the people could come forward: thus did progressivism govern. The biographer John Milton Cooper noted that Wilson was one of the last presidents to write his own speeches. His address, though brief, was full of fire and brimstone. Inveighing against the ruthlessness of business tycoons, he thundered, "We have been proud of our industrial achievements, but we have not hitherto stopped thoughtfully enough to count the human cost." There has been, he added, "something crude and heartless and unfeeling in our haste to succeed and be great." But with regard to his actual policies, the new president was reassuringly moderate. He wanted no draconian upheaval, just a "sober second thought." Bankers in particular were soothed when he declared, "We shall restore, not destroy. We shall deal with our economic system as it is and as it may be modified, not as it might be if we had a clean sheet of paper to write upon."

Wilson was the first (and thus far, the only) president with a Ph.D. He entered office with a well-conceived agenda and a sure sense of the powers of the presidency. The Sixty-second Congress having expired, he opted to convene a special session, in April, to at-

tack the tariff; the timing of bank reform was up for grabs.* Wilson
was at least mildly distracted by the arrest and, quickly following it,
the murder of the president of Mexico barely a week before he entered the White House. The violent revolution south of the border
would dog him throughout 1913, as he tried to focus on his domestic
program—a harbinger of the attention he would later devote to foreign affairs, specifically Europe. However, in March, Wilson put
Mexico to the side and received Glass, together with McAdoo, and
urged Glass to deliver a bill promptly. The congressman exited excit-
edly. "The prospect," he reported to Willis, "is that the President,
Mr. McAdoo and I will be in frequent consultation within the next
few weeks, and I shall want to be well up on every detail of our bill."

Glass then urged Willis, who was revising their draft, to work
in haste. For Glass, the interlude between legislative sessions was
blessed. He did not have to consult with other members (his committee had yet to be reconstituted) and he could focus on the mechanics
of how the system would work. He corresponded with the director of
the U.S. Mint, who had a useful suggestion (urging that private
banks be integrated into the new system through an exchange of
their gold for reserve notes) and who became an ally of Glass within
the administration.

As usual, Glass and Willis were busy fending off perceived threats.
Willis warned Glass that McAdoo, when building his Hudson River
tunnels, had received financing from Kuhn, Loeb (Warburg's firm)
and was said to be in Warburg's pocket. There is no evidence that this
was true. Untermyer represented a darker shadow. The attorney attempted to relaunch the Money Trust inquiry; when this failed, Untermyer tried to get to Wilson by cultivating a relationship with
Colonel House, who shared his taste for intrigue. Untermyer insinu-

---

* Congressional sessions were irregular. Frequently, after a presidential inauguration,
Congress did not meet for any extended period until the following December.

ated to House that the Glass bill would not solve the "vast" problem of concentration of credit—only, naturally, a bill that Untermyer had in mind would do that.

House took an interest in the banking bill, and his diary refers to repeated meetings not only with Untermyer but with Wall Street bankers such as Jack Morgan, Warburg, and Vanderlip. He also took Glass on a carriage ride to discuss the legislation. All were eager to meet with House, as his intimacy with Wilson was well known.* But closeness did not necessarily translate to influence. At a "family affair" at the White House at which the Colonel shared fish, veal cutlets, rice, peas and potatoes, and ice cream with the Wilsons, he casually suggested that he and McAdoo "whip the Glass measure into final shape." There is no evidence that Wilson endorsed this idea. House also conveyed a request from Henry Frick, the steel mogul, that the administration quietly resolve the government suit against U.S. Steel out of court. Wilson brusquely rejected this plea for corporate favoritism, replying that U.S. Steel should receive "the same consideration as any other, neither more nor less." The President was at ease with the Colonel and relied on him for emotional support, but on banking and other financial matters McAdoo carried far more weight.

Wall Street bankers, who had been spoiled by their warm relations with Taft, sensed that their influence in the White House was diminished. Vanderlip sourly complained that his "friendship" with Wilson did not seem to count for much. Jack Morgan opted to sell much of his firm's stake in National City to forestall public criticism. It was a sign that, under the new administration, banks were on a shorter leash, particularly on matters where they might be suspected of wielding undue influence. As Morgan put it, "We all feel that it behooves us to pay more or less attention to public feeling of that kind."

---

* Willis, for instance, had the impression that House "was apparently vested with very large powers."

Pierpont, the elder Morgan, had dropped from view since his appearance in Congress, embarking on a trip with family and friends to Egypt, where he was supporting archaeological treasure hunting. Nelson Aldrich and his family departed on the same boat as the Morgans. Lucy, the senator's eldest daughter, reported, "We have been practically one party [with the Morgans] since we left New York and we have gone about seeing the ruins together." Aldrich always had a taste for antiquities, perhaps never more than in his own twilight. In Cairo, the senator and Pierpont lunched with Lord Kitchener, the conqueror of Sudan. The families, glittering relics of the Gilded Age, traveled the Nile in a pair of private steamers, "stop[ping] at the same places." However, Morgan was fatigued and depressed. By March, each family was in Rome. Aldrich bought a pair of marble sphinxes and two Persian bowls and proceeded to Monte Carlo. From his art dealer, he heard, along with details relating to the packing of his art, disquieting news. Morgan, who had remained at the Grand Hotel in Rome, was seriously ill. On March 31, updating Aldrich on his sphinxes, the dealer added: "Sorry to say that Mr. Morgan is not at all well and all sorts of rumors are afloat." He died that day.

Morgan's passing symbolized the end of the era in which a single financier could hope to rescue the banking system. Walter Hines Page, Wilson's new ambassador to Great Britain, immediately observed that "a revision of the currency and banking laws, if a wise revision be made, will prevent any other such career." For one man to hold such power, Page correctly judged, "does not fit into the American scheme of life or business." Vanderlip, too, sensed the portent in Morgan's passing. "The king is dead," began his letter to Stillman. "There are no cries of, 'Long life the king,' for the general verdict seems to be that there will be no other king; that Mr. Morgan, typical of the time in which he lived, can have no successor, for we are facing other days."

CHAPTER TWELVE

THE "SLIME OF BRYANISM"

The germinal principle of the bill appears to be
distrust of banks and of bankers.

> —The New York Times, *June 20, 1913*

The banks may be the instruments, not the masters,
of business.

> —WOODROW WILSON, *before a joint session*
> *of Congress, June 23, 1913*

WHEN AMERICA last had a central bank, in 1836 (the year before
J. P. Morgan Sr.'s birth), the country was a financial innocent. Its
credit was borrowed in Europe; its stock market barely existed; its
most common mode of transportation was the horse. The United
States of 1913 was entirely different. The frontier had vanished; indus-
trialization was a fact. Ford's was churning out 170,000 Model Ts a
year. The New York Stock Exchange listed more than three hundred
companies, and corporate news was disseminated on glass-domed

stock tickers. The banking industry had mushroomed, thanks in large part to the greater willingness of people to deposit their savings. The heady progress of finance was, however, an unfulfilled promise to the great wash of industrial workers. Capital in its formative stage was undemocratic. Workers' pensions and other forms of savings were practically nonexistent. Leisure time was the province of the wealthy. America had far more banks than ever, but banks existed to serve business. Neither Carter Glass nor Paul Warburg would have understood the term "consumer loan." National City Bank loaned against trade, not against the purchase of automobiles. Banks, of course, provided a trust service to the Aldriches, the Vanderbilts, and their ilk, distributing the dividends on their shares, balancing the books when the families were in Newport or London. The great exception—the one respect in which bankers trafficked with a wider public—was in mortgages, which were mostly rural mortgages, and these were a source of friction as much as fulfillment. National banks did not issue real estate loans, and credit from state banks was never ample enough; the farmer subsisted on the anxious edge of foreclosure.

As far as rural and laboring Americans were concerned, banks belonged to privilege. If banking was to be reformed, people wanted a say in it, so that credit would be more widely distributed. Nelson Aldrich had approached reform as a technical puzzle whose solution could be engineered by competent experts. Carter Glass approached it as a political question. His task was to unite populist Democrats on one wing of the party with conservatives and businesspeople on the other. He counted on reform-minded bankers to be his allies. But bankers increasingly distrusted the Democrats and attached conditions for their support. They set a high price on collaboration. When Bryan Democrats attached their own conditions, a confrontation was inevitable.

Three questions divided reformers: Who should issue the new currency? To what degree should the system be centralized? And should bankers or politicians be in control? Of the three, the first—

the "money question"—will seem most puzzling to modern readers. Americans today think of "money" as paper that is minted by governments, but this was not always the case. A century ago, money—"notes"—still retained their ancient connection to credit. Notes were promises to be redeemed for coin or reliable securities, and who had more wherewithal to back up promises than banks, at least well-regulated banks? Governments had only the taxing power, which was considered unreliable. A 1910 tract asserted, "Currency should be based on credit which has real values back of it, and not on the credit of any national or local government." The report of the Indianapolis Monetary Convention, in 1898, had gone even further, labeling government money a fraud, for it "educates the people who use it in false notions." They begin to think of paper as "possess[ing] the virtue of money in and of itself."

Dissenters had often challenged the orthodox view, but never from a position of power. Now, however, William Jennings Bryan was secretary of state, with a loyal following among the majority in both houses of Congress. In particular, the chairman of the Senate Banking and Currency Committee, Robert Owen of Oklahoma (who had previously withstood a run on his bank), was a Bryan disciple. Owen, like Bryan, believed that government—not banks—should control the circulation of money. This view was heresy among conservatives, who equated government money with unrestrained issuance and inflation.

The only person who could hope to reconcile such differences was Wilson. Thanks to the Democrats having elected 114 first-time congressmen, the President had an enhanced power to affect legislation. With so many newcomers, Wilson was in a position to dominate.

Wilson launched his agenda early in April, addressing a joint session of Congress on the tariff. In typically soaring prose, he demanded that lawmakers abolish "even the semblance of privilege or of any kind of artificial advantage." Wilson's presence at the rostrum of the House of Representatives reversed a century-old custom by which presidents did not appear in Congress (Jefferson had considered it undemocratic, a practice too suggestive of English kings). Even Wilson was accused of mimicking royalty. In truth, his visit had a strategic purpose: he wanted to enhance the president's personal authority. Wilson found a symbolic way to demonstrate his reach later in the month, when, sitting at his desk in Washington, he switched on the lights of the new Woolworth Building in New York. The fifty-seven-story gothic skyscraper—the world's tallest—reaffirmed the mood of accelerating change. In May, Wilson claimed a substantive triumph, when the House passed the biggest tariff cut since the Civil War. Compounding the sense of galloping reform, the Seventeenth Amendment was ratified, mandating direct election of senators (an early Bryan idea come to fruition).

Banking reform proceeded on a parallel, if less visible, track. Congress was eager to recess and avoid the Washington summer, but Wilson was adamant that the members stay in town to work on banking. The President delegated the administration effort to his Treasury secretary. Moving quickly, McAdoo mapped the country into districts, trying to position the reserve centers so that no bank would be more than an overnight train ride from a supply of cash. He worked closely with Willis, who was revising the latest draft. The two met on a Sunday at McAdoo's home, and it is evident from Willis's correspondence that he regarded McAdoo's suggestions as close to commands. To attract votes from farm states, McAdoo inserted the secretary of agriculture on the central board, in place of the attorney general, who had no business being there. He also improved the bill's nomenclature, changing "National Reserve Bank" to "Federal Reserve Bank."

However, McAdoo became frustrated with Glass and Willis's secretive ways (it did not help that McAdoo developed a strong dislike for the prickly Willis). From McAdoo and others, pressure mounted on Glass and Willis to circulate a draft. In mid-April, McAdoo requested that Glass bring a copy of the bill to a Washington dinner party to which each man was invited. Promptly, the two got involved in a spirited discussion of it. As the evening ended, Colonel House, who was also present, asked if he could take the bill with him. Glass declined, saying it was his only copy. A few days later, Wilson ordered Glass to prepare a "digest" of the bill, which Willis did. This was the first crack in Glass and Willis's veil of secrecy.

House immediately conveyed Willis's digest to Paul Warburg, requesting that the banker supply an analysis—within twenty-four hours! Once again, Warburg exploited the chance to gain influence. Working in a frenzy, he delivered thirteen pages of pointed suggestions. As before, he urged a reduction in the number of Reserve Banks (the Willis digest stipulated twenty) with satellite branches, if necessary, in more remote territories. The principle he advanced was of "a large number of faucets" but a small number of reservoirs. In an era in which physical proximity of money was critical, Warburg understood the need for multiple branches, but insisted that a pooling of reserves was critical to the system's strength. Warburg also urged that state-chartered banks be allowed to join, so that the new system would be as inclusive as possible. To prevent banks from milking the system, he recommended that a ceiling be imposed on dividends. Warburg also suggested a reduction in reserve requirements.

His paper, dated April 22, was unsigned, but Willis immediately recognized its author. Now almost finished with his second draft, Willis was incensed by this encyclopedic critique. While giving it careful study, Willis advised Glass that the Warburg paper was "vicious" and also "extreme." Such remarks can be attributed only to Willis's monumental insecurities. Despite his sensitivity, however, most of Warburg's points were adopted.* Warburg's critique also served as a useful irritant in the waters. Previously, too little had been known—even in official Washington—for people to discuss the bill.

---

* For instance, states were permitted to subscribe, dividends were capped, and reserve requirements were cut.

Now, people had Warburg's analysis to chew over. Not for the first time, the German stirred controversy and debate.

Colonel House, who never missed an opportunity to stir the pot, stopped by McAdoo's apartment when, as it happened, McAdoo and Willis were reviewing the Warburg paper. With an air of mystery, House took McAdoo into another room, to confer in private. This surely irritated Willis—who needed little encouragement to suspect a conspiracy. After fifteen minutes or so, House reappeared, grabbed the Warburg paper, offering the dubious excuse that he had yet to read it, and left.

For as long as the bill remained secret, the process was subject to intrigue and to the interplay of personalities. Two days after the encounter at McAdoo's apartment, on May 4, Colonel House was invited to Greystone, Untermyer's estate north of New York City. Senator Owen, chairman of the Senate Banking Committee, had spent the night and was there as well. House presumably discussed what he knew of the Glass bill, and of Warburg's critique of it— both of which were news to Owen. Partly due to differences with Glass, partly from annoyance at being left out of the loop, Owen around this time resolved to write his own bill. The eventual co-sponsors of the Federal Reserve Act were now in a race against each other.

Coincidentally, Owen had been born in Lynchburg, Virginia, two years before Glass and a block from Glass's birthplace. Part Cherokee on his mother's side, he had the look of a statesman: tall with a swarthy complexion and black hair and dark eyes. Unlike Glass, Owen had been raised in a comfortable home, the son of a railroad president, but his father's early death and the Panic of 1873 reduced the family to poverty. A gifted student, Owen attended Washington and Lee University on scholarship, where he was valedictorian. In 1879, he moved to Indian Territory (present-day Oklahoma), where he taught school to orphan Cherokees and was admitted to the bar, specializing in Indian claims. He briefly edited the weekly newspaper *Indian*

Chieftain, and in 1885 he was appointed Indian Agent (a federal post) in Muskogee.

Pioneers were often jacks-of-all-trades, and Owen cultivated diverse business interests, including livestock and real estate. As he later noted in a campaign letter, he rode horseback, for one purpose or another, "all over Oklahoma." As a businessman, Owen witnessed a monetary system that was a crude form of barter. Muskogee had a population of 1,200, white, black, and red. Farmers and ranchers, who bought their necessities in Muskogee, would bring an animal to town as the basis for credit. If the farmer or rancher had a surplus after making a purchase, the merchant gave him scrip, which circulated as money. This was embryonic banking.

In 1890, Owen and other residents organized the First National Bank of Muskogee. Bandits being prevalent, an armed guard stood constant watch. But as Owen discovered, the bank had more to fear from its own customers. During the Panic of 1893, frightened depositors withdrew half of their funds, and the bank nearly failed.

Scarred by the near miss, Owen became a student of banking. He attended the Democratic convention of 1896, saw Bryan in his glory, and unsuccessfully proposed a measure to protect the country from future panics. In 1898 he traveled to European capitals to study central banking—the same mission Aldrich was to embark on a decade later. When Oklahoma was admitted to the union in 1907, Owen was elected one of its senators. His first speech on the Senate floor was an attack on Aldrich. Owen was a Jeffersonian Democrat, more progressive than Glass. The racial politics of the South wedded Glass to tradition; by contrast, promoting Indian claims nurtured Owen's taste for reform. He championed direct elections to the Senate, women's suffrage, an income tax. Having seen a banking panic firsthand, he gravitated to the Bryan view that government should issue the currency, to ensure that the currency did not run short. Glass, who favored bank currency, vehemently disagreed.

For Untermyer, whose feud with Glass was out in the open,

the chance to influence the legislation via Glass's Senate counter-part must have been a godsend. In an odd alliance of Wall Street insider and prairie populist, Untermyer offered to bring bankers to Greystone to give Owen a quick tutorial. In rapid succession, the senator was introduced to Vanderlip, Warburg, and Hepburn; the former two would correspond with him extensively. Through these contacts, Owen reached out to Professor Piatt Andrew, who essentially drafted his bill.

Notwithstanding that Owen was mentored by Aldrich's former colleagues, his bill was a loosely worded version of Glass's save for two key points. Owen thought the new institution's notes should be issued by the federal government, whereas Glass, of course, favored notes issued by the Reserve Banks and backed by their members' assets. Put simply, Owen wanted government money, Glass, private bank notes. Also, Owen wanted the entire Federal Reserve Board to be appointed by the president; Glass thought some of the directors should be chosen by bankers. In other words, on two pivotal issues, the Glass bill was closer to the bankers' position, while Owen, faithful to his hero Bryan, wanted the government in charge. Glass represented the Victorian age of laissez-faire while Owen favored twentieth-century progressivism, with its credo that even high finance should be subject to government control. One or the other would have to give.

At some point in May, Owen alerted Bryan that the Glass bill, which the Wilson administration was supporting, did violence to their shared principles. The chameleonlike Untermyer invited Bryan to lunch and delivered a similar warning. It was now only a matter of time before the President discovered he had a problem deep within his cabinet. On May 11, House alerted Wilson that Bryan was "waking up to the fact that the proposed bill was not to his liking and that it did not provide for direct government issue."

Four days later, House reiterated to the President: "I saw Primus [their code name for Bryan] today and had quite a talk with him. He brought up the currency question and I am very much afraid that he is a long way afield from your views." Bryan, who had been frustrated over his inability to see the bill, now asked that Glass walk him through it. House suggested, as an alternative, that Wilson meet with Bryan. The President sensed that such a meeting could be disastrous.

Instead, the assignment went to McAdoo. Initially, Bryan had not been happy with McAdoo's selection as Treasury secretary, suspecting he was a pawn of Wall Street, but in the cabinet the pair had quickly become friends. When they met to discuss the banking bill, however, McAdoo made no headway. Bryan's self-image, as well as his popular following, was rooted in the perception that he stood for the "people" against the banks. Public control of the banking system was a matter of high principle.

On May 20, the day after his unsuccessful meeting with Bryan, McAdoo uncorked one of the more bizarre episodes in the long campaign for a central bank. Convinced that the Glass bill would fly neither with bankers (who had been muttering their disapproval) nor with Bryan, McAdoo dashed off an entirely new plan, which he outlined in a memorandum to Colonel House. His notion was to snip through the hornet's nest of conflicting demands:

> We run against so much of prejudice upon the part of the bankers particularly, to any plan that does not fit their preconceived and established notions, that we shall, I think, have to cut away entirely from all the mazes and hazes of previous discussions and bring out something new and simple and direct.

The essence of the McAdoo plan was for a government-owned central bank, under the dominion of the Treasury Department. His plan was elegantly crafted, intended to please both sides. Bryan would get government control, Wall Street would get centralization as well as rationalization. There would be only four or five reserve centers, and all government notes and bank notes would be replaced by a single currency issued by the Treasury.

It is not certain who drafted the McAdoo plan; McAdoo had a hand in it, as did his assistant secretary, John Skelton Williams, who was an archenemy of Wall Street. The plan also bore the thumbprint of the ubiquitous Untermyer.

House immediately pitched the idea to Wilson, urging that he adopt a measure "along the lines suggested by Mr. Untermyer and one which Primus [Bryan] and Senator Owen will probably accept." The Colonel, who was in over his head, said the McAdoo scheme, save for its provision for government-issued money, was "not different from the one we have in mind," meaning the Glass bill. He also asserted that the McAdoo plan would find favor with bankers.

House was wrong on both counts; moreover, it was fantastic of him to think that Wilson would jettison a committee chairman with whom he had been working since the previous December. House had clearly been seduced by Untermyer, to whom he ascribed magical powers of persuasion. He recommended that Wilson smuggle Untermyer into the White House to set the McAdoo plan into action: "Pythias [McAdoo] or Owen could get him to Washington and when he was there you could arrange to see him for an hour in the evening and it is quite possible that no one would know."

House should have consigned this dubious plot twist to his anonymously published novel. The day after writing Wilson, as if acknowledging his need for a dose of fresh air, House sailed to England on the RMS *Mauretania*, the fastest liner on the seas, white hulled with four black smokestacks. The Colonel encountered, to their mutual surprise, Warburg on the same boat. Warburg, who was bound for the Swiss Alps, heard what was afoot and wrote a lengthy missive on board, which eventually reached the White House, denouncing both the Owen bill and the McAdoo plan for investing government with too much power over banking.

But Warburg's absence diminished his influence, and McAdoo was charging ahead. The Treasury secretary summoned Glass to his office, where he dropped the bombshell that he was promoting a government bank rather than the Glass bill.

"Are you serious?" said Glass.

"Hell, yes," McAdoo replied.

McAdoo seems to have caught the bug of nearly everyone involved in reform—thinking he could write a bill superior to the one on the table. Years later, he claimed he had proposed a government bank because, as he put it, "I could see clearly that the Federal Reserve Banks were destined to be . . . an integral part of public finance."

Glass recounted that he was "astounded" when he left the Treasury (Glass often affected shock when others took positions contrary to his). He must have realized that his work of the past year was about to be consigned to the dustbin. In despair, the chairman directed Willis to round up negative reactions to the McAdoo plan from bankers—a tactic the two had employed before.

Wilson now was in an awkward spot. He had three bills on his desk—two more than he wanted. He could not ignore a proposal from an important member of his cabinet; on the other hand, he was intent on preserving a solid front among Democrats in Congress. He wanted a bill that the leaders in both chambers backed, and which Wilson could then endorse as an "administration bill."

Toward the end of May, McAdoo met with Owen and Glass, with the hope of crafting some mutually agreeable solution. They made little progress. In June, when the House Banking Committee was officially reconstituted, Glass, now installed as chairman, complained to Willis, "I am all in the air and do not know what to say to members of my committee."

However, on June 6, Glass got an audience with the President. He brought with him telegrams from bankers affirming their opposition to the McAdoo plan. Glass read aloud an especially emphatic letter, from George Reynolds. Wilson seemed surprised; his interest in the

Treasury secretary's scheme evaporated on the spot. "I fear Mac is deceived," Wilson said, "but fortunately the thing has not gone so far it cannot be stopped."

With Glass reassured of Wilson's support, he confided in Hepburn, a banker in whom he trusted, "The chief point of danger now seems to be the apparent intractability of our friend Senator Owen." Glass's language suggests that he had come to regard bankers as his allies against the radicals in his party. Three days after seeing Wilson, Glass met with Owen. He found the senator in a conciliatory mood, willing to go along with most aspects of the Glass bill. However, they remained divided on the issue of control. Glass was willing to support a seven-person board with up to four directors—a majority—appointed by the president, in addition to three banker nominees. Owen insisted that all seven directors represent the public.

While the legislators were trying to hash out a deal, Wall Street laid an egg. During late May and early June, stocks plunged, approaching the levels of the previous panic. Credit markets tightened severely. Noting the prospect for a bumper wheat crop, which would burn through vaults of cash, traders became anxious about the prospect of a credit squeeze in autumn. In a frightening echo of 1907, higher interest rates in Europe were luring gold out of the United States. Vanderlip reported to Paris, "We will need the gold badly in the fall I am afraid." In a follow-up, he added, "The pessimism here in Wall Street is extreme."

McAdoo suspected that Wall Street might be contriving the disturbance to scramble the legislation. This was unlikely, but he moved to stabilize the situation by announcing his readiness (under the 1908 Aldrich-Vreeland Act, which had been hastily enacted after the previous panic) to issue emergency currency. Markets did promptly settle down. Regardless of how earnestly bankers trumpeted the virtues of laissez-faire, in times of unrest markets looked to Washington to provide stability. The fact that Aldrich-Vreeland, never more than a Band-Aid, was set to expire in 1914 gave further impetus to reform.

"Currency legislation," *The Wall Street Journal* opined, "should be pushed rapidly."

The unspoken obstacle was Bryan, and Wilson summoned him to the White House. The President, who had worked hard in the past year to mend their past differences, now asked for Bryan's support. Bryan wanted to remain loyal; however, when Wilson confirmed what was in the bill, the Commoner said he had no choice but to oppose it. Invoking, rather loosely, the legacy of Jefferson and Jackson, he said he could not violate the Democratic Party's long-standing commitment to government-issued money. Furthermore, Bryan objected to putting bankers on the board. He expressed "deep regret," and offered to mute his criticism and even to resign.

Wilson now faced a political crisis. He somberly told Tumulty, his secretary, "It begins to look as if Bryan and I have come to the parting of the ways on the currency bill." The two discussed the potential fallout should the secretary of state resign. Without Bryan's active help, banking reform would surely be dead.*

It was fortunate for Wilson that he was fresh from a triumph on the tariff. In recent weeks, corporate lobbyists (who formerly had worked so effectively with Aldrich) had descended on the Senate, aiming to gut the House measure. It had begun to look as though history would repeat—tariff reform in the House followed by a stealthy retreat in the upper chamber. But Wilson had a knack for channeling public outrage to political effect. Genuinely furious, he had exploded that protectionist lobbyists were so numerous in Washington that "a brick couldn't be thrown without hitting one of them." Having gotten the public's attention, he had maneuvered the Senate, where Democrats had only a thin majority, into conducting an inquiry into the conflicts of interest tainting numerous senators. During the first week

---

* According to Willis, since the Bryan faction in the House had no commitment to reform, "it was believed that the only way to get their support would be that of enlisting the direct aid of Mr. Bryan himself" (*The Federal Reserve System*, p. 210).

in June, the public was treated to a spectacle, as senator after senator confessed to personal investments that had been favored by duty protection ratified by their own votes. Senator Nathan Bryan of Florida testified to interests in an orange grove; William Jackson of Maryland that he was part owner of a lumber mill; Henry F. Lippitt of Rhode Island to holdings in cotton. The revelations were highly embarrassing. Although Republicans continued to engage in delaying tactics, they were now too scandalized to vote against reform. Senator Robert La Follette rejoiced, "The country is indebted to President Wilson for [blowing] the lid off the congressional lobby." Wilson had shown he could force business to back down.

WILSON WAS DETERMINED to be equally tough with bankers. However, banking was a more challenging subject. As he sifted through the maze of conflicting opinions, he summoned Louis Brandeis for a consultation at the White House. Brandeis was not a member of the administration, and in his law career he had focused on railroads and utilities—not banking. But Wilson had immense respect for him (bolstered by his effective advice during the campaign). Brandeis met with the President on June 11 and, as Wilson requested, memorialized his thoughts by letter immediately after. A few phrases will demonstrate that Brandeis regarded the financial class—insofar as it sought a public role—with contempt. Although he recognized that bankers were experts in their industry, he warned the President, "It is extremely dangerous to follow their advice even in a field technically their own." According to Brandeis, advice from financiers would inevitably be self-interested, and the conflict between the administration's goals and what bankers wanted was "irreconcilable." Therefore, concessions to bankers would prove "futile." He advised Wilson to insist on public control of the currency and to limit the role of bankers to a strictly advisory one.

Wilson must have expected that the fiery Brandeis would deliver such an impassioned response; most likely, it solidified the President in his own views. On the evening of June 17—six days after Brandeis's visit—Wilson held a parley with Glass, Owen, and McAdoo in the Cabinet Room of the White House, and informed them he had decided, as Glass put it, "to eliminate all banking representation from the Federal Reserve Board." The board would be composed of three cabinet-level officers (the Treasury secretary, the comptroller of the currency, and the agriculture secretary) and four presidential appointees. McAdoo, having given up his own plan with reluctance, agreed that government should be "in the saddle." Owen, of course, went along as well. Only Glass objected—vehemently. The Virginian, fearing that bankers would abandon the bill, actually took their side, protesting that it was an "injustice" to deny bankers (who were putting up the capital) a voice in the new entity. Resorting to a familiar tactic, Glass argued that Wilson's position would raise political obstacles, especially with Republicans in the Senate. The debate lasted two hours, but the President wouldn't budge. Not only did he opt for a fully political board, he scotched—at Bryan's insistence—a key demand of bankers: namely, that the government insulate them during the transition by fully protecting them against losses in their holdings of government bonds. (Under the prevailing system, these bonds were required to issue National Bank Notes, and thus benefited from artificially high demand; under the new system, their value was expected to drop.)

When Glass returned to the Raleigh Hotel, he ran into a fellow Banking Committee member, the Ohio Democrat Robert Bulkley, and kept him up until one a.m. stewing over Wilson's decision. Still unable to sleep, Glass wrote a note, in florid script on Raleigh letterhead, to Willis, advising him that the President had decided to make the board "an entirely government affair." In the morning, the still despairing Glass sent a missive to Wilson, pleading with him to reconsider what the congressman viewed as a "grave mistake." Glass was deluding himself: Wilson had deliberated at length and was not about to change his mind.

As Willis recognized, Wilson's decision heralded a change "of first rank." It was, Willis said, "a yielding of the classical doctrine of laissez-faire in banking in favor of the idea of public participation and direction." No single decision of Wilson better indicated the turn toward a larger federal presence in society. Democrats would be the party of small-government Jeffersonians no more.

Wilson promptly recalled Glass to the White House, where he hit him with another brick: Federal Reserve notes were to be "obligations of the United States," just as Bryan had demanded. This sounded to Glass like heresy—government money. However, Wilson elaborated that the government imprimatur would be mostly window dressing. The new notes would still be issued to member banks by the Federal Reserve Banks in exchange for safe and short-term bank loans, and only on condition that the Reserve Bank had gold in the vault equal to one-third of the notes issued. In other words—and just as Glass had demanded—reserve notes would still be bank money, and backed by specie, but with an added and perhaps redundant layer of government endorsement. "If we can hold to the substance of the thing and give the other fellow the shadow," Wilson said artfully, "why not do it, if thereby we may save our bill?"

Glass, feeling he had won after all, was immediately persuaded. Bryan, now, also agreed to support the bill. This meant that Owen would go along as well. It has been suggested that Bryan didn't realize that the notes would retain much of the character of private bank issues and that, in effect, he had been played. It is also possible that Bryan sensed that once paper currency—even in a superficial sense—was proclaimed to be an obligation of the United States, people would begin to think of money differently. The long march of the twentieth century would be toward government dollars (such as circulate today) unfettered by any link to either bank assets or to specie. Wilson's compromise was a step in that direction: a step, that is, toward fiat currency.

On June 20, the text of the bill (with the changes ordered by Wilson) was finally released and published in newspapers across the country. Editorial reaction was harsh. To conservative publishers, the notion of the federal government's controlling a large, private industry was new and profoundly shocking. Opinion writers said the bill represented a surrender to the philosophy of Bryan. The *New York Sun*, an organ of Wall Street, said the measure was "covered all over with the slime of Bryanism." If so, then the Reichsbank and the Bank of France, whose directors and governors, respectively, were appointed by the state, were covered with the same slime, a point the *Sun* overlooked. The more dispassionate *New York Times* conceded that the Glass bill had much to recommend it. Nonetheless, it termed the measure "radical" and judged it to be the work of bank-hating populists (which hardly described Carter Glass). The *Washington Post*, daunted by the prospect of a banking system run by political appointees, warily predicted that the power to be lodged in the new Federal Reserve Board could be "greater in some respects than the power now wielded by the President of the United States."

Wilson smoothly deflected the criticism. When a reporter noted that critics were calling it "the Bryanesque bill," the President retorted, "Those things don't count. It will be called all kinds of a thing before they get through with it."

The administration had more pressing concerns than editorial carping. Members of the House Banking Committee, realizing the bill had been prepared without their input, were in a sullen and rebellious mood. Wilson, at Glass's urging, invited the committee Democrats to the White House and implored them to support the bill (it eased his task that Bryan made his endorsement public). Nonetheless, the President confided to his friend Mary Peck that he was preoccupied with the banking bill—"Not an hour can I let it out of my mind." It was a difficult subject for him:

> It is not like the tariff, about which opinion has been forming long years through. There are almost as many judgments as there are men. To form a single plan and a single intention about it seems at times a task so various and so elusive that it is hard to keep one's heart from failing.

Presenting the legislation, Wilson broke with tradition again. On June 23, formally got up in black frock coat, gray trousers, and a dark cravat, the President returned to the Capitol. His wife and two of their daughters were seated in the President's pew. Speaker of the House Champ Clark (whom Wilson had bested at the Democratic convention) rapped his gavel, and Wilson, accompanied by Secret Service men, entered from a doorway in the rear. All rose, he ascended the rostrum, and Clark announced the President of the United States. Wilson read his speech, nodding on occasional words for emphasis. It took only nine minutes. He stressed—fittingly, on such a sweltering afternoon—that the hardship of working through the "heated season" was no excuse for delay. "We must act now," he said, snapping his jaws at the word, "at whatever sacrifice to ourselves."

Wilson depicted banking reform as a companion to still pending tariff reductions—together, the two measures would set business free from the twin shackles of arbitrary duties and inadequate credit. He cited three principles for banking reform. One was the cliché that the currency should be "elastic," by which he meant flexible in quantity, to meet the ebb and flow of demand. Another echoed Warburg: "Our banking laws must mobilize reserves," Wilson said. And this, he asserted, would accomplish a third purpose—abolishing the concentration of monetary resources "in [just] a few hands." Banks,

Wilson concluded ringingly, should be the instruments and not the masters of business.

THE AMERICAN BANKERS ASSOCIATION, members of whose currency commission were conveniently meeting in New York, at the Waldorf Hotel, now went on a counterattack. The view of midwestern bankers, including James Forgan, president of the First National Bank of Chicago, was emphatically negative. Bankers had urged reform for years; now that it looked as though reform could bring about federal control, they were not so happy.

Bankers generally applauded the aspect of individual Reserve Banks, which Willis had designed to be owned by banks and run by bankers—so-called bankers' banks. However, La Salle Street was uncomfortable with the central board—a public body—and unsettled that the Glass bill authorized Washington to determine the key interest rate, known as the discount rate, in each district.

Many bankers also objected to the compulsory shifting of reserves. Country banks would lose the interest they collected from depositing funds in banks in the city; city banks would lose control of the money. Breaking this dependent relationship was, of course, one of the primary purposes of the legislation. The goal was to establish collective reserves to replace the archaic pattern of every bank for itself. In practice, many bankers treated their vault reserves as a drug that—however harmful in theory—was impossible to give up. Laughlin observed, with justification, that the banks cared less about reform than about their "selfish private interests." It is also true that many bankers were frightened by the prospect of being forced to fundamentally alter how they did business.

Two days after Wilson's appearance on Capitol Hill, Glass, who was still feeling protective toward the industry, led a troop of bankers—including Wade of St. Louis, Reynolds of Chicago, and Sol Wexler from New Orleans, all influential members of the ABA's currency commission—to see the President. McAdoo and Owen were present, but it was Glass's show. The congressman was in the awkward position of providing moral support to the bankers as they lobbied for changes to his own bill. The hard-driving Wade, who had emigrated from Ireland in infancy and worked in construction as a boy before becoming a banker, struck a contrast with the scholarly Wilson, whose office was lined with leather-bound books. Wade spoke forcefully against Wilson's all-political board. "Will one of you gentlemen," the President shot back, "tell me in which civilized country of the earth there are important government boards of control on which private interests are represented?" A painful silence followed.

The bankers lost that round, but they won important concessions. Discount rates would be set by each individual Reserve Bank, subject to Washington's approval. (Given that banks would have more control at the Reserve Bank level, bankers were eager to shift power away from the center.) Second, the problematic government bonds would be refinanced, removing the threat of losses as banks transitioned to the new system. Third and most remarkably, banks would be permitted, at the discretion of the Reserve Board, to keep a portion of their reserves in banks downstream, as they had done for years. Wilson and Glass were foolish to give in on this point, which threatened the integrity of the system. In return, Glass believed he had won the bankers' promise of support.

The following day, June 26, Glass and Owen introduced identical bills in their respective chambers. Far from a radical manifesto, Glass-Owen struck a sensible middle ground, with power shared between the center and the regions and between the public and private domains.* Save for the concessions to Bryan, the proposed Reserve system was essentially faithful to what central bank partisans

---

* After June 26, the legislation that was to become the Federal Reserve Act was commonly referred to as both the "Glass-Owen" bill and the "Owen-Glass" bill. For the sake of consistency, this text will use "Glass-Owen."

such as Warburg had been preaching. Thus, reserve requirements had been cut and the number of Reserve Banks had been trimmed, to "not less than twelve" (still too many to Warburg's liking). Perhaps most remarkably, given the Democratic Party's hostility to centralism, Wilson's innocent "capstone" had evolved into something approaching the dominant central organ that Wall Street had been hankering for. As now proposed, the Federal Reserve Board had authority to require one Reserve Bank to lend money to another, supervise each Reserve Bank's issue of notes, examine their books, and, if it chose, remove their executives. Also dear to Wall Street's heart, Glass-Owen permitted the Reserve Banks to finance import and export trade.

No onlooker in 1913 could have predicted that one day the Fed's most well-advertised duty would be setting interest rates. The bill's primary purpose was to mobilize reserves, the better to avert a crisis, and to modernize the banking system. Its emphasis was on the mechanics of how the Reserve Banks would provide liquidity to banks— that is, by purchasing their short-term loans. However, an intriguing clause stated that interest rates should be adjusted "with a view to accommodating the commerce of the country and promoting a stable price level." Buried in that phrase was the suggestion of what became, through a subsequent act of Congress, the Fed's dual mandate— promoting growth and minimizing inflation.

Glass imagined that since the banks had (mostly) prevailed and since Bryan, too, had been placated, both his left and his right flank were covered. In fact, neither of them was. Harmony with the banks was shattered first. At the White House, Glass had understood the bankers to promise unwavering support. The bankers, actually, left Washington supportive of the bill in general, but still determined to fight for improvements. After conferring with colleagues, they realized that much of the industry was still opposed. Country banks found the requirement that they subscribe to stock in their local Reserve Bank too onerous. Chicago was terrified of losing deposits and wanted even more modifications to the reserves clause. Wall Street was exceedingly hostile to federal control. Warburg, summering in the Swiss alpine village of Sils-Maria, finally got hold of a copy of the bill and, though satisfied with most of its provisions, was horrified by the concessions to Bryan. He cabled House, "Is there anything I can do in the currency situation? It looks to me as if they were bungling it most terribly."* One by one, the Aldrich crowd was roused into resistance. Davison begged Aldrich to meet and plan a counterstrategy. Andrew penned a damning review of the bill, calling it "Bryanized."

The ABA was also critical, although some of its members were willing to bargain for half a loaf. Reynolds and Wade expected to support the bill, but wanted to see improvements first. Forgan, the closest that Chicago had to a J. P. Morgan, was simply opposed. At sixty-one, Forgan was older than other ABA leaders and, with his wide sideburns and handlebar mustache, considerably more steeped in nineteenth-century traditions. Forgan distributed to members of the House Banking Committee a pamphlet asserting that the bill would pose a danger to the country. *The New York Times,* parroting Forgan as well as New York bankers, hyperbolically submitted that the bankers' objections rendered the bill, in its present form, "dead and done for." As veterans of Gettysburg gathered in Washington to commemorate the fiftieth anniversary of the Civil War battle, the flimsy consensus on banking seemed to be melting in the summer heat.

Glass, who had mightily extended himself for the bankers, was livid. He regarded the bankers' renewed demands as a renunciation of their "agreement." Abruptly, he decided that his banker allies could not be trusted and shifted into what Willis was to describe as a state of "warfare." Glass withdrew his offer to compromise and reinstated language making it compulsory that banks pull their reserves from

---

* The mountain air did not lower Warburg's temperature. Toward the end of July he fumed to Colonel House that if Glass-Owen was enacted in its current state, "history will write down President Wilson as a complete failure and Bryan will once more have ruined the chances of the Democratic Party."

banks in the cities and park them, more securely, in the Federal Reserve banks, with a portion kept in their own vaults. Even if he had acted in pique, it was a sensible move that resurrected the bill's essential purpose.

Early in July, Glass and McAdoo attempted, once again, to mollify the bankers. The government's 2 percent bonds mysteriously began to trade lower, to a point where banks, which held some $700 million of these bonds, were threatened with serious losses. Banks had purchased these bonds so that, under the National Banking Act, they would be entitled to circulate bank notes. McAdoo and Glass sympathized with the banks, feeling that since the government now was changing the rules, bondholders should be protected. Evidently— to judge from the bonds' cascading prices—the recent changes to the bill had not done the trick. In short order, the bill was further amended, seemingly guaranteeing the bonds' value.

However, the bonds continued to plummet. McAdoo smelled a rat. Never very trusting of Wall Street, the onetime tunnel financier hotly accused New York bankers of conspiring to artificially drive down prices to frighten country banks and turn them against the bill.

Such a conspiracy was unlikely, but the ill will between Wall Street and the administration was not so easily repaired. In a public letter, Vanderlip threatened that if the legislation retained its noxious element of federal control, the country's seventy-five hundred national banks would feel free to recharter as state banks (for whom membership was voluntary), take their $11 billion in assets, and defect from the National Banking system. The threat to desert the new Federal Reserve—even before it was created—was a gun to the head. But if Vanderlip imagined that either McAdoo or Glass might back down, he was deluded. It was a measure of his remove that even while threatening to undermine the system, Vanderlip affected a haughty air of noblesse oblige, insisting that only businessmen—not public officials—should be trusted to look after the public interest. "There must, in fact, be a central bank and that is what the proposed measure creates," Vanderlip said curtly. "The objection is not to the powers granted but to the hands in which they are placed."

While McAdoo and Glass were sparring with banks, House Democrats began to savage the bill for being too kind to bankers. Wilson at first underestimated the threat. However, in mid-July, he confided to Ellen, who was spending her maiden summer as First Lady at an artists' colony in Cornish, New Hampshire, "We have a difficult Banking and Currency Committee to deal with in the House." Actually, it was more serious than that. Rural Democratic congressmen from the West and South, known as "agrarians," were much like the populist agitators of the nineteenth century. Rather than use silver-backed money to inflate commodity prices, the latest crop of populists wanted to channel more bank loans directly to farmers, who still made up some 30 percent of the U.S. population. Although the Glass-Owen bill specifically included bank loans to agriculture as being eligible for Federal Reserve discounts, the agrarians were wary of leaving the process up to bankers. They also feared that the new central bank would become too cozy toward member banks, and even, in an emergency, protect the banks from losses. (This fear would look prescient during the financial crisis of 2008.) However, agrarians were not opposed to government protection—they simply wanted it extended toward farmers rather than banks.

The spiritual leader of the agrarians was Robert Henry, a Texas Democrat who was chairman of the House Rules Committee. Henry was an engaging talker, who traded on his reputation for being close to Bryan and commanded loyalty among backcountry members of the Banking Committee. Henry insisted that the Federal Reserve Board should include a bona fide farmworker as well as a representative of organized labor. To bankers, this was worse than a board of politicians. Even more troubling to the orthodoxy, Henry challenged the basis of the new Federal Reserve notes. Mistrusting bankers, Henry disliked any sort of currency that was based on bank assets. He wanted the bill amended so that agricultural assets (such as warehouse receipts) would become the basis of money. This new money would be loaned, on generous terms, to farmers.

On July 23, the agrarians on the Banking Committee broke into open rebellion, proposing a controversial amendment to ban interlocking directorates (preventing any director from serving on the board of more than one national bank). The amendment was extraneous to monetary reform, and though it was sound from a corporate-governance perspective, in the context of the Glass-Owen legislation it was a volatile distraction. Knowing that it would extinguish whatever support still remained among bankers, Glass opposed it. The amendment was adopted over his protest. With his committee, and his bill, in crisis, fireworks erupted. James Ragsdale, a South Carolina ally of Henry, proposed a series of amendments to fundamentally alter the bill. The most eye-catching would direct the Reserve Banks to issue $700 million worth of loans divided among three new classes of United States currency (each to a powerful interest group): $300 million for ordinary business loans, $200 million for state projects such as bridges and roads, and $200 million to corn, cotton, and wheat farmers. In other words, bank credit was to be apportioned by the U.S. Congress. Bankers, who had considered this to be their job, were naturally appalled. The amendments, apparently inspired by Henry, were, according to the shocked editors of the *Times,* "quite beyond the pale of discussion." It was unclear whether Henry had the support of Bryan, which he seemed to be reckoning on. But plainly, Glass had lost control of the Banking Committee. Wilson would need to step in again.

CHAPTER THIRTEEN

"THE IMPOSSIBLE HAS HAPPENED"

Fleeing from the evils of Wall Street and a private
monopoly, we rush headlong and pell-mell into the
arms of a great public monopoly.
—REPRESENTATIVE THOMAS W. HARDWICK,
on the Glass-Owen bill

Isn't it wonderful?
—WOODROW WILSON TO ELLEN WILSON,
September 19, 1913, the day following House passage

OVER LATE JULY AND AUGUST, Wilson was buffeted by a series
of difficult challenges. As his biographer Arthur Link put it, "During
that epochal summer of 1913 Wilson and his advisers moved from
crisis to crisis." The revolution in Mexico had spun out of control,
with the strongman General Victoriano Huerta seizing dictatorial

powers and various rivals mounting armed attacks. The insecurity along the border, as well as the threat to American citizens and business interests, thrust the President into his first international crisis. Over the summer, he recalled America's ambassador, appointed a new envoy, and gave his first address on foreign policy, proclaiming of the turmoil to the south, "Those conditions touch us very nearly." Wilson was meanwhile struggling to push tariff reform to a vote in the Senate, its last lap before enactment. The measure included an income tax—the first ever in peacetime.

On Glass-Owen, the President was occupied at two levels: fending off threats from bankers and dealing with the revolt in the House Banking Committee. The latter in particular upset him. Intraparty strife was the virus that had undone Taft, and Wilson was determined not to give factionalism any quarter. He worked closely with Carter Glass, who provided the President with a list of nine troublesome committee members, asking Wilson to call them (that he complied is suggested by the check marks the President made beside each name). Wilson also insisted, in his public comments, that Glass-Owen would be approved without any significant changes. Although news reports were often pessimistic, the President reassured his wife, Ellen, "Discount what you see in the papers." He went on to explain, "It happens, by very hard luck, that practically *all* the men likely to oppose and give trouble, whether in the House or in the Senate, are on the committees now handling the matter. When once it is out of their hands, I believe that we shall have comparatively plain sailing."

The agrarians, led by Robert Henry, sought to fundamentally alter the bill, and Wilson's leadership was critical in overcoming them. He summoned several congressmen to the Oval Office, cajoling, imploring, and pressuring them to fall in line. A master of parliamentary process, the President calculated that the legislation would fare better in the full House than in the Banking Committee. Glass, therefore, moved it to a caucus of the House Democrats, where a favorable reception was considered likely. Once the caucus approved the measure, it would become binding on every Democrat in the House. Also at Wilson's prompting, Glass obtained a gag order on the fractious members of his committee.

However, the caucus deliberations, which had been expected to last only several days, dragged on for most of August. Henry was not a member of the Banking Committee, but in the caucus he had free rein. Henry charged that the bill was a redo of the Aldrich Plan of 1910 (which, in large part, it was) and that it violated the legacy of Jackson. More to the point, he quoted a speech by Bryan, when the Commoner had been in Congress, in opposition to then President Cleveland. The powerful implication was that Bryan also sided with Henry against the President now. Since Henry's chief demands— to substitute a more expansive currency, and to ban interlocking boards—were issues that Bryan had championed for most of his career, the threat was entirely credible.

Although the caucus debate was mostly superficial, it touched on the issue that had vexed Americans throughout their history: What is the proper basis of money? In modern times, the Fed influences the money supply by buying and selling Treasury securities (buying securities will add to the money supply). A member bank can also borrow from the discount window of the local Federal Reserve Bank by pledging many of the forms of collateral (such as its loans to customers) envisioned in 1913. However, the discount window is used on a limited basis—mainly when banks need liquidity to cover a shortfall. The 2008 financial crisis was a prime example, when banks—as envisioned by Paul Warburg—did pledge commercial paper, as well as other assets, to get loans from the Fed. But the ordinary channel through which banks get stacks of dollars to distribute to customers has evolved. Generally, banks request currency from their Reserve Bank, in return for which the Fed debits the account that each bank maintains at the Fed. Once again, during the financial crisis and its aftermath, the Fed made use of an improvised avenue for creating liquidity—directly purchasing assets such as Treasury bonds and certain mortgage-backed securities. These moves were controversial; at the margin, the determination of what sort of paper is worthy of being converted into "money" remains a matter of judgment and, to some extent, arbitrary.

The principle of the Glass-Owen bill was that the new Federal Reserve Banks would make this determination by deciding which bank loans to "discount," or exchange for reserve notes—that is, for money. The guidelines in the bill were favorable to commerce; for instance, Reserve Banks were authorized to discount commercial paper as well as bills of trade based on imports and exports.

Henry objected that the legislation "should be fair to the farmer and allow him to have money based on his assets upon the same terms." The point was hardly trivial. People held all sorts of financial assets—bills of lading, merchant IOUs, and so forth. Those that could be converted into currency would obviously be in a privileged position. Although the legislation permitted banks to convert agricultural loans to reserve notes, Henry continued to insist that farm assets—a warehouse receipt for grain, say—should be convertible directly into money. His proposal surely would have led to inflation. However, it's well to note that monetary arrangements are always man-made contrivances; none can claim perfection much less divine inspiration. Paul Volcker, the Fed chief during most of the 1980s, attempted to run policy by counting the total of money in circulation; he soon forsook this approach, known as "monetarism," because no useful definition of money existed.

Glass-Owen simply represented one of the better approaches of its day. The mechanism for converting bank loans into currency appealed to bankers because it seemed to place the new central bank in a passive position; the Fed would mint reserve notes only if, and as, banks presented it with acceptable commercial paper.* But there was

---

* This was the real bills theory discussed in chapter 1. I am indebted to Robert Craig West, *Banking Reform and the Federal Reserve*, especially pp. 153–54 and 172–73.

plenty of room for argument over just which paper should be "acceptable." Moreover, the legislation was slightly contradictory. On the one hand, it set a practical limit on how many notes the Reserve Banks could issue, by establishing rules on what sort of bank assets they could exchange for notes. On the other hand, the bill required the Reserve Banks to limit the circulation of notes to a set proportion of their gold (and to redeem their notes for gold on demand); this established an alternate set of monetary brakes. In effect, the legislation created two, not always consistent, limits on the circulation.

Wilson, of course, did not involve himself in questions of theory. His priority was to furnish a more "elastic" currency and to make the credit system more resilient by knitting the banks into a unified whole. The President's other expressed goal, to "democratize" banking, was mostly rhetoric.

When the bill was in caucus, Bryan asked Wilson to add language to placate the agrarians. Glass objected that "a lot of bunk was being handed out to the farmer." Nonetheless, he allowed a phrase to be inserted stating explicitly that the act did not prohibit banks from discounting paper "secured by staple agricultural products, or other goods, wares, or merchandise." It is doubtful that this clause changed any of the substance. It certainly did not satisfy Henry, who continued to push for radical changes.

Adding to the legislation's difficulties, Senator Robert Owen, who was overly impressed by monetary critics and cranks, gave out in an interview that he no longer advocated a regional reserve system—which, as the *Times* noted, "is the essence of the bill that bears his name." Owen may well have been influenced by the budding rebellion in the House. In any case, Wilson summoned Owen to the White House on August 20 (the day the senator's comments were published), jerking him back into line. Even though Owen's apostasy was quickly aborted, it was alarming on account of his closeness with Bryan. Glass concluded that only Bryan could get the bill unstuck. Soon, an opportunity presented itself.

On August 22, Henry addressed the House caucus, demanding that it support the ban on interlocking boards. Glass was ready for him. With a theatrical flourish, the bantam chairman retrieved from his pocket a letter that, he revealed—glancing at Henry—had been addressed to him from the secretary of state. Glass began to read. In the letter, Bryan noted that he had long advocated a ban on interlocking directorates. However, he said, "care must be taken not to overload a good measure with amendments, however good those amendments may be in themselves." Bryan went on in that statesmanlike vein, asserting that the bill was correct with regard to the few principal points that mattered. As for the rest, he authorized Glass to say that he, Bryan, stood entirely with the President—"I am with him on all the details."

Witnesses said the Democrats broke into cheers. Glass, never a gracious winner, recorded for posterity that Henry turned "white with anger." In any case, Henry was beaten. Wilson promised to address the issue of bank directors in a subsequent antitrust measure.[*] Although the caucus tarried for another week, it overwhelmingly approved Glass-Owen, with only minor changes.

Just as the caucus deliberations were reaching a climax, the currency commission of the American Bankers Association held a parley in Chicago and unanimously recommended a set of draconian amendments—without which, they strongly implied, support for the bill would be withheld.[†] The ringleader was James Forgan, who called Glass-Owen "unworkable" and crossed a line by tarring Glass, personally, as "incompetent." This was so strong that Forgan was forced

---

[*] In 1914 Wilson signed the Clayton Antitrust Act, prohibiting directors from serving on the boards of more than one bank when either of the banks had capital, surplus, and deposits aggregating to more than $5 million.

[†] Among other demands, the bankers wanted a central bank or at most a handful of Reserve Banks, rather than the twelve in Glass-Owen; they wanted three Reserve Board directors chosen by bankers; they wanted to let banks continue depositing some reserves in private banks; and they wanted membership in the new system to be voluntary.

to issue an apology. More important, the ABA's aggressive tactics backfired. Its supposedly "unanimous" vote, it developed, had been secured by railroading the two hundred bankers present and stifling dissent. Many of the bankers, led by George Reynolds, thought it would be wiser to negotiate with the administration and had urged a more conciliatory stance. An even wider chasm separated the big banks in Chicago, who dominated the proceedings, from smaller country banks. For instance, the ABA demanded that bankers be given a voice on the Federal Reserve Board; country bankers, fearful of their urban brethren, preferred to have oversight by the government. And despite the ABA's advocacy of a single central bank, rural bankers liked the idea of a regional network.

Word of the industry's divisions leaked to the Wilson administration. As Treasury Secretary McAdoo confided to Colonel House, "The action of the banks at Chicago, although upon the surface unanimous, was . . . far from reflecting the real sentiments of that meeting. I am advised that fully half of those present in their hearts favored the bill." McAdoo was further buoyed by evidence that, outside the banking fraternity, Glass-Owen was increasingly popular. The publisher of the influential *Charlotte Daily Observer* figured that Glass-Owen, if enacted, would "distribute the money over the whole U.S. much more equally." In North Carolina, he approvingly predicted, it would spare cotton millers from having to go to New York for money. The U.S. Chamber of Commerce conducted a field study in eleven states west of the Missouri River and reported "a strong desire" on the part of businesspeople for Congress to act. Based on such reports and on his own contacts with bankers and others, McAdoo felt confident enough to reject the Chicago manifesto out of hand. Parker Willis similarly urged Glass to ignore the ABA, whose conference he judged a "fiasco."

In the second week of September, Glass brought the bill to the House floor. Sensing that the members remained uncomfortable with the prospect of creating a powerful federal agency, Glass downplayed the legislation's impact. For the most part, he maintained, the bill would merely reassign powers that had long been exercised by the secretary of the Treasury and the comptroller of the currency. The Reserve Board, he suggested, would function as an "altruistic institution . . . with powers such as no man would dare misuse." This was remarkably naïve. Frank Mondell, a Republican from Wyoming, was more perceptive—or more candid—in recognizing the bill's landmark character. "Not only is its power, authority, and control vast," he warned of the prospective Fed, "but it is of a character which in practical operation would tend to increase and centralize."

Charles Lindbergh, another Republican opponent from the heartland, violently criticized the bill—among other reasons, for authorizing the Fed to operate overseas in support of foreign trade. Lindbergh's nativism was striking, since his constituents in Minnesota depended on exports and the congressman himself was an immigrant. But xenophobia had been a hallmark of monetary populists since the early days of the republic. It did not die easily. A generation later, when the United States was facing a mortal threat from Nazi Germany, Lindbergh's aviator son would urge America to stay out of "foreign" wars.

Owing to the Democrats' large majority, the debate in the House was brief. The Republicans tried to distract the chamber by proposing an amendment endorsing the gold standard (which the legislation had left untouched). As expected, some of the Democrats became aroused by the mention of the Republican metal and wanted to substitute "coin" for "gold," to include a place for silver. Fearing a tempest, Glass called Bryan. The Commoner had no interest in revisiting old crusades and advised that silver was "irrelevant." On September 18, the gold standard amendment was approved. Hours later, Glass-Owen passed by a thumping vote of 285–85. All but three Democrats voted in favor.

Glass could not have done it without Bryan, and Bryan, surely the least likely man to champion a central bank, had cooperated only due to Wilson's dogged courtship and careful compromising. Willis ascribed the credit "almost exclusively to the unswerving determination of the President." Wilson was elated. He wrote to his "own darling," Ellen, that he was overjoyed to see the bill pass "by so splendid a majority."

Nevertheless, the outlook in the Senate was problematic. Local control was less of a concern in the upper chamber, and many senators agreed with the ABA that twelve Reserve Banks were well too many. The Republicans on the Banking Committee favored a more centralized approach and so did two of the Democrats—Gilbert Hitchcock of Nebraska and James O'Gorman of New York. Another Democrat, James Reed of Missouri, was a demagogue and reflexively oppositional. Without those three, the Democrats' 7–5 majority on the committee would shrink to a 4–8 minority.

In contrast to the brisk proceedings in the House, the Senate committee scheduled extensive hearings, with a witness list that was stacked with fault-finding bankers. Forgan was the lead witness; he insisted that Congress ditch Glass-Owen for a single bank. Festus Wade, objecting to the bill's compulsory features, was even harsher. "To many of us, and I admit I am one, this bill is repulsive," the banker said. As such views were known, the purpose of the hearings was less to inform than to sow discord and delay.

Owen, who was not an effective chair, sought to cut the proceedings short, but the Democratic holdouts ganged up with the minority and the hearings dragged on. The list of witnesses included a hardware executive from Duluth, a lumber merchant from Minneapolis, a smattering of economists and lawyers, and a parade of bankers. The quarrelsome senators brazenly led their witnesses and tried to elicit negative comments. Despite their efforts, a rich diversity of viewpoints emerged. A telling exchange occurred between Senator Hitchcock and Thomas McRae, a country banker from Prescott, Arkansas, whose tiny institution boasted capital and surplus of a mere $150,000. McRae, like other Arkansas bankers, was accustomed to spreading his reserves among banks in New York, St. Louis, and Little Rock.

Under Glass-Owen, McRae would be forced to shift his reserves to the nearest Federal Reserve Bank. Hitchcock, emphasizing the bill's coercive character, tried to goad him into denouncing it. McRae did not bite.

> HITCHCOCK: You have the power to control it. Do you want all that wiped out, to have all your eggs put in one basket and no assurance that your paper will be discounted when you present it?
>
> McRAE: Your question assumes that the place where I can now present my paper will have plenty of money to accommodate me. This was not true in 1907.

McRae testified that, given the ever present threat of a panic, prudence required him to operate with an overabundance of cash. The cotton farmers in Prescott did their borrowing from March through the summer; when the loan season peaked, McRae generally put $2 million in the safe, just to have on hand. The money, in other words, sat idle. "The purpose of this bill," McRae volunteered, lecturing the senator, "is to require public funds of the United States to be kept in circulation."

But country bankers, with their deeply held suspicions of centralized banking, did have concerns. They were unhappy at being made to invest their capital in the Federal Reserve when dividends would be capped at 5 percent—less than they typically earned on loans. And they feared that under the new system, the cumbersome process for clearing checks would be overhauled, rationalizing a business on which they earned tidy fees.

Wall Street's view of the bill was ambiguous. Bankers were vocal with a few key criticisms but favored the bill's guiding principle of concentrating reserves. And they tended to be less oppositional in private. Warburg was a prime example. Appalled by the populist rhetoric of politicians, he adamantly opposed putting the banks under political control. In an article published just before he returned from Switzerland, Warburg fulminated that "in our country, with every untrained amateur a candidate for any office . . . a political management would prove fatal." Yet Warburg's criticisms, relayed from his mountain lair in Europe via Colonel House, were always intended to improve the Glass-Owen legislation—not to forestall it. Reform had been his idea, and he remained an avid supporter.

If Warburg's view was predictably double-edged, Frank Vanderlip's was maddeningly inconsistent. In midsummer, heading into an uncertain harvest, the head of America's largest bank had publicly warned Glass that the bill's weaknesses were such that it would be better not to have a bill at all; in the fall, as money market conditions eased, his mood improved. By late September, Vanderlip was confessing to James Stillman, "The more consideration I give to the currency bill, the more I am inclined to believe that we need not be frightened [of it]."

With bankers' opinions scattered and shifting, the industry could do little to break the impasse in the Senate Banking Committee. Inevitably, the responsibility defaulted to the President. Ellen Wilson had remained in Cornish through the Indian summer, and in that era, when long-distance telephoning was a luxury, even the First Family communicated via the mail. Wilson tried to reassure his fretful wife not to worry about the bill or its effect on him—"Don't be anxious about me," read one typical passage. Ellen, often depressed, disregarded him and inquired about the flood of worrisome news stories. Wilson was more candid with his friend Mary Peck, to whom he wrote in late September, "The struggle goes on down here without intermission. Why it should *be* a struggle is hard (cynicism put on one side) to say." Frustrated by the committee's refusal to act, the idealistic Wilson wondered why "public men" should have to be led "to what all the country knows to be their duty."

Once again, he moved on the tariff first. The President leaned full bore on the Senate, which (remarkably) approved more drastic cuts than the House. On October 3, using two gold pens, Wilson signed the Revenue Act of 1913, sharply reducing tariff rates from the Aldrich tariff of 1909. The measure also instituted an income tax of 1 percent above $4,000 and steeper rates on higher incomes. Secretary of Agriculture David Houston could scarcely believe it. "A progressive income tax!" he noted with astonishment. "I did not much think we should live to see these things." Vanderlip offered the jaundiced, and accurate, prophecy that the income tax would be "extremely annoying. The machinery of collection will make it as unpopular as the tax itself."

A cornerstone in the progressive agenda, the income tax was a harbinger of the coming era of big government. However, to Americans of the day, few of whom reached the threshold of taxation, the tariff cuts seemed more epochal.* For Wilson, who had always regarded the tariff as a burden on ordinary citizens to benefit northern manufacturers, the legislation fulfilled a long-standing dream. Yet the reform, he felt, would not be complete until Congress also reformed the banking system. Even at the White House signing ceremony, the President was mindful of unfinished business. "So I feel tonight," he offered poetically, "like a man who is lodging happily in the inn which lies half way along the journey."

Intent on cracking the whip over the Banking Committee, Wilson tabled plans for an extended vacation with Ellen in New Hampshire and put off a visit to Panama, where the American canal was nearing completion. Nor, he insisted, would he allow Congress to recess before the Senate dealt with Glass-Owen. Congress was still in the "special session" that had started in the spring. The regular session would begin on December 1. Wilson was adamant that the Senate give him a proper banking bill before that date, so he could then

---

* The tariff cuts were destined to be of little consequence. Within a year of the legislation, World War I had broken out, disrupting world trade. After the war, once Republicans were returned to office, tariff rates were raised again.

shift his focus to antitrust reform. But the opposition would not be quieted.

When the ABA held its annual convention in Boston, on October 8, some two thousand delegates ratified the criticisms drafted in Chicago and denounced Glass-Owen as "socialistic." A week later, Senator Nelson Aldrich emerged from the obscurity of his retirement and savaged the bill as a triumph of "Bryanism." Wilson could ignore Aldrich but the President was furious at the ABA. His mounting stack of mail—which he eagerly showed to visitors—was running heavily in support of the legislation. Both the Merchants' Association of New York and the U.S. Chamber of Commerce endorsed Glass-Owen early in October, suggesting that business was also on board. Wilson believed that the banks were trying to "poison" an otherwise favorable climate. Even though his suspicions had an element of truth, the industry was neither so united nor so calculating. America had more than 25,000 banks of various classes—some were opposed, some criticized Glass-Owen in the hope of landing a better deal, and some supported it.

Wilson next threatened to take the bill to a party caucus, essentially forcing the measure on Democrats in the Senate as he had in the House. However, given the strong opposition from Democratic senators, that step was problematic.* It also would guarantee the enmity of every Republican. The President then floated, as a trial balloon, the possibility of squeezing the refusenik senators by campaigning directly in their home states. But he realized he could not afford to alienate the Senate. He protested, a bit too loudly, to the *Washington Post,* "I never said any such thing. It is contrary to both my thought and character."

With the administration momentarily flummoxed, Treasury Secretary McAdoo invited Owen, the Senate Banking Committee chair-

---

* Legally, legislators would be free to defy a party caucus, and Senator Hitchcock made clear that he would do so.

man, aboard a revenue cutter, one of the armed ships then operated by the Treasury Department to enforce customs duties. Over two days, they anchored on the Potomac and talked strategy. On October 16, after the secretary had regrouped with his boss, Wilson unveiled a softer approach, inviting O'Gorman, Reed, and Hitchcock to separate conclaves at the White House.

Each of the three holdouts was a first-term senator with distinct reasons for defying the President. Hitchcock was a Nebraska rival to Bryan and the publisher of the influential *Omaha World-Herald*. He was fiercely independent, having abandoned the Republican Party of his father (who had also been a U.S. senator). He was not a man to bow to a president, and as a director of several Nebraska banks, Hitchcock genuinely preferred a central bank to the dozen Reserve Banks in Glass-Owen. O'Gorman's resistance was a matter of politics. A former New York judge, O'Gorman was an ally of Tammany Hall and eager to deliver the clubhouse its share of federal appointments. Wilson had seemingly slighted his need for patronage and was disdainful toward the machine, which had set O'Gorman against him. Reed, a former mayor of Kansas City, was opposed to Glass-Owen from the other political extreme—that is, he hewed to the Jacksonian tradition of opposition to any form of banking combination. Reed was a skillful speaker and a hard drinker who despised Wilson's self-righteousness. He styled himself a maverick but was contentious for its own sake, a point suggested by H. L. Mencken's later tribute: "The stature of such a man as Reed is not to be counted by his successes. The important thing is that he fights."

After the three renegades left the White House, Reed told reporters that for Glass-Owen to win the committee's support it would have to undergo drastic alteration. However, the tone of the resistance softened. Over the next several days, Reed and O'Gorman each delivered more encouraging remarks (Hitchcock was immovable). Wilson offered an olive branch by suggesting that he might be willing to compromise with proponents of a central bank by modestly reducing the number of Reserve Banks.

This more hopeful climate was shattered in less than an hour. On October 23, Vanderlip, the impulsive steward of National City Bank, appeared before the committee and dropped the equivalent of a bomb by proposing a radically different plan.

The genesis of Vanderlip's proposal was an appearance at the committee earlier in October. It is notable that, in his first testimony, although he found fault with various technical features of the bill, such as the vagueness of its definition of the powers of the Federal Reserve Board, he was supportive overall. He testified that the legislation would rechannel into ordinary commerce millions of dollars that were currently tied up in the stock market; moreover, he stated that the new Reserve Banks, with their ability to manipulate interest rates, would give the United States newfound power to discourage the flight of gold. Privately, he expressed himself more forcefully and more candidly: the prospect of lower reserve requirements, he wrote unblushingly to Stillman, would liberate National City from having to tie up so much of its capital, and thus permit it to aggressively expand. While Vanderlip's public testimony was more circumspect, it jarred some of the members into rethinking the legislation. In an illuminating exchange, Joseph Bristow, a Kansas progressive, asked whether he would advise amending Glass-Owen so that farm mortgages could be discounted for reserve notes. Positively not, Vanderlip replied, elaborating that it was a mistake to think of banks as (merely) creditors. "Banks," he averred, "are the great debtors of the country." To be sure of satisfying their depositors, their assets had to be in liquid form. This is why the bill stipulated ninety-day commercial loans as eligible for discount. Mortgages, being the *least* liquid paper, could not be readily converted into cash. Vanderlip's insight was validated nearly a century later: modern investment bankers created an entire industry out of converting mortgages into tradable and supposedly liquid securities, but during the 2008 meltdown, these wizards discovered that mortgages were not so liquid as they had imagined. Committee members in 1913 could not have known that, but Vanderlip's superior understanding left them dazzled.

After the hearing, O'Gorman and Hitchcock approached Vanderlip with the germ of an idea: Would he consider drawing up a new plan with a unitary central bank, owned by the government? The point of such a plan would be to appeal, simultaneously, to two political extremes. Democrats, progressives, and other traditional opponents of a central bank might be able to stomach such a body if control rested in public hands, and bankers might be willing to yield on control if the country were to create a centralized institution, on a par with those in Europe.

Vanderlip's initial reaction was dubious—he did not think credit decisions should be left to the government. However, he agreed to consider it. After mulling the idea for a couple of days, he heartily embraced it. Like others before him, he seems to have become seduced by the prospect of authoring a banking reform, and let vanity cloud his judgment. In any case, he eagerly wrote to Stillman on October 10, "If the legislation is perfected along the lines that I now feel confident it can be, the City Bank will for the first time begin to reap true benefit from its great capital."

Vanderlip then called Harry Davison, the congenial Morgan banker who had proved so useful on Jekyl Island (Warburg, who was about to board a liner home from Hamburg, was unavailable), and also Ben Strong, one of the more incisive thinkers in the industry. Very quickly, and with a hint of renewed conspiracy, the trio got to work. Vanderlip reported to Stillman:

> They came to my rooms in the Plaza and we deserted all meetings or telephone calls. The result was the creation of a plan that seemed to us of very great value; one that would meet every

economic principle, that could be accepted by bankers, so far as control is concerned, and that still was ingenious enough to have met the tenets of the Democratic Party and the political exigencies of the day.

Vanderlip's optimism was misplaced. The Democratic Party platform, of course, proscribed the establishment of a central bank. Also, by eliminating the Reserve Banks, the plan would do away with the one organizational layer that was to have been run by bankers—a change unlikely to appeal to the industry.

Nevertheless, Vanderlip, now intoxicated by his mission, eagerly decamped for Washington, his two confreres in tow. They put up at the Army and Navy Club, where Senator O'Gorman resided. Vanderlip corralled O'Gorman, telling him he had the requested plan. However, the senator denied having asked for a plan. Presumably, he had had second thoughts about confronting the President so publicly. He suggested that Vanderlip present the plan as his own.

So, a fortnight after his first appearance, the National City president returned to the committee room. He now proposed a central bank with twelve branches, wholly controlled by the federal government and (to appeal to progressives) its stock held by the public. The bait for bankers was that the plan included fewer compulsory features and, of course, it was more centralized. Vanderlip's most sensible idea was to drop the three cabinet officials from the Reserve Board, which would then be composed of seven members nominated by the president, upon the "advice and consent" of the Senate—and for terms of fourteen years rather than eight. These changes would lessen the president's control, tending to a less political and more professional body.

Republicans and the three renegade Democrats immediately endorsed his plan. No one on the committee seemed to notice that Vanderlip's proposal represented a complete about-face from his previous, fervent denunciations of government control.* No matter, the Vanderlip plan suddenly had eight votes on the Banking Committee, versus four for Glass-Owen.

Vanderlip now wrote to Wilson, immodestly suggesting that his plan was "quite along the lines of your own thoughts, as I understand them." He offered to call on the President, along with Davison and Strong, "to more fully explain" it.

Wilson was stunned. There was no chance, he knew, that the House would endorse a central bank. The Democrats remained the party of Jackson. Moreover, the process was too far along to contemplate such a drastic revision. The President had completely lost patience with the big banks, and his reply was curt:

> I am at a loss to understand how you can have come to think of the bank plan which you proposed to the [committee] yesterday as "being along the lines of my own thought." It is so far from being along the lines of my thought in this matter that it would be quite useless for me to discuss it with you and Mr. Davison and Mr. Strong.

Wilson reaffirmed his support for all the essentials of Glass-Owen and summoned the Senate Democratic leaders to the White House. His message was succinct: he would not let bankers dictate policy. Not for the first time, Vanderlip had overplayed his hand.†

Because the committee was unwilling to report a central bank against the wishes of the President, the members met in daily session, testing proposals to see if anything stuck. The Republicans voted in

---

* The inconsistency did not escape Glass, who sarcastically inquired, "If these things constituted 'unsound banking' in July" why were they not "unsound banking in November." (Glass, *An Adventure in Constructive Finance*, p. 194.)

† Vanderlip remained hopeful about his proposal. On November 15, he boasted to Stillman, "There is no question at all but what the plan which I have presented to the Committee has met with the approval of the intelligent thought of the country."

a block, so the rebellious Democrats acted as swing votes. Owen tried to cobble together a majority, and Wilson coordinated with Senate leaders, but they were clearly on the defensive. At the end of October, they suffered a defeat when the committee cut the number of Reserve Banks to only four (specifying New York, Chicago, St. Louis, and San Francisco). This was a fair-sized step toward a central bank, and unacceptable to Wilson or to Democrats in the House, since it would rob the system of its federal character. Similarly, the committee, over Owen and Wilson's objections, swung toward the Vanderlip notion of offering stock in the Reserve Banks to the public rather than to banks.

Wilson agreed to drop the secretary of agriculture and the comptroller of the currency from the Reserve Board but insisted that the Treasury secretary remain. This reflected the President's desire to have McAdoo, a trusted confidant (he then was courting Wilson's youngest daughter, who was a quarter of a century younger), oversee the Fed once it got going.

The President saw the contest as a power struggle from which retreat would be disastrous. In his prior career as an academician, he had admired the way leaders in the British Parliament commanded loyalty from the party; the American chief executive, he believed, was entitled to no less. He tended to react personally to disagreement, and having made up his mind, he viewed dissension from Democrats as disloyal.

Outside the halls of Congress, support for the administration bill continued to grow. Many bankers, fearful that the chaos in the Senate Banking Committee could leave the country with no reform at all, rallied to Glass-Owen. Wade, the St. Louis banker who in September had called the bill "repulsive," now did a complete flip. He was sure, he wrote reassuringly to Wilson, that the American people would not support a central bank. Glass-Owen was the only shot. Soon after, Glass debated Vanderlip at the Hotel Astor in New York, a gala event before eleven hundred people "gay with fashion and beauty." Glass seemed to get the better of it. Vanderlip trashed the bill and pouted over the President's refusal to see him; Glass's defense of a regional system resonated with the high-toned crowd, many of whom were bankers.

Wilson and Glass got a further boost on election day: Democratic victories in New Jersey, Maryland, and Massachusetts were seen as a ratification of the first-year president. Just as important, New York City's Democratic slate—handpicked by Tammany—was trounced. This weakened Senator O'Gorman's base, lessening his inclination to challenge the President. Indeed, O'Gorman immediately began to vote on the administration's side in the committee. Reed also began to waver. If O'Gorman was intimidated from further opposition, Link suggested, Reed was satisfied with his. Quietly, he abandoned the fight. Just days after the November 4 balloting, the committee (with the help of one Republican) reversed its previous action reducing the number of reserve banks.

Only Hitchcock continued to hold out. The senator bridled at Wilson's efforts to meddle in the committee and refused to be either persuaded or pushed. Hitchcock's implacable stance left the committee, in mid-November, firmly deadlocked at 6 votes to 6. The panel ruptured, its two factions now convening separately.

Vanderlip went on a speaking tour and boldly predicted that no legislation would be enacted until 1914, when he hoped a consensus would favor his plan. While he distanced himself from the Glass-Owen camp, Warburg, having just returned from Europe, avidly engaged the committee. Predictably, his energies were focused on making Glass-Owen more centralized by eliminating some of the Reserve Banks. Warburg's evolving concern reflected his appreciation of the still vast distances that separated American cities in the era before commercial aviation. He envisioned that a dozen Reserve Banks would be uncoordinated and, in some cases, undercapitalized. (The total capital of all national banks was only $1 billion, heavily concentrated in the Northeast.) Moreover, Washington itself was a provincial capital and anything but a commercial center. Warburg favored establishing pillars of banking in a few major cities rather than entrust the system to, as he put it, "a set of men who are out of touch with the daily business of the county, and situated at Washington."

Unlike Vanderlip, Warburg maintained a supportive stance in public and tried to modify the bill from within. He and Owen fortuitously shared a train ride from Washington to New York, affording Warburg the chance to lobby the senator at length. He tried to disabuse Owen of his "pet theories" of banking, which were laden with prairie suspicions. Owen held his ground, but once back in Washington, he began consulting Warburg on changes in the draft. Warburg was also called to mediate between the committee's warring factions. Although the attempt failed, members of both parties subsequently sought his counsel. Warburg also forwarded to McAdoo, Colonel House, and various senators a flood of correspondence from European bankers echoing his prescriptions.

Warburg's relentless lobbying seemed to bear fruit when, on November 20, the Owen faction cut the number of Reserve Banks to eight, the minimum that Wilson would accept. Warburg also persuaded Owen to make changes in the discounting section, a technical area of great interest to Warburg. Meanwhile, Hitchcock (with help from Vanderlip and Strong) prepared a separate bill, with only four Reserve Banks and public stock subscription. Even the four banks would be controlled by Washington—a very centralized scheme.

Although unwilling to vote for Owen's bill (the Senate counterpart of the measure that had passed in the House), Hitchcock at least acquiesced in a legislative maneuver that allowed reform to get out of committee. Since the panel could not endorse a bill, it simply referred *two* bills, recommending neither. Then, Wilson ordered the Senate Democrats to meet in caucus, to align the party behind the Owen bill. While Hitchcock insisted he would not comply with the caucus, Wilson had signaled that he considered the Owen bill a make-or-break test of loyalty.

Banking reform finally got to the Senate floor in December, at the start of the regular session. Wilson, in his annual message to Congress on December 2, urged the Senate to move with dispatch.* He emphasized the plan's benefit to farmers. Adding to the pressure on the upper chamber, the President put his plans for a Christmas vacation on hold, pending enactment. He also directed Democrats in the Senate to table plans for a holiday recess—not a trivial matter in an era when members could hardly fly home for a weekend. With Wilson riding herd, Senate leaders imposed a grueling schedule of day and night sessions lasting until eleven p.m. Even Vanderlip admitted that the President was becoming an exceptionally forceful executive. All pursed lips, the banker exclaimed, "I have never seen so much power wielded by any administration as Wilson seems to have."

The first order of business in the Senate was to choose between the Owen and the Hitchcock measures. As the debate began, Owen held a slim lead. But the Senate became embroiled in a paramount issue that, up until that point, had remained curiously offstage— inflation. Although all of the rival measures reaffirmed the country's commitment to the gold standard, there was understandable fear that the creation of a new machinery designed to foster access to credit would end up debasing the money. Senators hotly debated whether reserve notes themselves should be "legal tender"—or merely paper that could be redeemed for gold. The distinction was mostly theoretical, because the vast majority of citizens would choose to carry reserve notes rather than specie. Still, the Senate's legal tender standard, seeming to endow the Fed with greater license, alarmed monetary purists, since if it prevailed, the new Reserve Banks would be minting not just notes but "money."

Further stoking inflation fears, the Owen bill, as compared with the House measure, was more conducive to stimulating credit (credit is the basis of money; more of it leads to more dollars in circulation). For instance, at Warburg's urging, the Senate cut reserve require-

---

* The term "State of the Union" was not adopted until later.

ments below those in the House, enabling banks to issue more loans and, again, create more money. The most controversial feature in the Senate bill was a provision for a deposit guarantee. The notion of insuring deposits as a means of forestalling bank runs had been on the margins of the debate since 1907 and, of course, was favored by Bryan. It was considered a radical step—one that would encourage imprudent banking.

Nonetheless, Wall Street, which had visions of a muscular Federal Reserve that would pump up credit and arm American banks to do business overseas, preferred the Senate's version of Glass-Owen to the House's. The upper chamber not only permitted national banks to open foreign branches but explicitly permitted the new Reserve Banks to trade in securities "at home or abroad." The House bill, more faithful to Glass's original Princeton blueprint, was more cautious. For instance, the Senate employed forceful language in authorizing the Federal Reserve Board to compel one Reserve Bank to loan money to another. This was important, because it enabled the board to coax the various parts of the system into working as a whole. The language in the House was more restrictive.

Thanks to pressure from farm state senators, the Owen bill was also permissive toward farmers, extending to six months, instead of just ninety days, the agricultural paper eligible for discount (in practical terms, this meant that a rural bank could lend money to a farmer to cover the entire growing season, and redeem the loan at the local Federal Reserve Bank). Owen's bill also permitted national banks, for the first time, to write mortgages on farms. Not since the heyday of silver had a banking proposal gone so far to liberalize rural credits. Banking traditionalists, especially in the East, were terrified of the potential for inflation.

Such concerns boiled over on December 13, when Elihu Root, the senior senator from New York, delivered an eloquent peroration that attacked the Owen bill as an inflationary menace. Root, a Republican, was a prestigious figure, secretary of both war and state under Roosevelt (he had recently been awarded the Nobel Peace Prize) and an accomplished corporate lawyer. On the Senate floor, he charged that the "universal experience" of paper currency is the tendency to increase circulation. Inflation was a product of human nature, and "little by little business is enlarged with easy money. . . . Bankers are not free from it—they are human. The members of the Federal Reserve Board will not be free from it. . . . Regional bankers will not be free from it."

Root supplied facts and figures attesting to an increase in the money stock; he claimed that under the proposed legislation, money in circulation would rise without limit. In fact, if any country had defied the "universal experience" of inflation, it was the United States over the previous forty years. Prices had consistently fallen from the 1870s to the McKinley era. Since 1896, the trend had reversed, but in 1913 price levels remained no higher—probably, they were lower— than after the Civil War. Root was quite right to consider whether a new agency for circulating currency could lead to inflation, but he understated the bill's considerable safeguards. Although no explicit ceiling on the currency was written into the bills in either chamber, the Reserve Banks could issue notes only in exchange for qualified bank paper. Moreover, the Reserve Banks would have to back their notes with a gold reserve. The bill contained a safeguard of a different kind by authorizing the Reserve Banks for only twenty years. This replicated the limited authorization of the ill-fated first and second Banks of the United States. (In 1927, this sunset provision over the Fed would be abolished.)

While the Senate was trying to get its head around inflation, the President was in a state of seclusion. Always of delicate health, Wilson had been under a strain from the still escalating turmoil in Mexico, as well as from his self-imposed deadline on banking. He had not been well since attending the Army-Navy game on a blustery day, when he had caught a cold. Having seemed to recover, he had gone for a walk in a bracing wind, scorning an overcoat, and developed an infection. He was feeling "bum and blue," he confessed to Mary Peck.

His condition spread concern through the White House. Wilson's doctor ordered him abed and forbade visitors. He also insisted that the President take his rest in a southern clime, banking bill or no banking bill. Wilson stayed put but was inopportunely silent.

Luckily for Wilson, public support for the administration bill was mounting, especially from workaday bankers who much preferred the Owen version to the Hitchcock proposal. He also got support from Warburg, who defended the legislation against inflation charges. Even with the deadline approaching, Warburg peppered Senator Owen with suggestions for improving the bill. He also corresponded with business executives, trying to goad them into further lobbying. When Wade, the St. Louis banker, pronounced himself well satisfied with the bill as it stood, Warburg, still pushing a plan to concentrate the reserve banks, accused him of "throwing up [his] hands." This was a mere ten days before Christmas.

Glass had maintained a wary distance from Warburg, but as the legislation reached a climax relations between the two framers—one a self-educated southerner, the other a sophisticated European—considerably warmed. Warburg kept Glass closely informed of his discussions with senators, which Glass no doubt appreciated. After a lengthy chat at Glass's hotel, the Virginian stunned Warburg by urging him to consider a position (should it be offered) on the prospective Federal Reserve Board. As a recently naturalized citizen still craving acceptance, Warburg was deeply moved.

On December 17, after eighty hours of debate, Senate Democrats imposed a time limit on speeches and scheduled a vote for two days later. As a precaution, they acquiesced to a demand of Root and the inflation hawks and upped the gold backing for Federal Reserve notes from 33 percent to 40 percent. Wilson by now was well enough to appear in public. Showing no ill effects, he went for a ride—with his physician—in a closed motorcar and again refused to let Congress consider a recess. On the nineteenth, a Friday, the Senate considered the Hitchcock bill and voted it down 43–41. By this slimmest of margins it turned to the Owen bill. Hitchcock proclaimed that, the bill having been improved by his labors, he would accede. Six Republicans joined every Democrat for a resounding 54–34 vote in favor.

Warburg rifled off a congratulatory note to Owen. He revealed his true feelings about the Senate (including Owen) to a fellow European, to whom he groused, "It is a terribly tiring business to try to influence these hundred obstinate and ignorant men." Not that Warburg had tired of it. Even though he preferred the Senate bill to the House's, Warburg was far from satisfied and hoped that the "best work" still lay ahead. Unable to stop agitating, he implored the president of the U.S. Chamber of Commerce to lobby for last-minute changes in the conference committee.

The gap between the House and Senate bills was unusually large. The two bills differed on the number of Reserve Banks, the requirements for reserves, deposit insurance, the composition of the Reserve Board, and dozens of other points. Glass, worried to the end, saw "no prospect at all of an immediate agreement."

The conferees worked with surprising speed. The Senate prevailed on most of the headline issues. Reserve Banks were to be established in "not less than eight nor more than twelve cities" (the House had said at least twelve). The exact number and the locations would be chosen by an organization committee including the Treasury secretary. The Senate's sharp cuts to bank reserve requirements were also retained. (Today, reserve ratios are even lower than in 1913, reflecting the modern emphasis on promoting bank lending, although at an incremental cost to prudence.)* The conference committee also sweetened the pill for banks in a pair of changes still in force today: first, each bank's contribution to the Reserve system was reduced to a

---

* Reserve requirements were cut to 12 percent for country banks, 15 percent for middle-tier banks, and 18 percent for central reserve city banks. The previous standard was 15, 25, and 25 percent, respectively. Today, reserve requirements are zero up to $14.5 million of deposits, 3 percent up to $103.6 million of deposits, and 10 percent thereafter.

manageable 6 percent of its capital and surplus; additionally, the dividend that member banks would receive was raised, in accord with the Senate bill, also to 6 percent.

However, the House conferees, led by Glass, would not budge on "legal tender." Technically, Federal Reserve notes would not be lawful money until an act of Congress in 1933, although in a practical sense they were regarded as money from the outset. Glass was so worried about inflation that the conference deleted authority to print $1 and $2 bills (somehow regarded as more of a menace); the smallest denomination would be a $5 note. The Act called for gradual retirement of the Civil War–era National Bank Notes, but America's various other currencies—silver certificates, gold coins, greenbacks, and so forth—remained in circulation. Monetary uniformity would be long in coming.* Even reserve notes would carry distinctive engravings to designate the particular city of issue.

The conferees tackled the truly sticky points in a marathon session on Sunday, December 21. At the eleventh hour, due to inflation concerns, Glass refused to let banks count reserve notes in their vaults as "reserves"—a bitter disappointment to Warburg, though one he would later reverse.† The sharpest conflict was over the deposit guarantee. Bankers opposed it as an invitation to reckless banking. Although the idea of insurance did have support in the House, Glass thought the Senate's version was poorly structured. At 1:30 a.m. on Monday, the deposit guarantee was stricken. (Deposit insurance would finally be established when Glass was in the Senate, in the Glass-Steagall Act of 1933—too late to avert the Depression-era bank runs.)

Only the makeup of the board remained unsettled. The Senate

---

* While Federal Reserve notes make up more than 99 percent of the money in circulation today, some U.S. notes (greenbacks), as well as National Bank Notes and silver certificates, are still around. All remain legal tender.
† This was the same issue on which Warburg had debated Aldrich at Jekyl Island, but thanks to a subsequent amendment, Warburg prevailed. Thus, today, Federal Reserve notes in the vaults of banks are counted as reserves.

bill called for six appointees in addition to the Treasury secretary. The House fancied a board that was little more than an appendage of the White House, including three sitting members of the administration. The conference settled on just two—the Treasury secretary and the comptroller of the currency. McAdoo was in frequent contact with the negotiators and seems to have succeeded in bolstering the authority of the Treasury secretary. The power of the board was amplified; terms of members (later known as governors) were increased to ten years, in staggered sequence, so that no president could name a full board. It was now 4:10 a.m., not quite daybreak.

Colonel House arrived at McAdoo's home for breakfast and found the Treasury secretary, who had barely slept, in pajamas. For all of Monday, they waited for news from the Capitol; the bill would not be law until each chamber approved the conference report. In the evening, the Colonel went to the White House, where he dined alone with the Wilsons. The two friends were in an expansive mood; the prospect of great tidings in the offing led them to reflect on other historic moments. House asked the President how he rated the Gettysburg Address; Wilson said he rated it very highly. After dinner, the group retired to an upstairs sitting room by a fire. Although Wilson wanted to steer the discussion toward the imminent legislation, Ellen, who was in an agitated frame of mind, repeatedly brought up the topic of the couple's finances. The First Lady, who would be dead within the year, suggested that when Woodrow left office he could earn income from writing, as Roosevelt did. Wilson said the kind of books he wrote didn't sell as well. House offered to recommend some investments.

Finally, the men repaired to Wilson's study. House gave the President a list of potential Reserve Board nominees—certainly including Warburg—which they discussed at length. As they chatted, Wilson received periodic updates on the proceedings in the Capitol. House remarked on Wilson's successes over his first year, but Wilson was haunted by his experience at Princeton: he had had great success at the college, he recalled, until all of a sudden he had become embroiled in controversies with alumni and trustees. "He seemed to fear," Colonel House jotted down that evening, "that such a denouement might occur again."

That same evening, in the House of Representatives, Glass presented the conference report—the compromise bill. He elaborated on the conference changes and opened the floor to debate. The chairman found it necessary to refute a claim by Frank Vanderlip that the new notes would lack security and be a kind of fiat currency. Glass was pleased to note that Paul Warburg, "perhaps the greatest international banker in America," not only disagreed with Vanderlip but had been in Washington protesting that the security behind the notes was actually too exacting. The House discussed such matters for a couple of hours. Then it voted, adopting the conference report by an overwhelming margin.

The Senate met the following afternoon, December 23. It adopted the report with nearly a two-thirds majority. Wilson and his family, members of Congress, and others gathered in the Oval Office just before six o'clock. A print of the bill, on parchment, was placed on the flat-top mahogany desk, the last page folded for the President's signature. The color had returned to Wilson's cheeks. "I'll do the deed first," he noted, "and then I will have something to say." The President asked Glass, who had been hidden in the crowd, and Owen to stand more prominently beside his desk. Owen looked somber; Glass was beaming. At 6:02 p.m., nimbly shifting among four gold pens, Wilson signed the Federal Reserve Act into law. He expressed his "deep gratification" at being able to sign this bill. The previous banking law, he recalled, had been in place since the Civil War; the necessary "readjustments" had taken more than a generation to resolve. Monetary reform had been actively debated for twenty years. The President paid tribute to the "skill and patience" of Glass and Owen. He staked a partisan claim—that the Democratic Party, long distrusted, was now demonstrating its ability to govern. The Federal

Reserve Act, he added, was not a measure hostile to business as some had claimed, but "friendly and serviceable."

It was too late in the day, and too late in the year, for a long speech. The family's bags were already packed for Pass Christian, Mississippi, where the Wilsons—with the President's doctor—would spend the holidays, in a cottage overlooking the balmy waters of the Gulf Coast. At 10:45 p.m., the family boarded a railcar south.

It was a year since Glass, terrified of centralization, had visited the president-elect in Princeton. In twelve short months, Wilson had wrung from a party steeped in devotion to Andrew Jackson, and to the crudest anti-banking stereotypes, the filaments of a central bank. Agriculture Secretary David Houston wrote in his diary, "The impossible has happened." A loyal Democrat, refreshingly unbiased, Houston noted that the law had been adopted by a Congress "dominated by the Democrats, two thirds of whom had been unsound on currency questions," and that the majority of the Republicans had been similarly unsound.

Prospectively, the most dramatic change would be the replacement of the outmoded system of segregated banking reserves with a series of centrally directed Reserve Banks that would act—especially in an emergency—as lenders of last resort. The Act would also create a more adaptable currency and strengthen the organization and oversight of America's wobbly banks. That this would make Washington a more prominent player in the monetary system (and the sometime partner of the big New York banks) could not be doubted. Representative Lindbergh said acidly that the new law gave official sanction to the Money Trust. It was also charged that the new institution would be captive to the easy-money theories of Bryan. But the public was weary with the debate and ready to give the Federal Reserve System a try. Editorial reaction was generally favorable. The *New York Tribune* judged that the new system would be "a great advance upon any which this country has ever had." The *Times*, though muted, was thankful that the measure had been improved by the force of public opinion; the paper said the legislative history offered striking proof of the "efficiency of representative institutions." Even *The Wall Street Journal* grudgingly allowed that the final measure was better "than business dared to hope." Banks were also pleased. Although Vanderlip sourly hinted that National City would relinquish its charter in protest, most national banks quickly applied for membership in the Federal Reserve—some on the day the law was enacted.

Also on that day, Warburg sent a bittersweet note to Glass: "While my heart bleeds at many things that went into the bill, and at many things that were left out, I rejoice at the many good features that, after all, the law will contain." An incurable reformer, Warburg could not resist, even on the day of triumph, outlining points he had in mind for subsequent amendment. He did, at least, indulge a moment's pride in "the victory of which some of us have worked for so many years."

If Jackson had stood against the supposed evils of centralization, Warburg, more than anyone else, had recognized the weakness in stand-alone banking and crusaded to overcome the Jacksonian view. It was an American prejudice, a parochialism, which he as a foreigner had seen more clearly. Colonel House, long under his spell, wrote to Warburg on New Year's Day, "It is you that just now deserves the gratitude of your countrymen, and some day I shall tell them when and how you served them."

The Federal Reserve's creation closed the gap between American banks and the developed banking systems that Aldrich had seen in Europe, and readied the United States for financial leadership. It also closed a gap in American history. Since the days of the Founding Fathers, resistance to central authority had been entrenched in the culture; it was the spiritual sword wielded by the colonists in 1776 and by mistrustful populists ever since. But local autonomy had its limits. Notably, the Articles of Confederation had failed to deliver effective government, and so the country had embarked on the compromise of federalism. Only the country's banks had been left behind. When the subject was money, central authority had always been taboo; it was a demon that terrified the people. Fear of this demon had kept the country without any effective organization of its finances for seventy-five years. Now, three-quarters of a century after Andrew Jackson, the ghost was slain.

CHAPTER FOURTEEN

EPILOGUE

The measure itself was the result of the labors of
many men, extending over a long period.
—AGRICULTURE SECRETARY DAVID F. HOUSTON

Mr. Wilson experienced no lack of confidence in me.
—CARTER GLASS

[Carter Glass] is not the chief author . . . nor is he
entitled to the main credit.
—SAMUEL UNTERMYER

Mr. Glass himself could not have created such a bill.
—JAMES L. LAUGHLIN

A profanation of history.
—CARTER GLASS

It was not an "original proposal". . . . but, on the contrary, it was the digested product of elaborate and careful study of European banking experience as adapted to American necessities and requirements.

—H. Parker Willis

Glass and Willis have so falsified the record . . .

—Paul Warburg

Mr. Warburg has never made any statement regarding the authorship of the act.

—H. Parker Willis

Congress should realize that the Federal Reserve System is the child and property of both parties.

—Paul Warburg

It had little or no relationship in principle to the so-called Aldrich bill.

—H. Parker Willis

I feel for it, in a sense, as I would for my child.

—Paul Warburg

THE ENACTMENT of the Federal Reserve system, although a landmark in American history, was less an ending than a truce. Few of the battles of 1902–1913 were put to rest. The tension between centralism and local autonomy, between the public and Wall Street, and between an inflationary money-printing machine and countinghouse prudence persisted. Congress's internal quarrel over how much power to vest in the Fed endures to this day. The conflicts continued in part because the framers, not wishing to brook too much controversy, had been deliberately vague. As Frank Vanderlip wrote the week the Federal Reserve Act was passed, "The law is full of indirect and implied powers." The pressing issue of who would control the system was contested from the start, when William McAdoo ran the agency almost as a Treasury subbureau. It arose again in the 1920s, when the board in Washington battled the Reserve Bank of Chicago over control of the discount rate, and later, in the Truman era, when the White House attempted to impose its will on the board. Later still, Richard Nixon bullied his Fed chairman, Arthur Burns, into an inflationary stimulus policy in advance of the President's reelection.

Then, too, the issue of Wall Street influence was never resolved, no matter that the original Act created twelve supposedly equal banks. New York's was destined to be dominant, and its influence was as bitterly resented in the era of Lloyd Blankfein and Jamie Dimon as it was in 1913.

The basic federalist structure enacted a century ago remains in force; so does the essential purpose. Then as now, the Fed serves as a banker to other banks and the keeper of their reserves. Along with setting short-term interest rates and supervising the banking system, the Fed is in charge of the nation's monetary policy. Then as now, the Fed provides liquidity to the system, especially in times of crisis, so that banks may supply the country with adequate credit.

But the framers had created less a static machine than an organic institution that, inevitably, would be buffeted by presidents and economic cycles and repeatedly amended by Congress. Its charter—"to furnish an elastic currency" while defending the dollar through the mechanism of the gold standard—was fraught with tension. (It was further conflicted by the real bills idea that reserve notes should be printed only to provide for actual commercial activity.) The resolution of these debates was never a fixed point, but rather a range on a continuum that was destined to be fought over again and again. The Fed's failure during the Great Depression hardly proved that Elihu Root, the tradition-minded New York senator, had been wrong about the risk of inflation—only that he had overlooked the risks in the other direction. In the 1970s, the Federal Reserve vindicated Root when it destroyed the dollar with excessive money-printing.

Similarly, the framers argued over the proper type of bank paper acceptable for discount because of the risk of being either too liberal or too strict. A century later, Ben Bernanke reignited this debate with his frantic acquisitions of mortgage securities, Treasury bonds, and also the very commercial paper of which Paul Warburg was so enamored. Even the desirability of Wall Street control was a matter of degree. Wall Street, as Vanderlip was fond of saying, was as patriotic as anyplace else; more to the point, it had desirable expertise. In the 1980s, Fed chairman Paul Volcker, formerly of Chase Manhattan, vanquished double-digit inflation by jacking up interest rates, triggering a recession. Congress protested that Volcker was a tool of Wall Street. Representative Henry González (a Texas Democrat, just like the agrarian leader in 1913) threatened to impeach him. Volcker did his job. The New York Fed's intervention, in 1998, when it organized a rescue of a hedge fund that was scarily entwined with the biggest banks, was further along the continuum—that is, it reeked of Wall

Street influence. By then, Congress had amended the Fed's charter, stipulating more explicitly that its mission was to promote both full employment and stable prices. The Fed's evolution was neither steady nor direct, but over time its thrust was clear: power shifted toward the center, and its charter was interpreted more broadly—not just the narrow terrain of monetary policy, but to a large extent the economy as well.

Would Carter Glass or Paul Warburg approve of such things? It has become a commonplace that the founders of the Fed, were they to return to Washington, would scarcely recognize the colossus housed in the Marriner S. Eccles Federal Reserve Board Building. It is just as certain that the veterans, pro and con, of the founding era, would find validation of very disparate views. To Lindbergh, the Fed's bailouts of banks and of AIG in 2008, as well as the New York Fed's general coziness with Wall Street, would confirm his fears about the Money Trust. Just as surely, Warburg would applaud that, when the Great Recession came, the United States had a lender of last resort that could provide elasticity (all that "quantitative easing") so that banks were not forced to desperately hoard their reserves, and so that the meltdown did not become pandemic. In this sense, the debates that shroud the contemporary Fed are a replay of those of 1913.

America's abandonment of the gold standard *would* have shocked the founders, who took for granted that money had to be more than mere paper. More than anything, going off gold (which occurred in stages, culminating under Nixon) expanded the Fed's charter. It made the agency the supreme arbiter of the money supply. This was a significant departure from 1913. Originalism, however, is not an argument, although it may be a faith. The view that the Fed could have stayed fixed, a fossil from the Wilson era, seems hopelessly naïve. In truth, the Fed was forced to start adapting on the day it came into being, and by the time the founding generation had left the scene, the organization was already appreciably evolved.

It took some time, in 1914, for the Fed to become operational.

Although the Act specified eight to twelve Reserve Banks, McAdoo never considered fewer than twelve, probably because the Banks were hot political plums. He and Secretary of Agriculture Houston embarked on a ten-thousand-mile cross-country trip, where they heard pitches from scores of cities. McAdoo also commissioned a poll, asking bankers to name the city where they would want their Reserve Bank. Political favoritism was said to influence the selections, but there is no evidence of this. McAdoo's selections closely mirrored the bankers' poll.* Perhaps this was done to induce banks to join the new system; overwhelmingly, they did. Even at the start, the New York Fed was by far the most powerful, with four times the capital of Atlanta's.

Wilson guaranteed a Wall Street presence on the board by nominating Warburg. His appointment was controversial with the Senate Banking Committee, which was nervous about Warburg's connection to Kuhn, Loeb. Under badgering from senators, Warburg promised to sever himself from the firm (which he was not required to do, since investment banks were not part of the Federal Reserve System). Not until November 1914 was the Reserve system—banks and board, including Warburg—up and running.

By then, the war in Europe was raging. The founders could scarcely have anticipated the war or its effect on the new system. In many ways, the world for which the agency had been designed ceased to exist. In the United States, the guns of August triggered a financial crisis. As the Fed was not yet operational, McAdoo authorized banks to issue emergency currency. He pressed the New York Stock Exchange to close (to prevent European belligerents from selling American securities and withdrawing gold). And it remained closed until December.

---

* Reserve Banks were placed in New York, Boston, Philadelphia, Richmond, Atlanta, Cleveland, Chicago, St. Louis, Kansas City, Minneapolis, Dallas, and San Francisco. Those twelve were also the top-ranking cities in the bankers' poll, with the single exception of Cleveland, which was swapped by McAdoo for Cincinnati.

Even as the Fed got going, it remained under the Treasury's thumb. Due to the war, McAdoo exercised czarlike powers. He repeatedly clashed with Warburg, who thought the central bank should be independent from the executive, and who attempted to persuade the board to seek greater powers from Congress. A third party emerged in the power struggle: the Reserve Bank of New York, run by Benjamin Strong, the Wall Street insider and intimate of the Jekyl Island group. Because the Act did not make clear exactly where the levers of authority lay, the Fed's first years were marked by a profound competition among the Reserve Banks, the board, and the Treasury Department.

Various members of the founding generation did battle to ensure that the Act was implemented according to their designs. Glass warily monitored the Fed from Congress and was often at odds with Warburg, as was H. Parker Willis, who had been appointed secretary to the board. The debate over whether the Fed would be a so-called central bank was replayed in repeated battles for control over the discount rate (the benchmark interest rate). According to the statute, each Reserve Bank was entitled to set the rate in its district, but they were subject to board "review and determination." This language provided a fertile field for disputes. Glass was active on each side. As a congressional overseer, Glass favored the periphery over the center. Then, in 1918, he was appointed Treasury secretary and evidenced an unseen Hamiltonian impulse when he blocked the Reserve Banks from hiking rates. In 1927, when in the Senate, Glass reverted to Jeffersonian form, protesting that an imperious board was behaving too much like, in his words, a "central bank."

After America entered the war, McAdoo leaned on the board to keep rates low and the Fed dutifully complied. The Reserve Banks further assisted war finance by purchasing bank credits backed by Treasury notes and bonds. They also bought government securities on the open market. This tacitly redirected the Fed from its intended method of operation. As the Reserve Banks fell in step with war finance, their assets became concentrated in government securities rather than the bank commercial paper to which the framers had devoted so much energy.

However, if the war temporarily thrust the Fed into a subservient role, it also broadened its field of action. Many people had envisioned that, apart from emergencies, the agency would play a passive role—as the Act put it, simply "discount[ing] notes, drafts, and bills of exchange arising out of actual commercial transactions." Harvard's Oliver Sprague had predicted an extreme degree of passivity, testifying just before enactment, "After the institution has been going ten or fifteen years it will almost run itself." This would soon seem ludicrous. In fairness, centralizers such as Warburg always wanted a more dynamic agency. Within a year of the Fed's founding, so did the board. In its first annual report, the board signaled its disposition to be proactive. Its duty, it asserted, "is not to await emergencies but by anticipation to do what it can to prevent them."

Just as Wall Street had hoped, the Fed's emergence, coupled with the war, catapulted America's standing in world finance. By keeping Britain and France afloat, the United States, long a debtor nation, suddenly became a significant creditor. In return for exports of food, arms, and other supplies, gold poured into American harbors. After America's entry into the war, Congress fulfilled Warburg's insistent demands and amended the Act to widen the board's powers. The amendments greatly increased the Fed's note-issuing capacity; notes in circulation doubled within months. And the Reserve Banks, by issuing more notes, were able to soak up much of the bullion previously stashed in people's pockets and in the vaults of member banks. The Fed's enlarged and unified gold cache elevated the dollar's status as an international currency.

However, the war put Warburg in an awkward spot. Given that he had two banker brothers still in Hamburg—one an adviser to the German government—Warburg became an easy target for international conspiracy theorists and closet anti-Semites, groups that would hound the Fed in the future. In May 1918, to spare Wilson the embarrassment of a prolonged renomination battle, Warburg offered his resignation.* He stressed his utter allegiance to the United States and indicated he would continue to serve if the President desired. No doubt, Warburg was hoping that Wilson would insist. There was no question of his loyalty, and bankers rallied to his cause. But his tussles with McAdoo had damaged his standing in the administration, and he faced opposition on the Senate Banking Committee, in particular from the mercurial chairman, Robert Owen. After letting Warburg dangle for months, in August Wilson accepted his resignation. For Warburg, it was a devastating, and an irrecuperable, loss.

For the next decade, the Fed's most effective leader (and its last connection to the founding generation) was Benjamin Strong. His first task was to nip inflation, which skyrocketed after the war. After a battle with the Treasury Department, Strong hiked the discount rate, leading to a severe but brief depression. Bank failures rose sharply; however, there was no money shortage and no liquidity crisis. The mechanism of 1913 worked.

In the 1920s, the Reserve Banks shifted their emphasis from making discount loans to individual member banks to so-called open market interventions. Trading by Reserve Banks developed a liquid market in short-term Treasury securities. Such interventions became the Banks' chief tool for influencing interest rates and credit conditions—and not just on an emergency basis, but as an ongoing ballast to the economy. Significantly, in 1923, the Reserve Banks formed the Open Market Investment Committee, which attempted to conduct monetary policy on a coordinated basis. Although still a good distance from the bureaucratic giant of later years, such concerted action nudged the Fed closer toward being a central bank.

---

* The original Reserve Board members were appointed to terms of varying lengths; Warburg's term expired that year.

Nonetheless, confusion over the board's and the Reserve Banks' respective powers persisted. The uncertainty would do serious harm; it contributed to the Fed's ineffectualness during the Great Depression.

The Fed's framers had assumed that the new institution would take its place, with other central banks, in a world in which exchange rates and capital flows were regulated and kept reasonably stable by international gold movements. But after World War I, with Europe hobbled by debts (and in Germany's case, reparations), this system broke down. Europe's insolvency put America under a severe strain.

Strong attempted to navigate these turbulent monetary seas, but his death in 1928 left the Fed without a capable hand at the tiller. The next year, Warburg, who monitored the Fed like an anxious parent, criticized the agency's weakened leadership for letting stock market operators seize the reins of money creation. He warned that if their "orgies of unrestrained speculation" were permitted to spread—that is, if credit continued to flow to the stock market and to other speculative assets—it would lead to a general depression throughout the country. Three years later, during the depths of the Great Depression, the sixty-four-year-old Warburg died in New York City. The Fed would face the tempestuous 1930s without the cream of its founding generation, and without anyone else of equal caliber.

The other sojourners to Jekyl Island were, by then, gone from the scene. Harry Davison had remained the dominant partner at Morgan's, but shifted his focus after the war to philanthropic ideas for reconstruction and relief. In 1922 he succumbed, his grace intact, to a lethal brain tumor. During the war, Piatt Andrew went to Europe and organized an ambulance squadron, the American Field Service, to serve with French divisions at the front. He was awarded the Croix de Guerre from France. In 1920, he was elected to Congress, where he later became a staunch enemy of the New Deal, but the professor was never again influential in banking. Frank Vanderlip, ever the eager international financier, seized on the Federal Reserve Act to build a vast network of overseas lending offices. But he fell out with James

Stillman, who did not approve of National City's expansion, especially when the Russian Revolution led to losses. After the war, Vanderlip became passionately interested in European recovery schemes, to the displeasure of the bank's directors, who replaced him with Stillman's son. Two years before his death in 1937, Vanderlip published a memoir in which he recalled the week on Jekyl Island as "the highest pitch of intellectual awareness that I have ever experienced."

Nelson Aldrich did not shake his bitterness that Glass's bill, rather than his, was embraced by the public and enacted by Congress. He clung to his belief that banks should be supervised by bankers—not by government. Improbably, he was hoping for a Republican revival and new legislation when, in April 1915, he died, leaving an estate worth approximately $16 million. Aldrich's heirs, as if shadowed by the patriarch's sullied reputation, were more self-conscious aristo-crats. His daughter, Abby Aldrich Rockefeller, became a noted col-lector. Far more progressive than her father, she helped to found the Museum of Modern Art. Her son Nelson, a liberal Republican, was a big-spending governor of New York and vice president of the United States; another of the senator's grandsons, David Rockefeller, chief executive of Chase Manhattan, was the quintessential banker in the postwar era, when globe-trotting bankers were willing, and subject, partners to government.

William McAdoo married Wilson's daughter Eleanor, in a White House ceremony, in the spring of 1914. Since Wilson was counting on McAdoo to shape the Federal Reserve, he refused to accept his son-in-law's offer to resign. After the war, the ambitious McAdoo left the government and ran, unsuccessfully, for president.

Colonel House accompanied Wilson to Paris in 1918 to represent the United States in the peace negotiations at Versailles. His eager-ness to accede to French and Italian demands, at a time when Wilson was ailing, led to a rift. The two men were never friends again.

Historians regard Woodrow Wilson's first term as one of the most successful ever, and the Federal Reserve Act as its crowning achievement. Wilson's fear that early success would be followed by controversy proved prophetic. In 1916, widowed and already happily remarried, he narrowly won reelection, campaigning on the slogan "He kept us out of war." A month into his second term, America joined the fight. Full of postwar ideals, Wilson negotiated the Treaty of Versailles and earnestly sought its approval by the Senate. Then he suffered a debilitating stroke. Senator James Reed, beaten by Wilson during the Federal Reserve legislation, helped to thwart his dream of an American-led League of Nations—a bitter disappointment. Wilson died in 1924.

Carter Glass, who as a junior representative had studied banking in his hotel room at nights, became a Senate authority on finance. He sponsored an amendment to create the Securities and Exchange Commission as a stand-alone agency rather than, as had been proposed, part of the Federal Trade Commission. Thus, he played a pivotal role in the three major financial reforms—the Fed, the SEC, and the Glass-Steagall Act—of the twentieth century. Within the upper chamber, he oversaw the Banking Act of 1935, which strengthened the Reserve Board—the little "capstone" that had once appalled him. The 1935 act divorced the board from the executive branch, removing the Treasury secretary and the comptroller of the currency from the directors' table, and lengthened terms to fourteen years (all as Vanderlip had proposed in 1913). Otherwise, Glass was a persistent thorn in the New Deal's side. He remained committed to states' rights and helped to block federal efforts to lift the poll tax. When he died in 1946, he was the last member of Congress born in the antebellum South. *The New York Times* eulogized, "He is generally regarded as the father of the Federal Reserve Act."

For as long as they lived, the framers fought bitterly over this assessment. Eight of the founding generation wrote memoirs or accounts of the creation of the Federal Reserve. Owen and Glass got into a nasty scrap over who was entitled to the lion's share of the credit for the bill's passage. Owen hit the press first, with a slim volume in 1919. He later denounced the Fed, which he said had become a tool of the big banks. Glass was less bothered by Owen than by Charles Seymour, a Yale professor who got access to the files of Colonel House, from which he stitched a sensational narrative, *The Intimate Papers of Colonel House*, exaggerating House's role in the Fed's enactment. Glass's own memoir, *An Adventure in Constructive Finance*, published in 1927, devoted nearly fifty pages to refuting Seymour, whose book he termed "an amusing fiction," and which he did not find amusing at all.

Glass's account was highly self-serving, unctuously praising Wilson as the unerring helmsman and leaving no doubt that the honor of realizing Wilson's program had belonged to Glass. By overstating Wilson's role, Glass was able to ignore those who had preceded Wilson—and who had preceded Glass. Parker Willis, who wrote an exhaustive, 1,750-page history of the bill, took a more expansive approach, although he also concentrated on the period after he and Glass had begun to draft a bill. Neither Glass nor Willis cited Victor Morawetz—a stinging omission, since Morawetz had been the first to propose a regional banking plan. Even more unkindly, Willis all but ignored his former professor, James Laughlin, to whom he had eagerly turned for advice when he was sketching out a plan in 1912. Willis's comment on the plan that Laughlin had helpfully supplied when Willis and Glass were preparing to see Wilson was especially uncharitable. "This bill," he coldly informed posterity, "when received by Mr. Glass was filed with numerous other bills . . . transmitted to the Committee and received the same consideration."

Willis reserved his greatest animus for the Aldrich Plan and for its intellectual author, Warburg. Unlike Glass, who came to appreciate the German-born banker despite their disagreements, Willis resented Warburg's reputation for brilliance and lobbied to keep him off the Reserve Board. In his book, Willis ungraciously characterized Warburg's role as "simply that of a critic . . . and a critic whose recommendations were not adopted"—a narrow and highly misleading

268 | AMERICA'S BANK

synopsis. Willis also claimed that of all the antecedent bills from which the Federal Reserve Act borrowed, it was *least* indebted to the Aldrich Plan. Willis managed to make this topsy-turvy assertion even while acknowledging that in drafting the Act, he had made "use of such features of the Aldrich bill as were considered to be desirable or even in various places the use of language drawn from or modeled after the language implied in the Aldrich bill." In other words, he had copied from it.

Willis's book did not provoke a response, at least immediately, but Glass's did. Samuel Untermyer, whose feud with Glass had never been repaired, quickly responded to excerpts of *An Adventure in Constructive Finance* with all of his old vinegar, calling it an "interesting work of imagination." Untermyer said Glass had slighted the contribution of Owen (not a disinterested comment, since he, Untermyer, had worked with Owen in the spring of 1913). Moreover, Untermyer claimed that the Reserve Act was "the direct outcome of the disclosures of the dangerous concentration of the control of money and credits by the Pujo investigating Committee"—of which, of course, Untermyer had been counsel. In other words, Untermyer's investigation led to the Federal Reserve Act.

Warburg claimed that Glass's book inspired him to write his two-volume tome on the Fed's enactment and early years, *The Federal Reserve System*. Warburg probably would have written it anyway, but Glass's book, which Warburg privately referred to as "vicious," gave Warburg his purpose: he wanted to add historical perspective and balance to the Glass narrative of a Democratic Congress legislating over the will of Republicans and of truculent bankers. Warburg saw the Act—which *was* the work of Democrats—as the culmination of many previous proposals, including by Republicans and by bankers such as himself. He wanted the Federal Reserve to be seen as one of America's great monuments—"like the old cathedrals of Europe"— whose preservation would require a national and shared commitment. When Warburg was writing, in the late 1920s, America had lived with the Fed for less than twenty years. If the agency were to survive—by no means assured then, and perhaps not today—it was imperative, he wrote, that it have bipartisan support, and therefore, that it be seen "not as the work of a single party," but as the product of years of work by people across the spectrum.

To rebut the notion that financiers had been antagonistic to reform, Warburg emphasized the role of bankers and economists who had instigated the reform discussions arising out of the 1907 Panic. Even in 1913, he rightly pointed out, bankers were hardly the uniformly hostile lobby that Glass depicted, the savage critiques of the American Bankers Association notwithstanding. Most of all, Warburg sought to establish a place of honor for the Aldrich Plan. While Glass portrayed the Aldrich Plan as a counterreform intended to institutionalize the Money Trust and block any genuine reforms, Warburg presented it as an evolutionary step that, in conjunction with the Citizens' League publicity campaign, prepared the public for eventual legislation.

Warburg's book was also self-serving, and his sarcasm betrayed his dislike of Willis and of Glass. However, he presented his case as perhaps only he could, methodically setting forth the Aldrich bill and, on facing pages, the Reserve Act. This "juxtaposition of texts," which stretched to over two hundred pages including explanatory comment, demonstrated, even to Glass's admirers, that the Aldrich bill was the nearest ancestor to the Glass-Owen bill. Milton Friedman and Anna Schwartz would call the bills "identical in many details" and "very similar in general structure." It is doubtful that the Reserve Act would have passed without Wilson's leadership or Glass's tenacity, but it would have looked quite different without the Aldrich bill, which itself sprang from Congress's idea (in hindsight, an inspired one) of creating a commission to study reform. The Aldrich trip to Europe was vital because the models for central banking came from Europe. Warburg supplied the intellectual rigor. Having traced the failings of American banking to the country's phobia of centralization, he labored unceasingly to cure it. Warburg was the anti-Jackson. But as Warburg acknowledged, there were many theorists and contributors besides himself. Asked once about the identity of the Fed's "father," he replied that he didn't know, but that judging from the number of men who claimed the honor, "its mother must have been a most immoral woman."

As the joke implied, the Fed's parentage was mixed. It drew from both American traditions, Hamiltonian and Jacksonian. Some said the banks got all they wanted—that, in effect, the Money Trust won out. But they did not get control of the Reseve Board, and that was a very great concession. For National City to submit to Washington, in so many particulars and regulatory details, was more than it had ever done before. Control was to be shared—private or quasi-private banks but a government board. Similarly, the organization was split—Federal on top, regional below. The character of the money was also a compromise. The essential bargain was to respect the federalist character of American politics while overcoming its fierce resistance to centralization.

The Federal Reserve Act did not guarantee sound monetary policy any more than the establishment of Congress could guarantee good laws. Policy would be the burden of those in power—as disputatious today as in 1913. However, the Act unified the banking system, which unquestionably made it stronger. It created an institution for regulating the money supply, a difficult task but a necessary one for societies too advanced to depend on the vagaries of mining gold. It provided flexibility to respond to financial shocks and economic headwinds and thus made the system more resilient. It was an imperfect bill—nonetheless, after a decade of debate, division, panic, study, conspiracy, party platforms, elections, and legislative work, it was a highly worthy achievement.

ACKNOWLEDGMENTS

Many people helped me with this book. I am grateful to Sarah Binder, Michael D. Bordo, J. Lawrence Broz, Gary Gorton, Richard S. Grossman, Douglas A. Irwin, William L. Silber, and Ellis Tallman—super scholars and historians who provided me with encouragement and help, in some cases often, in all cases graciously. I am grateful, as well, to John Hunter for a stimulating tour of the Jekyll Island Museum and historic site, and to Michelle A. Smith, nonpareil assistant to the Federal Reserve Board, and to the Fed's Sara Messina, for tracking down some details on the operation of the present-day central bank. To my friend José Souto, your legwork on Wall Street is not forgotten. Alex Beam, Neil Barsky, Ron Chernow, and David Moss—that would be three writer-historians and one journalist-filmmaker: four good friends—provided advice, answered queries, and encouraged me as only colleagues can. Who could ask for more? Jeffry Frieden, Geoffrey Lewis, Matthew Lowenstein, Mitch Rubin, Jeffrey Tannenbaum, and Mark Williams (five friends and a certain relative) read every word of this book in progress. With each of you, editing calls were a labor of love, even as they were instructional and frank. To a writer in the midst, that is as good as it gets. My sister Jane Ruth Mairs lent her sharp editor's eye when I needed it. My in-laws, Janet and Gil Slovin, and my mother, Helen

Lowenstein, read and absorbed more about bankers, populists, and turn-of-the-century politicians than I had a right to expect. None of you feigned neutrality; your partisanship on my behalf was richly appreciated.

Apart from the narrative in the book, there is a narrative *of* the book, which every author lives from the moment of inception until the distant moment of publication. The early going, in the summer of 2012, was difficult indeed. I have countless family and friends to thank for sustaining me in that time, not least my cousins Michael and Carol Lowenstein and Wendy and Neil Sandler. When research and other aspects of everyday life had all but come to a standstill, Dr. Virany Hillard, my daughter's surgeon at Westchester Medical Center, together with her colleagues and staff, turned an enveloping nightmare into a story of redemption, now steadily receding in the rearview mirror. I must also mention Lisa Berkower (and Mitch, too)—in whose warm abode, and at whose polished-walnut dining room table, I labored on this book. Next time, I promise to use coasters.

When bad things happen you discover who your friends are. Melanie Jackson, my agent, and Ann Godoff, my editor, demonstrated by word and deed that their personal feeling trumped editorial and business concerns. Hard to forget that. I am as grateful as ever to Melanie for her professionalism and loyalty. Ann's insights and discerning judgment made a telling difference on every page; I am also deeply grateful to her for believing, from the beginning, that a hundred-year-old banking story could be brought to exciting life. I am also indebted to the entire crew at Penguin Press; with them, publishing remains an art form and a collaboration. Last and assuredly not least, Judy, my wife, read and critiqued this book numerous times. She read it on buses, planes, and trains; she read it upstairs and downstairs; she read it in fair weather and, during our present epic winter, foul. Her dedication was remarkable; her literary skills are equally formidable. Judy told me at the outset she was a reader. She did not divulge that she is also a superior editor and critic. For her generosity, her talent, and her love, I am profoundly grateful.

ROGER LOWENSTEIN
Boston, March 2015

NOTES

UNPUBLISHED PAPERS AND COLLECTIONS

The principal archives consulted for this book, which are often cited in the notes that follow, can be found in these locations:

Nelson W. Aldrich Papers: Manuscript Division, Library of Congress, Washington, D.C.

A. Piatt Andrew Papers: Hoover Institution Archives, Stanford, California.

Carter Glass Collection: Albert and Shirley Small Special Collections Library, University of Virginia, Charlottesville, Virginia.

Edward M. House Papers: Manuscripts and Archives, Sterling Memorial Library, Yale University, New Haven, Connecticut.

Thomas W. Lamont Papers: Baker Business Historical Collections, Harvard University, Cambridge, Massachusetts.

James Laurence Laughlin Papers: Manuscript Division, Library of Congress, Washington, D.C.

Pierpont Morgan Papers and J. P. Morgan Jr. Papers: Morgan Archives, Morgan Library and Museum, New York, New York.

George W. Perkins Sr. Papers: Rare Book and Manuscript Library, Butler Library, Columbia University, New York, New York.

Frank A. Vanderlip Papers: Rare Book and Manuscript Library, Butler Library, Columbia University, New York, New York. (All quoted letters from "Part B.")

Paul Moritz Warburg Papers: Manuscripts and Archives, Sterling Memorial Library, Yale University, New Haven, Connecticut.

Henry Parker Willis Papers: Rare Book and Manuscript Library, Butler Library, Columbia University, New York, New York.

The Aldrich Papers warrant elaboration. They include Aldrich's papers and correspondence, as well as his personal financial records, over his lengthy (1879–1911) congressional career and beyond, and the archives of the National Monetary Commission, which Aldrich directed. They also include detailed notes compiled by Jeannette P. Nichols and Nathaniel W. Stephenson for the latter's biography, *Nelson W. Aldrich:*

A Leader in American Politics (1930), along with associated correspondence. These notes include material culled from interviews and from other archival sources, including the papers of Paul Warburg and of Piatt Andrew. When possible, the origin of such material is indicated with an annotation such as "Biographer's notes" or the parenthetical "(from Warburg Papers)." Whatever their source, the materials in the Aldrich Papers represent a treasure trove.

I benefited from several exceptional unpublished works and dissertations, cited more fully below but worthy of mention here. They include: Harry Edward Poindexter, "From Copy Desk to Congress: The Pre-Congressional Career of Carter Glass" (1966); Michael Clark Rockefeller, "Nelson W. Aldrich and Banking Reform: A Conservative Leader in the Progressive Era" (1960); Jerome L. Sternstein, "Nelson W. Aldrich: The Making of the 'General Manager of the United States,' 1841–1886" (1959); and William Diamond, *The Economic Thought of Woodrow Wilson* (1943).

Among the most valuable published sources were the memoirs, biographies, diaries, and compilations of the main characters, including of Aldrich, Piatt Andrew, William Jennings Bryan, Harry Davison, Carter Glass, Colonel Edward M. House, William G. McAdoo, J. P. Morgan, Robert L. Owen, Theodore Roosevelt, William Howard Taft, Frank Vanderlip, Paul Warburg, H. Parker Willis, and Woodrow Wilson. Three merit particular mention: Warburg's two-volume *The Federal Reserve System: Its Origin and Growth—Reflections and Recollections* (1930); Willis's *The Federal Reserve System: Legislation, Organization and Operation* (1923); and *The Papers of Woodrow Wilson*. The Wilson Papers, a massive undertaking edited by Arthur S. Link, comprise sixty-nine volumes and were published between 1966 and 1994; I consulted volume 8 (1970) and volumes 18–29 (1975–80).

INTRODUCTION

2 **Alexander Hamilton proposed:** Ron Chernow, *Alexander Hamilton* (New York: Penguin Press, 2004), 347.

2 **To modern eyes, the Bank:** Richard Grossman, *Wrong: Nine Economic Policy Disasters and What We Can Learn from Them* (Oxford: Oxford University Press, 2013), 45. Grossman's third chapter, "Establish, Disestablish, Repeat," is an elegant summary of the purposes of central banking internationally and of America's first two aborted experiments.

3 **But the Bank was doomed:** Ibid., 45.

4 **"object of intense hatred":** Alexis de Tocqueville, *Democracy in America* (1835; repr., New York: Library of America, 2004), 448.

4 **"Americans are obviously preoccupied":** Ibid., 443.

4 **For the opposition to central banking:** Grossman, *Wrong,* 43.

4 **when Jackson was elected president:** Richard Hofstadter, *The American Political Tradition and the Men Who Made It* (New York: Knopf, 1991), 69.

4 **They relied less on labor:** Robert Kuttner, *Debtors Prison: The Politics of Austerity vs. Possibility* (New York: Knopf, 2013), 183–85.

5 **Jefferson in particular was:** Hofstadter, *American Political Tradition,* 36.

5 **The U.S. dollar was a second-rate currency:** Ed Conway, *The Summit: Bretton Woods, 1944, J. M. Keynes and the Reshaping of the Global Economy* (New York: Pegasus, 2015), 39,

citing Barry Eichengreen, *Exorbitant Privilege: The Rise and Fall of the Dollar and the Future of the International Monetary System* (New York: Oxford University Press, 2011), 32.

CHAPTER ONE: THE FORBIDDEN WORDS

11 **"I am in favor of a national bank"**: Illinois Ancestors, speech available at www .illinoisancestors.org/lincoln/firstspeech.html. Accounts of the speech differ, but there is no doubt that during the 1840s Lincoln frequently advocated a national bank.

11 **"to carry with him the coin necessary"**: Andrew McFarland Davis, National Monetary Commission, *The Origin of the National Banking System*, 61st Cong., 2d sess. (Washington, D.C.: Government Printing Office, 1910), 12–13.

12 **"the frequently worthless issues"**: Ibid., 13–14, quoting John Jay Knox, "By a Western Banker," *Hunt's Merchants' Magazine*, January 1863. Knox was later U.S. comptroller of the currency.

12 **In theory, these notes**: Ibid., 12–14.

12 **"The speculator comes to Indianapolis"**: Ibid., 20–21.

12 **"with no other security than"**: Ibid., 19, quoting Cooke's memoirs.

12 **8,370 varieties of notes**: Ibid., 25, quoting *Chicago Tribune*, February 13, 1863.

13 **"Counterfeit Detectors"**: Ibid., 23, 24.

13 **However, note circulation was**: Alexander Dana Noyes, National Monetary Commission, *History of the National-Bank Currency*, 61st Cong., 2d sess. (Washington, D.C.: Government Printing Office, 1910), 10–14, 18; and Richard T. McCulley, *Banks and Politics During the Progressive Era: The Origins of the Federal Reserve System, 1897–1913* (New York: Garland, 1992), 21–23.

14 **"the vast demands of the war"**: Davis, *The Origin of the National Banking System*, 103.

14 **"This system of currency has"**: McCulley, *Banks and Politics During the Progressive Era*, 15.

15 **"for purely speculative purposes"**: Carter Glass, *An Adventure in Constructive Finance* (Garden City, N.Y.: Doubleday, 1927), 61–62.

15 **note circulation sharply declined**: McCulley, *Banks and Politics During the Progressive Era*, 21–23; and Milton Friedman and Anna Jacobson Schwartz, *A Monetary History of the United States, 1867–1960* (Princeton, N.J.: Princeton University Press, 1971), 31–32.

16 **"we could no longer claim"**: Richard H. Timberlake Jr., *The Origins of Central Banking in the United States* (Cambridge, Mass.: Harvard University Press, 1978), 158–59.

17 **less peasants than little businessmen**: Alexis de Tocqueville, *Democracy in America* (1835; repr., New York: Library of America, 2004), 644.

17 **There were fewer bank notes issued**: McCulley, *Banks and Politics During the Progressive Era*, 18, 19–20.

17 **Carter Glass was one of those**: For details on Robert Glass, as well as on Carter Glass, see Harry Edward Poindexter, "From Copy Desk to Congress: The Pre-Congressional Career of Carter Glass," Ph.D. diss., University of Virginia, 1966, 37–38. See also Rixey Smith and Norman Beasley, *Carter Glass* (New York: Longmans, Green and Co., 1939), 3–36; James E. Palmer Jr., *Carter Glass: Unreconstructed Rebel* (Roanoke: Institute of American Biography, 1938), 12–33; and Matthew Fink, "The Unlikely Reformer: Carter Glass's Approach to Financial Legislation" (unpublished manuscript), 4.

17 **Glass's view of this calamity**: Poindexter, "From Copy Desk to Congress," 137.

18 **"But when I see the merciless forces":** Ibid., 224, 183.

18 **from 1867 to 1897:** Friedman and Schwartz, *Monetary History of the United States*, 24, 41, and 91.

18 **a bushel of winter wheat:** George Frederick Warren, *Crop Yields and Prices, and Our Future Food Supply* (Ithaca, N.Y.: Cornell University Press, 1914), 196.

18 **"You do not want an honest dollar":** Timberlake, *Origins of Central Banking in the United States*, 161–62.

19 **"the fate of the Western institution":** Alexander D. Noyes, "The Banks and the Panic of 1893," *Political Science Quarterly* 9, no. 1 (March 1894), 17.

19 **The Panic of 1893 exposed:** Ibid., especially 16–18, 24; and Robert L. Owen, *The Federal Reserve Act* (New York: Century, 1919), 2–3.

20 **"Fear of a silver basis prevailed":** Barton Hepburn, *A History of Currency in the United States* (New York: Macmillan, 1924), 349–50.

20 **forced to go hat in hand:** James Grant, *Money of the Mind: Borrowing and Lending in America from the Civil War to Michael Milken* (New York: Farrar, Straus and Giroux, 1992), 74.

20 **Morgan turned a profit:** Vincent P. Carosso, *The Morgans: Private International Bankers, 1854–1913* (Cambridge, Mass.: Harvard University Press, 1987), 339.

20 **Glass believed, on no evidence:** Poindexter, "From Copy Desk to Congress," 177.

20 **"It is just the money power":** Ibid., 206–7.

21 **Virginia's farmers were ruined:** Ibid., 125.

21 **Cleveland held that people should:** The precise Cleveland quote, widely cited, is "Though the people support the government; the government should not support the people."

21 **party bosses insisted that he stand for gold:** Nelson W. Aldrich Papers, Reel 59. Technically, McKinley promised to support a bimetallic system (gold and silver) if other nations did as well. Because most of Europe had no intention of switching, practically speaking, this meant that the Republicans were the party of gold.

22 **His editorials, a daily barrage:** Poindexter, "From Copy Desk to Congress," 15, 204, 224, and 234.

22 **Bryan did not analyze issues:** Richard Hofstadter, *The American Political Tradition and the Men Who Made It* (New York: Knopf, 1991); see especially 188–91.

23 **Eyewitnesses reported a momentary silence:** Robert A. Degen, *The American Monetary System: A Concise Survey of Its Evolution Since 1896* (Lexington, Mass: D.C. Heath, 1987), 95; and Poindexter, "From Copy Desk to Congress," 246–47.

23 **a noted Princeton professor:** John Milton Cooper Jr., *Woodrow Wilson* (New York: Knopf, 2009), 73.

24 **Rather than a currency based on government bonds:** "Report of the Monetary Commission to the Executive Committee of the Indianapolis Monetary Convention" (1897), available at openLibrary.org. See especially p. 37, discussing the phasing out of the requirement for depositing government bonds, and p. 43.

24 **"not a proper function of the Treasury Department":** *Annual Report of the Secretary of the Treasury on the State of the Finances*, 1896, lxxiii.

25 **"adjust itself automatically and promptly":** "Report of the Monetary Commission," 4.

25 **getting the government out of banking:** *Annual Report of the Secretary of the Treasury on the State of the Finances*, 1897, lxxiv–lxxvi; and Timberlake, *Origins of Central Banking in the United States*, 172.

26 **What further amplified the Treasury's:** McCulley, *Banks and Politics During the Progressive Era*, 56–57.

26 **"Money is plentiful throughout the country":** Arthur A. Housman to J. P. Morgan, June 14, 1899, J. P. Morgan Jr. Papers.

26–27 **"The cry everywhere":** Henry Morgenthau, *All in a Life-Time* (New York: Doubleday, 1922), 73.

27 **"havoc was wrought in the regular ongoing":** *Annual Report of the Secretary of the Treasury on the State of the Finances*, 1899, xc, xcii, xciv, and xcv.

27 **Legislators were irate that Gage:** A. Piatt Andrew, "The Treasury and the Banks Under Secretary Shaw," *Quarterly Journal of Economics* 21, no. 4 (August 1907), 528–29, 567.

27 **"orders for the transfer of existing bank credits":** *Annual Report of the Secretary*, 1899, xci; and *Annual Report of the Secretary of the Treasury on the State of the Finances*, 1901, 74.

27 **This 90 percent:** Friedman and Schwartz, *Monetary History of the United States*, 135–36, 139.

27 **"ruling principle of self-preservation":** *Annual Report of the Secretary*, 1901, 76.

28 **a raid on Northern Pacific:** Friedman and Schwartz, *Monetary History of the United States*, 142.

28 **"We justly boast of our political system":** *Annual Report of the Secretary*, 1901, 73-74, 77.

CHAPTER TWO: PRIVILEGED BANKER, SELF-MADE SENATOR

29 **"Under our clumsy laws, the currency":** Alexander D. Noyes, "The Banks and the Panic of 1893," *Political Science Quarterly* 9, no. 1 (March 1894).

29 **"The study of monetary questions":** Henry Dunning MacLeod, National Monetary Commission, *An Address by Senator Nelson W. Aldrich Before the Economic Club of New York*, November 29, 1909, 61st Cong., 2d sess. (Washington, D.C.: Government Printing Office, 1910), 26.

29 **Beginning in 1887:** Author interview with Mark Williams.

30 **Critics roundly debated whether Shaw:** A. Piatt Andrew, "The Treasury and the Banks Under Secretary Shaw," *Quarterly Journal of Economics* 21, no. 4 (August 1907), 519–68; see especially 530–38 and 540–42. See also Richard T. McCulley, *Banks and Politics During the Progressive Era: The Origins of the Federal Reserve System, 1897–1913* (New York: Garland, 1992), 102.

30 **"I was not here for three weeks":** Harold Kellock, "Warburg, the Revolutionist," *The Century Magazine* 90 (n.s. 68—May to October 1915).

30 **Paul seemed to make money:** Ron Chernow, *The Warburgs: The Twentieth-Century Odyssey of a Remarkable Jewish Family* (New York: Random House, 1993), 40.

31 **Overall, his field study:** Kellock, "Warburg, the Revolutionist."

31 **running the family bank:** Chernow, *The Warburgs*, 69.

31 **Warburg was shocked by the primitiveness:** Paul M. Warburg, *The Federal Reserve System: Its Origin and Growth—Reflections and Recollections* (New York: Macmillan, 1930), 1:14–16.

31 **approximately fifteen thousand banks:** "Changes in the Number and Size of Banks in the United States, 1834–1931, Material Prepared for the Information of the Federal Reserve System by the Federal Reserve Committee on Branch, Group, and Chain Banking," 3, available at http://fraser.stlouisfed.org/docs/historical/federal%20reserve%20history/frcom_br_gp_ch_banking/changes_in_banks_1834_1931.pdf. This report gives

a figure of 13,925 banks in 1900; by 1903 the total was slightly higher than 15,000. The report was written for a Fed committee appointed in 1930, J. H. Riddle, executive secretary and director of research.

32–33 **"How is the great international financier?":** This anecdote is from Warburg, *Federal Reserve System,* 1:18–19, except for the detail on Edward Harriman, which is from the research notes collected by Jeannette Paddock Nichols and Nathaniel W. Stephenson for the latter's biography found in the Nelson W. Aldrich Papers, Reel 61. (These research notes are found in various reels of the Aldrich Papers and all are hereinafter cited as "Biographer's notes.")

34 **Aldrich had high aspirations:** Jerome L. Sternstein, "Nelson W. Aldrich: The Making of the 'General Manager of the United States,' 1841–1886," A.B. thesis, Brooklyn College, 1959, 199–200.

34 **"its splendid white marble staircase":** Nathaniel Wright Stephenson, *Nelson W. Aldrich: A Leader in American Politics* (New York: Scribner's, 1930), 11–12.

34 **His father, a skilled machinist:** Biographer's notes, Aldrich Papers, Reel 58.

34 **Aldrich felt acutely:** Sternstein, "Nelson W. Aldrich," 9.

34 **Rejection furnished Aldrich:** Ibid., 38–41; the letter to Abby is on p. 32.

34 **Aldrich elevated himself:** Biographical details on Senator Aldrich generally come from Stephenson, *Nelson W. Aldrich.* The impression that Aldrich felt entitled to membership in the aristocracy is informed by Nelson W. Aldrich Jr., *Old Money: The Mythology of Wealth in America* (1988; repr., New York: Allworth Press, 1996), in particular p. 14; this is also the source for the *objets* (p. 26) and the land acquisition (p. 27). Details about the château come from Biographer's notes, Aldrich Papers, Reel 58; Aldrich, *Old Money,* 26; and Stephenson, *Nelson W. Aldrich,* 192.

35 **"most earnest and cherished hope":** Sternstein, "Nelson W. Aldrich," 150–51.

35 **a rambling tour of Europe:** Ibid., 84–100.

35 **"a basis for his commitment":** Ibid., 105.

35 **"If I am deeply impressed":** Quoted in ibid., 105–6.

35 **smiled rather than laughed out loud:** Biographer's notes, Aldrich Papers, Reel 58. See also Aldrich, *Old Money,* 13–21.

36 **Rarely did he debate:** Biographer's notes, Aldrich Papers, Reel 59.

36 **"side whiskers close cut":** Stephenson, *Nelson W. Aldrich,* 44.

36 **"a blindness to inessentials":** Sternstein, "Nelson W. Aldrich," 159.

36 **Rhode Island legislative bosses:** Sternstein, "Nelson W. Aldrich," 52–53; and Aldrich, *Old Money,* 15–16.

36 **the hot issue was the tariff:** Author's correspondence with Douglas A. Irwin.

37 **had 170 volumes shipped:** Biographer's notes, Aldrich Papers, Reel 58.

37 **"the general liberty of trade":** Adam Smith, *The Wealth of Nations* (1776).

37 **highest concentration of industry:** Sternstein, "Nelson W. Aldrich," 194.

37 **family that ran the Sugar Trust:** There is a rich literature on Aldrich's relationship with the Sugar Trust; see especially Jerome L. Sternstein, "Corruption in the Guilded Age Senate: Nelson W. Aldrich and the Sugar Trust," *Capitol Studies: A Journal of the Capitol and Congress* 6, no. 1 (Spring 1978), as well as Biographer's notes, Aldrich Papers, Reel 59; and Sternstein, "Nelson W. Aldrich," 236. Other details in this paragraph come from Sternstein, "Nelson W. Aldrich," 191, 198–201, 236, 248, 255–56, 260, and 262.

37 **persuading William McKinley:** Biographer's notes, Aldrich Papers, Reel 59.

37–38 bankers desperate to halt: Michael Clark Rockefeller, "Nelson W. Aldrich and Banking Reform: A Conservative Leader in the Progressive Era," A.B. thesis, Harvard College, 1960, 6.

38 "Our currency is as good as gold": Barton Hepburn, *A History of Currency in the United States* (New York: Macmillan, 1924), v–xvi.

38 "Aldrich is a great man": Sternstein, "Nelson W. Aldrich," 4.

38 "would adopt it as his own": Hepburn, *History of Currency*, v–xvi.

39 This "stupid condition": *Banking and Currency Reform: Hearings Before the Subcommittee of the Committee on Banking and Currency, Charged with Investigating Plan of Banking and Currency Reform and Reporting Constructive Legislation Thereof*, 62nd Cong., 3rd sess., House of Representatives, January 7, 1913 (Washington, D.C.: Government Printing Office, 1913), 77, available at http://books.google.com/books?id=pcoqAAAAYAAJ&printsec=frontcover&source=gbs_ge_summary_r&cad=0#v=onepage&q&f=false.

39 "To a person trained under": Warburg, *The Federal Reserve System*, 1:17.

39 "a lively and intimate daily exchange": Ibid., 1:14–15.

40 "Once started, the poor check": James G. Cannon and David Kinley, National Monetary Commission, *Clearing Houses and Credit Instruments* (Washington, D.C.: Government Printing Office, 1911), 6:70–73.

40 more than two hundred trusts: Richard Hofstadter, *The Age of Reform: From Bryan to F.D.R.* (New York: Vintage, 1955), 168–69, 232.

40–41 America had far more banks: Kellock, "Warburg, the Revolutionist."

41 "there existed as many disconnected": Warburg, *The Federal Reserve System*, 1:12.

41 Warburg frequently unburdened himself: "Aldrich Becomes Converted to Idea of a Central Bank, May–October, 1908," Aldrich Papers, Reel 61 (from Warburg Papers).

41 His one innovation was to suggest: "What Congress Left Undone," *The Outlook* 73, no. 11 (March 14, 1903), available at www.unz.org/Pub/Outlook-1903mar14-00597a02. See also Rockefeller, "Nelson W. Aldrich and Banking Reform," 6; Stephenson, *Nelson W. Aldrich*, 210; Robert H. Wiebe, *Businessmen and Reform: A Study of the Progressive Movement* (Chicago: Elephant, 1989), 64; and McCulley, *Banks and Politics During the Progressive Era*, 104–5.

42 A card-playing companion of J. P. Morgan: Jerome L. Sternstein, "King Leopold II, Senator Nelson W. Aldrich, and the Strange Beginnings of American Economic Penetration of the Congo," *African Historical Studies* 2, no. 2 (1969).

43 "it became easy for Aldrich": Rockefeller, "Nelson W. Aldrich and Banking Reform," 50.

43 Many articles focused on the gross inequities: Arthur Weinberg and Lila Weinberg, eds., *The Muckrakers: The Era in Journalism That Moved America to Reform—The Most Significant Magazine Articles of 1902–1912* (New York: Simon and Schuster, 1965), xiv, xv, and xix.

44 "the chief exploiter of the American people": David Graham Phillips, "The Treason of the Senate," *Cosmopolitan*, March 1906. The previous year, Aldrich had been the focus of another broadside: Lincoln Steffens, "Rhode Island: A State for Sale," *McClure's Magazine* 24, no. 4 (February 1905).

44 "look no way but downward": Weinberg and Weinberg, *The Muckrakers*, xvii.

44 Critics also thought the attacks: Ibid., xvi–xvii, 70.

44 America had 3,800 of them: Ibid., xiii, xiv.

CHAPTER THREE: JITTERS ON WALL STREET

46 **"There is just as true patriotism"**: Vanderlip to Woodrow Wilson, October 29, 1912, telegram, Frank A. Vanderlip Papers, Box 1-4.

46 **Schiff feared that America's prosperity**: Cyrus Adler, *Jacob H. Schiff: His Life and Letters* (1928; repr., Grosse Pointe, Mich.: Scholarly Press, 1968), 1:277–79. The $100 million figure comes from A. Piatt Andrew, "The Treasury and the Banks Under Secretary Shaw," *The Quarterly Journal of Economics* 21, no. 4 (August 1907), 542–43.

47 **the hidebound National Banking system**: Biographer's notes, Nelson A. Aldrich Papers, Reel 61, which makes reference to the "hard-boiled" loyalty shown by American bankers toward the National Banking Act.

47 **Vanderlip had grown up**: Biographical details in this and the next paragraph come from Frank A. Vanderlip with Boyden Sparkes, *From Farm Boy to Financier* (New York: D. Appleton-Century, 1935); the opinion of Roosevelt is found on 80–82.

48 **ferried four eggs**: Anna Robeson Burr, *James Stillman: The Portrait of a Banker* (New York: Duffield, 1927), 185.

48 **Even though the U.S. economy had grown**: Henry Parker Willis, *The Federal Reserve System: Legislation, Organization and Operation* (New York: Ronald Press, 1923), 486. The 40 percent figure was given during the 1913 Senate debate on the Federal Reserve Act; in 1906, the percentage most likely was less, but it was still impressively high.

49 **the dollar would overtake the pound**: J. Lawrence Broz first proposed the thesis that American bankers lobbying for a central bank were motivated, at least in part, by their private interest in seeing the dollar become an international currency. See Broz's "The Origins of Central Banking: Solutions to the Free-Rider Problem," *International Organization* 52, no. 2 (Spring 1998), 231–68, as well as his "Origins of the Federal Reserve System: International Incentives and the Domestic Free-Rider Problem," *International Organization* 53, no. 1 (Winter 1999), 39–70. See also Adler, *Jacob H. Schiff*, 280–81, which quotes Schiff at the New York Chamber of Commerce: "Our merchants who buy goods in China, Japan, South America, and elsewhere must, to our mortification, still settle their transactions in London, Paris, or Germany, just as the very money we loaned to Japan recently had to be remitted to London."

49 **"unable to make use of their credit"**: "The Currency," report by the Special Committee of the Chamber of Commerce, New York State, submitted October 4, 1906, and adopted November 1, 1906, available at https://archive.org/stream/currencyreportoonewyrich /currencyreportoonewyrich_djvu.txt.

50 **"a majority of the bankers"**: Ibid.

50 **"New York bankers are, with few exceptions"**: Richard T. McCulley, *Banks and Politics During the Progressive Era: The Origins of the Federal Reserve System, 1897–1913* (New York: Garland, 1992), 89–90.

50 **"If you go away from New York City"**: Adler, *Jacob H. Schiff*, 284–85.

51 **"The immediate effect has been"**: Vanderlip to James Stillman, April 27, 1906, Vanderlip Papers, Box 1-2. Details on Stillman's mansion from Burr, *James Stillman*, 248, 275. See also Kerry A. Odell and Marc D. Weidenmier, "Real Shock, Monetary Aftershock: The 1906 San Francisco Earthquake and the Panic of 1907," *Journal of Economic History* 64, no. 4 (December 2004).

51 **"The drain which California"**: Vanderlip to James Stillman, May 4, 1906, Vanderlip Papers, Box 1-2.

52 **In April and three times later:** Andrew, "The Treasury and the Banks Under Secretary Shaw," 543.

52 **a short-term loan of $10 million:** Ibid., 545.

52 **"granaries and warehouses were empty":** *Annual Report of the Secretary of the Treasury on the State of the Finances,* 1906, 39, 41.

52 **"business men returned to their desks":** Ibid., 41–42.

53 **"with great benefit":** Ibid., 39, 42.

53 **The total funds at his disposal:** Richard H. Timberlake Jr., *The Origins of Central Banking in the United States* (Cambridge, Mass.: Harvard University Press, 1978), 220–21.

53 **fully 11 percent:** Harold van B. Cleveland and Thomas F. Huertas, *Citibank: 1812–1970* (Cambridge, Mass: Harvard University Press, 1985), 49.

53 **"had begun to smell kerosene":** McCulley, *Banks and Politics During the Progressive Era,* 123.

53 **"a ring of powerful Wall Street speculators":** Timberlake, *The Origins of Central Banking in the United States,* 179.

53 **"finds its level about as quickly":** *Annual Report of the Secretary,* 1906, 42–43.

53 **some future "autocrat":** Timberlake, *The Origins of Central Banking in the United States,* 179.

54 **"Outside relief in business":** Andrew, "The Treasury and the Banks Under Secretary Shaw," 544, 559, 561, and 565.

54 **Shaw immodestly suggested:** Shaw specifically claimed that if he was given $100 million to be deposited with or withdrawn from banks at his pleasure, and was permitted to set reserve requirements, he could avert any panic that threatened either the United States or Europe: see *Annual Report of the Secretary,* 1906, 46, 49.

55 **the ABA championed a bill:** McCulley, *Banks and Politics During the Progressive Era,* 92–93; and Robert H. Wiebe, *Businessmen and Reform: A Study of the Progressive Movement* (Chicago: Elephant, 1989), 63–64.

55 **But the prospect of branch banking:** McCulley, *Banks and Politics During the Progressive Era,* 92, 95–97, 124, and 133; and Michael Clark Rockefeller, "Nelson W. Aldrich and Banking Reform: A Conservative Leader in the Progressive Era," A.B. thesis, Harvard College, 1960, vi, x, and xi.

55 **"The bankers are still divided":** Wiebe, *Businessmen and Reform,* 65.

55 **the system was run by "God":** Henry F. Pringle, *The Life and Times of William Howard Taft* (New York: Farrar and Rinehart, 1939), 2:716.

55 **"abhorrence of both extremes":** Paul M. Warburg, *The Federal Reserve System: Its Origin and Growth—Reflections and Recollections* (New York: Macmillan, 1930), 1:12.

56 **"You ought to write":** Harold Kellock, "Warburg, the Revolutionist," *The Century Magazine* 90 (n.s. 68—May to October 1915).

57 **"The Bank of England is extremely nervous":** Vanderlip to James Stillman, March 22, 1907, Vanderlip Papers, Box 1-2.

57 **London raised its interest rate:** Andrew, "The Treasury and the Banks Under Secretary Shaw," 548 (also the source for Reichsbank).

57 **directing British banks to liquidate:** O. M. W. Sprague, National Monetary Commission, *History of Crises Under the National Banking System,* 61st Cong., 2d sess. (Washington, D.C.: Government Printing Office, 1910), 241.

57 **"the Wall Street boom punctured":** McCulley, *Banks and Politics During the Progressive Era,* 125.

57 **Wall Street tried to replace:** Ibid., 119; and Sprague, *History of Crises,* 241.

57 **"I have felt for some time"**: Cleveland and Huertas, *Citibank*, 51–52.
58 **"buoyancy and hopefulness"**: Perkins to J. P. Morgan, April 30, 1907, George W. Perkins Sr. Papers, Box 9.
58 **"a great number of people and houses"**: Perkins to J. P. Morgan, May 31, 1907, ibid.
58 **"make loans for any length of time"**: Perkins to J. P. Morgan, June 19, 1907, ibid.
58 **"a partial fulfillment of hopes"**: "Currency Outlook Under Aldrich Law," *The New York Times*, March 4, 1907.
58 **"There seems to be a general feeling"**: Perkins to J. P. Morgan, May 27, 1907, Perkins Papers, Box 9.

CHAPTER FOUR: PANIC

59 **"A panic grows"**: Walter Bagehot, *Lombard Street: A Description of the Money Market* (London, 1873), 20.
59 **"Who is to be Mr. Morgan's successor?"**: Ida Tarbell, "The Hunt for a Money Trust, III. The Clearing House," *American Magazine*, July 1913, 42.
59 **"The present head of the department"**: Richard H. Timberlake Jr., *The Origins of Central Banking in the United States* (Cambridge, Mass.: Harvard University Press, 1978), 184.
60 **"Not so *loud*, please, Mr. Street"**: Frank A. Vanderlip with Boyden Sparkes, *From Farm Boy to Financier* (New York: D. Appleton-Century, 1935), 165–67.
60 **"a little let-up in general business"**: Perkins to J. P. Morgan, July 12, 1907, George W. Perkins Sr. Papers, Box 9.
60 **The New York money market tightened:** Jon Moen and Ellis W. Tallman, "The Bank Panic of 1907: The Role of Trust Companies," *The Journal of Economic History* 52, no. 3 (September 1992), 617.
61 **"There is nothing special to report"**: Perkins to J. P. Morgan, October 3, 1907, Perkins Papers, Box 9.
61 **"We are all very well"**: Perkins to J. P. Morgan, October 12, 1907, ibid.
61 **manipulate a copper-mining stock:** The speculator, whose name I omitted to avoid deluging the reader with an abundance of characters, was Frederick Augustus Heinze, one of the three so-called copper kings of Butte, Montana. The mining stock was that of United Copper Company. This account is largely based on O. M. W. Sprague, "The American Crisis of 1907," *The Economic Journal* 18, no. 71 (September 1908).
62 **And while a dollar in the national banks:** Jon R. Moen and Ellis W. Tallman, "Why Didn't the United States Establish a Central Bank Until After the Panic of 1907?" (unpublished manuscript, September 2007), 27, table 3; the figures are for New York City only. Note the precise reserve figures were 5.8 percent (5.8 cents per dollar of deposits) for trusts and 25.7 percent for banks.
62 **"had been of an extreme character"**: Sprague, "The American Crisis of 1907," 357.
62 **two of the Morse banks:** Ibid., 358.
62 **Morse seems to have ratted out:** "Knickerbocker Will Be Aided," *The New York Times*, October 22, 1907. This article says that Morse urged the New York Clearing House to continue its probe into other banks, and that Morse and Barney were "at odds."
62 **Barney and the unsavory Morse:** Robert F. Bruner and Sean D. Carr, *The Panic of 1907: Lessons Learned from the Market's Perfect Storm* (Hoboken, N.J.: John Wiley and Sons, 2007), 75–76. Bruner and Carr also maintain that growing rumors of the two men's connections both contributed to Barney's downfall and "gained credence" when Barney was forced to resign.

62 private railcar: Vincent P. Carosso, *The Morgans: Private International Bankers, 1854–1913* (Cambridge, Mass.: Harvard University Press, 1987), 536.

63 Davison was immediately confronted: New York Clearing House, Minutes, October 21, 1907, cited in Moen and Tallman, "Why Didn't the United States Establish a Central Bank," 12.

63 The sidewalk in front was besieged: "Pays Out $8,000,000 and Then Suspends," *The New York Times*, October 23, 1907.

63 "stacks of green currency": Quoted in Bruner and Carr, *The Panic of 1907*, 78.

63 green-marbled public area: Ibid.

63 "The consternation of the faces": Lester V. Chandler, *Benjamin Strong, Central Banker* (Washington, D.C.: Brookings Institution, 1958), 28.

63 "with Mr. Morgan presiding": "Knickerbocker Will Not Open," *The New York Times*, October 23, 1907.

64 "This, then, is the place": Thomas W. Lamont, *Henry P. Davison: The Record of a Useful Life* (New York: Harper and Brothers, 1933), 76.

64 Harry Davison had been reared in: Ibid., especially 15.

64 Strong had been raised: Background on Strong from Chandler, *Benjamin Strong;* see also "Mrs. Strong Kills Herself," *The New York Times*, May 11, 1905; and Lamont, *Henry P. Davison*, 59–62.

65 "making figures as we went along": Carosso, *The Morgans*, 539–40.

65 the fifth straight of panicky conditions: Ibid., 540–41; and Jean Strouse, *Morgan, American Financier* (New York: Random House, 1999), 579.

65 By then, a new crisis was erupting: Carosso, *The Morgans*, 542.

66 the Treasury's surplus was exhausted: *Annual Report of the Secretary of Treasury on the State of the Finances*, 1907, 53–54. Cortelyou said his hands were "virtually tied."

66 "We sat quietly": Vanderlip, *From Farm Boy to Financier*, 174–75.

66 Grateful tributes streamed in to: The letters of appreciation to Morgan can be found in the Pierpont Morgan Papers, Box 7, book 12. See also Ron Chernow, *The House of Morgan: An American Banking Dynasty and the Rise of Modern Finance* (New York: Grove Press, 1990), 125; "J. P. Morgan Has a Cold," *The New York Times*, October 26, 1907; and "Lord Rothschild's Tribute to Morgan," *The New York Times*, October 26, 1907.

66 New York's trusts lost: Author interview with Ellis W. Tallman, who cited call reports of the New York Superintendent of Banking. According to Tallman, from August 22 to December 19, 1907, deposits in New York City trusts fell 47.8 percent. The figure was inflated by the shuttering of the Knickerbocker, but even if the Knickerbocker is omitted from the calculation, deposits fell a hefty 33.7 percent.

67 With panic spreading, clearinghouses: A. Piatt Andrew, "Substitutes for Cash in the Panic of 1907," *The Quarterly Journal of Economics* 22, no. 4 (August 1908), 509.

67 banks were forced to hand out: O. M. W. Sprague, National Monetary Commission, *History of Crises Under the National Banking System*, 61st Cong., 2d sess. (Washington, D.C.: Government Printing Office, 1910), 290.

67 Many railroads, mining companies: Andrew, "Substitutes for Cash in the Panic of 1907," 510–13.

67 By mid-November, approximately half: Ibid., 501; the exact figures in the survey were 71 of 145 cities. In addition, Sprague, *History of Crises*, reports that 60 of 110 established clearinghouses made use, specifically, of loan certificates (p. 290). Quotations and other details in this paragraph come from Andrew, "Substitutes for Cash in the Panic of 1907," especially 497, 504, and 507–8.

68 **$500 million of cash substitutes:** Andrew, "Substitutes for Cash in the Panic of 1907," 515. Andrew calculated (p. 507) that $238 million, or nearly half of the estimated total of cash substitutes, consisted of "regular" clearinghouse certificates, including $101 million of such certificates in New York.

68 **"to a greater or lesser degree":** Ibid., 501–2.

68 **Council Bluffs . . . Providence:** Ibid., 502A. For banks' discretion, see also Sprague, *History of Crises,* 287.

68 **in many states they encouraged banks:** Andrew, "Substitutes for Cash in the Panic of 1907," 498–500; and Sprague, *History of Crises.*

68 **"the most extensive and prolonged breakdown":** Andrew, "Substitutes for Cash in the Panic of 1907," 497.

68 **"drafts on Philadelphia, Boston":** "Bankers Discuss Causes of Flurry," *The New York Times,* December 3, 1907.

68 **Even the suggestion that banks:** Sprague, *History of Crises,* 276. Sprague succinctly observed: "Suspension increases enormously the propensity to hoard money."

68 **safe-deposit boxes:** A. Piatt Andrew, "Hoarding in the Panic of 1907," *The Quarterly Journal of Economics* 22, no. 2 (February 1908), 293–95.

69 **plunged by $350 million:** Sprague, "The American Crisis of 1907," 367. In "Hoarding in the Panic of 1907" (p. 293), Andrew suggests the far smaller figure of $230 million of currency that "passed out of the banks and disappeared from sight between August and December."

69 **However, hoarding by individuals:** Elmus Wicker, *The Great Debate on Banking Reform: Nelson Aldrich and the Origins of the Fed* (Columbus: Ohio State University Press, 2005), 39.

69 **"It is said that many of our people":** *Annual Report of the Secretary of the Treasury on the State of the Finances,* 1907, 53.

69 **"We were broke with a pocket full of money":** *Banking and Currency Reform: Hearings Before the Subcommittee of the Committee on Banking and Currency, Charged with Investigating Plan of Banking and Currency Reform and Reporting Constructive Legislation Thereof,* 62nd Cong., 3rd sess., House of Representatives January 7, 1913 (Washington, D.C.: Government Printing Office, 1913), 262, available at http://books.google.com/books?id=pcoq AAAAYAAJ&printsec=frontcover&source=gbs_ge_summary_r&cad=0#v=onepage &q&f=false.

69 **bolstered their reserves:** Andrew, "Hoarding in the Panic of 1907," 296–97 (for San Antonio, Indianapolis, Wichita, Portland, and Galveston).

69 **Vanderlip sourly surmised:** Vanderlip, *From Farm Boy to Financier,* 171.

69 **well below the legal minimum:** Myron T. Herrick, "The Panic of 1907 and Some of Its Lessons," *Annals of the American Academy of Political and Social Science* 31 (March 1, 1908), 9. The cumulative reserve deficit of the national banks in New York City was $54 million, the largest ever.

69 **Charges and countercharges flew:** See, for instance, Sprague, "The American Crisis of 1907," 367.

69 **The problem was that the system:** Sprague, *History of Crises,* 304.

70 **a town without a fire department:** Paul M. Warburg, *The Federal Reserve System: Its Origin and Growth—Reflections and Recollections* (New York: Macmillan, 1930), 2:125.

70 **Britain had not experienced a banking suspension:** Andrew, "Hoarding in the Panic of 1907," 290.

70 **America had been scorched:** J. Lawrence Broz, "Origins of the Federal Reserve System:

International Incentives and the Domestic Free-Rider Problem," *International Organization* 53, no. 1 (Winter 1999), 44. The five severe crises occurred in 1873, 1884, 1890, 1893, and 1907.

70 **"All institutions had to run":** Timberlake, *The Origins of Central Banking in the United States,* 183–84.

70 **Quickly on the heels of the Panic:** Sprague, "The American Crisis of 1907," 368; and Milton Friedman and Anna Jacobson Schwartz, *A Monetary History of the United States, 1867–1960* (Princeton, N.J.: Princeton University Press, 1971), 156. From December 1906 to November 1907, the Dow Industrials fell 40.9 percent.

71 **"Too late now, Mr. Stillman":** Warburg, *The Federal Reserve System,* 1:18–19.

71 **"a modern central bank":** "Mr. Warburg Urges Government Bank," *The New York Times,* November 14, 1907.

71 **One episode in particular soured:** This account is based on Strouse, *Morgan, American Financier,* 582–88.

72 **"group of financiers who withhold":** Ibid., 589.

72 **"unreasoning *dis*trust and pessimism":** Ibid. (italics added).

72 **"inscrutable and mysterious power":** Lucy D. Chen, "Banking Reform in a Hostile Climate: Paul M. Warburg and the National Citizens' League" (working paper, April 2010), available at www.fas.harvard.edu/~histecon/crisis-next/1907/docs/Chen-Warburg_Final _Paper.pdf.

73 **"statesmen"—leaders in society:** William Diamond, *The Economic Thought of Woodrow Wilson* (Baltimore: Johns Hopkins University Press, 1943), 78–79.

73 **"this turmoil of undefined wickedness":** "Dr. Wilson Defines Material Issues," *The New York Times,* November 24, 1907.

73 **Columbia University sponsored:** The title page of *The Currency Problem and the Present Financial Situation,* a book reproducing the Columbia lectures, can be found in the Nelson W. Aldrich Papers.

74 **Warburg unapologetically advised:** Paul M. Warburg, "American and European Banking Methods and Bank Legislation Compared," February 3, 1908, reprinted in Warburg, *The Federal Reserve System,* 2:43, 48, and 54.

74 **introduced the arguments for centralization to a wider public:** Wicker, *The Great Debate on Banking Reform,* 38.

74 **a "modified" central bank:** Warburg's plan was published as a letter to the *Times* on November 14, 1907, under the headline "Mr. Warburg Urges Government Bank." Warburg, in his later collection of speeches and essays (*The Federal Reserve System,* 2:29–36), recycled a version of this plan under the more memorable title "A Plan for a Modified Central Bank"; he said it had been published on November 12. The discrepancy between dates is unexplained.

74 **an umbrella organization of clearinghouses:** Warburg, "A Plan for a Modified Central Bank," in Warburg, *The Federal Reserve System,* 2:34–35.

74 **never permit the system to truly change:** Warburg, *The Federal Reserve System,* 1:31.

74 **Aldrich, now sixty-six:** The biographical details on Aldrich in this paragraph are from Michael Clark Rockefeller, "Nelson W. Aldrich and Banking Reform: A Conservative Leader in the Progressive Era," A.B. thesis, Harvard College, 1960, 12–13.

75 **Gazing on Aldrich for the first time:** Notes found in Aldrich Papers, Reel 61. See also Warburg, *The Federal Reserve System,* 1:31–32.

75 **Schiff advised that it would be a grave mistake:** Notes found in Aldrich Papers, Reel 61.

75 **Four days later:** Warburg, *The Federal Reserve System,* 1:32.

76 **"Did not the last panic":** Paul Warburg to Aldrich, December 31, 1907, Aldrich Papers, Reel 61; reprinted in Warburg, *The Federal Reserve System*, 1:555–57.

CHAPTER FIVE: THE CROSSING

77 **"This central reserve, or whatever name":** *Banking and Currency Reform: Hearings Before the Subcommittee of the Committee on Banking and Currency, Charged with Investigating Plan of Banking and Currency Reform and Reporting Constructive Legislation Thereof,* 62nd Cong., 3rd sess., House of Representatives, January 7, 1913 (Washington, D.C.: Government Printing Office, 1913), 69, available at http://books.google.com/books?id=pcoqAA AAYAAJ&printsec=frontcover&source=gbs_ge_summary_r&cad=0#v=onepage&q&f =false.

77 **"Well timed reform alone averts revolution":** Theodore Roosevelt to Everett Colby, October 3, 1913; George W. Perkins Sr. Papers, Box 13.

77 **Congress crafted a legislative response:** Harold Kellock, "Warburg, the Revolutionist," *The Century Magazine* 90 (n.s. 68—May to October 1915).

78 **But 1908 did not start auspiciously:** Paul Warburg to Hon. Theodore E. Burton, April 30, 1908, in Paul M. Warburg, *The Federal Reserve System: Its Origin and Growth— Reflections and Recollections* (New York: Macmillan, 1930), 1:553–54.

78 **The Aldrich bill proposed:** See various items in Nelson W. Aldrich Papers, Reel 61, including "Aldrich Becomes Converted to Idea of a Central Bank, May–October 1908"; as well as Michael Clark Rockefeller, "Nelson W. Aldrich and Banking Reform: A Conservative Leader in the Progressive Era," A.B. thesis, Harvard College, 1960, 18–19; Henry Parker Willis, *The Federal Reserve System: Legislation, Organization and Operation* (New York: Ronald Press, 1923), 45–46; and Richard T. McCulley, *Banks and Politics During the Progressive Era: The Origins of the Federal Reserve System, 1897–1913* (New York: Garland, 1992), 152–54.

78 **"We are all thoroughly disgusted":** Perkins to J. P. Morgan, May 22, 1908, Perkins Papers, Box 9.

79 **There was little enthusiasm:** McCulley, *Banks and Politics During the Progressive Era,* 153–54.

79 **"Thoughtful students of economic history":** Speech of Senator Nelson W. Aldrich on S. Bill No. 3023, February 10, 1908, quoted in Warburg, *The Federal Reserve System,* 1:32.

79 **Given carte blanche to do as little:** James Grant, *Money of the Mind: Borrowing and Lending in America from the Civil War to Michael Milken* (New York: Farrar, Straus and Giroux, 1992), 122–23. Tallies of the number of National Monetary Commission volumes differ. Andrew cites thirty-five volumes; see Andrew to Woodrow Wilson, November 23, 1911, A. Piatt Andrews Papers, Box 22, folder 7; however, Andrew L. Gray, Andrew's grandnephew, cites twenty-three volumes in "Who Killed the Aldrich Plan?" *The Bankers Magazine* 54 (Summer 1971), 62–74.

80 **Aldrich did seek help:** "Minutes of Meetings of Monetary Commission, 1908–1911" and "Chronology on Monetary Commission Work of Senator Aldrich," both in Aldrich Papers, Reel 61. Regarding the recommendation of Davison, see Perkins to J. P. Morgan, July 14, 1908, Perkins Papers, Box 9.

80 **Morgan had been so impressed:** Jean Strouse, *Morgan, American Financier* (New York: Random House, 1999), 602.

80 **"It is understood Davison":** Perkins to J. P. Morgan, July 23, 1908, telegram, Perkins Papers, Box 9.

80 **was furiously lobbying Congress to weaken:** Correspondence in the Perkins Papers

(Box 9) documents efforts for antitrust relief, both in general and specifically for International Harvester and U.S. Steel, each the fruit of Morgan-orchestrated mergers. See also Robert H. Wiebe, *Businessmen and Reform: A Study of the Progressive Movement* (Chicago: Elephant, 1989), 46–47. On rate fixing, Perkins's April 21, 1908, letter to Morgan (also in Perkins Papers, Box 9) contains this gem: "The most important thing that really has been accomplished—and it is very important—is that at least we have succeeded in getting practically all the railroad Presidents together in an agreement to raise freight rates. We had a great deal of difficulty in convincing Mr. [George Frederick] Baer, Mr. [Henry] Walters and one or two others that this ought to be done. They have finally come into line and yesterday, at a meeting of the Presidents here, they all agreed to the principle and gave out a statement to that effect. . . . It is estimated that this ought to add about $100,000,000 a year to the railroads' revenues." Finally, my understanding of the Morgan ethos was indelibly affected by reading *The House of Morgan: An American Banking Dynasty and the Rise of Modern Finance* (New York: Grove Press, 1990); for that and more, I am indebted to its author, my friend Ron Chernow.

81 **"the levelest headed man in the country":** William Howard Taft to Aldrich, June 27, 1908, Aldrich Papers, Reel 61.

81 **"make men good by law":** McCulley, *Banks and Politics During the Progressive Era*, 160.

82 **Taft denounced the Oklahoma plan:** Ibid., 159–61.

82 **Aldrich told the press his aim:** "Aldrich Satisfied with Currency Law," *The New York Times*, August 1, 1908.

82 **Aldrich reserved a $260 suite:** North German Lloyd Steamship Co. to Arthur P. Shelton, July 23, 1908, Aldrich Papers, Reel 27.

82 **Davison had sailed ahead:** Perkins to Morgan, July 23, 1908, George W. Perkins Sr. Papers.

82 **Aldrich exhaustively prepared:** Nathaniel Wright Stephenson, *Nelson W. Aldrich: A Leader in American Politics* (New York: Scribner's, 1930), 335–36.

82 **he took unusual precautions:** Ibid., 336; and Aldrich Papers, Reel 61.

82 **Professor Andrew brought banking textbooks:** Aldrich Papers, Reel 27; Rockefeller, "Nelson W. Aldrich and Banking Reform," 28; and Stephenson, *Nelson W. Aldrich*, 335.

82 **Andrew hailed from La Porte:** Typed "Family History," A. Piatt Andrew Papers, Box 43, folder 8.

83 **At Princeton he had studied:** Andrew to W. G. Brown, December 5, 1911, ibid., Box 22, folder 7.

83 **teacher to the young Franklin D. Roosevelt:** "Family History." Andrew's social outings with FDR are mentioned in his *Diary of Abram Piatt Andrew, 1902–1914*, ed. E. Parker Hayden Jr. and Andrew L. Gray (Princeton, N.J., 1986).

83 **Economics in the Gilded Age:** Andrew, *Diary;* for Andrew's government salary, see Aldrich Papers, Reel 58.

83 **the Bank of England acquired:** Walter Bagehot, *Lombard Street: A Description of the Money Market* (London, 1873). Bagehot stresses that the duty as lender of last resort was merely tacit, not written down or "acknowledged"—see especially pp. 25, 71.

84 **In the famous phrase of Walter Bagehot:** Bagehot, *Lombard Street*, 19, 21; see also ibid., 66-67, 78.

84 **roughly twenty in all:** Forrest Capie, Charles Goodhart, and Norbert Schnadt, "The Development of Central Banking" (1994), available at http://eprints.lse.ac.uk/39606/1

/The_development_of_central_banking_%28LSERO%29.pdf. Specifically, its table 1.2, "The Number of Central Banks 1900–1990" (p. 6), states there were eighteen in 1900 and twenty in 1910. Background on central bank history and development is based on J. Lawrence Broz's trenchant "The Origins of Central Banking: Solutions to the Free-Rider Problem," delivered at the 1996 Annual Meeting of the American Political Science Association, and published in *International Organization* 52, no. 2 (Spring 1998), 231–68.

84 **the big three of European banking:** Bagehot, *Lombard Street,* 16, 28, and 84–85.

85 **In Germany, management was in the hands:** National Monetary Commission, *Interviews on the Banking and Currency Systems of England, Scotland, France, Germany, Switzerland, and Italy,* 61st Cong., 2d sess. (Washington, D.C.: Government Printing Office: 1910), 336.

85 **Morgan lost no time in requesting:** Stephenson, *Nelson W. Aldrich,* 336.

85 **Interviews at the Bank of England:** Biographer's notes, Aldrich Papers, Reel 61.

85 **naïve and unprepared:** Stephenson, *Nelson W. Aldrich,* 335.

85 **Matters improved after a few days:** "Minutes of Meetings of Monetary Commission."

85 **Aldrich also enlisted George Reynolds:** Stephenson, *Nelson W. Aldrich,* 335; and Rockefeller, "Nelson W. Aldrich and Banking Reform," 32.

85 **Davison took the lead:** Biographer's notes, Aldrich Papers, Reel 61; and Rockefeller, "Nelson W. Aldrich and Banking Reform," 28.

85 **Commercial banks kept:** Bagehot, *Lombard Street,* 11–13.

85 **had relatively little gold:** J. Lawrence Broz, "The Domestic Politics of International Monetary Order: The Gold Standard," in *Contested Social Orders and International Politics,* ed. David Skidmore (Nashville: Vanderbilt University Press, 1997), 53–91.

85 **Aldrich liberally buying economics books:** Biographer's notes, Aldrich Papers, Reel 61; and Stephenson, *Nelson W. Aldrich,* 337–38.

86 **the group ventured to Berlin:** Andrew, *Diary;* and "Chronology on Monetary Commission Work of Senator Aldrich."

86 **a dispatch written by Napoleon:** National Monetary Commission, *An Address by Senator Nelson W. Aldrich Before the Economic Club of New York,* November 29, 1909, 61st Cong., 2d sess. (Washington, D.C.: Government Printing Office, 1910), 28.

86 **suggested that Aldrich gather:** Frank A. Vanderlip with Boyden Sparkes, *From Farm Boy to Financier* (New York: D. Appleton-Century, 1935), 211.

86 **Andrew and the Davisons:** Andrew, *Diary.*

86 **the interviews:** Biographer's notes, Aldrich Papers, Reel 61; and National Monetary Commission, *Interviews.*

86 **Davison and Aldrich pressed their hosts:** National Monetary Commission, *Interviews;* quotes come from pp. 31–32, 356, 201–2, and 212, respectively.

87 **fifty-eight meetings:** Rockefeller, "Nelson W. Aldrich and Banking Reform," 23; and Aldrich Papers, Reel 29.

88 **Reynolds, the Chicago banker, maintained:** Stephenson, *Nelson W. Aldrich,* 339.

88 **safari in Africa:** Discussion of Roosevelt's pending trip was public within weeks of the election: see, for example, "Explorers See Roosevelt," *The New York Times,* November 21, 1908.

88 **"I like your ideas":** This anecdote is drawn from Warburg, *The Federal Reserve System,* 1:56, and from "Aldrich Becomes Converted to Idea of a Central Bank, May–October 1908," Aldrich Papers, Reel 61.

88 **"It is easy to imagine":** Warburg, *The Federal Reserve System*, 1:56–57.

89 **Warburg jumped into the fray:** Paul Warburg to Piatt Andrew, December 14, 1908, Aldrich Papers, Reel 28; and Warburg, *The Federal Reserve System*, 1:33–34, 57.

89 **a monument to his decades:** "Money Commission Meets," *The New York Times*, November 23, 1908.

89 **"he doesn't like being pilloried continually":** "Aldrich Weary of Senate," ibid., November 2, 1908.

89 **Aldrich intended to devote:** "Senator Aldrich Tells of His Trip," ibid., November 19, 1908.

90 **The commission certainly had plenty:** National Monetary Commission correspondence, Aldrich Papers, Reel 27. For New York State, see a banking department letter to Arthur Shelton, July 23, 1909, ibid.

90 **"Really, gentlemen, I have nothing to say":** Rockefeller, "Nelson W. Aldrich and Banking Reform," 31–32, quoting the *Milwaukee Journal*.

90 **Butler asked whether Aldrich:** Nicholas Murray Butler to Aldrich, January 25, 1909, Aldrich Papers, Reel 29; Aldrich's reply is in ibid.

90 **Woodrow Wilson turned down an invitation:** "Chronology on Monetary Commission Work of Senator Aldrich"; Frank Vanderlip to Aldrich, December 1, 1908, Aldrich Papers, Reel 28; and Vanderlip, *From Farm Boy to Financier*, 211.

91 **"What I am anxious to do":** Henry F. Pringle, *The Life and Times of William Howard Taft* (New York: Farrar and Rinehart, 1939), 1:382 (italics added).

91 **bruised his mentor's ego:** Ibid., 384, 387–88.

91 **conversation at dinner was strained:** Ibid., 392.

91 **"It is coming to be an open secret":** Vanderlip to Lord Revelstoke (Edward Charles Baring), January 27, 1909, Vanderlip Papers, Box 1–3. For a full and compelling account of the Taft-Roosevelt relationship, see Doris Kearns Goodwin's *The Bully Pulpit: Theodore Roosevelt, William Howard Taft, and the Golden Age of Journalism* (New York: Simon and Schuster, 2013).

CHAPTER SIX: **PROGRESSIVISM**

92 **"Neither the political prejudice":** *Nelson W. Aldrich*, National Monetary Commission, *An Address by Senator Nelson W. Aldrich Before the Economic Club of New York*, November 29, 1909, 61st Cong., 2d sess. (Washington, D.C.: Government Printing Office, 1910), 27.

92 **"Financial questions are perplexing":** Taft quoted in "Taft Advocates Currency Reform," *The New York Times*, June 23, 1911.

93 **He was bombarded with pleas:** Letters from U.S. Steel (April 6, 1909) and National Biscuit (April 19, 1909) to Aldrich are in Nelson W. Aldrich Papers, Reel 31; letter from Royal Weaving's Joseph Ott to Aldrich (May 6, 1909) is in ibid., Reel 32.

93 **Against these letters Aldrich had:** Ibid., Reels 31–33; see especially Reel 33, which contains Secretary of State Philander C. Knox to Aldrich, May 26, 1909, enclosing translation of a note from the Turkish embassy.

93 **Always at ease working:** Nathaniel Wright Stephenson, *Nelson W. Aldrich: A Leader in American Politics* (New York: Scribner's, 1930), 351.

94 **"for a speedy end of the Tariff wrangle":** Paul Warburg to A. Piatt Andrew, July 26, 1909, Aldrich Papers, Reel 35.

94 **Andrew at least kept the Monetary Commission:** A. Piatt Andrew, *Diary of Abram Piatt Andrew, 1902–1914*, ed. E. Parker Hayden Jr. and Andrew L. Gray (Princeton, N.J., 1986), entries for June 29, 1909 (Wright), and April 27, 1910 (Gettysburg).

94 **The tariff work thrust Aldrich:** For the Taft-Aldrich relationship during the tariff

legislation, see Henry F. Pringle, *The Life and Times of William Howard Taft* (New York: Farrar and Rinehart, 1939), 1:411–15; and Doris Kearns Goodwin, *The Bully Pulpit: Theodore Roosevelt, William Howard Taft, and the Golden Age of Journalism* (New York: Simon and Schuster, 2013), 593–94, 597. The source for the White House portico is Stephenson, *Nelson W. Aldrich,* 351. Taft's letter to Aldrich of July 29, 1909 (Aldrich Papers, Reel 35), in which the President remarks, "I regret exceedingly to differ with you upon this subject . . . ," is suggestive of Taft's reluctance to confront Aldrich.

94 **The President had more success:** Walter Nugent, *Progressivism: A Very Short Introduction* (New York: Oxford University Press, 2010), 84.

94 **Aldrich did agree, reluctantly:** See the fascinating recollection "Notes on an Interview with A. Piatt Andrew," February 1, 1934, on mimeograph in the A. Piatt Andrew Papers. The interviewer, Andrew L. Gray, wrote that "Aldrich told me in personal conversations that his own inclination would have been to liberalize [reduce the duties] considerably but that he could not do so without letting down his old associations who had stuck by him through thick and thin."

94 **"meets the full approval":** James W. Van Cleave of the National Association of Manufacturers to Aldrich, May 19, 1909, Aldrich Papers, Reel 33. For appraisals of the Payne-Aldrich tariff, see Pringle, *William Howard Taft,* 1:425; Robert H. Wiebe, *Businessmen and Reform: A Study of the Progressive Movement* (Chicago: Elephant, 1989), 95; Stephenson, *Nelson W. Aldrich* 357–58; and Arthur S. Link, *Wilson,* vol. 2, *The New Freedom* (Princeton, N.J.: Princeton University Press, 1956), 178.

95 **Senator Jonathan Dolliver of Iowa:** Goodwin, *The Bully Pulpit,* 593.

95 **La Follette and other progressives:** Richard T. McCulley, *Banks and Politics During the Progressive Era: The Origins of the Federal Reserve System, 1897–1913* (New York: Garland, 1992), 226.

95 **Albert B. Cummins:** "Cummins Will Give No Quarter in Fight," *The New York Times,* November 7, 1909.

95 **"distrusted, disliked, even hated":** "Aldrich the Master of Details," *Current Literature* 47 (August 1909), 145–47.

96 **a second European study tour:** "Chronology on Monetary Commission Work of Senator Aldrich," Aldrich Papers, Reel 61. For the meeting with Churchill, see Michael Clark Rockefeller, "Nelson W. Aldrich and Banking Reform: A Conservative Leader in the Progressive Era," A.B. thesis, Harvard College, 1960, 34–35; and Stephenson, *Nelson W. Aldrich,* 362.

96 **The bankers in his circle:** Various correspondence in Aldrich Papers, Reels 35–37.

96 **a barnstorming tour in the West:** Stephenson, *Nelson W. Aldrich,* 363.

96 **"I am particularly pleased":** Henry Davison to Aldrich, August 6, 1909, Aldrich Papers, Reel 35.

97 **"some interests of mine":** Aldrich to Porfirio Diaz, August 28, 1909, ibid., Reel 36.

97 **Aldrich by now was a very wealthy man:** Stephenson, *Nelson W. Aldrich,* 367; Carrere and Hastings (architects) to Aldrich, July 15, 1910, Aldrich Papers, Reel 42; and Senator Boies Penrose to Aldrich, March 25, 1910, ibid., Reel 41. Reel 61 of ibid. is replete with stock transactions, many of them substantial.

97 **Even ordinary Americans:** Various correspondence, Aldrich Papers, Reels 30, 37. Ravenscroft's book appeared in 1911.

97 **The most interesting proposal:** Victor Morawetz, *The Banking and Currency Problem in the United States* (New York: North American Review Publishing, 1909); see especially 45–46, 84–86.

97 **"Wall Street influences"**: "Taft with Aldrich for a Central Bank," *The New York Times,* September 15, 1909.

97 **nine midwestern cities:** "Chronology on Monetary Commission Work of Senator Aldrich."

98 **"one which will satisfy the manufacturers"**: Rockefeller, "Nelson W. Aldrich and Banking Reform," 35, 54.

98 **Local coverage tended:** National Monetary Commission (probably A. Piatt Andrew) to Paul Warburg, November 19, 1909, and unidentified Milwaukee newspaper clipping, both in Aldrich Papers, Reel 61.

98 **"What do you do when you"**: Quoted in Rockefeller, "Nelson W. Aldrich and Banking Reform," 74.

98 **"the ghost of Andrew Jackson"**: *An Address by Senator Nelson W. Aldrich Before the Economic Club of New York.*

98 **Although Warburg and he:** Paul M. Warburg, *The Federal Reserve System: Its Origin and Growth—Reflections and Recollections* (New York: Macmillan, 1930), 1:57.

98 **"The universal American nation"**: Paul Moritz Warburg Papers, Folder 91.

99 **Warburg believed that if Americans:** Warburg, *The Federal Reserve System,* 2:160.

99 **Aldrich decreed that the next stage:** "Minutes of Meetings of Monetary Commission, 1908–1911," Aldrich Papers, Reel 61.

99 **Aldrich's address suggested just how:** *An Address by Senator Nelson W. Aldrich Before the Economic Club of New York;* quotes on 17, 19.

100 **"The insurgents have been showing"**: Vanderlip to James Stillman, January 21, 1910, Frank A. Vanderlip Papers, Box 1-3; see also Vanderlip to James Stillman, February 11, 1910, ibid.

100 **Progressivism embodied an attitudinal shift:** Nugent's *Progressivism* is a worthy introduction to the subject.

100 **To judge from newspaper sales:** According to the website Press Reference (www .pressreference.com/Sw-Ur/United-States.html), the number of newspapers in the United States hit a peak in 1910, at 2,600.

100 **less—not more—tolerant:** Pringle, *William Howard Taft,* 1:413.

100 **for much of the winter:** Vanderlip to Stillman, January 21, 1910.

101 **"One cannot help feeling very confident"**: Warburg to Nelson Aldrich, December 24, 1909, Warburg Papers.

101 **"It is a scheme based upon conditions"**: Warburg, *The Federal Reserve System,* 1:35–46, 2:118.

101 **"These sectional reserve banks"**: Ibid., 1:85–86, 2:160–61.

101 **In a second lecture in 1910:** Ibid., 1:42–48; quote on 45–46.

102 **The "United Reserve Bank" lecture:** Ibid., 36–37.

102 **Roosevelt disembarked in New York:** "Million Join in Welcome to Roosevelt," *The New York Times,* June 19, 1910; Pringle, *William Howard Taft,* 1:538–55, especially 551 and 553–54; and Goodwin, *The Bully Pulpit,* 640–41.

102 **"We have had no national leadership"**: Theodore Roosevelt to Henry Cabot Lodge, August 17, 1910, quoted in James Chace, *1912: Wilson, Roosevelt, Taft and Debs—The Election That Changed the Country* (New York: Simon and Schuster, 2004), 56.

102 **Roosevelt conveniently overlooked:** Wiebe, *Businessmen and Reform,* 91; and Pringle, *William Howard Taft,* 1:420.

103 **"My intercourse with Aldrich"**: Notes (quoting Roosevelt letter to Lodge, September 10, 1909), Aldrich Papers, Reel 61.

103 **As progressives battled for control:** Arthur S. Link, *Woodrow Wilson and the Progressive Era, 1910–1917* (New York: Harper and Row, 1954), 5. Reel 42 in the Aldrich Papers contains extensive correspondence and material relating to the Bristow charge. See also "Rubber, Aldrich and the Tariff," *The New York Times,* July 28, 1910; "Bristow Makes New Charge," *The New York Times,* July 26, 1910; "Insurgents Gained Four," *The New York Times,* August 4, 1910; and "Senator Bristow and Senator Aldrich," *The Outlook,* August 27, 1910.

103 **a private railroad car:** Goodwin, *The Bully Pulpit,* 643.

103 **"Roosevelt is certainly making":** Vanderlip to James Stillman, September 2 and September 9, 1910, Vanderlip Papers, Box 1-3.

104 **a far more radical agenda:** Chace, *1912,* 56. In his famous "New Nationalism" speech, delivered in Osawatomie, Kansas, on August 31, 1910, Roosevelt said, "Every man holds his property subject to the general right of the community to regulate its use to whatever degree the public welfare may require it." He also called for a "moral awakening."

104 **Although he supported the notion of financial reform:** In his speech at Osawatomie, Roosevelt said: "It is of profound importance that our financial system should be promptly investigated, and so thoroughly and effectively revised as to make it certain that hereafter our currency will no longer fail at critical times to meet our needs."

104 **Aldrich intended to wait out:** Aldrich's correspondence (in the Aldrich Papers) documents that he was closely, and anxiously, monitoring the 1910 campaign.

104 **"The political pot is boiling here":** Perkins to J. P. Morgan, October 11, 1910, George W. Perkins Sr. Papers.

105 **The collision hurled him several feet:** "Aldrich Not Badly Hurt," *The New York Times,* October 22, 1910; William H. Taft to Aldrich, October 21, 1910, Aldrich Papers, Reel 43. That Aldrich was already planning a trip is confirmed by a letter Frank Vanderlip wrote to James Stillman, in which Vanderlip reported that Aldrich "met with what came very near being a severe auto accident" and that the mishap "has naturally postponed the conference that was in mind": Frank A. Vanderlip with Boyden Sparkes, *From Farm Boy to Financier* (New York: D. Appleton-Century, 1935), 212.

105 **On election day:** Results in Nugent, *Progressivism,* 89.

105 **"It is hardly an exaggeration":** Frederick Jackson Turner, "Social Forces in American History," *American Historical Review* 16, no. 2, 217–33. Turner had delivered the essay to the American Historical Association in Indianapolis on December 28, 1910.

105 **"We shall appeal to the thoughtful men":** "Keep Politics Out of Finance—Aldrich," *The New York Times,* November 12, 1910. The occasion was the annual dinner of the Academy of Political Science of New York.

106 **His plan was so secret:** "Minutes of Meetings of Monetary Commission."

CHAPTER SEVEN: JEKYL ISLAND

107 **"A Banker uses the money of others":** Walter Bagehot, *Lombard Street: A Description of the Money Market* (London, 1873), 9. Apparently, the words up to the semicolon are Ricardo's and the rest is a paraphrasing or interpretation from Bagehot.

107 **"Public utility is more truly the object":** "Report of the Secretary of the Treasury on the Subject of a National Bank," read to the House of Representatives, December 15, 1790.

107 **Aldrich insisted on absolute secrecy:** Narrations of Jekyl trip sourced to the Warburg Papers, "Jekyl Island Conference, Nov. 18-26, 1910" and "Jekyl Island Conference Nov. 18, 1910," are in Nelson W. Aldrich Papers, Reel 61 (hereinafter Warburg Narration 1

and 2, respectively). The narrations are in the third person, but were written by either Warburg or someone with close access to him.

108 **Aldrich also recruited Frank Vanderlip:** Warburg Narration 1; and "Notes on an Interview with A. Piatt Andrew," February 1, 1934, A. Piatt Andrew Papers.

108 **six co-conspirators:** Vanderlip's 1935 memoir, *From Farm Boy to Financier* (witten with Boyden Sparkes; New York: D. Appleton-Century), says Ben Strong was also at Jekyl. This seems highly unlikely. In a letter to Stillman on November 29, 1910 (the day after his return), Vanderlip described a party of only six. Warburg Narrations 1 and 2 include only the six named participants. Andrew also cites the same six participants in "Notes on an Interview with A. Piatt Andrew." Finally, the earliest public account of the trip, a cursory mention in an article by B. C. Forbes, "Men Who Are Making America," *Leslie's Weekly* 123, no. 42 (October 19, 1916), identifies Aldrich, Andrew, and the three bankers (omitting Aldrich's secretary, Shelton) and specifically mentions that "later" Strong "was called into frequent consultation" and "joined the first-name club." This suggests that the subsequent close identification of Strong with the Jekyl party (Strong, of course, was to become the first president of the New York Federal Reserve Bank) blurred Vanderlip's later recollection, which was not published until twenty-five years after the trip. One final corroborating bit of evidence is that the Jekyl Island trip was not mentioned in Lester V. Chandler's thorough-seeming 1958 biography of Strong.

108 **It was Davison who arranged:** Warburg Narration 1; and Vanderlip, *From Farm Boy to Financier*, 213–14. Some accounts say Warburg purchased a gun, but his son James said he "borrowed a lethal weapon" as camouflage: James Warburg, *The Long Road Home* (Garden City, N.Y.: Doubleday, 1964), 29.

109 **"On what kind of an errand":** Warburg Narrations 1 and 2 are the source for the entire train encounter between Warburg and Vanderlip.

109 **Aldrich set a workmanlike:** Warburg Narration 2; and Vanderlip, *From Farm Boy to Financier*, 215. Disappointingly, Andrew's diary contains no entries for the several months leading up to and including the Jekyl trip.

109 **"Now gentlemen, this is all very pretty":** Warburg Narration 1.

110 **For the next eight days:** Vanderlip to James Stillman, November 29, 1910, Frank A. Vanderlip Papers, Box 1-3; and Vanderlip, *Farm Boy to Financier*, 215.

110 **The Jekyl Island Club, founded in 1885:** Description of club history and setting from my visit to Jekyll Island (as a footnote later in the chapter explains, the spelling of the island's name was changed years later); author interview with John Hunter, director of historical resources for Jekyll Island Authority; and displays at Jekyll Island Museum, January 18, 2013. For Morgan arranging that there were no other guests, see Michael Clark Rockefeller, "Nelson W. Aldrich and Banking Reform: A Conservative Leader in the Progressive Era," A.B. thesis, Harvard College, 1960, 35.

110 **"We were working so hard":** Vanderlip, *From Farm Boy to Financier*, 216. Vanderlip's memoir recounts that Davison and Strong went swimming and riding. For reasons stated in endnote for page 108 (on Notes pages 293–94), it is unlikely Strong was there, and since Andrew was an indefatigable athlete—in particular a swimmer and rider—and close to Davison, it is likely he meant Davison and *Andrew*.

110 **Aldrich set the pace:** Warburg Narration 1; and "The Drafting of the Aldrich Plan: Meeting of the Statesmen at Jekyl Island," Aldrich Papers, Reel 61 (hereinafter Warburg Narration 3).

111 **his ideas on how to structure it:** Vanderlip to Stillman, November 29, 1910.

111 **Warburg favored a stronger government role:** Warburg Narrations 1 and 3; and Mi-

chael A. Whitehouse, "Paul Warburg's Crusade to Establish a Central Bank in the United States," *The Region* (publication of Federal Reserve Bank of Minneapolis), May 1989.

111 **tension arose:** Warburg Narration 1; and Vanderlip, *From Farm Boy to Financier*, 216.

111 **The pair reached an impasse:** Warburg Narrations 1 and 3; Vanderlip, *From Farm Boy to Financier*, 216; and Thomas W. Lamont, *Henry P. Davison: The Record of a Useful Life* (New York: Harper and Brothers, 1933), 98–100, 101.

112 **"The notes must count":** Warburg Narration 1.

112 **wild turkey and oyster stuffing:** Vanderlip, *From Farm Boy to Financier*, 216.

112 **With the basic points of the reform:** Warburg Narration 1; and Lamont, *Henry P. Davison*, 100.

112 **The final, crucial task:** Warburg Narration 1.

112 **Aldrich prevailed on the issue of reserves:** Ibid.

113 **Each participating bank would belong:** The description of the Aldrich Plan in this passage comes from Rockefeller, "Nelson W. Aldrich and Banking Reform," especially 39–45; "Aldrich Money Plan Avoids Central Bank," *The New York Times*, January 18, 1910; Paul M. Warburg, *The Federal Reserve System: Its Origin and Growth—Reflections and Recollections* (New York: Macmillan, 1930), 1:58–62; Elmus Wicker, *The Great Debate on Banking Reform: Nelson Aldrich and the Origins of the Fed* (Columbus: Ohio State University Press, 2005), 67–69; and Richard T. McCulley, *Banks and Politics During the Progressive Era: The Origins of the Federal Reserve System, 1897–1913* (New York: Garland, 1992), 234–40.

113 **Governance in the association:** Rockefeller, "Nelson W. Aldrich and Banking Reform," 41; McCulley, *Banks and Politics During the Progressive Era*, 236, 237; and "Aldrich Money Plan Avoids Central Bank."

114 **"It was strictly a bankers' bank":** Warburg, *The Federal Reserve System*, 1:59–60.

114 **bankers—not government—would be in control:** McCulley, *Banks and Politics During the Progressive Era*, 234.

115 **"These are business questions":** Rockefeller, "Nelson W. Aldrich and Banking Reform," 44–45.

116 **Warburg suggested they also organize:** "Introducing the Aldrich Plan to the Bankers and the General Public," Aldrich Papers, Reel 61. See also Warburg Narration 1; and Warburg, *The Federal Reserve System*, 1:58.

116 **The group disbanded quietly:** Vanderlip, *From Farm Boy to Financier*, 217.

116 **"I am back from Jekyl Island":** Vanderlip to Stillman, November 29, 1910.

116 **"Zivil was greatly pleased":** Ibid.

116 **Aside from a couple of vague allusions:** As discussed in an earlier note, the article by B. C. Forbes, "Men Who Are Making America," appeared in *Leslie's Weekly* on October 19, 1916. It is probable that either Forbes or his source had been at the train depot in Brunswick, Georgia, to greet the unlikely "duck hunters." See also Warburg, *The Federal Reserve System*, 1:58, 60. The authorized biography was Stephenson's *Nelson W. Aldrich*.

117 **"secret meetings of the international bankers":** Eustace Mullins, *The Secrets of the Federal Reserve* (1952; repr., n.p.: Bankers Research Institute, 1983).

117 **to establish a cartel:** G. Edward Griffin, *The Creature from Jekyll Island: A Second Look at the Federal Reserve*, 3rd ed. (Westlake Village, Calif.: American Media, 1998). See, for instance, pp. 19–20: "Most of Warburg's writing and lecturing on this topic was eyewash for the public. To cover the fact that a central bank is merely a cartel which has been legalized, its proponents had to lay down a thick smoke screen of technical jargon. . . .

There was not the slightest glimmer that, underneath it all, was a master plan which was designed from top to bottom to serve private interests at the expense of the public. . . . The consequences of wealth confiscation by the Federal-Reserve mechanism are now upon us."

118 **the centenary of the Aldrich mission:** Mark Thornton of the Ludwig von Mises Institute presented a paper at the "Birth and Death of the Fed" conference on Jekyll Island, February 26–27, 2010. Ron Paul was one of the conferees. Ben Bernanke, the Federal Reserve chairman, appeared as part of a subsequent conference, on November 4–6, 2010, co-sponsored by the Atlanta Federal Reserve Bank and Rutgers University.

118 **"the main business of a bank":** Frank Vanderlip to Glass, July 24, 1913, Carter Glass Collection, Box 16.

118 **They wanted a more resilient banking system:** For a further exploration of the bankers' motives, see McCulley, *Banks and Politics During the Progressive Era,* 229–332.

118 **Vanderlip's correspondence makes emphatically clear:** On the very day Vanderlip returned to work from Jekyl Island, he stressed in a letter to Aldrich his eagerness to see the "enlargement of the powers of national banks" via the opening of foreign branches. In this letter, Vanderlip pointedly noted that it was a matter "upon which I have had several conferences with the President [Taft]." Appearing to defer to Aldrich's discretion, Vanderlip wrote that he understood that the senator might object to separating the international issue from the broader one of banking reform. Unwilling to let the matter rest, however, he added, "Of course, it is unnecessary for me to say that we deem it extremely desirable so to extend the powers of national banks as either to permit foreign branches or permit the organization of banks to conduct foreign business." Vanderlip to Aldrich, November 28, 1910, can be found in both Aldrich Papers, Reel 43, and Vanderlip Papers, Box 1-3.

119 **While sequestered on the island:** Warburg Narration 1.

119 **they orchestrated a two-pronged attack:** "Introducing the Aldrich Plan to the Bankers and the General Public"; and Rockefeller, "Nelson W. Aldrich and Banking Reform," 58, 59–60. The western bankers included Forgan and Reynolds in Chicago and Festus J. Wade in St. Louis.

119 **Warburg bombarded Aldrich:** Paul Warburg to Aldrich, December 6, 1910, Aldrich Papers, Reel 43.

119 **"Will you please find out from Mr. N":** Paul Warburg to Andrew, December 18, 1910, Andrew Papers, Box 22, folder 7.

120 **"I hear all kinds of things that Senator Aldrich":** Warburg Narration 1.

120 **the American Academy of Political and Social Science:** "Senator Aldrich Would Weld Greater Banking System," *The New York Times,* January 8, 1911; and Warburg, *The Federal Reserve System,* 1:62.

120 **press accounts grew steadily:** "Senator Aldrich Ill," *The New York Times,* January 6, 1911; and "Aldrich Is Ill in Bed," ibid., January 13, 1911.

120 **His Jekyl confreres tactfully:** "Introducing the Aldrich Plan to the Bankers and the General Public"; and Warburg, *The Federal Reserve System,* 1:62. Mrs. Aldrich's diary entry is quoted in Aldrich Papers, Reel 61. The advice of Aldrich's doctor comes from Aldrich to Henry Davison, January 26, 1911, telegram, Aldrich Papers, Reel 44.

121 **Aldrich's ill-timed absence:** "Introducing the Aldrich Plan to the Bankers and the General Public"; and Warburg, *The Federal Reserve System,* 1:61–62.

121 **"Laughlin, did you ever see":** A. Piatt Andrew, *Diary of Abram Piatt Andrew, 1902–1914,* ed. E. Parker Hayden Jr. and Andrew L. Gray (Princeton, N.J., 1986); and James

L. Laughlin, *The Federal Reserve Act: Its Origin and Problems* (New York: Macmillan, 1933), 16–17.

122 **"undue favoritism with the central bank":** Warburg to Samuel Sachs, January 12, 1911, Paul Moritz Warburg Papers, Box 1, folder 1.

122 **the Jekyl conspirators minus Aldrich:** Andrew, *Diary;* "Notes on an Interview with A. Piatt Andrew"; and "Introducing the Aldrich Plan to the Bankers and the General Public."

122 **"for their criticism and action":** A copy of Aldrich's letter to commission vice chair Edward B. Vreeland, typed and edited in Aldrich's hand, dated January 16, 1911, is in the Aldrich Papers, Reel 44. See also Rockefeller, "Nelson W. Aldrich and Banking Reform," 45.

122 **Aldrich himself was absent:** Aldrich's telegram of January 16, 1911, to James Forgan states, "My doctors say that it is necessary for me to go South at once" (Aldrich Papers, Reel 44); he apparently left that day. See also Andrew's note of the same date to Forgan, in ibid., Reel 61; and "Aldrich Goes to Georgia," *The New York Times,* January 17, 1911.

123 **the debate over the Aldrich Plan:** "Aldrich Money Plan Avoids Central Bank," *The New York Times,* January 18, 1911; and "Shaw Denounces the Plan," ibid., January 19, 1911.

123 **His colleagues' strategy:** "Bankers Here Approve Plan: Paul M. Warburg Declares It Is Well Adapted to Conditions in This Country," ibid., January 18, 1911; "Introducing the Aldrich Plan to the Bankers and the General Public"; Warburg, *The Federal Reserve System,* 1:62–63, 567–71; and Rockefeller, "Nelson W. Aldrich and Banking Reform," 63–64.

123 **bankers were the generals:** Warburg made this observation, retrospectively, in *The Federal Reserve System,* 1:60–61.

CHAPTER EIGHT: INTO THE CRUCIBLE

127 **"We want the views":** Michael Clark Rockefeller, "Nelson W. Aldrich and Banking Reform: A Conservative Leader in the Progressive Era," A.B. thesis, Harvard College, 1960, 46.

129 **the approval of James Forgan and George Reynolds:** Ibid., 61.

129 **"I am very sorry to bother you":** Henry Davison to Aldrich, January 23, 1911, telegram, Nelson W. Aldrich Papers, Reel 44.

129 **The retreat took place:** Shelton invitation to bankers, January 23, 1911, ibid., Reel 44; "Minutes of Meetings of Monetary Commission, 1908–1911," ibid., Reel 61; and Biographer's notes, ibid. See also James Forgan to Andrew, January 17, 1911, A. Piatt Andrew Papers, Box 22, folder 7; Rockefeller, "Nelson W. Aldrich and Banking Reform," 61; and Richard T. McCulley, *Banks and Politics During the Progressive Era: The Origins of the Federal Reserve System, 1897–1913* (New York: Garland, 1992), 242–44.

130 **"Every attempt to do my work":** Quoted in Nathaniel Wright Stephenson, *Nelson W. Aldrich: A Leader in American Politics* (New York: Scribner's, 1930), 383–85.

130 **"Am improving so slowly":** Aldrich to Henry Davison, January 26, 1911, telegram, Aldrich Papers, Reel 44. For details of Aldrich's recuperation, see the diary of Abby Aldrich excerpted in ibid., Reel 61.

131 **The result was to make the Reserve Association:** Loose notes, ibid., Reel 61; Forgan to Andrew, January 17, 1911; A. Piatt Andrew to Warburg, March 30, 1911, Paul Moritz Warburg Papers; Rockefeller, "Nelson W. Aldrich and Banking Reform," 62; and Robert Craig West, *Banking Reform and the Federal Reserve* (Ithaca, N.Y.: Cornell University Press, 1974), 84. For brevity, the account in the text omitted a step. After the ABA

currency committee approved the Aldrich Plan in March, the organization's executive committee, meeting in early May in Nashville, ratified that decision.

131 Warburg, while reaping a victory: Laughlin to Paul Warburg, June 8, 1911, James Laurence Laughlin Papers, Box 4, Paul M. Warburg folder.

131 Shrewdly, he told the press: "Currency Reform: Its Popular Side," *The New York Times,* July 26, 1911. Warburg's account is in Paul M. Warburg, *The Federal Reserve System: Its Origin and Growth—Reflections and Recollections* (New York: Macmillan, 1930), 1:69–70, which more generally discusses his involvement in organizing the National Citizens' League. See also Lucy D. Chen, "Banking Reform in a Hostile Climate: Paul M. Warburg and the National Citizens' League" (working paper, April 2010), 12, available at http://www.fas.harvard.edu/~histecon/crisis-next/1907/docs/Chen-Warburg_Final _Paper.pdf; Laughlin to Warburg, June 8, 1911, as well as other correspondence in Laughlin Papers, Box 4, Paul M. Warburg folder; and Warburg's correspondence in the Aldrich Papers, Reel 61.

132 The Citizens' League's publicity was similarly: Warburg, *The Federal Reserve System,* 1:72, 68; and Chen, "Banking Reform in a Hostile Climate," 15.

132 The league's strategy was also controversial: Warburg, *The Federal Reserve System,* 1:131; Rockefeller, "Nelson W. Aldrich and Banking Reform," 66; and Chen, "Banking Reform in a Hostile Climate."

132 But Laughlin had a prickly, self-important streak: The view of Willis, Roosevelt, and others that Laughlin should distance the league from Aldrich comes from James L. Laughlin, *The Federal Reserve Act: Its Origin and Problems* (New York: Macmillan, 1933), 38, 43, and 78. See also the untitled essay on the Citizens' League in the Aldrich Papers, Reel 61.

132 consider submitting a plan of his own: "Notes for Mrs. Nichols in Life of Aldrich" (accompanies letter to Jeannette P. Nichols, February 7, 1927), Laughlin Papers, Box 2, Nelson W. Aldrich folder; see also notes from Warburg Papers in Aldrich Papers, Reel 61; Laughlin, *The Federal Reserve Act,* 51; and Warburg, *The Federal Reserve System,* 1:76, 89.

132 Aldrich became newly despondent: "Notes for Mrs. Nichols in Life of Aldrich."

132 A rift opened: Laughlin, *The Federal Reserve Act,* 44–48; and Gabriel Kolko, *The Triumph of Conservatism: A Reinterpretation of American History, 1900–1914* (New York: The Free Press of Glencoe, 1963), 188. For Warburg's dislike of Laughlin, see Biographer's notes, Aldrich Papers, Reel 58.

133 Relations were further strained: James Laughlin to James Forgan, August 13, 1911, Aldrich Papers, Reel 61; Laughlin, *The Federal Reserve Act,* 44–48; Stephenson, *Nelson W. Aldrich,* 395; and "Notes for Mrs. Nichols in Life of Aldrich."

133 was leaked to the *Times*: "To Rid Money Plan of Aldrich's Name," *The New York Times,* July 6, 1911; the editorial, "A Campaign for Monetary Reform," appeared in the *Times* the next day, July 7.

133 put intense pressure on Laughlin: Laughlin, *The Federal Reserve Act,* 44. Forgan was among those who pressured Laughlin to cooperate with Aldrich.

133 a parley on Aldrich's yacht: Lester V. Chandler, *Benjamin Strong, Central Banker* (Washington, D.C.: Brookings Institution, 1958), 32, recounts that Strong, who was increasingly engaged with the topic of central banking, discussed the Aldrich Plan "at length" with Aldrich on the senator's yacht in August 1911. See also A. Piatt Andrew, *Diary of*

Abram Piatt Andrew, 1902–1914, ed. E. Parker Hayden Jr. and Andrew L. Gray (Princeton, N.J., 1986), which records five days in July and August on which he met with Aldrich, often with other parties, on his yacht, usually to discuss the Aldrich Plan.

133 **a bimonthly newsletter:** Rockefeller, "Nelson W. Aldrich and Banking Reform," 66.

133 **Touring the South:** Laughlin, *The Federal Reserve Act,* 64, 74–75, 80–81, and 93. See also, for Laughlin's publicity campaign, McCulley, *Banks and Politics During the Progressive Era,* 244–45. Laughlin says the league's periodical was bimonthly, but various others, including Warburg (*The Federal Reserve System,* 1:73), say it appeared biweekly.

133 **state banking associations signed on:** Numerous telegrams and letters from individual state associations, Aldrich Papers, Reel 45; Andrew to William H. Taft, August 28, 1911, Andrew Papers, Folder 7; George Reynolds to Laughlin, July 14, 1911, Laughlin Papers, Box 4, G. M Reynolds folder; and Rockefeller, "Nelson W. Aldrich and Banking Reform," 66.

133 **Treasury Secretary MacVeagh was harder:** "Taft Advocates Currency Reform," *The New York Times,* June 23, 1911; "MacVeagh Indorses Aldrich Bank Plan," *The New York Times,* November 12, 1911; "Memorandum Concerning Public Aspects of Mr. MacVeagh's Administration," Andrew Papers, Box 22, folder 4; Andrew to Senator W. Murray Crane, June 29, 1912, ibid., Box 20, folder 24; and "Notes on an Interview with A. Piatt Andrew, Feb. 1, 1934," ibid., Box 2, folder 10, which states, "Senator Aldrich had little regard for Secretary MacVeagh." See also Andrew Gray, "Who Killed the Aldrich Plan?" *The Bankers Magazine* 54 (Summer 1971), available at http://books.google.com /books?id=RAB3ynybvoUC&lpg=PA216&dq=andrew+gray+who+killed+the+aldrich +plan&source=bl&ots=eNjeHvf9IF&sig=D8DUQr5tcU2CcjUPBEjVqYD9NX4&hl =en&sa=X&ei=UtEDU5rfFu3IogHmgoDYCA&output=reader&pg=GBS.PA216.)

134 **Aldrich's return to action:** The public hearings are documented in Arthur Shelton to C. H. Huttig (president of the Third National Bank, St. Louis), October 13, 1911, Aldrich Papers, Reel 46; "Minutes of Meetings of Monetary Commission"; and Rockefeller, "Nelson W. Aldrich and Banking Reform," 65.

134 **a round of speeches:** Paul Warburg to Aldrich, October 15, 1911, Aldrich Papers, Reel 46 (for Aldrich speeches in Indiana on October 26 and Chicago on November 11); and Rockefeller, "Nelson W. Aldrich and Banking Reform," 65, which notes that Aldrich also spoke in Kansas City and (in the East) in Philadelphia and New York. In addition, he addressed the ABA in New Orleans in November.

134 **control would be "impossible":** "Money Trust Could Not Buy Control," *Journal of Commerce,* October 23, 1911; a clipping was found in Warburg Papers, Folder 91.

134 **The first inkling of trouble:** The National City episode is largely drawn from the splendid account in Harold van B. Cleveland and Thomas F. Huertas, *Citibank: 1812– 1970* (Cambridge, Mass.: Harvard University Press, 1985), 62–68. The National City letter was dated June 28, 1911; it is quoted in "Giving Up Control of Outside Banks," *The New York Times,* November 4, 1911.

135 **openly colluded in others:** One notorious example of collusion concerned the National Bank of Commerce, the second-largest bank in New York. Morgan, Baker, and Stillman all owned slices of the bank and jointly directed its management and board. When National City conceived of its investment affiliate, the affiliate acquired Vanderlip's share of the Bank of Commerce, so that National City now became a partner with two other Wall Street titans—Morgan and Baker.

135 The Citizens' League was alarmed: John Farwell to Paul Warburg, July 20, 1911, Aldrich Papers, Reel 61 (from Warburg Papers). The *Times* quote comes from "The National City Company," November 4, 1911. See also "Giving Up Control of Outside Banks."

135 "was as remote to the managers": Paul Warburg to John Farwell, July 24, 1911, Laughlin Papers, Box 4, Paul M. Warburg folder.

136 "could not have come out": McCulley, *Banks and Politics During the Progressive Era*, 245.

136 "My intuition is": Vanderlip to Stillman, June 20, 1911, Frank A. Vanderlip Papers, Box 1-4.

136 In November, Vanderlip wisely defused: "The National City Company"; "Giving Up Control of Outside Banks"; Cleveland and Huertas, *Citibank*, 66; McCulley, *Banks and Politics During the Progressive Era*, 259; and Henry F. Pringle, *The Life and Times of William Howard Taft* (New York: Farrar and Rinehart), 2:676.

137 Lindbergh saw a parallel plot: "Wants a Bank Inquiry," *The New York Times*, July 9, 1911.

137 Bryan's plan was not developed: Laughlin, *The Federal Reserve Act*, 155–56.

137 "absolute commercial and industrial slavery": Bryan quoted in Rockefeller, "Nelson W. Aldrich and Banking Reform," 79.

138 Warburg spent an evening: Paul Warburg to Andrew, December 14, 1911, Andrew Papers, Folder 7.

138 La Follette proclaimed: "La Follette Invades Taft's Home State," *The New York Times*, December 28, 1911.

138 Lurking in the shadows of the La Follette: James Neal Primm, *A Foregone Conclusion* (St. Louis: Federal Reserve Bank of St. Louis, 1989), chapter 2, "Banking Reform, 1907–1913"; available at www.stlouisfed.org/foregone/chapter_two.cfm.

139 Vanderlip sized up the turbulent politics: Numerous letters of Vanderlip to James Stillman are in Vanderlip Papers, Box 1-4; see, for instance, April 6, April 15, June 20, July 21, and September 29, 1911.

139 the former president regarded it: In *William Howard Taft*, Pringle writes that previously "there was an outside chance that harmony, of a sort, might be achieved again. But it was not possible after the steel suit" (2:673). See also Doris Kearns Goodwin, *The Bully Pulpit: Theodore Roosevelt, William Howard Taft, and the Golden Age of Journalism* (New York: Simon and Schuster, 2013), 667–68.

139 Morgan, who had been troubled: J. P. Morgan Jr. to Henry Davison, June 5, 1911, J. P. Morgan Jr. Papers, Box 5, book 8.

139 "felt that all the old moorings": Vanderlip to James Stillman, October 17, 1911, Vanderlip Papers, Box 1-4.

139 in New Orleans: *Proceedings* of the 37th Annual Convention of the American Bankers Association, available at http://books.google.com/books?id=LBgaAQAAIAAJ&pg=PA340&lpg=PA340&dq=american+bankers+association,+proceedings+of+the+37th+annual+convention&source=bl&ots=dMH2bntf6H&sig=kT-uZ68Z3jQYHwsBaXmcgtsm4E&hl=en&sa=X&ei=ldsQU6y2HuLF0gG714DoDw&ved=0CCcQ6AEwAA#v=onepage&q=american%20bankers%20association%2C%20proceedings%20of%20the%2037th%20annual%20convention&f=false].

140 Banks were given greater license: See McCulley, *Banks and Politics During the Progressive Era*, 235–40.

140 Aldrich received a five-minute ovation: "Bankers Indorse Aldrich Money Plan."

140 La Follette was making opposition: Rockefeller, "Nelson W. Aldrich and Banking

Reform," 79. For La Follette's Hamilton speech, see "LaFollette serves notice on Aldrich Plan, Dec. 30, 1911, Phil. N.Am. Dec. 31," Aldrich Papers, Reel 61.

140 **Newspaper coverage was withering:** A newspaper clipping found in Aldrich Papers, dated December 7, 1911 (the name of the paper is clipped off) states matter-of-factly that the "chief purpose" of the Aldrich plan was "to concentrate financial power in the hands of a very few men." For the *Rocky Mountain News* quote, see Rockefeller, "Nelson W. Aldrich and Banking Reform," 76.

141 **a body with "semi-public" powers:** National Monetary Commission, *Letter from Secretary of the National Monetary Commission Transmitting, Pursuant to Law, the Report of the Commission*, 62d Cong., 2d sess., January 9, 1912 (Washington, D.C.: Government Printing Office, 1912), 14.

141 **In December, Representative Lindbergh:** McCulley, *Banks and Politics During the Progressive Era*, 257.

141 **met in nearly daily session:** Rockefeller, "Nelson W. Aldrich and Banking Reform," 83.

141 **New York banks, which held 20 percent:** Warburg, *The Federal Reserve System*, 1:413. That they could elect three of thirty-nine representatives is my analysis, based on *Letter from Secretary of the National Monetary Commission*, 12–13.

141 **Aldrich confessed to Taft:** "Aldrich Sees Taft," *The New York Times*, December 14, 1911. In the spring of 1911, Vanderlip was already writing Stillman, "It may interest you to know that Taft has practically abandoned hope of re-election to a second term" (Vanderlip to Stillman, April 15, 1911).

141 **Andrew sent the former president:** Theodore Roosevelt to Andrew, December 2, 1911, Andrew Papers, Folder 23; for thirty-five volumes, see Andrew to Woodrow Wilson, November 23, 1911, ibid., Folder 7.

141 **the governor was a leading candidate:** Arthur S. Link, *Woodrow Wilson and the Progressive Era, 1910–1917* (New York: Harper and Row, 1954), 11.

141 **"current is drifting very strongly":** Vanderlip to Stillman, July 21, 1911.

142 **"Ever since I have had":** John Milton Cooper Jr., *Woodrow Wilson* (New York: Knopf, 2009), 28.

142 **As a mature political scientist:** Woodrow Wilson, "An Historical Essay, September 15, 1893: A Calendar of Great Americans," in Arthur S. Link, ed., *The Papers of Woodrow Wilson* (Princeton, N.J.: Princeton University Press, 1966–1989), 8:368–80.

142 **"The supporters of the second bank":** Woodrow Wilson, *A History of the American People*, vol. 7, *Critical Changes and Civil War* (New York: Harper and Brothers, 1906), 45–46.

142 **"proved itself":** Ibid., 47.

142 **"I was born a politician":** Wilson's letter to Turner is quoted in Arthur S. Link, *Woodrow Wilson: A Brief Biography* (Cleveland: World, 1963), 28–29.

142 **the silver campaign of Bryan in 1896:** House to Woodrow Wilson, October 16, 1911, Edward M. House Papers, Box 119a. In this letter, Colonel House relates gossip about Wilson's non-support of Bryan in 1896. See also the confirming response of a Wilson aide, October 17, 1911, ibid.

142 **George Harvey:** Cooper, *Woodrow Wilson*, 91, 106, and 120.

143 **his eye on the White House:** Ibid., 64; Link, *Woodrow Wilson: A Brief Biography*, 47–49.

143 **"the greatest monopoly in this country":** Paolo E. Coletta, *William Jennings Bryan* (Lincoln: University of Nebraska Press, 1969), 2:128; and "Gov. Wilson and the Aldrich Plan," *The New York Times*, September 1, 1911 (citing Wilson's August 26 interview with *The Outlook*).

143 **"everyone south of Canal Street":** Edward House to William Jennings Bryan, December 6, 1911, Aldrich Papers, Reel 61. For Wilson's distancing himself from Harvey, see Cooper, *Woodrow Wilson*, 141; and James Chace, *1912: Wilson, Roosevelt, Taft and Debs—The Election That Changed the Country* (New York: Simon and Schuster, 2004), 132–35.

144 **Andrew sent Wilson the Monetary Commission:** Andrew to Woodrow Wilson, November 23, 1911, Andrew Papers, Folder 7; Woodrow Wilson to Andrew, November 27, 1911, ibid.; and Laughlin, *The Federal Reserve Act*, 176–77.

144 **William Garrett Brown:** William Garrett Brown to Andrew, December 4, 1911, Andrew Papers, Folder 7; Andrew to Brown, December 5, 1911, ibid.; and Andrew and Brown letters, Aldrich Papers, Reel 61 (from Andrew Collection). See also House to Woodrow Wilson, December 15, 1911, House Papers, Box 119a.

144 **Wilson began to receive entreaties:** Cooper, *Woodrow Wilson*, 182–83. Further biographical details of House can be found in Louis Gould, "Wilson's Man in Paris," *The Wall Street Journal*, January 17–18, 2015.

145 **"I have been with Mr. Bryan":** House to Woodrow Wilson, November 18, 1911, House Papers, Box 119a; and Chace, *1912*, 139.

145 **in 1900 and 1908:** Coletta, *William Jennings Bryan*, 2:44.

145 **Bryan came to dinner:** Cooper, *Woodrow Wilson*, 141–42.

145 **knowing how Bryan felt:** House to Wilson, December 15, 1911.

145 **addressing him as "My dear friend":** Woodrow Wilson to House, December 22, 1911, House Papers, Box 119a.

145 **"He is like my second personality":** Cooper, *Woodrow Wilson*, 192.

145 **House pursued Bryan's support:** Coletta, *William Jennings Bryan*, 2:35–38; and Colonel House's assistant to Wilson, December 30, 1911, House Papers, Box 119a.

CHAPTER NINE: **THE GREAT CAMPAIGN**

147 **"The Democratic members":** Warburg to James Laughlin, April 22, 1912, Paul Moritz Warburg Papers, Folder 3. I have slightly shortened the quote; the passage in its entirety reads, "The Democratic members of the committee, leaving aside Pujo, are absolutely unfit to ever produce anything; they simply have not got the knowledge."

147 **"No one class can comprehend":** "Wilson's reference to Aldrich Plan (Phil. Press, Jan. 9, 1912)," January 8, 1912, Nelson W. Aldrich Papers, Reel 61.

148 **"I got in the motor":** "Filing of Report of Monetary Commission, Jan. 8, 1912 (from Andrew Coll., Gloucester)," ibid. The National Monetary Commission formally expired in March.

148 **"The bankers of the country":** "Wilson's reference to Aldrich Plan."

148 **faced three rivals for the nomination:** Arthur S. Link, *Woodrow Wilson and the Progressive Era, 1910–1917* (New York: Harper and Row, 1954), 11–12: and John J. Broesamle, *William Gibbs McAdoo: A Passion for Change, 1863–1917* (Port Washington, N.Y.: Kennikat Press, 1973), 48–50

149 **"predatory wealth":** "Attitude of Wilson, Daniels, Kern and Bryan toward Aldrich Plan, Jan. 11, 1912," Aldrich Papers, Reel 61 (from Warburg Papers).

149 **"In conversation with Mr. William":** "Attitude of Wilson toward Aldrich plan, Jan., 1912: A memo to Mr. Warburg, from Mr. Dinwiddie, Jan. 26, 1912," ibid. (from Warburg Papers).

149 **He and Andrew were invited to a luncheon:** "Monetary Plan and Roosevelt, 1912," ibid. (from Andrew Papers). This document quotes Andrew's letter to his parents of January 26, 1912, which described the luncheon.

149 **"Why not give Mr. Warburg"**: Paul M. Warburg, *The Federal Reserve System: Its Origin and Growth—Reflections and Recollections* (New York: Macmillan, 1930), 1:77–78.

149 **In February, Roosevelt formally declared:** Doris Kearns Goodwin, *The Bully Pulpit: Theodore Roosevelt, William Howard Taft, and the Golden Age of Journalism* (New York: Simon and Schuster, 2013), 580–82, 678, and 681; James Chace, *1912: Wilson, Roosevelt, Taft and Debs—The Election That Changed the Country* (New York: Simon and Schuster, 2004), 31, 107, and 108; and Henry F. Pringle, *The Life and Times of William Howard Taft* (New York: Farrar and Rinehart, 1939), 1:318, 327, and 329, and 2:562, 749, 768, and 769.

150 **language in their platforms:** Warburg, *The Federal Reserve System*, 1:77.

150 **"Why should not Wall Street"**: Alfred Owen Crozier, *U.S. Money vs. Corporation Currency: "Aldrich Plan"* (Cincinnati: Magnet, 1912), 9, 205.

151 **He turned down all speaking invitations:** Aldrich to James Forgan, January 31, 1912, telegram, Aldrich Papers, Reel 47; and Nathaniel Wright Stephenson, *Nelson W. Aldrich: A Leader in American Politics* (New York: Scribner's, 1930), 405. For Aldrich's stock portfolio, see correspondence in Aldrich Papers, Reel 47.

151 **"grim granite and slate"**: Nelson W. Aldrich Jr., *Old Money: The Mythology of Wealth in America* (1988; repr., New York: Allworth Press, 1996), 26.

151 **The Democrats wrangled over the scope:** For the origins of the Pujo hearings, see Richard T. McCulley, *Banks and Politics During the Progressive Era: The Origins of the Reserve System, 1897–1913* (New York: Garland, 1992), 260–64.

152 **"The questions will be put"**: J. P. Morgan Jr. to Henry Davison, April 26, 1912, J. P. Morgan Jr. Papers, Book 9.

152 **"wild imaginings"**: Vanderlip to James Stillman, July 28, 1911, Frank A. Vanderlip Papers, Box 1-4.

152 **In March, the Banking Committee:** "To Split Money Inquiries," *The New York Times*, March 6, 1912. The next month, Laughlin made the point to Warburg that a separate legislative process was preferable. Referring to Samuel Untermyer, named as counsel to lead the Money Trust inquiry, Laughlin wrote, "Whatever Mr. Untermyer's pyrotechnics, the Sub-Committee on the bill will continue its quiet work" (James Laughlin to Warburg, April 25, 1912, Warburg Papers, Box 1, folder 3).

153 **Glass was a Bryan Democrat:** For a detailed account of Glass's early career, which documents the central role of racial politics for Glass and his Virginia contemporaries, see Harry Edward Poindexter, "From Copy Desk to Congress: The Pre-Congressional Career of Carter Glass," Ph.D. diss., University of Virginia, 1966.

153 **"misguided Negroes"**: Rixey Smith and Norman Beasley, *Carter Glass* (New York: Longmans, Green and Co., 1939), 49.

153 **However, he had no false pride:** James E. Palmer Jr., *Carter Glass: Unreconstructed Rebel* (Roanoke: Institute of American Biography, 1938), 54.

153 **Willis was close to Laughlin:** McCulley, *Banks and Politics During the Progressive Era*, 292.

154 **protect his "baby"**: Andrew to Paul Warburg, March 25, 1912, A. Piatt Andrew Papers, Box 22, folder 7.

154 **"simply have not got the knowledge"**: Warburg to James Laughlin, April 22, 1912, Warburg Papers, Box 1, folder 3.

154 **As a southerner, Glass was suspicious:** For evidence that Glass, early in 1912, was in fact hostile to centralization, see H. Parker Willis to Laughlin, March 30, 1912, James Laurence Laughlin Papers, Box 2.

154 **However, with Warburg prodding Laughlin:** Warburg to Laughlin, April 22, 1912; in

this letter, Warburg warns Laughlin, "I am worried about [Willis's] articles in the *Journal of Commerce*. He writes against centralization of reserves." See also Lucy D. Chen, "Banking Reform in a Hostile Climate: Paul M. Warburg and the National Citizens' League" (working paper, April 2010), 19, available at www.fas.harvard.edu/~histecon /crisis-next/1907/docs/Chen-Warburg_Final_Paper.pdf.

154 **"From recent information, I am inclined":** James Laughlin to Willis, June 14, 1912, Henry Parker Willis Papers, Box 7.

154 **The subcommittee finessed this delicate issue:** Henry Parker Willis, *The Federal Reserve System: Legislation, Organization, Operation* (New York: Ronald Press, 1923), 133–34. No notes from the subcommittee work in 1912 survive.

155 **That spring, Willis scratched out the beginnings:** Willis to James Laughlin, June 17, 1912, Willis Papers, Box 7; and "Glass Wins Again in Sixth District," *Richmond Times Dispatch*, August 9, 1912.

155 **Samuel Untermyer:** Vanderlip to James Stillman, May 4, 1912, Vanderlip Papers, Box 1–4; Morgan Jr. to Davison, April 26, 1912; McCulley, *Banks and Politics During the Progressive Era*, 265–66; and Vanderlip to James Stillman, April 23, 1912, Vanderlip Papers, Box 1-4 ("The whole thing runs back to Unterrmyer's ambition to go to the Senate"). For background on Untermyer, see McCulley as well as Gabriel Kolko, *The Triumph of Conservatism: A Reinterpretation of American History, 1900–1914* (New York: The Free Press of Glencoe, 1963), 220.

155 **lucrative stock deals:** Vanderlip to James Stillman, May 17, 1912, Vanderlip Papers, Box 1-4; this letter observes of a deal to sell a big block of Seaboard Company stock that "business as well as politics make strange bed fellows and one of the participants will be Samuel Untermyer for $1,000,000."

155 **"unpleasant":** Jean Strouse, *Morgan: American Financier* (New York: Random House, 1999), 9.

155 **Untermyer made quiet overtures:** Vanderlip to Stillman, April 27, 1912, Vanderlip Papers, Box 1-4; and Warburg to Samuel Untermyer (replying to Untermyer's luncheon invitation), May 29, 1912, Warburg Papers, Box 1, folder 3.

155 **The congressman was warned:** James Laughlin to Willis, May 5, 1912, Willis Papers, Box 7, advising Willis that Glass should occupy the field "in order to anticipate Untermyer." Willis certainly relayed this information to Glass.

155 **Untermyer had been born in Lynchburg:** The family was not long tenured in the South. Untermyer's parents were German Jews who emigrated from Bavaria. When his father died, shortly after the Civil War, the rest of the family moved to New York.

156 **"Baseball men are more optimistic":** "Major Leagues' Clubs Ready for Long Battle," *The New York Times*, April 7, 1912. The other new stadiums were in Detroit and Cincinnati.

156 **opposed to "social relations":** Chace, *1912*, 214. For the early state of the race, see Wilson to Josephus Daniels, January 18, 1912, in Arthur S. Link, ed., *The Papers of Woodrow Wilson* (Princeton, N.J.: Princeton University Press, 1966–1989), 24:64–65; John Milton Cooper Jr., *Woodrow Wilson* (New York: Knopf, 2009), 151–53; and Broesamle, *William Gibbs McAdoo*, 52–53.

157 **"chiefly to men's minds":** Arthur S. Link, *Wilson*, vol. 2, *The New Freedom* (Princeton, N.J.: Princeton University Press, 1956), 149.

157 **Meanwhile, Bryan beseeched Wilson:** William Jennings Bryan to Wilson, April 1, 1912, in *The Papers of Woodrow Wilson*, 24:273; and "Southwest Georgia Greets Gov. Wilson with Big Reception," press clipping of April 18, in ibid., 24:344.

157 **procure a statement from Bryan:** Paolo E. Coletta, *William Jennings Bryan* (Lincoln: University of Nebraska Press, 1969), 2:44. For newspaper endorsements, see Cooper, *Woodrow Wilson*, 151, 154.

157 **La Follette, whose campaign:** Goodwin, *The Bully Pulpit*, 670, 673–74. For Taft and Roosevelt name-calling, see Chace, *1912*, 111–12.

158 **Roosevelt's stated reason for running:** "Roosevelt Denies Taft Is Progressive," *The New York Times*, April 4, 1912; see also Pringle, *William Howard Taft*, 2:772–73, 776–77.

158 **a generally sound record:** Goodwin, *The Bully Pulpit*, 627; and Walter Nugent, *Progressivism: A Very Short Introduction* (New York: Oxford University Press, 2010), 89–90.

158 **letting voters overturn decisions:** Pringle, *William Howard Taft*, 2:768; and Goodwin, *The Bully Pulpit*, 679. For background on Taft's attitude on labor, see Pringle, *William Howard Taft*, 2:619–25. Wall Street's relationship with Roosevelt was complicated by his support for such Morgan-sponsored trusts as U.S. Steel. As Chace (*1912*, 204) and Vanderlip (Vanderlip to James Stillman, October 20, 1910, Vanderlip Papers, Box 1-3) document, the House of Morgan had turned against Roosevelt by 1912. Perkins was the exception. However, many financiers were also dismayed by Taft, due to his vigorous antitrust policy.

158 **"In years past he has done":** Lamont to W. J. Oliver, September 3, 1912, Thomas W. Lamont Papers, Box 123-6.

158 **Two days later, Piatt Andrew:** A. Piatt Andrew, *Diary of Abram Piatt Andrew, 1902–1914*, ed. E. Parker Hayden Jr. and Andrew L. Gray (Princeton, N.J., 1986), entries for April 27, 29, and 30, 1912; for the dinner with Warburg, see ibid., entry for April 15.

159 **Archie Butt:** Goodwin, *The Bully Pulpit*, 690–92, 571.

159 **"The horror of the thing":** Vanderlip to James Stillman, April 22, 1912, Vanderlip Papers, Box 1-4.

159 **Taft felt compelled:** Goodwin, *The Bully Pulpit*, 693–94; and Pringle, *William Howard Taft*, 2:774, 781–82, Taft's quotations in this paragraph are from "Taft Opens Fire on Roosevelt," *The New York Times*, April 26, 1912.

159 **the league ratcheted up:** James L. Laughlin, *The Federal Reserve Act: Its Origin and Problems* (New York: Macmillan, 1933), 65–67.

159 **he and Warburg continued to tussle:** Laughlin to W. J. Lauck, May 25, 1912, Laughlin Papers, Box 3, W. J. Lauck folder; and Laughlin, *The Federal Reserve Act*, 54, 65–67.

160 **Speakers were booked:** Speakers Bureau Reports for weeks ending June 8 and June 15, 1912, Warburg Papers, Box 8, folder 108; and Publicity Report for week ending June 8, 1912, ibid., pp. 4–5.

160 **"directing public opinion into definite channels":** Publicity Report for week ending June 15, 1912, ibid. The *Herald* article can also be found in Warburg Papers.

160 **Laughlin was hopeful that businessmen:** For examples of the Citizens' League's outreach to both businessmen and editorial writers in Arkansas, as well as information on membership fees and a directory of the forty states with league offices, see Warburg Papers, Box 8, folder 108. This folder contains a flyer titled "ATTENTION! $$$ FOR YOU— IT'S YOUR BUSINESS $$$," as well as the letter to editorial writers from the Arkansas Division, addressed to "Editorial Writer," May 11, 1912.

160 **Laughlin's earlier insistence on keeping:** Publicity Report for week ending June 8, 1912 ("Following the national conventions, which, it is confidently expected, will both declare for a non-partisan revision of the banking and currency laws"); and Publicity Report for week ending June 15, 1912 ("It is anticipated that the Republican plank will be a frank endorsement of the plan of the National Monetary Commission").

160 **In several southern states:** See "Work of National Citizens League to get safe state Dem. Planks in 1912, along Aldrich bill lines, although ostensibly denouncing said bill, May 1912," Aldrich Papers, Reel 61 (from Warburg Papers). This document quotes from several of Laughlin's letters to Warburg in the spring of 1912.

161 **"The country will":** Laughlin to William Jennings Bryan, June 3, 1912, Laughlin Papers, W. J. Bryan folder.

161 **steer the Republican platform:** Andrew, *Diary*, entries for June and July 1912; Franklin MacVeagh to Andrew (undated), Andrew Papers, Box 22, folder 1; Franklin MacVeagh to Andrew, April 23, 1912, ibid., folder 3; and Andrew to Franklin MacVeagh, May 10, 1912, ibid., Box 20, folder 20.

161 **"I can not think":** William H. Taft to Andrew, July 2, 1912, ibid., Box 22, folder 7. See also Franklin MacVeagh to Andrew, June 24, June 28, June 29, and July 2, 1912, and Andrew to Franklin MacVeagh, June 28, 1912, all in ibid., folder 3; and Andrew to Nelson Aldrich, June 26, 1912, ibid., Box 20, folder 23. Various correspondence in the Andrew Papers documents that Andrew made public a letter airing his complaints with MacVeagh.

162 **He was even less effective:** Nugent, *Progressivism*, 91; Pringle, *William Howard Taft*, 2:804–5; Goodwin, *Bully Pulpit*, 705–6; and McCulley, *Banks and Politics During the Progressive Era*, 259. The Republican platform is available from American Presidency Project at www.presidency.ucsb.edu/ws/?pid=29633.

162 **"fever [of] excitement":** Andrew, *Diary*, entry of June 19, 1912.

162 **"We stand at Armageddon":** Pringle, *William Howard Taft*, 2:803, 809.

163 **"The Republicans have met":** Wilson to Mary Allen Hulbert Peck, June 23, 1912, in *The Papers of Woodrow Wilson*, 24:495.

163 **Laughlin, Willis, and Andrew converged on Baltimore:** For Laughlin, see typed material on Citizens' League, Warburg Papers, Box 8, folder 108; for Willis, see Willis to James Laughlin, June 17, 1912, Willis Papers, Box 7; and for Andrew, see Andrew, *Diary*, entry for June 1912. The description of Baltimore comes from Broesamle, *William Gibbs McAdoo*, 57.

163 **"The day is gray and grizzly":** Wilson to Mary Allen Hulbert Peck, June 17, 1912, in *The Papers of Woodrow Wilson*, 24:481–82.

163 **"a convention of progressives":** Wilson to William Jennings Bryan, June 22, 1912, in ibid., 493.

CHAPTER TEN: **WOODROW'S MIRACLE**

164 **"A democratic nation is richer":** Speech in Frankfort, Kentucky, February 9, 1912, in Arthur S. Link, ed., *The Papers of Woodrow Wilson* (Princeton, N.J.: Princeton University Press, 1966–1989), 24:141–46.

164 **"The Aldrich Plan is 60 to 70 percent correct":** Vanderlip to James Stillman, September 20, 1912, Frank A. Vanderlip Papers, Box 1-4; and Henry Parker Willis, *The Federal Reserve System: Legislation, Organization and Operation* (New York: Ronald Press, 1923), 139–40. The two sources give generally consistent though not identical accounts of Wilson's remark.

164 **"We oppose the so-called Aldrich bill":** The Democratic platform is available from American Presidency Project at: www.presidency.ucsb.edu/ws/?pid=29590. For Bryan's authorship of the platform, see Paolo E. Coletta, *William Jennings Bryan* (Lincoln: University of Nebraska Press, 1969), 2:62; and Michael Kazin, *A Godly Hero: The Life of William Jennings Bryan* (New York: Knopf, 2006), 188.

165 At the outset, Bryan threw the convention: Convention details from John J. Broe-samle, *William Gibbs McAdoo: A Passion for Change, 1863–1917* (Port Washington, N.Y.: Kennikat Press, 1973), 58–60; James Chace, *1912: Wilson, Roosevelt, Taft and Debs—The Election That Changed the Country* (New York: Simon and Schuster, 2004), 150; Coletta, *William Jennings Bryan*, 2:59–64, and William Gibbs McAdoo, *Crowded Years: The Reminiscences of William G. McAdoo* (Boston: Houghton Mifflin, 1931), 145. Michael Kazin, a Bryan biographer, says that even though Bryan's wife was eager for him to launch a fourth campaign in 1912, Bryan was sincere in his expressed desire not to run (*A Godly Hero*, 184).

165 At Sea Girt, the governor anxiously: "Wilson Serene as Voting Goes On," *The New York Times*, June 29, 1912.

166 "My nomination was a sort of political miracle": Wilson to Mary Allen Hulbert Peck, July 6, 1912, in *The Papers of Woodrow Wilson*, 24:541. Convention details come from "Murphy and Bryan in a Deadlock," *The New York Times*, June 20, 1912; "Break to Wilson Seems at Hand as Convention Adjourns Till Today; He Leads on the 42nd Ballot," *The New York Times*, July 2, 1912; Broesamle, *William Gibbs McAdoo*, 61–62; Chace, *1912*, 154; John Milton Cooper Jr., *Woodrow Wilson* (New York: Knopf, 2009), 156; Arthur S. Link, *Woodrow Wilson and the Progressive Era, 1910–1917* (New York: Harper and Row, 1954), 13; and Arthur S. Link, *Woodrow Wilson: A Brief Biography* (Cleveland: World, 1963), 54.

166 more coherence to his evolving views: Link, *Wilson and the Progressive Era*, 20, stresses that Wilson remained a Jeffersonian. For Wilson's idealistic view of businessmen, see William Diamond's insightful *The Economic Thought of Woodrow Wilson* (Baltimore: Johns Hopkins University Press, 1943), 51–55; Diamond curtly dismisses the question of Wilson's leftward evolution, observing tartly (p. 87), "Precisely why Wilson underwent this change is a problem for his biographer." Cooper's very good biography, *Woodrow Wilson*, cites opportunism as a partial answer but does not attempt a definitive answer, noting (p. 106), "When, how and why Woodrow Wilson became a progressive would become hotly debated questions after he entered politics."

167 "middle class is being more and more squeezed": Speech in Frankfort, Kentucky, February 9, 1912, 141–46; and Richard Hofstadter, *The Age of Reform* (New York: Knopf, 1955), 225.

167 "government by experts": Chace, *1912*, 203. For background on Wilson's and Roosevelt's views on the trusts, see ibid., 166, 194–203; Cooper, *Woodrow Wilson*, 163; Diamond, *Economic Thought of Woodrow Wilson*, 63–65; Hofstadter, *Age of Reform*, 223–28; Doris Kearns Goodwin, *The Bully Pulpit: Theodore Roosevelt, William Howard Taft, and the Golden Age of Journalism* (New York: Simon and Schuster, 2013), 667–70; Gabriel Kolko, *The Triumph of Conservatism: A Reinterpretation of American History, 1900–1914* (New York: The Free Press of Glencoe, 1963), 209; and Alpheus Thomas Mason, *Brandeis: A Free Man's Life* (New York: Viking, 1956), 377.

167 he had few misgivings about federal authority: See Cooper, *Woodrow Wilson*, 10. Elsewhere Cooper notes that Wilson "had never been able to swallow the legacies of state rights and limited government" that Democrats inherited from Jefferson (p. 143). For Wilson's "Tory" remark, see Diamond, *Economic Thought of Woodrow Wilson*, 42. Even as early as Wilson's graduate thesis, *Congressional Government: A Study in American Politics* (1885), he deplored the sectionalism in Congress as frustrating the purposes of the federal government: "These petty barons, some of them not a little powerful, but none of them within reach [of] the full powers of rule, may at will exercise an almost despotic sway within their own shires, and may sometimes threaten to convulse even the realm itself" (p. 30).

168 **"I do not know enough about this subject":** Acceptance speech, August 7, 1912, in *The Papers of Woodrow Wilson*, 25:12, 14.

169 **"I am for big business and I am against trusts":** Speech in Sioux City, Iowa, September 17, 1912, in ibid., 152. Wilson meant that while he was against monopolization he had no trouble with a business growing large by lawful means—but this was a distinction surely beyond the average voter. Wilson also said in his acceptance speech of August 7, "Power in the hands of great business men does not make me apprehensive, unless it springs out of advantages which they have not created for themselves" (ibid, p. 11). On Brandeis's influence on the campaign, see Broesamle, *William Gibbs McAdoo*, 66; Cooper, *Woodrow Wilson*, 162–67; Kolko, *The Triumph of Conservatism*, 208–9; Link, *Wilson and the Progressive Era*, 20–21; and Mason, *Brandeis*, 377–80.

169 **He made the fair point:** Chace, *1912*, 206.

169 **Wilson also supported labor:** Diamond, *Economic Thought of Woodrow Wilson*, 54–55, 70; and Link, *Woodrow Wilson: A Brief Biography*, 53.

169 **Wall Street was as divided:** Due to Perkins's role in the Roosevelt campaign, the Morgan-sponsored U.S. Steel was extremely uncomfortable with Perkins's presence on its board. Jack Morgan asked Perkins—at least three times—to resign; Perkins refused: see J. P. Morgan Sr. to Perkins, August 18 and September 3, 1912, and Perkins's memorandum of September 4 documenting Morgan's telephone call that day, all in George W. Perkins Sr. Papers, Box 12. For Morgan and Carnegie's support of Taft and Schiff's support of Wilson, see Chace, *1912*, 204. The senior Morgan aide Thomas Lamont also supported Taft: Lamont to W. J. Oliver, September 3, 1912, Thomas W. Lamont Papers, Box 123-6. For Warburg's support of Wilson, see Ron Chernow, *The Warburgs: The Twentieth-Century Odyssey of a Remarkable Jewish Family* (New York: Random House, 1993), 140. Kolko's *The Triumph of Conservatism*, 211, notes other prominent Jews supporting Wilson, including Henry Morgenthau Jr. and Bernard Baruch. For Untermyer's gift and Vanderlip's response, see Vanderlip to James Stillman, September 27, 1912, Vanderlip Papers, Box 1-4.

169 **he told an editorial writer:** McCulley, *Banks and Politics During the Progressive Era*, 270–71. Aside from bankers, Citizens' League members also contacted Wilson: see Paul M. Warburg, *The Federal Reserve System: Its Origin and Growth—Reflections and Recollections* (New York: Macmillan, 1930), 1:79; and James L. Laughlin, *The Federal Reserve Act: Its Origin and Problems* (New York: Macmillan, 1933), 113–14.

170 **His campaign utterances:** See, for example, Wilson's speech in Columbus on September 20, 1912, in *The Papers of Woodrow Wilson*, 25:203, in which his principal recommendation for currency reform was "You've got to make it elastic."

170 **"You don't understand politics":** Frank A. Vanderlip with Boyden Sparkes, *From Farm Boy to Financier* (New York: D. Appleton-Century, 1935), 225–26.

170 **Morgenthau reported to New York bankers:** Vanderlip to Stillman, September 20, 1912; and Willis, *The Federal Reserve System*, 139–40.

170 **Wilson continued his courtship:** Cooper, *Woodrow Wilson*, 168; and Coletta, *William Jennings Bryan*, 2:81.

171 **Laughlin was the only petitioner with:** Laughlin, *The Federal Reserve Act*, 177–79.

171 **"the better part of an entire day":** Samuel Untermyer to Wilson, November 6, 1912, in *The Papers of Woodrow Wilson*, 25:528–29; Wilson's response, dated November 12, is in ibid., 542.

171 **"formulated, tentatively, a substitute":** Carter Glass to Wilson, November 7, 1912, in *The Papers of Woodrow Wilson*, 25:530–31; Wilson's response, dated November 14, is in ibid., 547.

171 **"short vacation":** Wilson to Ira Remsen, November 14, 1912, ibid.

171 **a conference between Willis and Untermyer:** H. Parker Willis to Glass, November 7, 1912, Carter Glass Collection, Box 25/26. The conference had occurred the day before, November 6, which itself was the day after the election.

172 **"Mr. Untermyer contemplates":** Ibid.

172 **"the main ideas of the Aldrich bill":** Ibid.

172 **"impertinent activity":** Glass to Arsène Pujo, November 8, 1912; Glass to Arsène Pujo, November 12, 1912; and Arsène Pujo to Glass, November 11, 1912, telegram, all in ibid., Box 64. See also "Laughlin's untitled and undated retrospective memorandum" (typed), James Laurence Laughlin Papers, Glass bill folder.

172 **"Moral: Put not your trust":** James Laughlin to Willis, November 21, 1912, H. Parker Willis Papers, Box 7.

173 **"been working on various phases":** Willis to Glass, November 7, 1912.

173 **In mid-November, Glass hosted Laughlin:** Laughlin to Willis, November 21, 1912; "Laughlin's untitled and undated retrospective memorandum"; and Laughlin, *The Federal Reserve Act*, 115, 117–19, and 120–21.

173 **Glass, in fact, was still laboring to understand:** Colonel House recorded that Glass admitted his lack of expertise: see Edward House to Wilson, November 28, 1912, in *The Papers of Woodrow Wilson*, 25:564. Glass's lack of expertise was also on display in a December 14, 1912, letter to Willis: "As I said to you last night, quite a number of questions present themselves to my mind" (Willis Papers, Box 1). Furthermore, Laughlin later wrote that Glass was "slow in taking in the banking principles," although once he grasped them he was "firm in his position and was a good fighter for what he believed" ("Laughlin's untitled and undated retrospective memorandum"). See also Robert Craig West, *Banking Reform and the Federal Reserve, 1863–1923* (Ithaca, N.Y.: Cornell University Press, 1974), 94.

173 **"too prone to be suspicious":** Glass to H. Parker Willis, December 9, 1912, Glass Collection, Box 25/26.

173 **"allowed little or nothing to become public":** Warburg, *The Federal Reserve System*, 1:81.

174 **"sound banking" principles:** Ibid., 81–82. For the Morawetz article, see West, *Banking Reform and the Federal Reserve*, 95.

174 **"I fear, Mr. Glass":** Carter Glass, *An Adventure in Constructive Finance* (Garden City, N.Y.: Doubleday, 1927), 32–37.

174 **"I think the quicker you see him":** Edward House to Wilson, November 28, 1912, in *The Papers of Woodrow Wilson*, 25:563–64.

175 **In December, Untermyer turned:** "Five Men Control $368,000,000 Here," *The New York Times*, December 11, 1912.

175 **Morgan regarded public testimony:** See, for example, Jean Strouse, *Morgan, American Financier* (New York: Random House, 1999), 5.

175 **"by special train with half a dozen":** Vanderlip to James Stillman, December 20, 1912, Vanderlip Papers, Box 1-4.

175 **"No, sir; the first thing is character":** House Committee on Banking and Currency, *Report of the Committee Appointed Pursuant to House Resolutions 429 and 504 to Investigate the Concentration of Control of Money and Credit*, 62d Cong., 3d sess., submitted February 28, 1913 (Washington, D.C.: Government Printing Office, 1913), 136; available

at https://fraser.stlouisfed.org/docs/historical/house/money_trust/montru_report.pdf. (Hereinafter cited as Pujo Report.)

175 as later witnesses would demonstrate: See, for example, the testimony of George F. Baker, ibid., 1503.

176 "You are an advocate of combination and cooperation": Ibid., 1050.

176 Untermyer deliberately zeroed in on railroads: Ibid., 1019, 1034, and 1035.

176 had at times been "blundering": Vanderlip to Stillman, December 20, 1912.

176 Laughlin proposed that monetary policy: Laughlin Papers, Plan D folder.

177 Warburg also dashed off a fourteen-page: Warburg to Henry Morgenthau, December 7, 1912, Paul Moritz Warburg Papers, Box 1, folder 3. Warburg's plan was, characteristically, elaborated in great detail. He proposed to Morgenthau that Congress enact *two* pieces of legislation, one for a bank with branches, another providing for a national clearinghouse. Warburg's letter to Colonel House of December 19, 1912 (Edward M. House Papers, Box 114a) documents that the plan was conveyed to House, which surely means that Wilson was advised of it.

177 Glass also met with Piatt Andrew: A. Piatt Andrew, *Diary of Abram Piatt Andrew, 1902–1914,* ed. E. Parker Hayden Jr. and Andrew L. Gray (Princeton, N.J., 1986), entry for December 14, 1912. Apparently at their breakfast meeting, Glass advised Andrew of his continuing worries about securing the Banking Committee chairmanship. Three days later, Aldrich wrote Andrew (A. Piatt Andrew Papers, Box 3, folder 17), offering to help Glass gain the chairmanship, presumably by putting in a word with his friends in Congress. This suggests that Aldrich, by then of course retired, was held in higher esteem by congressional Democrats than their public utterances suggested. Lastly, in another example of pressure for a central bank, the economist Charles Conant urged Glass to endorse a "concentration" of reserves (Glass to Willis, December 9, 1912).

177 "deluged with letters": Glass to H. Parker Willis, December 14, 1912, Glass Collection, Box 25/26.

177 Glass's every instinct was to try: James Laughlin to Willis, December 21, 1912, Willis Papers, Box 7. On Glass's irritation over the attention Untermyer received from newspapers, see, for example, Glass to H. Parker Willis, December 3, 1912, Glass Collection, Box 25/26. For Glass's efforts to screen witnesses, see West, *Banking Reform and the Federal Reserve,* 97–100.

177 "Mr. Hulbert is a very sharp critic": Willis to Carter Glass, December 14, 1912, Willis Papers, Box 1.

178 Glass put off seeing him: Laughlin's query regarding authorship is missing; Willis's reply of December 18, 1912 (Laughlin Papers, Glass bill file) says: "As to authorship of the forthcoming measure, custom dictates that the Chairman's name shall be given to any bill that may be reported." Laughlin had proposed to Willis on December 2 that they and Glass meet promptly in Baltimore to discuss Laughlin's progress. On December 6, when Laughlin received word from Willis that Glass wanted to put off a meeting until January, Laughlin realized his role would be strictly consultative. He immediately wired Glass, "Telegram received much disappointed at postponement." More expressions of hurt followed. Notwithstanding his bruised feelings, Laughlin continued to revise his plan for Willis and Glass's benefit, and succeeded in meeting Glass at his hotel on December 21. (See Laughlin correspondence of December 6, 7, and 21, 1912, in Willis Papers, Box 7.)

178 "I was considerably taken": Laughlin to H. Parker Willis, December 7, 1912, Laughlin Papers, Glass bill file.

178 **The only audience Glass wanted was with Wilson:** Carter Glass to Wilson, December 14, 1912, in *The Papers of Woodrow Wilson,* 25:588–89; Carter Glass to Wilson, December 18, 1912, in ibid., 608; and "The President-Elect Back from Bermuda," *The New York Times,* December 17, 1912.

CHAPTER ELEVEN: **THE PRINCETON DEPOT**

179 **"The ghost of Andrew Jackson stalked":** Carter Glass, *An Adventure in Constructive Finance* (Garden City, N.Y.: Doubleday, 1927), 110–11.

179 **"I do not care what you call it":** *Banking and Currency Reform: Hearings Before the Subcommittee of the Committuee on Banking and Currency, Charged with Investigating Plan of Banking and Currency Reform and Reporting Constructive Legislation Thereof,* 62d Cong., 3rd sess., House of Representatives, January 14, 1913, 233; available at http://books.google.com/books?id=pcoqAAAAYAAJ&printsec=frontcover&source=gbs_ge_summary_r&cad=0#v=onepage&q&f=false.

179 **Glass was anxious to meet:** Carter Glass to Willis, December 23, 1912, Henry Parker Willis Papers, Box 1; and Glass to H. Parker Willis, December 19, 1912, Carter Glass Collection, Box 25/26.

179 **intensely agitated by the pressure:** See, for example, Willis to Carter Glass, December 21, 1912, Willis Papers, Box 20, in which Willis warned Glass to expect a "sharp fight" from bankers lobbying for a central bank. Such missives inevitably distressed Glass.

180 **"Confined by attack of cold":** James E. Palmer Jr., *Carter Glass: Unreconstructed Rebel* (Roanoke: Institute of American Biography, 1938), 76. Glass's telegram about his arrival is in Willis Papers, Box 1.

180 **"the only place in the world":** William Diamond, *The Economic Thought of Woodrow Wilson* (Baltimore: Johns Hopkins University Press, 1943), 16.

180 **Glass's family:** Harry Edward Poindexter, "From Copy Desk to Congress: The Pre-Congressional Career of Carter Glass," Ph.D. diss., University of Virginia, 1966, 4.

180 **free of any southern accent:** John Milton Cooper Jr., *Woodrow Wilson* (New York: Knopf, 2009), 23; for Wilson's feelings about the Civil War, see ibid., 34.

180 **"He did not doubt":** Diamond, *Economic Thought of Woodrow Wilson,* 15.

180 **Princeton was bitterly cold:** Glass, *An Adventure in Constructive Finance,* 81–82; and Rixey Smith and Norman Beasley, *Carter Glass* (New York: Longmans, Green and Co., 1939), 90–92.

181 **Glass was painfully aware:** Glass to H. Parker Willis, December 29, 1912, Glass Collection, Box 25/26.

181 **nothing so formal as a draft:** Smith and Beasley, *Carter Glass,* 90.

181 **What Glass and Willis proposed:** The most comprehensive source for what was presented at Princeton is Henry Parker Willis, *The Federal Reserve System: Legislation, Organization and Operation* (New York: Ronald Press, 1923), 141–47. See also James L. Laughlin, *The Federal Reserve Act: Its Origin and Problems* (New York: Macmillan, 1933), 127–28; and Glass, *An Adventure in Constructive Finance,* 81–85. Warburg gives his interpretation in Paul M. Warburg, *The Federal Reserve System: Its Origin and Growth—Reflections and Recollections* (New York: Macmillan, 1930), 1:82.

182 **the banking system should be organized:** For Willis and Glass's intent, see Willis to Glass, December 19, 1912, which states, "The effect of these changes will be to strengthen the reserve banks very greatly as against the large national banks of New York and other central reserve cities." For "local field," see Willis, *The Federal Reserve System,* 145.

182 **"in regard to centralization":** Willis, *The Federal Reserve System,* 141.

182 The president-elect suggested: Whether Wilson definitively affirmed that a central bank would be superior is unknowable, but it seems likely. All we have is the account of Willis, who averred that the president-elect "recognized the fact that such an organization was politically impossible even if economically desirable" (ibid., 146).

182 "You are far on the right track": Wilson to Carter Glass, December 31, 1912, in Arthur S. Link, *The Papers of Woodrow Wilson* (Princeton, N.J.: Princeton University Press, 1966–1989), 25:650; Glass, *An Adventure in Constructive Finance*, 81–82; and Willis, *The Federal Reserve System*, 146, 147.

183 "perhaps, an hour with Mr. Wilson": Glass to Willis, December 29, 1912.

183 "We may ourselves have in readiness": Carter Glass to Wilson, December 29, 1912, in *The Papers of Woodrow Wilson*, 25:641–42.

183 "It is clear to me": Glass to Willis, December 29, 1912.

184 "I am not entirely convinced": Carter Glass to Willis, January 3, 1913, Willis Papers, Box 1.

184 Forgan, the leader: James Laughlin to Willis, January 10, 1913, ibid., Box 7.

185 Glass and Willis did not even disclose: Gabriel Kolko, *The Triumph of Conservatism: A Reinterpretation of American History, 1900–1914* (New York: The Free Press of Glencoe, 1963), 225–26; Robert Craig West, *Banking Reform and the Federal Reserve, 1863–1923* (Ithaca, N.Y.: Cornell University Press, 1974), 113–15; and Willis, *The Federal Reserve System*, 151.

185 "in good humor toward the hearings": Willis to Carter Glass, December 31, 1912, Willis Papers, Box 20.

185 "no one would claim": *Banking and Currency Reform: Hearings Before the Subcommittee of the Committee on Banking and Currency*, 4.

186 "Would you say that we should do nothing": The quoted portions of Warburg testimony come from ibid., 77, 67, 69, and 73. Warburg was not at all candid about his involvement with the Aldrich Plan (he referred sympathetically to the "framers" of the Plan, without divulging that he himself was one of them).

187 Glass repeatedly trotted out: Glass was upfront about his political motivations. In his cross-examination of Festus Wade, the chairman observed, "The situation, frankly, has its political aspects. I do not mean to say that anybody is proposing to mix politics with the reformation of the currency; but understand that the majority members of this committee are confronted by the platform declaration of the Democratic Party against the so-called Aldrich Plan" (ibid., 206).

187 "no scheme would be considered": Warburg, *The Federal Reserve System*, 1:89.

187 Prominent bankers: Willis to Carter Glass, January 18, January 20, and January 23, 1912, all in Willis Papers, Box 20; and James Neal Primm, *A Foregone Conclusion* (St. Louis: Federal Reserve Bank of St. Louis, 1989), chapter 2, "Banking Reform 1907–1913"; available at www.stlouisfed.org/foregone/chapter_two.cfm.

187 Warburg recast his latest plan: Warburg, *The Federal Reserve System*, 1:89–90; see also Willis to Glass, January 20, 1913.

187 Warburg's point: Warburg, *The Federal Reserve System*, 1:170.

187 "The tantalizing puzzle . . . safe-deposit vaults": This is my construction from two separate quotations: "tantalizing puzzle" is from ibid.; the longer part of the quotation is from the same volume, (p. 85), and in the same context—i.e., evaluating Glass's regional plan—but was used there by Warburg in evaluating Morawetz's plan back in 1909.

187 Glass didn't trust him: Primm, *A Foregone Conclusion*, chapter 2; see also Arthur S.

Link, *Wilson*, vol. 2, *The New Freedom* (Princeton, N.J.: Princeton University Press, 1956), 205.

188 **Warburg returned the favor:** Warburg, *The Federal Reserve System*, 1:58.

188 **Wilson was eager:** Woodrow Wilson to Glass, January 9, 1913, Glass Collection, Box 1. For the January 15 date of the draft, see Willis, *The Federal Reserve System*, 147.

188 **to keep its provisions secret:** Willis to Carter Glass, January 21, 1913, Willis Papers, Box 20; Willis to Glass, January 23, 1913, Willis Papers, Box 20; and James Laughlin to Willis, January 21, 1913, ibid., Box 7 (Laughlin all but begs, "I hope some way can be devised by which we can have a chance to know what the committee bill will be"). See also Warburg, *The Federal Reserve System*, 1:82.

188 **"outside the breastworks":** Laughlin, *The Federal Reserve Act*, 136. The Trenton meeting was held on January 30.

188 **The document Glass took:** The Trenton draft was reprinted in Willis, *The Federal Reserve System*, 1531–53. Willis says the draft included a "limited" guaranty (ibid., 147); however, it consisted only of a plan for partial payment to depositors of failed banks and only up to the banks' estimated asset values—that is, what depositors would receive without such a plan. For open market operations, see ibid., 1543; for compulsory membership and "not less than 15," see ibid., 1532.

188 **In other respects, the Trenton draft bore a striking resemblance:** The gold provision of the Trenton draft—among other criteria, reserve banks would be required to hold gold equal to 50 percent of their outstanding note circulation—is in ibid., 1548.

189 **The bills were also similar in scope:** West, *Banking Reform and the Federal Reserve*, 106, noted the bills' organizational similarity. See also Willis, *The Federal Reserve System*, 1543–44, for the agency's functioning as the government's fiscal arm; and West, *Banking Reform and the Federal Reserve*, 108, for similar systems. In *The Federal Reserve System*, 1:178–368, Warburg prints the texts of the Aldrich Plan and the Federal Reserve Act side by side, demonstrating their similarity, including in their language. Even as Willis denied any claim of the Aldrich bill to paternity, he admitted the similarity in language in his book: "This, however, did not prevent the use of such features of the Aldrich bill as were considered to be desirable or even in various places the use of language drawn from or modeled after the language implied in the Aldrich bill" (Willis, *The Federal Reserve System*, 526–27).

189 **The biggest was that:** West, *Banking Reform and the Federal Reserve*, 110; and Willis, *The Federal Reserve System*, 1544–47.

189 **Willis would contend:** Willis, *The Federal Reserve System*, 523–25. See also "Aldrich Bill Compared [by Willis] with Federal Reserve Act," Nelson W. Aldrich Papers, Reel 61, which states, "It was not drawn, even largely, from any single source, but is the product of comparison, selection, and refinement upon the various materials, ideas, and data rendered available throughout a long course of study and agitation."

189 **"was not derived from":** Willis, *The Federal Reserve System*, 523. In 1916, Glass similarly asserted that the Aldrich bill and his own "differ[ed] in principle, in purpose and in processes" (Warburg, *The Federal Reserve System*, 1:407). On the other hand, a neutral observer, West (*Banking Reform and the Federal Reserve*, 112), says that "the bills are very similar." This topic is treated at greater length in the epilogue.

189 **As inauguration day neared, Wilson agonized:** House diary entry, December 19, 1912, in *The Papers of Woodrow Wilson*, 25:614; House to Woodrow Wilson, January 9, January 29, and February 5, 1913, all in Edward M. House Papers, Box 119a; and Cooper, *Woodrow Wilson*, 189. House was not the only naysayer on Brandeis, but he was the most decisive—see, for instance, House to Wilson, November 22, 1912, House Papers, Box 119a; and House diary entry, February 26, 1913, in *The Papers of Woodrow Wilson*, 27:137. Although House's November 22 letter bore ugly, anti-Semitic overtones, impugning Brandeis's "Hebrew traits of mind," House probably feared Brandeis's influence rather than his ethnicity. See also Cooper, *Woodrow Wilson*, 183, 185, and 190. Wilson's acquiescence is from Arthur S. Link, *Woodrow Wilson and the Progressive Era, 1910–1917* (New York: Harper and Row, 1954), 30. House declined Wilson's offer of a cabinet post in his letter of January 9, House Papers, Box 119a.

190 **Wilson made an inspired choice:** Cooper, *Woodrow Wilson*, 181, 205.

190 **into "bitter poverty":** John J. Broesamle, *William Gibbs McAdoo: A Passion for Change, 1863–1917* (Port Washington, N.Y.: Kennikat Press, 1973), 4. For background on McAdoo prior to his entry into politics, see ibid, especially 4–31; William Gibbs McAdoo, *Crowded Years: The Reminiscences of William G. McAdoo* (Boston: Houghton Mifflin, 1931); Cooper, *Woodrow Wilson*, 145–46; and Richard T. McCulley, *Banks and Politics During the Progressive Era: The Origins of the Federal Reserve System, 1897–1913* (New York: Garland, 1992), 293–94.

190 **McAdoo was not a Wall Street insider:** Broesamle, *William Gibbs McAdoo*, 24, 78, and 123. He recounts that Kuhn, Loeb provided assistance to the tunnel entity in 1913.

191 **business was unsettled:** Robert H. Wiebe, *Businessmen and Reform: A Study of the Progressive Movement* (Chicago: Elephant, 1989), 125–26; for McAdoo's view of the federal government's role, see, for instance, McAdoo, *Crowded Years*, 61.

191 **an address in January:** Cooper, *Woodrow Wilson*, 185.

191 **the Democrats were eager:** "Draft of Currency Bill," Glass Collection, Box 16. This document is undated and unsigned although it appears to be from early 1913. Containing notes, probably by either Willis or Glass, it argues for fast action on currency reform as an "offset to tariff criticism, because it would essentially appeal to business men." See also Willis to Representative Charles A. Korbly, February 8, 1913, Willis Papers, Box 20.

191 **His goal was to unshackle:** See, for instance, Link, *The New Freedom*, 203.

191 **"to take away from certain":** Joseph P. Tumulty, *Woodrow Wilson as I Know Him* (Garden City, N.Y.: Doubleday, Page, 1921), 170.

191 **a scorching indictment:** Untermyer was quite sarcastic in questioning Vanderlip, viz, "Of how many corporations are you a director Mr. Vanderlip; can you remember?": Pujo Report.

192 **"Have you ever competed for any securities":** Ibid., 1542.

192 **"well-defined identity and community":** Ibid., 129.

192 **Public revulsion was nearly uniform:** James Grant, *Money of the Mind: Borrowing and Lending in America from the Civil War to Michael Milken* (New York: Farrar, Straus and Giroux, 1992), 125.

193 **twenty-five thousand individual banks:** This figure was widely used, including in the Pujo Report, 251. According to Robert A. Degen, *The American Monetary System: A Concise Survey of Its Evolution Since 1896* (Lexington, Mass.: D.C. Heath and Company, 1987), 10, the total of banks in 1914 was twenty-eight thousand, a doubling from 1900. The minority report within the Pujo Report (also p. 251), says the resources of New York banks amounted to 23.2 percent of those nationally in 1900 and 18.9 percent of the total in 1912. The main body of the Pujo Report (p. 55) says the twenty largest banks in New York City held approximately 43 percent of the resources of banks in the city in 1911, up from 35 percent in 1901.

193 **net earnings of the national banks:** "160,980,084 Earned by National Banks," *The New York Times,* December 9, 1913.

193 **"When Mr. Morgan gave the word":** Pujo Report, 360.

194 **"gradually gathering to itself":** Ida Tarbell, "The Hunt for a Money Trust, III. The Clearing House," *American Magazine,* July 1913.

194 **Wilson rode to the Capitol alongside:** "Wilson Goes to Meet Taft," *The New York Times,* March 5, 1913; "How Wilson Was Sworn In," *The New York Times,* March 5, 1913; and Cooper, *Woodrow Wilson,* 198, 201.

194 **"We have been proud":** Inaugural Address, March 4, 1913, in *The Papers of Woodrow Wilson,* 27:151.

195 **the president of Mexico:** Francisco I. Madero was overthrown in a coup on February 18, 1913, and executed four days later.

195 **"I will be in frequent consultation":** Carter Glass to Willis, March. 20, 1913, Willis Papers, Box 1.

195 **Glass then urged Willis:** Carter Glass to Willis, March 10, March 13, and March 20, 1913, all in ibid. Glass, in his memoir, recalled it was a "distinct advantage" that Congress was out of session and that the Banking Committee was not yet constituted, as it stripped him of the obligation to confer (*An Adventure in Constructive Finance,* 93–94).

195 **the director of the U.S. Mint:** George Evan Roberts to Glass, March 13, 1913, Glass Collection, Box 14; and Willis, *The Federal Reserve System,* 209.

195 **Willis warned Glass:** Willis to Carter Glass, March 13, 1913, Willis Papers, Box 20.

195 **relaunch the Money Trust inquiry:** Samuel Untermyer to House, March 13, 1913, House Papers, Box 112; House to Samuel Untermyer, March 17, 1913, ibid.; and Samuel Untermyer to House, March 31, 1913, ibid.

196 **House took an interest in the banking bill:** Charles Seymour, *The Intimate Papers of Colonel House, Arranged as a Narrative by Charles Seymour* (Boston: Houghton Mifflin, 1928), 161, citing House diary entries of March 13 (re Vanderlip) and March 27, 1913 (re Morgan). Warburg wrote frequently to House: see his letters of January 6, January 16, and February 18, 1913, in House Papers, Box 114a.

196 **He also took Glass:** House diary entry of March 25, 1913, in *The Papers of Woodrow Wilson,* 27:227.

196 **"whip the Glass measure into final shape":** Ibid.

196 **"the same consideration as any other":** House diary entries of March 22 and March 24, 1913, in ibid., 215, 223.

196 **McAdoo carried far more weight:** Cooper, *Woodrow Wilson,* 193.

196 **his "friendship" with Wilson:** Vanderlip to James Stillman, April. 26, 1913, Frank A. Vanderlip Papers, Box 1-5.

196 **"We all feel that it behooves":** J. P. Morgan Jr. to James Stillman, March 12, 1913, J. P. Morgan Jr. Papers, Book 11.

197 **Nelson Aldrich and his family:** "European trip, 1913. The Morgans. Lucy Aldrich to Lucy Greene," Aldrich Papers, Reel 61. For Aldrich art purchases, see A. Imbert to Aldrich, March 21, March 25, and March 31, 1913, ibid., Reel 47.

197 **"a revision of the currency and banking laws":** Page is quoted is Vincent P. Carosso, *The Morgans: Private International Bankers, 1854–1913* (Cambridge, Mass.: Harvard University Press, 1987), 646.

197 **"The king is dead":** Vanderlip to James Stillman, April 4, 1913, Vanderlip Papers, Box b1-5.

CHAPTER TWELVE: **THE "SLIME OF BRYANISM"**

198 **"The germinal principle":** "Banking Under Federal Control," *The New York Times*, June 20, 1913.

198 **"The banks may be the instruments":** Arthur S. Link, *Woodrow Wilson and the Progressive Era, 1910–1917* (New York: Harper and Row), 48.

198 **The United States of 1913:** Data on Model Ts available at www.mtfca.com/encyclo /fdprod.htm; for the New York Stock Exchange, see Lance F. Davis, *International Capital Markets and American Economic Growth: 1820–1914* (New York: Cambridge University Press, 1994), 63. The rising propensity of people to deposit money in banks is a persistent theme of Milton Friedman and Anna Jacobson Schwartz, *A Monetary History of the United States, 1867–1960* (Princeton, N.J.: Princeton University Press, 1971); see, for instance, 15, 56–68, 122, and 164. Andrew Frame, *Elastic Currency* (Philadelphia: Annals of American Academy of Political Science, 1908), 12, states that individual deposits tripled from 1890 to 1908, to nearly $18 billion. By 1914, total deposits topped $21 billion— see Federal Reserve Bank of St. Louis, "Banking and Monetary Statistics, 1914–1941," 17, a report available at http://fraser.stlouisfed.org/docs/publications/bms/1914-1941 /BMS14-41_complete.pdf.

199 **bankers increasingly distrusted:** Vanderlip to James Stillman, May 12, 1913, Frank A. Vanderlip Papers, Box 1-5.

200 **"Currency should be based on credit":** William P. Goodwin, *Money, Credit Currency, and a Currency Plan* (Providence, R.I., 1910), 11.

200 **"educates the people who use it":** "Report of the Monetary Commission to the Executive Committee of the Indianapolis Monetary Convention" (1897), 40; available at openLibrary.org.

200 **Wilson was in a position to dominate:** Link, *Wilson and the Progressive Era*, 35.

200 **"even the semblance of privilege":** "Congress Cheers Greet Wilson," *The New York Times*, April 9, 1913. For the reversal of custom, see John Milton Cooper Jr., *Woodrow Wilson* (New York: Knopf, 2009), 214; and Arthur S. Link, *Woodrow Wilson: A Brief Biography* (Cleveland: World, 1963), 180. An index of joint sessions of Congress documents that (outside of inauguration days) Wilson was the first president since John Adams to appear in joint session: http://history.house.gov/Institution/Joint-Sessions/ 60-79.

201 **Even Wilson was accused:** Cooper, *Woodrow Wilson*, 214.

201 **he wanted to enhance:** "Congress Greets Wilson," *The New York Times*, April 9, 1913.

201 **Wilson was adamant:** Link, *Wilson and the Progressive Era*, 35; "Wilson Preparing for Business Boom," *The New York Times*, April 29, 1913; and "Federal Control of Interest Rate," *The New York Times*, April 30, 1913.

201 **McAdoo mapped the country:** Glass to H. Parker Willis, April 11, 1913, Carter Glass Collection, Box 47. That Willis and McAdoo met on Sunday, April 13, is from Willis to Carter Glass, April 16, 1913, Henry Parker Willis Papers, Box 20; they would also have a work session at McAdoo's home on Saturday, May 3. For the bill's new nomenclature, see Willis to Carter Glass, May 5, 1913, ibid.

201 **However, McAdoo became frustrated:** John J. Broesamle, *William Gibbs McAdoo: A Passion for Change, 1863–1917* (Port Washington, N.Y.: Kennikat Press, 1973), 100, 95.

201-2 **a Washington dinner party:** Carter Glass, *An Adventure in Constructive Finance* (Garden City, N.Y.: Doubleday, 1927), 52–53; and Henry Parker Willis, *The Federal Reserve System: Legislation, Organization and Operation* (New York: Ronald Press, 1923), 169.

202 **thirteen pages of pointed suggestions:** Glass, *An Adventure in Constructive Finance*, 48–49; and Paul M. Warburg, *The Federal Reserve System: Its Origin and Growth— Reflections and Recollections* (New York: Macmillan, 1930), 1:91–92. Warburg's analysis appears in his appendix, ibid., 613–25.

202 **"a large number of faucets":** Warburg, *The Federal Reserve System*, 1:613–14; a synopsis of his points follows in ibid., 614–25. The figure of twenty reserve banks can be found in Willis, *The Federal Reserve System*, 171.

202 **His paper, dated April 22:** Warburg, *The Federal Reserve System*, 1:92.

202 **"vicious" and also "extreme":** Willis to Carter Glass, April 29, 1913, Willis Papers, Box 1; and Willis to Carter Glass, April 28, 1913, ibid., Box 20.

203 **House reappeared, grabbed:** Willis to Carter Glass, May 2, 1913, ibid.

203 **Colonel House was invited:** Samuel Untermyer to House, May 3, 1913, Edward M. House Papers, Box 112.

203 **Owen had been born in Lynchburg:** For biographical details on Senator Owen, see Kenny L. Brown, "A Progressive from Oklahoma: Senator Robert Latham Owen, Jr.," *The Chronicles of Oklahoma* 62 (Fall 1984); Wyatt W. Belcher, "Political Leadership of Robert L. Owen," *The Chronicles of Oklahoma* 31 (Winter 1953–54); and Oklahoma Historical Society, "Oklahoma's First Senator Dies," *Chronicles of Oklahoma* 25, p. 178, available at http://digital.library.okstate.edu/Chronicles/contents.html.

204 **As a businessman, Owen:** "A Tribute to the Memory of Robert Latham Owen by the Officers and Directors of The First National Bank and Trust Co., Muskogee, Ok.," September 26, 1947, Special Collections and University Archives (Coll. no. 1931.001), McFarlin Library, University of Tulsa, Tulsa, Oklahoma; and Robert Owen to L. M. Nichols, March 5, 1912, L. M. Nichols Papers, Western History Collections, University of Oklahoma Libraries, Norman, Oklahoma, Box N-11, folder 4.

204 **frightened depositors withdrew half:** Robert L. Owen, *The Federal Reserve Act* (New York: Century, 1919), 2–3.

204 **Owen became a student of banking:** For the 1896 Democratic convention and Owen's European trip, see ibid., 5–9. For his speech in Congress, see "Characters in Congress— Senator Robert Latham Owen of Oklahoma," *The New York Times*, March 1, 1908. See also press clippings in L. M. Nichols Papers, Western History Collections, Box N-11, folder 4.

204 **For Untermyer, whose feud with Glass:** Samuel Untermyer to Glass, April 16, 1913, Glass Collection, Box 15/16; enclosed with this letter is one from R. C. Williken advising Untermyer that Glass "has done everything he could to discredit the great and important work performed by you [Untermyer] on the 'Money Trust' committee." Untermyer, of course, had been trying to poach on Glass's turf for nearly a year. For Owen and Untermyer, see Untermyer's self-published *Who Is Entitled to the Credit for the Federal Reserve Act? An Answer to Senator Carter Glass* (New York, 1927), 10, reproducing a letter from Owen to Untermyer of May 14, 1927, which states: "At your home you made various engagements for me to meet severally Frank A. Vanderlip, A. Barton Hepburn, Paul Warburg and others whose intimate views I desired in framing the Federal Reserve Act." See also Vanderlip to Robert Owen, May 31, 1913, Vanderlip Papers, Box 1-5. Warburg and Owen corresponded numerous times, but not until that fall.

205 **Owen reached out:** A. Piatt Andrew, *Diary of Abram Piatt Andrew, 1902–1914*, ed. E. Parker Hayden Jr. and Andrew L. Gray (Princeton, N.J., 1986), entries for May 19 through May 23, and also May 30.

205 **a loosely worded version:** Willis, *The Federal Reserve System*, 240.

205 **Untermyer invited Bryan to lunch:** Untermyer, *Who Is Entitled to the Credit for the Federal Reserve Act?* 12, 15.

205 **"waking up to the fact that the proposed bill":** House diary entry of May 11, 1913, Arthur S. Link, ed., *The Papers of Woodrow Wilson* (Princeton, N.J.: Princeton University Press, 1966–1989), 27:413.

205 **"I saw Primus":** House to Wilson, May 15, 1913, in ibid., 436. See also Willis, *The Federal Reserve System,* 245.

206 **Instead, the assignment went to McAdoo:** Broesamle, *William Gibbs McAdoo,* 78, 97.

206 **Convinced that the Glass bill:** Willis, *The Federal Reserve System,* 194–95.

206 **"We run against so much":** McAdoo to House, May 20, 1913, House Papers, Box 73.

206 **The essence of the McAdoo plan:** Willis, *The Federal Reserve System,* 206; Richard T. McCulley, *Banks and Politics During the Progressive Era: The Origins of the Federal Reserve System, 1897–1913* (New York: Garland, 1992), 295; and Broesamle, *William Gibbs McAdoo,* 101.

207 **It is not certain who drafted:** According to Broesamle, *William Gibbs McAdoo,* 80, Williams harbored a "pathological" dislike of Wall Street. On Williams's role, see also ibid., 104, and Willis, *The Federal Reserve System,* 194–95.

207 **"along the lines suggested":** House to Wilson, May 20, 1913, in *The Papers of Woodrow Wilson,* 27:458. A copy of this letter can also be found in Glass Collection, Box 14.

207 **"Pythias [McAdoo] or Owen could get him":** House to Wilson, May 20, 1913. Years later, in response to then Senator Glass's published account of this affair, Untermyer denied any involvement, tartly adding, "Glass is either dreaming or senile" (Samuel Untermyer to Robert Owen, May 10, 1927, Glass Collection, Box 24). It is possible the idea for Untermyer to sneak into the White House—never acted upon—was House's alone. However, Untermyer's broader denial of any role in McAdoo's plan does not stand up. House's May 20 letter to Wilson, written the day after he had spoken to Untermyer, was replete with specifics ("Untermyer tells me that some of the bankers here would approve," etc.). Also, Untermyer had been working to bring Owen together with bankers, and it is consistent with such efforts that he would have assisted in trying to hatch a compromise between them.

207 **RMS *Mauretania*:** Warburg, *The Federal Reserve System,* 1:97–98.

208 **"Are you serious?":** Glass, *An Adventure in Constructive Finance,* 100–101; and William Gibbs McAdoo, *Crowded Years: The Reminiscences of William G. McAdoo* (Boston: Houghton Mifflin, 1931), 243–44.

208 **"I could see clearly that":** McAdoo, *Crowded Years,* 222.

208 **Glass recounted that he was "astounded":** "Glass, *An Adventure in Constructive Finance,* 101. For collecting negative reactions, see Willis to Carter Glass, June 5, 1913, Willis Papers, Box 20.

208 **as an "administration bill":** Willis to Carter Glass, May 27, 1913, Willis Papers, Box 1; see also Willis, *The Federal Reserve System,* 241.

208 **McAdoo met with Owen and Glass:** Vanderlip to James Stillman, May 24, 1913, Vanderlip Papers, Box 1-5.

208 **"I am all in the air":** Carter Glass to Willis, June 6, 1913, Willis Papers, Box 1.

208 **Glass got an audience:** Glass to Woodrow Wilson, June 7, 1913, Glass Collection, Box 64; Glass to A. Barton Hepburn, June 7, 1913, ibid.; and Glass to Willis, June 6, 1913. Among those who provided letters were Hepburn, Reynolds, and the Chicago banker E. D. Hulbert. Some letters were delivered to Wilson the following day. The Wilson

quote ("I feel Mac is deceived") is recounted by Glass in *An Adventure in Constructive Finance,* 107–9. See also Rixey Smith and Norman Beasley, *Carter Glass* (New York: Longmans, Green and Co., 1939), 106, citing a "flood" of protests from bankers and economists.

209 "The chief point of danger": Glass to Hepburn, June 7, 1913.

209 He found the senator: Glass to H. Parker Willis, June 9, 1913, Glass Collection, Box 47. Glass's letter said Owen was in agreement on the "essential principles," but since they continued to differ on the issue of government vs. banker control, this was incorrect. For specifics on their negotiations, see Owen, *The Federal Reserve Act,* 74–75.

209 Wall Street laid an egg: The Dow Jones Industrials traded as low as 57 in late 1907. By May 1909 they were back in the low 90s, approximately their level before the Panic. For the next few years they traded mostly in the 80s and 90s. On March 4, Wilson's inauguration, the average closed at 80. After the May–June swoon, it stood (on June 10) at 72.

209 "We will need the gold badly": Vanderlip to Stillman, May 24, 1913, Vanderlip Papers, Box 1-5; his follow-up letter is dated June 6, 1913, ibid., and see also a further letter to Stillman of June 13, also in ibid. See also various market reports in the first week of June, such as "Stocks Lowest in Five Years," *The New York Times,* June 5, 1913, and "Review and Outlook," *The Wall Street Journal,* June 9, 1913.

209 McAdoo suspected that Wall Street: William McAdoo to House, June 18, 1913, House Papers, Box 73; and "Financial Markets," *The New York Times,* June 13, 1913.

210 "should be pushed rapidly": "Review and Outlook."

210 he had no choice but to oppose: Paolo E. Coletta, *William Jennings Bryan* (Lincoln: University of Nebraska Press, 1969), 2:130–31; Joseph P. Tumulty, *Woodrow Wilson as I Know Him* (Garden City, N.Y.: Doubleday, Page, 1921), 178; and William Jennings Bryan and Mary Baird Bryan, *The Memoirs of William Jennings Bryan* (New York: Haskell House, 1971), 369–70. These three books give consistent accounts of the Wilson-Bryan meeting, though none supply a date. "Deep regret" is from Bryan and Bryan. As evidence of Bryan's desire to be supportive, he had told his brother to hold back articles on banking reform in *The Commoner,* the family periodical, until Wilson's position became known.

210 "It begins to look as if": Tumulty, *Woodrow Wilson as I Know Him,* 178.

210 "a brick couldn't be thrown": "Wilson Denounces Tariff Lobbyists," *The New York Times,* May 27, 1913.

211 the public was treated to a spectacle: For a general account of the tariff debate, see Cooper, *Woodrow Wilson,* 216–18; Link, *Wilson and the Progressive Era,* 36–42; and Link, *Wilson,* vol 2, *The New Freedom* (Princeton, N.J.: Princeton University Press, 1956), 177–94 (La Follette quote on p. 190).

211 "It is extremely dangerous": Louis Brandeis to Wilson, June 14, 1913, in *The Papers of Woodrow Wilson,* 27:520; see also Alpheus Thomas Mason, *Brandeis: A Free Man's Life* (New York: Viking, 1956), 397–99.

212 "to eliminate all banking representation": Glass's account of this meeting is from Carter Glass to Willis, June 17, 1913, Willis Papers, Box 1, and from Glass, *An Adventure in Constructive Finance,* 112–14.

212 "in the saddle": William G. McAdoo to House, June 18, 1913, House Papers, Box 73.

212 an "injustice" to deny bankers: Owen, *The Federal Reserve Act,* 74; and Willis, *The Federal Reserve System,* 250. See also "Find Many Flaws in Bill: Democrats Divided on Currency Measure," *The New York Times,* June 21, 1913. For Wilson's choosing a fully political board, see Broesamle, *William Gibbs McAdoo*, 110–11. Owen's description of the meeting appears in his *The Federal Reserve Act*, 74–76.

212 **Still unable to sleep, Glass:** Glass to Willis, June 17, 1913; and Glass to Woodrow Wilson, June 18, 1913, Glass Collection, Box 8.

213 **"a yielding of the classical doctrine":** Willis, *The Federal Reserve System*, 256, 258.

213 **"If we can hold to the substance":** Glass, *An Adventure in Constructive Finance*, 123–25.

213 **Bryan didn't realize that the notes:** James Neal Primm, *A Foregone Conclusion* (St. Louis: Federal Reserve Bank of St. Louis, 1989), chapter 2, "Banking Reform, 1907–1913"; available at www.stlouisfed.org/foregone/chapter_two.cfm. For Bryan's reaction to Wilson's compromise solution, see Coletta, *William Jennings Bryan*, 2:132.

214 **"covered all over with the slime":** *New York Sun* quoted in Link, *The New Freedom*, 216. For the *New York Times*'s reaction, see "The President's Views on Banking," *The New York Times*, June 24, 1913, and "A Radical Banking Measure," ibid., June 21, 1913.

214 **"greater in some respects":** "Vast Scope of the New Currency Bill," *Washington Post*, June 22, 1913.

214 **"Those things don't count":** Press conference, June 26, 1913, in *The Papers of Woodrow Wilson*, 28:8.

214 **Wilson, at Glass's urging, invited:** Glass, *An Adventure in Constructive Finance*, 127–28, 130; William McAdoo to Wilson, June 18, 1913, in *The Papers of Woodrow Wilson*, 27:536; and Coletta, *William Jennings Bryan*, 2:133. See also Broesamle, *William Gibbs McAdoo*, 108–10.

215 **"Not an hour can I let":** Wilson's letter to Peck of June 22, 1913, is quoted in both Link, *The New Freedom*, 213–14, and Cooper, *Woodrow Wilson*, 220.

215 **the President returned to the Capitol:** Link, *The New Freedom*, 214; and "Money Reform Now, Is Wilson's Demand," *The New York Times*, June 24, 1913. Wilson's speech appears in *Cong. Rec.* S2132–33 (June 23, 1913).

216 **Bankers had urged reform:** "Forgan Denounces Bill," *The New York Times*, June 24, 1913; and "Bankers Clear Up the Currency Plan," ibid.

216 **the Glass bill authorized Washington:** Willis, *The Federal Reserve System*, 256–67. In deference to the banks, Willis scotched proposals to let individuals either do business with the Reserve Banks or own stock in them.

216 **The goal was to establish collective:** Willis to Carter Glass, May 26, 1913, Willis Papers, Box 1; "Financial Markets," *The New York Times*, June 20, 1913; "Bankers Clear Up the Currency Plan"; Willis, *The Federal Reserve System*, 273–74, 394–95; and James L. Laughlin, *The Federal Reserve Act: Its Origin and Problems* (New York: Macmillan, 1933), 141–42, 146–48 (quote on 148).

217 **Wade spoke forcefully against:** Glass, *An Adventure in Constructive Finance*, 112–16. See also Primm, *A Foregone Conclusion*, chapter 2; and "Money Bill Goes In; No Voice for Banks," *The New York Times*, June 27, 1913.

217 **they won important concessions:** Amended provisions to the bill reprinted in Willis, *The Federal Reserve System*, 1605, 1608, and 1609. See also ibid., 394–95; Laughlin, *The Federal Reserve Act*, 149; "Money Bill Goes In; No Voice for Banks"; and Link, *Wilson: The New Freedom*, 217.

217 **struck a sensible middle ground:** Wiebe, *Businessmen and Reform*, 130. It is my interpretation that the bill was essentially faithful to what Warburg's camp wished. Furthermore, in *The Federal Reserve System* (1:101), Warburg describes the bill, aside from the

"harmful changes" made to accommodate Bryan, as, "in the main, sound and highly commendable." Similarly, Vanderlip's first reaction to the published bill, even more favorable, was that it didn't contain "any serious financial heresies" (Vanderlip to M. J. M. Smith, June 19, 1913, Vanderlip Papers, Box 1-5).

218 **"not less than twelve":** Willis, *The Federal Reserve System*, 1596. The version of the bill submitted June 26 cut reserve requirements to 20, 20, and 15 percent for central reserve, reserve city, and country banks, respectively (ibid., 1609–10), down from the previous standard of 25, 25, and 15 percent. For powers of the reserve board: see ibid., 1603; for its import and export provisions, ibid., 1604.

218 **the mechanics of how the Reserve Banks:** McCulley, *Banks and Politics During the Progressive Era*, 297.

218 **"with a view to accommodating":** Willis, *The Federal Reserve System*, 1605. The "dual mandate" was enacted in the Federal Reserve Reform Act of 1977.

218 **Glass imagined that since the banks:** See Glass, *An Adventure in Constructive Finance*, 118–21. For Chicago's terror, see George Reynolds to Glass, July 7, 1913, Glass Collection, Box 16: "The more I study the matter, the more I am convinced that the drastic and revolutionary requirement that all of the bank reserves of the country should be taken away from existing banks and placed with the Federal Reserve Banks, would have a much more far-reaching, detrimental effect upon business than any of you people have contemplated."

219 **Warburg, summering:** Warburg, *The Federal Reserve System*, 1:101; Paul Warburg to House, July 1913, telegram, House Papers, Box 114a.

219 **Davison begged Aldrich:** Henry Davison to Aldrich, July 3, 18, and 23, 1913, Nelson W. Aldrich Papers, Reel 47.

219 **calling it "Bryanized":** A. Piatt Andrew, "The Bryanized Banking Bill," *Boston Evening Transcript*, June 25, 1913.

219 **The ABA was also critical:** See Festus Wade to Glass, July 1, 1913, Glass Collection, Box 28; and Festus Wade to Glass, July 3, 1913, ibid., Box 37 (both moderate in tone). See also George Reynolds to Glass, July 7, 1913, ibid., Box 16, in which Reynolds, though diffident, professes not to be "hostile" toward the legislation. Wiebe, *Businessmen and Reform*, 131, 215, adds texture on the variation of banker opinions. See also Glass, *An Adventure in Constructive Finance*, 118, 120–21; Gabriel Kolko, *The Triumph of Conservatism: A Reinterpretation of American History, 1900–1914* (New York: The Free Press of Glencoe, 1963), 232–34; and Willis, *The Federal Reserve System*, 395.

219 **Forgan distributed to members:** Willis, *The Federal Reserve System*, 276.

219 **"dead and done for":** "Amend or Abandon," *The New York Times*, June 29, 1913.

219 **Glass, who had mightily extended himself:** Glass to Solomon Wexler, July 3, 1913, Glass Collection, Box 27; in this letter, Glass accused Wexler of reneging on their understanding. See also Glass, *An Adventure in Constructive Finance*, 118, 120–21; Willis, *The Federal Reserve System*, 395 and ("warfare") 396; and Laughlin, *The Federal Reserve Act*, 146.

219 **"history will write down":** Paul Warburg to House, July 22, 1913, House Papers, Box 114a.

220 **$700 million of these bonds:** "The Government and Its Bonds," *The New York Times*, July 14, 1913. The issue was covered extensively in the press. The changes gave holders of the 2 percent bonds the right to refund 5 percent of their bonds each year for new

securities with a higher interest rate, and for retirement at par of any outstanding bonds in twenty years.

220 **However, the bonds continued to plummet:** "Drop in 2s a Bank Plot, Says McAdoo," *The New York Times,* July 29, 1913; see also Broesamle, *William Gibbs McAdoo,* 109–10.

220 **the country's seventy-five hundred national banks:** "160,980,084 Earned by National Banks," *The New York Times,* December 9, 1913; the precise numbers were 7,514 national banks and $11.186 billion in assets.

220 **"There must, in fact, be":** Frank Vanderlip to Glass, July 24, 1913, Glass Collection, Box 16.

221 **"We have a difficult Banking":** Wilson to Ellen Axson Wilson, July 20, 1913, in *The Papers of Woodrow Wilson,* 28:44–45.

221 **made up some 30 percent:** "Growing a Nation: The Story of American Agriculture," available at www.agclassroom.org/gan/timeline/farmers_land.htm.

221 **specifically included bank loans:** See section 13, "Rediscounts," of the bill draft in Willis, *The Federal Reserve System,* 1603–4. On the fears of agrarians, see, for instance, Kolko, *The Triumph of Conservatism,* 234, citing the belief of Representative Joe Eagle (D-Tx.) that the proposed Fed would adopt a "paternalistic relationship" toward its member banks.

221 **The spiritual leader of the agrarians:** On Henry and the radical rebellion, see Glass, *An Adventure in Constructive Finance,* 131–34; Link, *The New Freedom,* 219–21; and Kolko, *The Triumph of Conservatism,* 234.

222 **a series of amendments:** The radical amendments proposed in the House Banking Committee were covered extensively in the press; for example, these articles appeared that week in *The New York Times:* "Put Reserve Notes on a Gold Basis" (July 22, 1913), "Radicals Propose New Currency Bill" (July 23), "Tangle over Money Bill" (July 24), and "Urge Cotton, Wheat and Corn Currency" (July 25).

222 **"quite beyond the pale of discussion":** "Farmers' Money," ibid., July 26, 1913.

CHAPTER THIRTEEN: **"THE IMPOSSIBLE HAS HAPPENED"**

223 **"Fleeing from the evils":** Robert Craig West, *Banking Reform and the Federal Reserve* (Ithaca, N.Y.: Cornell University Press, 1974), 117–18.

223 **"Isn't it wonderful?":** Wilson to Ellen Axson Wilson, September 19, 1913, in Arthur S. Link, ed., *The Papers of Woodrow Wilson* (Princeton, N.J.: Princeton University Press, 1966–1989), 28:301.

223 **"During that epochal summer":** Arthur S. Link, *Woodrow Wilson and the Progressive Era, 1910–1917* (New York: Harper and Row, 1954), 50.

224 **"Those conditions touch us very nearly":** "Wilson Message; Gamboa's Reply," *The New York Times,* August 28, 1913; see also "Wilson Suggests Plan to Mexico," ibid., August 5, 1913; and John Milton Cooper Jr., *Woodrow Wilson* (New York: Knopf, 2009), 239–40.

224 **that he complied is suggestd:** Joseph Patrick Tumulty memorandum to Wilson, July 28, 1913 (with adjoining editor's note), in *The Papers of Woodrow Wilson,* 28:90.

224 **in his public comments:** Wilson press conferences of July 28 and August 14, 1913, in ibid., 89–90, 151.

224 **"Discount what you see":** Wilson to Ellen Axson Wilson, July 27, 1913, in ibid., 84–85.

225 **Glass obtained a gag order:** "Wilson Plan Is Adopted," *The New York Times,* July 29, 1913.

225 **dragged on for most of August:** The Glass-Owen bill was taken up by the Democratic caucus on August 11 and not approved until August 28.

225 Henry charged that the bill: For Representative Henry's references to Jackson, see James Neal Primm, *A Foregone Conclusion* (St. Louis: Federal Reserve Bank of St. Louis, 1989), chapter 2, "Banking Reform, 1907–1913"; available at www.stlouisfed.org/fore gone/chapter_two.cfm. For Henry's reference to Aldrich Plan and his reading of Bryan, see "Money Bill Faces Crisis in Caucus," *The New York Times*, August 18, 1913.

226 "should be fair to the farmer": "Money Bill Faces Crisis in Caucus."

227 which paper should be "acceptable": Even Willis, who had drafted the bill, admitted he had great difficulty framing a definition of acceptable commercial paper: see *Banking and Currency: Hearings Before the Committee on Banking and Currency, on H.R. 7837 (S. 2639)*, U.S. Senate, 63rd Cong., 1st sess., vol. 3, available at https://fraser.stlouisfed .org/publication/?pid=429.

227 Bryan asked Wilson to add: William Jennings Bryan to Wilson, August 6, 1913, in *The Papers of Woodrow Wilson*, 28:121; Paolo E. Coletta, *William Jennings Bryan* (Lincoln: University of Nebraska Press, 1969), 2:134; and Link, *Wilson and the Progressive Era*, 50.

227 "a lot of bunk": "Banks as Public Utilities," *The New York Times*, August 16, 1913.

227 "secured by staple agricultural products": Henry Parker Willis, *The Federal Reserve System: Legislation, Organization, Operation* (New York: Ronald Press, 1923), 1624–25.

227 Owen's apostasy: Owen's defection and return to the fold was registered in a pair of embarrassing *New York Times* headlines, the first of which, "Owen Turns Critic of Currency Bill," appeared on August 20, 1913, followed, the next day, by "Owen Still Loyal to Currency Bill."

228 Glass began to read: Carter Glass, *An Adventure in Constructive Finance* (Garden City, N.Y.: Doubleday, 1927), 131–39, especially 139; William Jennings Bryan to Glass, August 22, 1913, Carter Glass Collection, Box 67; and "Bryan Letter Routs Currency Radicals," *The New York Times*, August 23, 1913.

228 "white with anger": Glass, *An Adventure in Constructive Finance*, 139; and "Bryan Letter Routs Currency Radicals."

228 it overwhelmingly approved: One change was paring reserve requirements for country banks, from 15 percent of deposits to 12: see "Caucus Adopts Currency Bill," *The New York Times*, August 29, 1913. Another alteration was the wording on farm credit.

228 a set of draconian amendments: "Bankers Want Only One Federal Bank," *The New York Times*, August 24, 1913. Forgan's "unworkable"and "incompetent" come from "Bankers Optimistic on Currency Law," ibid., August 23, 1913. Forgan's apology came in his letter to Glass of August 25 (Henry Parker Willis Papers, Box 20), in which he humbly pronounced, "I have to sincerely apologize for the way in which I referred to you in my speech before the Bankers Conference here last Friday." See also, on the bankers conference, Robert H. Wiebe, *Businessmen and Reform* (Chicago: Elephant, 1989), 131–35; and Richard T. McCulley, *Banks and Politics During the Progressive Era: The Origins of the Federal Reserve System, 1897–1913* (New York: Garland, 1992), 298.

229 Its supposedly "unanimous" vote: *Banking and Currency: Hearings*, testimony of H. A. Moehlenpah, vol. 2, 1539–65. Moehlenpah, president of the Wisconsin Bankers Association, testified that when he tried to dissent, Reynolds objected, "We must go to the men at Washington, to the Administration, with a solid front, and if you have any objection . . . make it personally." When Hepburn closed off debate with his gavel, another banker exclaimed, "God, this steam roller is working fine." For the number of bankers present, see Vanderlip to James Stillman, August 29, 1913, Frank A. Vanderlip Papers, Box 1-5.

229 led by George Reynolds: "Bankers Optimistic on Currency Law"; Primm, *A Foregone Conclusion,* chapter 2; and Wiebe, *Businessmen and Reform,* 133–34.

229 country bankers, fearful of their urban: H. A. Moehlenpah testified (*Banking and Currency: Hearings,* 2:1539–65), "If it is a choice between the control of this new system by the Government [or] the bankers, you will get a very large majority of them who will say let the Government keep control of it."

229 "The action of the banks": William McAdoo to House, August 27, 1913, Edward M. House Papers, Box 73.

229 McAdoo was further buoyed: McAdoo to House, August 5, 1913, ibid., referring to the many letters McAdoo has received on the legislation, and concluding, "It has gone well."

229 "distribute the money": D. A. Tompkins, publisher of the *Daily Observer,* quoted in Arthur S. Link, *Wilson,* vol. 2, *The New Freedom* (Princeton, N.J.: Princeton University Press, 1956), 223.

229 U.S. Chamber of Commerce conducted: Harry Wheeler to Carter Glass, August 13, 1913, reprinted in Willis, *The Federal Reserve System,* 417–21. For evidence of support among businesspeople for the bill, see Glass's mail from correspondents in varied commercial fields in various boxes of the Glass Collection, in particular Box 19; Link, *The New Freedom,* 223; and Wiebe, *Businessmen and Reform,* 133–34.

229 his own contacts with bankers: See, for instance, "Coast Bankers See McAdoo," *The New York Times,* August 15, 1913. For McAdoo's rejection of the Chicago demands, see "Wilson Stands Firm on Currency Bill," ibid., August 26, 1913, in which McAdoo said "constructive criticism" would be "carefully considered"—a polite way of saying he did not regard this manifesto as constructive. For "fiasco," see H. Parker Willis to Glass, August 25, 1913, Glass Collection, Box 19. See also Link, *The New Freedom,* 227.

229 Glass downplayed: Lester V. Chandler, *Benjamin Strong, Central Banker* (Washington, D.C.: Brookings Institution, 1958), 11.

230 "altruistic institution": Richard H. Timberlake Jr., *The Origins of Central Banking in the United States* (Cambridge, Mass.: Harvard University Press, 1978), 192.

230 "Not only is its power": West, *Banking Reform and the Federal Reserve,* 118.

230 Charles Lindbergh, another Republican opponent: Willis, *The Federal Reserve System,* 364–72.

230 the debate in the House: Ibid., 125. For the gold standard debate, see Glass, *An Adventure in Constructive Finance,* 153; Coletta, *William Jennings Bryan,* 2:135; and Link, *The New Freedom,* 227. See also "Money Bill Passes House, 285 to 85," *The New York Times,* September 19, 1913.

231 "the unswerving determination of the President": Willis, *The Federal Reserve System,* 438.

231 "by so splendid a majority": Wilson to Ellen Axson Wilson, September 19, 1913, in *The Papers of Woodrow Wilson,* 28:301.

231 the Senate was problematic: For the political orientation of the Senate, and of its Banking Committee, see West, *Banking Reform and the Federal Reserve,* 130–31; "Bankers Find Clash over Currency Bill," *The New York Times,* September 3, 1913; and Link, *The New Freedom,* 228.

231 Forgan was the lead witness: Forgan appeared before the committee on September 2, followed the next day by Wade; their testimony appears in *Banking and Currency: Hearings,* 1:25, 126. The prolongation of the hearings and its effect on delaying the bill were widely reported: see, for instance, all in *The New York Times,* "Moves Delay in Senate" (September 5, 1913), "Wilson Aims to Win Senate Support" (September 20), "May Reduce Reserve Banks" (September 26), and "Test for Currency Bill" (September 28). See also Cooper, *Woodrow Wilson*, 223.

232 **"You have the power to control it":** Thomas McRae's September 29 testimony and his cross-examination by Hitchcock appear in *Banking and Currency: Hearings*, 2:1275–88.

232 **But country bankers, with their deeply held suspicions:** See for instance the August 2, 1913, letter from W. S. Fant, president of the First National Bank of Weatherford, Texas, to Glass, arguing that as "money [interest rates] is always high," bankers had better outlets for their capital (Glass Collection, Box 19). For check clearing, see "Bankers Want Only One Federal Bank," *The New York Times*, August 24, 1913.

232 **Wall Street's view of the bill:** Warburg later commented, in *The Federal Reserve System: Its Origin and Growth—Reflections and Recollections* (New York: Macmillan, 1930), 1:105, "The bill, at every stage of its development, represented a great triumph of the fundamental principles for which banking reformers had striven, namely, concentration and mobilization of reserves combined with an elastic note issue."

232 **tended to be less oppositional:** Primm, *A Foregone Conclusion.*, chapter 2.

233 **"in our country, with every":** "Money Bill as Bad, Good, Partly Good," *The New York Times*, September 28, 1913, quoting Warburg's article in the October 1913 issue of *North American Review*. See also Gabriel Kolko, *The Triumph of Conservatism: A Reinterpretation of American History, 1900–1914* (New York: The Free Press of Glencoe, 1963), especially 235–36; Kolko's thesis is that banker "opposition" was essentially a ruse.

233 **Vanderlip's was maddeningly inconsistent:** Frank Vanderlip to Glass, July 24, 1913, Glass Collection, Box 16; Vanderlip to James Stillman, September 27, 1913, Vanderlip Papers, Box 1-5. Also, Vanderlip took a middle ground in an August 29 letter to Stillman (ibid.).

233 **With bankers' opinions scattered:** Primm, *A Foregone Conclusion*, chapter 2.

233 **"Don't be anxious":** Wilson to Ellen Axson Wilson, July 27, 1913, in *The Papers of Woodrow Wilson*, 28:84–85. For Ellen's disregarding her husband, see for instance her letter of September 4 (ibid., 257), in which she asks him, "Is there fresh trouble about the currency bill—as the papers report?" Two days later (ibid., 260), she frets, "I am so concerned at the reports about the currency bill. They say you are fighting desperately with your back to the wall." Wilson tries to soothe her nerves, replying on September 9 (ibid., 267), "I am perfectly well. . . . The Senate is tired, some of the members of its committee are irritable and will have to be indulged." For Wilson's September 28 letter to Peck, see ibid., 336–37; he also confesses to his old friend that he was fearful he might "lose his patience and suffer the weakness of exasperation." An editor's note in ibid. (257) emphasizes that by early September, Republican and some Democratic senators were making clear that they intended to hold "lengthy hearings" on the currency bill.

233 **The President leaned:** Cooper, *Woodrow Wilson*, 217–18; for the Revenue Act of 1913, see Link, *The New Freedom*, 194 (Link also quotes David Houston's letter to W. H. Page of September 12, 1913). The detail of signing the law with two gold pens comes from "Wilson Signs New Tariff Law," *The New York Times*, October 4, 1913.

234 **"extremely annoying":** Vanderlip to James Stillman, September 12, 1913, Vanderlip Papers, Box 1-5.

234 **"So I feel tonight":** "Wilson Signs New Tariff Law."

234 **Wilson tabled plans:** "Foes of Money Bill Get Together," *The New York Times*, October 1, 1913. For Wilson's timetable, see "Money Bill Fight May Take a Month," ibid., October 14, 1913. At his October 6 press conference (in *The Papers of Woodrow Wilson*,

28:364–65), Wilson publicly expressed confidence that the bill would pass in the special session.

234 Wilson was adamant: "Altered Money Bill May Satisfy Wilson," *The New York Times,* October 17, 1913.

235 When the ABA held its annual convention: For the ABA trashing of the bill as well as Wilson's reaction, see press conference of October 9, 1913, as well as private correspondence to Ralph Pulitzer on October 9 and to Senator John Sharp Williams on October 11, all in *The Papers of Woodrow Wilson,* 28:378–89; "2,000 Bankers Hit Money Bill Hard," *The New York Times,* October 9, 1913; Willis, *The Federal Reserve System,* 403; Link, *The New Freedom,* 229; Link, *Wilson and the Progressive Era,* 51; Glass, *An Adventure in Constructive Finance,* 193; and Richard J. Ellis, ed., *Speaking to the People; The Rhetorical Presidency in Historical Perspective* (Amherst: University of Massachusetts Press, 1998), 170. See also *Proceedings* of the 39th Annual Convention of the Americans Bankers Association, available at http://babel.hathitrust.org/cgi/pt?id=njp.32101066788 769;view=1up;seq=11.

235 Aldrich emerged from the obscurity: Aldrich's address was delivered on October 15 at the annual dinner of the Academy of Political Science: see Michael Clark Rockefeller, "Nelson W. Aldrich and Banking Reform: A Conservative Leader in the Progressive Era," A.B. thesis, Harvard College, 1960, 89; Primm, *A Foregone Conclusion;* and "Aldrich Sees Bryan Back of Money Bill," *The New York Times,* October 16, 1913. Interestingly, Andrew said the Aldrich speech was "too denunciating"—one of the few times he ever criticized his former boss: A. Piatt Andrew, *Diary of Abram Piatt Andrew, 1902–1914,* ed. E. Parker Hayden Jr. and Andrew L. Gray (Princeton, N.J., 1986), entry of October 15, 1913. For Wilson's mail on the bill, see "Money Bill Delay Stirs Up President," *The New York Times,* October 7, 1913. For the endorsements from the Merchants' Association of New York and the U.S. Chamber of Commerce, see Link, *The New Freedom,* 235.

235 more than 25,000 banks: "Banking and Monetary Statistics, 1914–1941," Federal Reserve Bank of St. Louis, 16; available at http://fraser.stlouisfed.org/docs/publications/ bms/1914-1941/BMS14-41_complete.pdf.

235 Wilson next threatened: For Wilson's threats to take his fight either to the people or to a Democratic caucus, see these four articles in *The New York Times,* all from the fall of 1913: "Wilson May Stump for Currency Bill" (October 3), "Money Bill Delay Stirs Up President" (October 7), "To Urge Money Bill as a Party Measure" (October 8), and "Bankers Views in Senate" (October 10). See also Link, *Wilson and the Progressive Era,* 51; Link, *The New Freedom,* 230; Primm, *A Foregone Conclusion,* chapter 2; and, most especially, Ellis, *Speaking to the People,* 170, which includes Wilson's comment to the *Washington Post.*

236 they anchored on the Potomac: Broesamle, *William Gibbs McAdoo,* 113.

236 unveiled a softer approach: "Altered Money Bill May Satisfy Wilson," *The New York Times,* October 17, 1913; Cooper, *Woodrow Wilson,* 223; and Link, *The New Freedom,* 231.

236 Each of the three holdouts: For background on the three renegade senators, see Cooper, *Woodrow Wilson,* 223, 225, and 623; Primm, *A Foregone Conclusion;* and Link, *The New Freedom,* 228. On Hitchcock, in particular, see Thomas W. Ryley, *Gilbert Hitchcock of Nebraska: Wilson's Floor Leader in the Fight for the Versailles Treaty* (Lewiston, N.Y.: Edwin Mellen Press, 1998), especially 58–62. For "O'Gorman's resistance," see Kenneth E. Miller, *From Progressive to New Dealer: Frederic C. Howe and American Liberalism* (University Park: Pennsylvania State University Press, 2010), 205–6. The *New York Times* coverage of O'Gorman's efforts to secure patronage in the spring of 1913 documents that Wilson ignored O'Gorman on his first significant local appointment, for U.S. Attorney in the Southern District of New York, and was set to ignore him again, for collector of customs—but then reversed course and appointed O'Gorman's man: see "Marshall Named for Wise's Place," *The New York Times,* April 16, 1913; "Test for O'Gorman on Collectorship," ibid., April 18, 1913; "Polk Out of Race; O'Gorman's Victory," ibid., April 30, 1913; and "Mitchel Nominated for Port Collector," ibid., May 8, 1913. On Reed, see Daniel McCarthy, "Show Me a Statesman," *The University Bookman* 46, no. 3 (Fall 2008), a review of Lee Meriwether's *Jim Reed, Senatorial Immortal*) that is available at www.kirkcenter.org/index.php/bookman/article/show-me-a-statesman/.

236 **"The stature of such a man":** H. L. Mencken, "James A. Reed of Missouri," *American Mercury,* April 1929; available at http://truthbasedlogic.com/ownman.htm.

236 **After the three renegades:** *The Papers of Woodrow Wilson,* 28:369–70; and "Altered Money Bill May Satisfy Wilson," *The New York Times,* October 17, 1913.

236 **more encouraging remarks:** Wilson to James O'Gorman, October 21, 1913, in *The Papers of Woodrow Wilson,* 28:421; and Wilson to James Reed, October 23, 1913, in ibid., 425.

236–37 **he might be willing to compromise:** "Wilson Won't Fight Money Bill Changes," *The New York Times,* October 21 1913. According to Link, *Wilson: The New Freedom,* 231, the President seemed on the verge of coming to terms with O'Gorman and Reed.

237 **The genesis of Vanderlip's proposal:** See Vanderlip testimony in *Banking and Currency: Hearings,* 3:1933–2037 and 2052–69, October 8, 1913. In a September 24, 1913, letter to James Stillman (Vanderlip Papers, Box b1-5), Vanderlip noted that he first met with O'Gorman and Reed in White Sulfur, West Virginia, in mid-September; the two senators expressed their opposition to the bill and encouraged him to appear before the committee. See also Vanderlip to James Stillman, October 10, 1913, ibid.

237 **Privately, he expressed himself:** Vanderlip to Stillman, October 10, 1913.

237 **"are the great debtors of the country":** *Banking and Currency: Hearings,* 3:2056, October 8, 1913.

238 **a unitary central bank:** Vanderlip to Stillman, October 10, 1913; and Vanderlip to James Stillman, October 27, 1913, Vanderlip Papers, Box 1-5.

238 **"If the legislation is perfected":** Vanderlip to Stillman, October 10, 1913.

238 **"They came to my rooms":** Vanderlip to Stillman, October 27, 1913.

239 **Vanderlip's optimism was misplaced:** Predictably, Glass did cite the Baltimore platform as incompatible with the Vanderlip plan: see "Wilson Upholds Glass Money Bill," *The New York Times,* October 25, 1913.

239 **He suggested that Vanderlip:** Vanderlip to Stillman, October 27, 1913.

239 **He now proposed a central bank:** For accounts of Vanderlip's second appearance before the committee and its reaction, see *Banking and Currency: Hearings,* 3:2911–67, October 23, 1913; and "Currency Outlook Suddenly Changed," *The New York Times,* October 24, 1913.

240 **"quite along the lines":** Frank Vanderlip to Wilson, October 23, 1913, in *The Papers of Woodrow Wilson,* 28:428.

240 **"I am at a loss":** Wilson to Frank Vanderlip, October 24, 1913, in ibid., 430.

240 **His message was succinct:** Link, *Wilson: The New Freedom,* 233–34; and Cooper, *Woodrow Wilson,* 224.

240 **see if anything stuck:** "Strong Support for Central Bank," *The New York Times,* October 29, 1913.

241 **Wilson coordinated with Senate leaders:** Link, *Wilson and the Progressive Era,* 49. The

debate in the committee regarding the number of reserve banks was covered extensively in *The New York Times:* see, for instance, "Split on Regional Banks" (October 31, 1913) and "Cut Regional Banks to Four at Start" (November 1, 1913).

241 swung toward the Vanderlip notion: "Would Curb Banks in Regional System," *The New York Times,* November 2, 1913.

241 Wilson agreed to drop: "Split on Regional Banks"; "Wilson Is Blamed for Currency Halt," *The New York Times,* November 11, 1913.

241 he viewed dissension: Ryley, *Gilbert Hitchcock of Nebraska,* 59, 63.

241 Outside the halls of Congress: Link, *Wilson: The New Freedom,* 235; and Primm, *A Foregone Conclusion,* chapter 2.

241 he wrote reassuringly: Festus J. Wade to Wilson, October 25, 1913, in *The Papers of Woodrow Wilson,* 28:444.

241 "gay with fashion and beauty": Glass, *An Adventure in Constructive Finance,* 168–74; and Primm, *A Foregone Conclusion,* chapter 2. Owen also participated in the debate, which was sponsored by the Economic Club of New York: see "Wall Street Defended to Owen and Glass," *The New York Times,* November 11, 1913.

242 Wilson and Glass got a further boost: "Fusion Mayoral Candidate Thrashes Tammany," *The New York Times,* November 5, 1913; and "Wilson Is Cheered by Party Triumphs," ibid., November 6, 1913. For O'Gorman's and Reed's shifts, see "Yield to Wilson on Regional Banks," ibid., November 8, 1913. Link's suggestion is in *Wilson and the Progressive Era,* 51. Although Reed's and O'Gorman's resistance had seemed to weaken even before the election (see "Strong Support for Central Bank"), their support for Glass-Owen didn't gel until November. See also Ryley, *Gilbert Hitchcock of Nebraska,* 64. For a longer and satirical account of the effect of the election on the holdouts, especially O'Gorman, see "Revolt Against President Wilson Ends in a Fiasco," *The New York Times,* November 16, 1913.

242 The senator bridled: Ryley, *Gilbert Hitchcock of Nebraska,* 59; and "Wilson Is Blamed for Currency Halt."

242 six votes to six: Vanderlip to James Stillman, November 15, 1913, Vanderlip Papers, Box b1-5; and "Brighter Outlook for Currency Bill," *The New York Times,* November 14, 1913.

242 Vanderlip went on a speaking tour: Vanderlip to Stillman, November 1, 1913, Vanderlip Papers, Box 1-5; and Vanderlip to Stillman, November 15, 1913.

242 only $1 billion: "160,980,084 Earned by National Banks," *The New York Times,* December 9, 1913. More precisely, the figure was $1.068 billion.

243 "a set of men": Warburg to Robert Owen, November 10, 1913, Paul Moritz Warburg Papers, Folder 12.

243 He and Owen fortuitously: Warburg, *The Federal Reserve System,* 1:120–21; the train ride occurred on November 10, 1913.

243 a flood of correspondence: The Warburg Papers are rife with correspondence (in English, German, and French) from October to December with bankers from Great Britain and numerous countries on the Continent. Many sources attest to Warburg's lobbying: for instance, see Paul Warburg to House, November 14, 1913, and November 28, 1913, House Papers, Box 114a; Warburg to Robert Owen, October 30, 1913, Warburg Papers, Folder 7; Warburg to Owen, November 10 (including a schematic diagram by Warburg illustrating a preferred arrangement of reserve banks); most especially, Warburg to Robert Owen, November 24, 1913 (seeking final copies of the two bills referred by the committee to the Senate), Warburg Papers, Folder 106; Warburg to William McAdoo,

November 6, 1913, cited in Warburg, *The Federal Reserve System*, 1:114; and Warburg to William McAdoo, November 20, 1913, cited in ibid., 124. Warburg and Jacob Schiff also paid a visit to Colonel House on November 17—see Charles Seymour, *The Intimate Papers of Colonel House, Arranged as a Narrative by Charles Seymour* (Boston: Houghton Mifflin, 1928), 165.

243 **cut the number of Reserve Banks:** Willis, *The Federal Reserve System*, 471; and "Senate to Tackle Three Money Bills," *The New York Times*, November 21, 1913. The headline's reference to "three" bills was misleading if technically accurate: the count included the Glass-Owen bill as passed by the House, which had no support in the Senate and was referred as a formality; only the version of Glass-Owen as modified in the Senate committee and the Hitchcock bill were referred with any hope of consideration.

243 **changes in the discounting section:** Warburg, *The Federal Reserve System*, 1:113–14.

243 **a separate bill:** Vanderlip to J. P. Morgan Jr., November 18, 1913, Vanderlip Papers, Box 1-5. See also "Senate to Tackle Three Money Bills."

243 **Although unwilling to vote for Owen's bill:** Ryley, *Gilbert Hitchcock of Nebraska*, 64; see also "Brighter Outlook for Currency Bill," *The New York Times*, November 14, 1913. On the legislative maneuver see Link, *The New Freedom*, 233–34; Willis, *The Federal Reserve System*, 468; and James L. Laughlin, *The Federal Reserve Act: Its Origin and Problems* (New York: Macmillan, 1933), 167–68.

243 **Then, Wilson ordered:** Laughlin, *The Federal Reserve Act*, 167–68; and "Party Conference to Push Money Bill," *The New York Times*, November 26, 1913.

243 **While Hitchcock insisted:** "Caucus Vote to Be Binding," *The New York Times*, November 29, 1913; and Coletta, *William Jennings Bryan*, 2:137.

244 **in his annual message:** "Wilson Triumphs with Message," *The New York Times*, December 3, 1913; see also "An Annual Message to Congress," December 2, 1913, in *The Papers of Woodrow Wilson*, 29:5.

244 **Adding to the pressure:** Press conference of December 1, 1913, in *The Papers of Woodrow Wilson*, 28:600; "To Push Money Bill at Night Sessions," *The New York Times*, November 27, 1913; and "Adopt Long Hours to Pass Money Bill," *The New York Times*, December 7, 1913.

244 **"I have never seen so much power":** Vanderlip to. J. P. Morgan Jr., November 18, 1913.

244 **Owen held a slim lead:** "Money Bill Faces Close Senate Vote," *The New York Times*, November 24, 1913.

244 **But the Senate became embroiled:** Timberlake, *The Origins of Central Banking in the United States*, 201–2, notes that the inflation debate surfaced only in December. For contemporaneous discussion on whether reserves should be legal tender, see, for example, the *New York Times*'s outraged editorial of November 16, 1913, "Bryanizing the Money Bill," as well as Vanderlip's second appearance before the Senate, *Banking and Currency: Hearings*, vol. 3. See also Willis, *The Federal Reserve System*, 456–57, 467–68.

244–45 **the Senate cut reserve requirements:** Glass, *An Adventure in Constructive Finance*, 210.

245 **"at home or abroad":** Willis, *The Federal Reserve System*, 1654; the House language (ibid., 1626) was less explicit. However, the House version also permitted national banks to open overseas branches.

245 **coax the various parts:** The two versions can be compared in ibid: Senate, 1651; House, 1623. See also West, *Banking Reform and the Federal Reserve*, 212.

245 **farm state senators:** The Senate bill permitted farm mortgages for five years. The House bill also permitted such mortgages, but only for durations of one year. See Willis, *The Federal Reserve System*, 1633–34, 1664.

246 **"little by little":** "Root Sees Peril in Money Bill," *The New York Times,* December 14, 1913.

246 **Prices had consistently fallen:** Although calculations of inflation before 1913 are necessarily estimates, various indices of wholesale prices did exist. *Historical Statistics of the United States, 1789–1945,* prepared by the Census Bureau (Washington, D.C.: Government Printing Office, 1949), 231–32, shows a general wholesale index falling from 127 in 1865, the year the Civil War ended, to 100 in 1873. It hit bottom at 71 in 1896, and recovered to 100 in 1912, where it remained in 1913. The index was a composite of various subindices, including ones for commodities, farm products, hides, and leather. A contemporaneous source, Charles A. Conant, a banking specialist who testified before the Interstate Commerce Commission in 1913, noted that wholesale prices had plunged from 1880 to 1896, and subsequently regained much, though not all, the lost ground: "Why Prices Are Up," *The New York Times,* December 14, 1913. Conant testified that a wholesale index fell to 90.4 in 1896, "more than 40 per cent below the prices of 1880," implying that the index was above 150 in 1880. In 1912, Conant's index stood at 133.6, still below the figure implied for 1880. Moreover, the decline in prices began well before 1880. A later pair of experts, Milton Friedman and Anna Jacobson Schwartz, in *A Monetary History of the United States, 1867–1960* (Princeton, N.J.: Princeton University Press, 1971), 32–33, estimate that from 1867 to 1879 prices fell at an annual rate of 3.5 percent (some indices give even faster rates of decline). Regardless, the post–Civil War trend was clearly, and consistently, down. Even in the later expansionary phase, inflation was relatively restrained. From the trough of the recession in 1896, prices rose at a rate of just under 3 percent through 1900, hardly surprising given the severity of the contraction. Thereafter—that is, from 1900 to 1912— inflation was measured at precisely 2 percent per annum.

246 **he had caught a cold:** See the following entries in volume 29 of *The Papers of Woodrow Wilson:* Wilson to Mary Allen Hulbert Peck, December 8, 1913 (p. 23); diary entries of House, December 12 (pp. 32–33), December 14 (p. 34), and December 16 (p. 36). See also William McAdoo to House, December 7, 1913, House Papers, Box 73.

247 **Luckily for Wilson, public support:** George Reynolds to Glass, December 18, 1913, telegram, Glass Collection, Box 42; Willis, *The Federal Reserve System,* 507–8; Link, *The New Freedom,* 235; and Kolko, *The Triumph of Conservatism,* 241.

247 **Warburg peppered Senator Owen:** Warburg to Robert Owen, December 4, 1913, Warburg Papers, Folder 11; and Warburg to Robert Owen, December 15, 1913, ibid., Folder 12. See also Warburg, *The Federal Reserve System,* 1:121.

247 **He also corresponded with business executives:** H. A. Wheeler to Warburg, December 13, 1913, Warburg Papers, Folder 12; Solomon Wexler to Warburg, December 15, 1913, telegram, ibid.; Warburg to H. E. Hammond, December 17, 1913, ibid.; and Charles D. Norton to Warburg, December 17, 1913, ibid. See also various Warburg correspondence in the Warburg Papers with officials of Merchants' Association of New York and the New York Chamber of Commerce.

247 **"throwing up [his] hands":** Festus J. Wade to Warburg, December 10, 1913, ibid., Folder 11; and Festus J. Wade to Warburg, December 15, 1913, ibid, Folder 12. On Warburg's latest plan, see Warburg, *The Federal Reserve System,* 1:122–24, as well as numerous items of correspondence toward the end of 1913 in the Warburg Papers.

247 **relations between the two framers:** Warburg, *The Federal Reserve System,* 1:115; and Glass to Paul Warburg, November 22, 1913, Glass Collection, Box 8.

247 **Warburg kept Glass closely informed:** Glass, *An Adventure in Constructive Finance,* 209. See also Warburg, *The Federal Reserve System,* 1:115–17, reproducing two letters attesting to their frequent contact. On December 15, 1913, Warburg wrote to Glass on a favorite technical subject, rediscounting. Three days later he anxiously followed up, "I have not heard from you concerning the rediscount clause."

247 the Virginian stunned Warburg: Warburg, *The Federal Reserve System*, 1:125. See also Glass to Paul Warburg, December 24, 1913, Glass Collection, Box 8, in which Glass repeated the suggestion that Warburg consider a Federal Reserve Board post.

247 On December 17, after eighty: Willis, *The Federal Reserve System*, 503; and "Democrats Heed Root's Warning," *The New York Times*, December 18, 1913.

247 he went for a ride: "President Takes a Drive," *The New York Times*, December 18, 1913; and Laughlin, *The Federal Reserve Act*, 169. For the votes on December 19, see "Currency Bill Passes Senate," *The New York Times*, December 20, 1913; one Progressive also voted in favor.

248 Warburg rifled off a: Warburg to Robert Owen, December 19, 1913, Warburg Papers, Folder 12.

248 "It is a terribly tiring business": Warburg to Arthur Spitzer, December 19, 1913, ibid., Folder 11. See also Warburg's letter of December 19 to Harry A. Wheeler, president of the U.S. Chamber of Commerce, in ibid., Folder 12; and Warburg, *The Federal Reserve System*, 1:121.

248 "no prospect at all": Timberlake, *The Origins of Central Banking in the United States*, 202.

248 The conferees worked with surprising speed: The House-Senate conference dealt with dozens of individual items. The conference changes are detailed in Willis, *The Federal Reserve System*, 511–19; and Glass, *An Adventure in Constructive Finance*, 212–19; in addition, high (and low) points are treated in Warburg, *The Federal Reserve System*, 1:126–29. See also Glass's speech to the House of Representatives, December 22, 1913, in Glass Collection, Box 22, as well as "Money Bill May Be Law To-day," *The New York Times*, December 22, 1913, and "Money Bill Goes to Wilson To-day," "Currency Bill Conference Report," and "Changes Made in the Bill," all from ibid., December 23. For a more detailed comparison, in his *The Federal Reserve System*, Willis reprinted the House bill (p. 1614), as well as the Senate bill (p. 1637), and those versions may be contrasted with the final Federal Reserve Act (p. 1667).

249 "legal tender": Willis, *The Federal Reserve System*, 456–57, 467–68; for $1 and $2 bills, see "Changes Made in the Bill"; for distinctive engravings, see "Currency Bill Conference Report."

249 The conferees tackled the truly sticky points: "Money Bill May Be Law To-day"; and "Money Bill Goes to Wilson To-day." For Warburg's bitter disappointment, see Warburg, *The Federal Reserve System*, 1:121–23, 128–29.

249 Only the makeup of the board remained: "Money Bill May Be Law To-day"; and "Money Bill Goes to Wilson To-day." For analysis of this issue, see West, *Banking Reform and the Federal Reserve*, 132–33.

250 bolstering the authority: Warburg, *The Federal Reserve System*, 1:128; Seymour, *The Intimate Papers of Colonel House*, 139; Broesamle, *William Gibbs McAdoo*, 115; and Willis, *The Federal Reserve System*, 518. For amplifying the power of the board, see Willis, *The Federal Reserve System*, 518. Glass, *An Adventure in Constructive Finance*, 215, is the source for 4:10 a.m. Terms of board members in the House bill were to have been eight years; in the Senate bill, six years.

250 who had barely slept, in pajamas: Seymour, *The Intimate Papers of Colonel House*, 139. For House's evening at the White House, see House diary, December 22, 1913, in *The Papers of Woodrow Wilson*, 29:55.

251 **Glass presented the conference report:** Glass's December 22, 1913, speech is in Glass Collection, Box 22; see also Willis, *The Federal Reserve System*, 511; and "Money Bill Goes to Wilson To-day." The House vote was 298–60.

251 **"I'll do the deed first":** "Wilson Signs the Currency Bill; Promises Friendly Aid to Business," *The New York Times*, December 24, 1913. Wilson asking Glass and Owen to come closer is from Glass, *An Adventure in Constructive Finance*, 227. For the President's departure, see these *New York Times* articles: "Wilson's Vacation Plans" (December 21, 1913), "President Off for a Rest" (December 24), and "President Wilson Spends Happy Day" (December 26).

252 **"The impossible has happened":** Warburg, *The Federal Reserve System*, 1:129.

252 **"dominated by Democrats":** Ibid.

252 **Representative Lindbergh said acidly:** Link, *The New Freedom*, 239.

252 **"a great advance":** The *New York Tribune*'s opinion was quoted in "Result Will Be Good, Is Opinion of Press," a compendium of editorial reactions from other newspapers, *The New York Times*, December 24, 1913; the *Times*'s own editorial, "An Important Omission," appeared on December 25. For other editorial commentary, in the main positive, see the December 22 issues of *Philadelphia Bulletin*, *Cincinnati Enquirer*, *Chicago Post*, and *New York Mail* (all of which were excerpted in the *Times* compendium), as well as the *Boston Daily Globe* (December 22), the *Washington Post* (December 24), and the *Lawrence* (Mass.) *Journal-World* (December 24).

253 **"than business dared to hope":** "Review and Outlook," *The Wall Street Journal:* December 29, 1913, which also mentioned that the banks were pleased. See also "Owen Bill Is Liked," *The New York Times*, December 21, 1913.

253 **Although Vanderlip sourly hinted:** Vanderlip to James Stillman, December 29, 1913, Vanderlip Papers, Box 1-5; this letter includes "I feel firmly that I would rather take my chances under the legislature of the State of New York . . . than under the federal government so far as banking charter rights are concerned." For the applications for membership, see "Banks Eager to Enter," *The New York Times*, December 23, 1913, as well as an untitled item in ibid., December 24, 1913.

253 **"While my heart bleeds":** Paul Warburg to Glass, December 23, 1913, Glass Collection, Box 7.

253 **"It is you that just now":** House to Paul Warburg, January 1, 1914, House Papers, Box 114a.

CHAPTER FOURTEEN: EPILOGUE

255 **"The measure itself was the result":** Houston's diary entry of December 23, 1913, cited in Warburg, *The Federal Reserve System:Its Origin and Growth—Reflections and Recollections* (New York: Macmillan, 1930), 1:129.

255 **"Mr. Wilson experienced":** Carter Glass, *An Adventure in Constructive Finance* (Garden City, N.Y.: Doubleday, 1927), 36.

255 **"[Carter Glass] is not the chief author":** Samuel Untermyer, *Who Is Entitled to the Credit for the Federal Reserve Act?* (New York, 1927), foreword.

255 **"Mr. Glass himself":** James L. Laughlin, *The Federal Reserve Act: Its Origin and Problems* (New York: Macmillan, 1933), 136–37.

255 **"A profanation of history":** Glass, *An Adventure in Constructive Finance*, 20, commenting on Charles Seymour's *The Intimate Papers of Colonel House*.

256 **"It was not an 'original proposal'"**: Henry Parker Willis, *The Federal Reserve System: Legislation, Organization and Operation* (New York: Ronald Press, 1923), 523.

256 **"Glass and Willis have so"**: Paul Warburg to Laughlin, June 27, 1929, James Laurence Laughlin Papers, Paul M. Warburg folder.

256 **"Mr. Warburg has never made"**: Willis, *The Federal Reserve System*, 530.

256 **"Congress should realize"**: Warburg to Laughlin, June 27, 1929.

256 **"It had little or no relationship"**: Willis, *The Federal Reserve System*, 523.

256 **"I feel for it"**: Warburg quoted in "Our First Line of Financial Defense," *The New York Times*, August 18, 1918.

257 **"The law is full of indirect"**: Vanderlip to James Stillman, December 29, 1913, Frank A. Vanderlip Papers, Box 1-5.

259 **It took some time, in 1914**: Roger T. Johnson, *Historical Beginnings . . . The Federal Reserve* (Federal Reserve Bank of Boston, 2010), chapter 3, "Making the System Work," available at https://www.bostonfed.org/about/pubs/begin.pdf; and Sarah Binder and Mark Spindel, "Monetary Politics: Origins of the Federal Reserve," *Studies in American Political Development* 27, no. 1 (April 2013), 1–13.

260 **the guns of August**: William L. Silber, *When Washington Shut Down Wall Street: The Great Financial Crisis of 1914 and the Origins of America's Monetary Supremacy* (Princeton, N.J.: Princeton University Press, 2007); see especially chapter 4. The emergency currency was issued under the 1908 Aldrich-Vreeland Act—which had been set to expire in 1914 but, providentially, had been extended for a year by the Federal Reserve Act.

261 **Even as the Fed got going**: Robert Craig West, *Banking Reform and the Federal Reserve* (Ithaca, N.Y.: Cornell University Press, 1974), 208–9, 215; Ron Chernow, *The Warburgs: The Twentieth-Century Odyssey of a Remarkable Jewish Family* (New York: Random House, 1993), 187; John J. Broesamle, *William Gibbs McAdoo: A Passion for Change, 1863–1917* (Port Washington, N.Y.: Kennikat Press, 1973), 115–16; and Silber, *When Washington Shut Down Wall Street*.

261 **Glass warily monitored**: Willis to Carter Glass, August 18, 1914, Henry Parker Willis Papers, Box 1; Warburg, *The Federal Reserve System*, 1:493, 495–96.

261 **repeated battles for control**: West, *Banking Reform and the Federal Reserve*, 219, 222.

261 **their assets became concentrated**: See ibid., 186–87, 190, 215, and 218; and Broesamle, *William Gibbs McAdoo*, 115–16.

262 **the agency would play a passive role**: Lester V. Chandler, *Benjamin Strong, Central Banker* (Washington, D.C.: Brookings Institution, 1958), 14, notes that the language of the bill suggested a passive approach. West makes a similar point in *Banking Reform and the Federal Reserve*, 202, 205, and 192.

262 **"After the institution has been going"**: For Sprague's testimony, see *Banking and Currency: Hearings Before the Committee on Banking and Currency, on H.R. 7837 (S. 2639),* U.S. Senate, 63rd Cong., 1st sess., 1:362, Septermber 6, 1913, available at https://fraser.stlouisfed.org/publication/?pid=429.

262 **"is not to await emergencies"**: West, *Banking Reform and the Federal Reserve*, 182.

262 **catapulted America's standing**: Ibid., 178.

262 **Warburg's insistent demands**: Warburg, *The Federal Reserve System*, 1:137–77 (chapter 7). Warburg began his campaign for remedial legislation as soon as the ink on the original Act was dry. In January 1914, he made (in elegant cursive) a list of items entitled "Points where changes may be made" (Warburg Papers, Folder 107). Also found in his

files (Folder 104), apparently from a year or two later, is a typed list entitled "Amendments to Federal Reserve Act which are to be pushed." See also his eleven-page letter to Glass recommending amendments in 1916, reproduced in Warburg, *The Federal Reserve System*, 1:707. For the Fed soaking up much of the bullion, see West, *Banking Reform and the Federal Reserve*, 176–77; Robert L. Owen, *The Federal Reserve Act* (New York: Century, 1919), 95–97; and Warburg, 1:149–57. In particular, Warburg states, "The importance of this new legislation can scarcely be overstated, for it was the amendment relating to reserves which enabled the Reserve System to corral and mobilize the country's gold and thereby to finance, as well as it did, the unparalleled demands of the war" (p. 157). For an excellent summary of the 1917 amendments and its effects, including a chart documenting the increased note circulation, see Raymond P. H. Fishe, "The Federal Reserve Amendments of 1917: The Beginning of a Seasonal Note Issue Policy," *Journal of Money, Credit, and Banking* 23, no. 3 (August 1991), part I.

263 **to spare Wilson the embarrassment:** Chernow, *The Warburgs*, 187–89, captures the painful saga of Warburg's departure, including Owen's opposition to his renomination. For his support from bankers, see "Want Warburg to Stay," *The New York Times*, July 23, 1918. Although Owen and Warburg collaborated on the legislation, Owen never seems to have overcome his suspicion of Warburg as an international banker. Late in 1913, Owen offhandedly referred to Warburg's firm, Kuhn, Loeb, as "representatives of the Rothschilds"—close to a blood libel, given that the claim (wholly unfounded) was used by anti-Semites to impugn Kuhn, Loeb's loyalty. See *Banking and Currency: Hearings*, 2:1867. For more on the tension between Owen and Warburg, see Warburg, *The Federal Reserve System*, 1:498.

263 **a severe but brief depression:** Gary Gorton and Andrew Metrick, "The Federal Reserve and Financial Regulation: The First Hundred Years" (working paper, August 2013), and Willis, *The Federal Reserve System*, 1405–6, both credit the Fed with averting a panic. See also West, *The Federal Reserve and Banking Reform*, 193–94.

263 **Bank failures rose sharply:** Milton Friedman and Anna Jacobson Schwartz, *A Monetary History of the United States, 1867–1960* (Princeton, N.J.: Princeton University Press, 1971), 235.

263 **the Reserve Banks shifted their emphasis:** Gorton and Metrick, "Federal Reserve and Financial Regulation"; and West, *The Federal Reserve and Banking Reform*, 187–88, 190, and 219. Gorton and Metrick make the point that in 1913, the founders had no notion that active intervention in markets would weigh so heavily in the Fed's activities. Warburg (*The Federal Reserve System*, 1:176) tacitly admitted the point in acknowledging that "the importance of a definite open-market policy . . . is better understood today than it was when the Federal Reserve Act was written."

263 **ongoing ballast to the economy:** See West, *The Federal Reserve and Banking Reform*, 224; and Federal Reserve Bank of Richmond, "Federal Reserve History: The Fed's Formative Years," available at http://www.federalreservehistory.org/Events/DetailView/60.

264 **"orgies of unrestrained speculation":** "Warburg Assails Federal Reserve," *The New York Times*, March 8, 1929.

264 **Davison had remained:** Priscilla Roberts, "World War I as Catalyst and Epiphany: The Case of Henry P. Davison," *Diplomacy and Statecraft* 18, no. 2 (June 2007), 315–50.

264 **Frank Vanderlip, ever the eager:** Priscilla Roberts, "Frank A. Vanderlip and the National City Bank During the First World War," *Essays in Economic and Business History* 20, no. 2 (2002), 8; Vanderlip's memoir, written with Boyden Sparkes, is *From Farm Boy to Financier* (New York: D. Appleton-Century, 1935).

265 in April 1915, he died: Nelson W. Aldrich Jr., *Old Money: The Mythology of Wealth in America* (1988; repr., New York: Allworth Press, 1996), 22. The figure of $16 million is an estimate.

265 The two men were never: Lewis Gould, "Wilson's Man in Paris," *The Wall Street Journal*, January 17–18, 2015.

266 "He is generally regarded": "Carter Glass," *The New York Times*, May 29, 1946.

266 Owen and Glass got into a nasty: See the Federal Reserve profile of Owen available at www.federalreservehistory.org/People/DetailView/92. Owen's 1919 memoir was *The Federal Reserve Act*.

267 He later denounced the Fed: See Owen's foreword to Gertrude M. Coogan's populist tract, *Money Creators: Who Creates Money? Who Should Create It?* (Chicago: Sound Money Press, 1935), a distillation of paranoid theories of the day, which Owen warmly endorsed.

267 "when received by Mr. Glass": Laughlin, *The Federal Reserve System*, 533.

267 lobbied to keep him off the Reserve Board: H. Parker Willis to Glass, December 25, 1913, Carter Glass Collection, Box 42.

267 "simply that of a critic": Willis, *The Federal Reserve System*, 526, 530; the quotation at the end of the paragraph is from 526–27. Willis's book is full of backhanded swipes at Warburg. His statement (p. 439) that the Reserve System "was eventually placed for operation very largely in the hands of persons who had antagonized the adoption of the measure" can only be read as a derogatory comment on Warburg's elevation to the board. Willis's assertion (p. 528) that the Aldrich bill was "based upon German experience," whereas the Federal Reserve Act was (supposedly) modeled after the Bank of England, was an attempt to use Warburg's origins to taint the legacy of the Aldrich bill.

268 "interesting work of imagination": Untermyer, *Who Is Entitled to the Credit for the Federal Reserve Act?* foreword; the quotation later in the paragraph is from ibid.

268 Warburg claimed that Glass's book: Warburg to Laughlin, June 27, 1929.

268 "like the old cathedrals of Europe": Warburg, *The Federal Reserve System*, 1:10.

269 "not as the work of a single party": Ibid., 7.

269 To rebut the notion that financiers: Ibid., 133.

269 Friedman and Anna Schwartz would call: Friedman and Schwartz, *Monetary History of the United States*, 171. Robert C. West reached the same conclusion in his detailed *Banking Reform and the Federal Reserve*, 112. The Glass "admirer" is James E. Palmer Jr., author of the sycophantic *Carter Glass: Unreconstructed Rebel* (Roanoke: Institute of American Biography, 1938): see p. 71.

270 "its mother must have been": James Warburg, *The Long Road Home* (Garden City, N.Y.: Doubleday, 1964), 29.

INDEX

Page numbers beginning with 274 refer to endnotes.